P9-CJY-946

PRAISE FOR

KING LEOPOLD'S GHOST

"A superb synoptic history of European misdemeanor in central Africa."
—Jeremy Harding, *New York Times Book Review*

"An absorbing and horrifying account."
—Luc Sante, *San Francisco Chronicle*

"Carefully researched and vigorously told, *King Leopold's Ghost* does what good history always does — expands the memory of the human race."
—Fritz Lanham, *Houston Chronicle*

"A superb, engrossing chronicle."
— *Publishers Weekly*

"Hochschild's book is a rare thing in possessing both scholarly worth and the virtues of a novel. This is an extraordinary book."
— *Boston Sunday Globe*

"[Hochschild] spins engrossing yarns of kings and colonels, of distant station chiefs and feverish missionaries."
—James Zug, *Philadelphia Inquirer*

"A remarkably engaging work of popular history: extensively researched, well written and difficult to put down."
—Scott McLemee, *Newsday*

"Spellbinding."
—Robert Taylor, *Seattle Post-Intelligencier*

"Hochschild has produced a history like none other. A hundred years ago, enlightened people in the Western world were outraged by a holocaust in Africa which left millions dead ... Yet today not one person in a thousand could say what the fuss was all about, unless, of course, they have already read this amazing book."
—Tariq Ali, *Financial Times*

"A fascinating account of the creation of the Belgian Congo by that strange, greedy, cruel monarch Leopold, king of the Belgians ... A haunting book."
—K. Anthony Appiah, *New York Review of Books*

"A book of terrible beauty . . . *King Leopold's Ghost* is essential reading for the new century."
—Tom Sandborn, *Vancouver Sun*

"Hochschild has assembled the most remarkable facts and dramatis personae, added a keen appreciation for sociopolitical nuances in turn-of-the-century Europe and America, and produced a splendid new popular history."
—Gail Gerhart, *Foreign Affairs*

"Hochschild has written a moving and important book about wickedness triumphant and defeated. His Leopold merits a place among the great modern enemies of civilization."
—Algis Valiunas, *American Spectator*

"Adam Hochschild tells the story of the Belgian colonization in Africa with the talent of a great journalist and the verve of a passionate partisan. [He] shows the birth, around 1900, of the idea that independent pressure, exerted in the name of human rights, can make the powerful give way. Something which is important to us all."
—Jean Soublin, *Le Monde*

"Engrossing and horrifying . . . The book begins as an account of evil; it ends as an account of people of conscience."
—Philip Kennicott, *St. Louis Post-Dispatch*

"An awesome tale, very well researched and well told, and as Hochschild makes clear, it was a tragedy with continuing consequences."
—Martin Klein, *Toronto Globe and Mail*

"*King Leopold's Ghost* has a riveting cast of characters: heroes, villains and bit players, all extraordinary, all compelling tangles of neuroses and ambitions, all wonderfully drawn."
—Ronan Bennett, *Observer*

"This is a harrowing story, told with a crisp incisiveness . . . We knew of this skeleton in the colonial cupboard . . . but we did not know it was quite so ugly."
—Charles Nicholl, *Daily Telegraph*

BOOKS BY ADAM HOCHSCHILD

Half the Way Home: A Memoir of Father and Son

The Mirror at Midnight: A South African Journey

The Unquiet Ghost: Russians Remember Stalin

Finding the Trapdoor: Essays, Portraits, Travels

*King Leopold's Ghost: A Story of Greed, Terror,
and Heroism in Colonial Africa*

A STORY of GREED,

TERROR, and HEROISM

in COLONIAL AFRICA

A MARINER BOOK

Houghton Mifflin Company

BOSTON   NEW YORK

King
Leopold's
Ghost

Adam
Hochschild

First Mariner Books edition 1999

Copyright © 1998 by Adam Hochschild
All rights reserved

For information about permission to reproduce selections from
this book, write to Permissions, Houghton Mifflin Company,
215 Park Avenue South, New York, New York 10003.

Library of Congress Cataloging-in-Publication Data
  Hochschild, Adam.
    King Leopold's ghost : a story of greed, terror, and heroism in
  colonial Africa / Adam Hochschild.
      p.   cm.
    Includes bibliographical references and index.
    ISBN 0-395-75924-2
    ISBN 0-618-00190-5 (pbk.)
      1. Congo (Democratic Republic)—Politics and government
  —1885–1908. 2. Congo (Democratic Republic)—Politics and govern-
  ment. 3. Forced labor—Congo (Democratic Republic)—History—
  19th century. 4. Forced labor—Congo (Democratic Republic)—
  History—20th century. 5. Indigenous peoples—Congo (Democratic
  Republic)—History—19th century. 6. Indigenous peoples—Congo
  (Democratic Republic)—History—20th century. 7. Congo
  (Democratic Republic)—Race relations—History—19th century. 8.
  Congo (Democratic Republic)—Race relations—History—20th cen-
  tury. 9. Human rights movements—History—19th century. 10.
  Human rights movements—History—20th century.   I. Title.
  DT655.H63   1998
  967.5—DC21   98-16813   CIP

Printed in the United States of America

QUM 10 9 8 7

Book design by Melodie Wertelet
Map by Barbara Jackson, Meridian Mapping, Oakland, California
Photo credits appear on page 352.

In somewhat different form, portions of chapters 9 and 19 appeared
in *The New Yorker,* and portions of chapters 5 and 16 in *The American
Scholar.*

FOR
DAVID HUNTER

CONTENTS

CONTENTS

PART II: A KING AT BAY

KING
LEOPOLD'S
GHOST

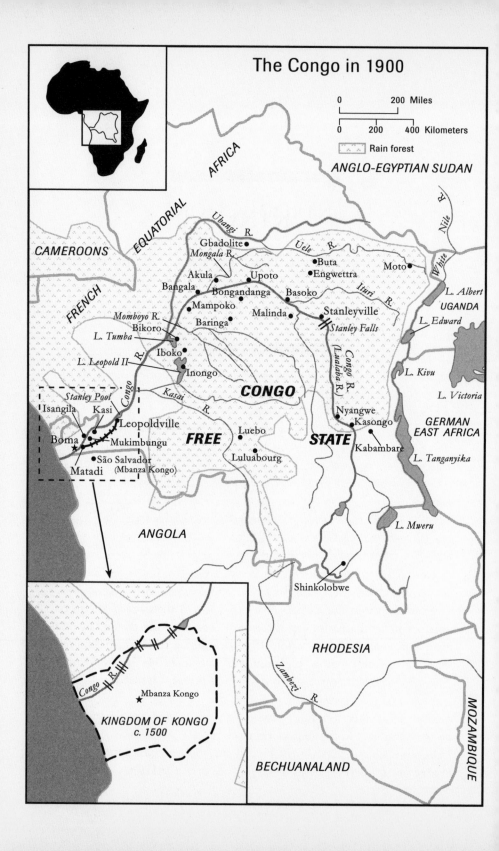

INTRODUCTION

T HE BEGINNINGS of this story lie far back in time, and its reverbera-
tions still sound today. But for me a central incandescent moment,
one that illuminates long decades before and after, is a young man's flash
of moral recognition.

The year is 1897 or 1898. Try to imagine him, briskly stepping off a
cross-Channel steamer, a forceful, burly man, in his mid-twenties, with a
handlebar mustache. He is confident and well spoken, but his British
speech is without the polish of Eton or Oxford. He is well dressed, but
the clothes are not from Bond Street. With an ailing mother and a wife
and growing family to support, he is not the sort of person likely to get
caught up in an idealistic cause. His ideas are thoroughly conventional.
He looks — and is — every inch the sober, respectable businessman.

Edmund Dene Morel is a trusted employee of a Liverpool shipping
line. A subsidiary of the company has the monopoly on all transport of
cargo to and from the Congo Free State, as it is then called, the huge
territory in central Africa that is the world's only colony claimed by one
man. That man is King Leopold II of Belgium, a ruler much admired
throughout Europe as a "philanthropic" monarch. He has welcomed
Christian missionaries to his new colony; his troops, it is said, have fought
and defeated local slave-traders who preyed on the population; and for
more than a decade European newspapers have praised him for investing
his personal fortune in public works to benefit the Africans.

Because Morel speaks fluent French, his company sends him to Belgium every few weeks to supervise the loading and unloading of ships on

the Congo run. Although the officials he works with have been handling this shipping traffic for years without a second thought, Morel begins to notice things that unsettle him. At the docks of the big port of Antwerp he sees his company's ships arriving filled to the hatch covers with valuable cargoes of rubber and ivory. But when they cast off their hawsers to steam back to the Congo, while military bands play on the pier and eager young men in uniform line the ships' rails, what they carry is mostly army officers, firearms, and ammunition. There is no trade going on here. Little or nothing is being exchanged for the rubber and ivory. As Morel watches these riches streaming to Europe with almost no goods being sent to Africa to pay for them, he realizes that there can be only one explanation for their source: slave labor.

Brought face to face with evil, Morel does not turn away. Instead, what he sees determines the course of his life and the course of an extraordinary movement, the first great international human rights movement of the twentieth century. Seldom has one human being — impassioned, eloquent, blessed with brilliant organizing skills and nearly superhuman energy — managed almost single-handedly to put one subject on the world's front pages for more than a decade. Only a few years after standing on the docks of Antwerp, Edmund Morel would be at the White House, insisting to President Theodore Roosevelt that the United States had a special responsibility to do something about the Congo. He would organize delegations to the British Foreign Office. He would mobilize everyone from Booker T. Washington to Anatole France to the Archbishop of Canterbury to join his cause. More than two hundred mass meetings to protest slave labor in the Congo would be held across the United States. A larger number of gatherings in England — nearly three hundred a year at the crusade's peak — would draw as many as five thousand people at a time. In London, one letter of protest to the *Times* on the Congo would be signed by eleven peers, nineteen bishops, seventy-six members of Parliament, the presidents of seven Chambers of Commerce, thirteen editors of major newspapers, and every lord mayor in the country. Speeches about the horrors of King Leopold's Congo would be given as far away as Australia. In Italy, two men would fight a duel over the issue. British Foreign Secretary Sir Edward Grey, a man not given to overstatement, would declare that "no external question for at least thirty years has moved the country so strongly and so vehemently."

This is the story of that movement, of the savage crime that was its target, of the long period of exploration and conquest that preceded it, and of the way the world has forgotten one of the great mass killings of recent history.

❧

I knew almost nothing about the history of the Congo until a few years ago, when I noticed a footnote in a book I happened to be reading. Often, when you come across something particularly striking, you remember just where you were when you read it. On this occasion I was sitting, stiff and tired, late at night, in one of the far rear seats of an airliner crossing the United States from east to west.

The footnote was to a quotation by Mark Twain, written, the note said, when he was part of the worldwide movement against slave labor in the Congo, a practice that had taken five to eight million lives. Worldwide movement? Five to eight million lives? I was startled.

Statistics about mass murder are often hard to prove. But if this number turned out to be even half as high, I thought, the Congo would have been one of the major killing grounds of modern times. Why were these deaths not mentioned in the standard litany of our century's horrors? And why had I never before heard of them? I had been writing about human rights for years, and once, in the course of half a dozen trips to Africa, I had been to the Congo.

That visit was in 1961. In a Leopoldville apartment, I heard a CIA man, who had had too much to drink, describe with satisfaction exactly how and where the newly independent country's first prime minister, Patrice Lumumba, had been killed a few months earlier. He assumed that any American, even a visiting student like me, would share his relief at the assassination of a man the United States government considered a dangerous leftist troublemaker. In the early morning a day or two later I left the country by ferry across the Congo River, the conversation still ringing in my head as the sun rose over the waves and the dark, smooth water slapped against the boat's hull.

It was several decades later that I encountered that footnote, and with it my own ignorance of the Congo's early history. Then it occurred to me that, like millions of other people, I had read something about that time and place after all: Joseph Conrad's *Heart of Darkness.* However, with my college lecture notes on the novel filled with scribbles about Freudian overtones, mythic echoes, and inward vision, I had mentally filed away the book under fiction, not fact.

I began to read more. The further I explored, the more it was clear that the Congo of a century ago had indeed seen a death toll of Holocaust dimensions. At the same time, I unexpectedly found myself absorbed by the extraordinary characters who had peopled this patch of history. Although it was Edmund Dene Morel who had ignited a movement, he was not the first outsider to see King Leopold's Congo for what it was and to try hard to draw the world's attention to it. That role was played by George Washington Williams, a black American journalist and historian, who, unlike anyone before him, interviewed Africans about their experience of their white conquerors. It was another black American, William Sheppard, who recorded a scene he came across in the Congo rain forest that would brand itself on the world's consciousness as a symbol of colonial brutality. There were other heroes as well, one of the bravest of whom ended his life on a London gallows. Then, of course, into the middle of the story sailed the young sea captain Joseph Conrad, expecting the exotic Africa of his childhood dreams but finding instead what he would call "the vilest scramble for loot that ever disfigured the history of human conscience." And looming above them all was King Leopold II, a man as filled with greed and cunning, duplicity and charm, as any of the more complex villains of Shakespeare.

As I followed the intersecting lives of these men, I realized something else about the terror in the Congo and the controversy that came to surround it. It was the first major international atrocity scandal in the age of the telegraph and the camera. In its mixture of bloodshed on an industrial scale, royalty, sex, the power of celebrity, and rival lobbying and media campaigns raging in half a dozen countries on both sides of the Atlantic, it seemed strikingly close to our time. Furthermore, unlike many other great predators of history, from Genghis Khan to the Spanish conquistadors, King Leopold II never saw a drop of blood spilled in anger. He never set foot in the Congo. There is something very modern about that, too, as there is about the bomber pilot in the stratosphere, above the clouds, who never hears screams or sees shattered homes or torn flesh.

Although Europe has long forgotten the victims of Leopold's Congo, I found a vast supply of raw material to work with in reconstructing their fate: Congo memoirs by explorers, steamboat captains, military men; the records of mission stations; reports of government investigations; and those peculiarly Victorian phenomena, accounts by gentleman (or sometimes lady) "travelers." The Victorian era was a golden age of letters and diaries; and often it seems as if every visitor or official in the Congo kept a voluminous journal and spent each evening on the riverbank writing letters home.

One problem, of course, is that nearly all of this vast river of words is by Europeans or Americans. There was no written language in the Congo when Europeans first arrived, and this inevitably skewed the way that history was recorded. We have dozens of memoirs by the territory's white officials; we know the changing opinions of key people in the British Foreign Office, sometimes on a day-by-day basis. But we do not have a full-length memoir or complete oral history of a single Congolese during the period of the greatest terror. Instead of African voices from this time there is largely silence.

And yet, as I immersed myself in this material, I saw how revealing it was. The men who seized the Congo often trumpeted their killings, bragging about them in books and newspaper articles. Some kept surprisingly frank diaries that show far more than the writers intended, as does a voluminous and explicit instruction book for colonial officials. Furthermore, several officers of the private army that occupied the Congo came to feel guilty about the blood on their hands. Their testimony, and the documents they smuggled out, helped to fuel the protest movement. Even on the part of the brutally suppressed Africans, the silence is not complete. Some of their actions and voices, though filtered through the records of their conquerors, we can still see and hear.

The worst of the bloodshed in the Congo took place between 1890 and 1910, but its origins lie much earlier, when Europeans and Africans first encountered each other there. And so to reach the headwaters of our story we must leap back more than five hundred years, to a time when a ship's captain saw the ocean change its color, and when a king received news of a strange apparition that had risen from inside the earth.

"THE TRADERS ARE
KIDNAPPING OUR PEOPLE"

W HEN EUROPEANS began imagining Africa beyond the Sahara, the continent they pictured was a dreamscape, a site for fantasies of the fearsome and the supernatural. Ranulf Higden, a Benedictine monk who mapped the world about 1350, claimed that Africa contained one-eyed people who used their feet to cover their heads. A geographer in the next century announced that the continent held people with one leg, three faces, and the heads of lions. In 1459, an Italian monk, Fra Mauro, declared Africa the home of the roc, a bird so large that it could carry an elephant through the air.

In the Middle Ages, almost no one in Europe was in a position to know whether Africa contained giant birds, one-eyed people, or anything else. Hostile Moors lived on Africa's Mediterranean coast, and few Europeans dared set foot there, much less head south across the Sahara. And as for trying to sail down the west African coast, everyone knew that as soon as you passed the Canary Islands you would be in the Mare Tenebroso, the Sea of Darkness.

> In the medieval imagination [writes Peter Forbath], this was a region of uttermost dread . . . where the heavens fling down liquid sheets of flame and the waters boil . . . where serpent rocks and ogre islands lie in wait for the mariner, where the giant hand of Satan reaches up from the fathomless depths to seize him, where he will turn black in face and body as a mark of God's

vengeance for the insolence of his prying into this forbidden mystery. And even if he should be able to survive all these ghastly perils and sail on through, he would then arrive in the Sea of Obscurity and be lost forever in the vapors and slime at the edge of the world.

It was not until the fifteenth century, the dawn of the age of ocean navigation, that Europeans systematically began to venture south, the Portuguese in the lead. In the 1440s, Lisbon's shipbuilders developed the caravel, a compact vessel particularly good at sailing into the wind. Although rarely more than a hundred feet long, this sturdy ship carried explorers far down the west coast of Africa, where no one knew what gold, spices, and precious stones might lie. But it was not only lust for riches that drove the explorers. Somewhere in Africa, they knew, was the source of the Nile, a mystery that had fascinated Europeans since antiquity. They were also driven by one of the most enduring of medieval myths, the legend of Prester John, a Christian king who was said to rule a vast empire in the interior of Africa, where, from a palace of translucent crystal and precious stones, he reigned over forty-two lesser kings, in addition to assorted centaurs and giants. No traveler was ever turned away from his dinner table of solid emerald, which seated thousands. Surely Prester John would be eager to share his riches with his fellow Christians and to help them find their way onward, to the fabled wealth of India.

Successive Portuguese expeditions probed ever farther southward. In 1482, an experienced naval captain named Diogo Cão set off on the most ambitious voyage yet. As he sailed close to the west African coast, he saw the North Star disappear from the sky once his caravel crossed the equator, and he found himself much farther south than anyone from Europe had ever been.

One day Cão came upon something that astounded him. Around his ship, the sea turned a dark, slate-tinged yellow, and brownish-yellow waves were breaking on the nearby beaches. Sailing toward the mouth of an inlet many miles wide, his caravel had to fight a current of eight to nine knots. Furthermore, a taste of the water surrounding the ship revealed that it was fresh, not salt. Cão had stumbled on the mouth of an enormous silt-filled river, larger than any a European had ever seen. The impression its vastness made on him and his men is reflected in a contemporary account:

> For the space of 20 leagues [the river] preserves its fresh water
> unbroken by the briny billows which encompass it on every side;
> as if this noble river had determined to try its strength in pitched
> battle with the ocean itself, and alone deny it the tribute which
> all other rivers in the world pay without resistance.

Modern oceanographers have discovered more evidence of the great river's strength in its "pitched battle with the ocean": a hundred-mile-long canyon, in places four thousand feet deep, that the river has carved out of the sea floor.

Cão went ashore at the river's mouth and erected a limestone pillar topped with an iron cross and inscribed with the royal coat of arms and the words: "In the year 6681 of the World and in that of 1482 since the birth of our Lord Jesus Christ, the most serene, the most excellent and potent prince, King João II of Portugal did order this land to be discovered and this pillar of stone to be erected by Diogo Cão, an esquire in his household."

The river where he had landed would be known by Europeans for most of the next five hundred years as the Congo. It flowed into the sea at the northern end of a thriving African kingdom, an imperial federation of two to three million people. Ever since then, geographers have usually spelled the name of the river and the eventual European colony on its banks one way, and that of the people living around its mouth and their indigenous kingdom another.

The Kingdom of the Kongo was roughly three hundred miles square, comprising territory that today lies in several countries. Its capital was the town of Mbanza Kongo — *mbanza* means "court" — on a commanding hilltop some ten days' walk inland from the coast and today just on the Angolan side of the Angola–Congo border. In 1491, nine years and several voyages after Diogo Cão's landfall, an expedition of awed Portuguese priests and emissaries made this ten-day trek and set up housekeeping as permanent representatives of their country in the court of the Kongo king. Their arrival marked the beginning of the first sustained encounter between Europeans and a black African nation.

The Kingdom of the Kongo had been in place for at least a hundred years before the Portuguese arrived. Its monarch, the ManiKongo, was chosen by an assembly of clan leaders. Like his European counterparts, he sat on a throne, in his case made of wood inlaid with ivory. As symbols of royal authority, the ManiKongo carried a zebra-tail whip, had the skins and heads of baby animals suspended from his belt, and wore a small cap.

In the capital, the king dispensed justice, received homage, and reviewed his troops under a fig tree in a large public square. Whoever approached him had to do so on all fours. On pain of death, no one was allowed to watch him eat or drink. Before he did either, an attendant struck two iron poles together, and anyone in sight had to lie face down on the ground.

The ManiKongo who was then on the throne greeted the Portuguese warmly. His enthusiasm was probably due less to the Savior his unexpected guests told him about than to the help their magical fire-spouting weapons promised in suppressing a troublesome provincial rebellion. The Portuguese were glad to oblige.

The newcomers built churches and mission schools. Like many white evangelists who followed them, they were horrified by polygamy; they thought it was the spices in the African food that provoked the dreadful practice. But despite their contempt for Kongo culture, the Portuguese grudgingly recognized in the kingdom a sophisticated and well-developed state — the leading one on the west coast of central Africa. The ManiKongo appointed governors for each of some half-dozen provinces, and his rule was carried out by an elaborate civil service that included such specialized positions as *mani vangu vangu,* or first judge in cases of adultery. Although they were without writing or the wheel, the inhabitants forged copper into jewelry and iron into weapons, and wove clothing out of fibers stripped from the leaves of the raffia palm tree. According to myth, the founder of the Kongo state was a blacksmith king, so ironwork was an occupation of the nobility. People cultivated yams, bananas, and other fruits and vegetables, and raised pigs, cattle, and goats. They measured distance by marching days, and marked time by the lunar month and by a four-day week, the first day of which was a holiday. The king collected taxes from his subjects and, like many a ruler, controlled the currency supply: cowrie shells found on a coastal island under royal authority.

As in much of Africa, the kingdom had slavery. The nature of African slavery varied from one area to another and changed over time, but most slaves were people captured in warfare. Others had been criminals or debtors, or were given away by their families as part of a dowry settlement. Like any system that gives some human beings total power over others, slavery in Africa could be vicious. Some Congo basin peoples sacrificed slaves on special occasions, such as the ratification of a treaty between chiefdoms; the slow death of an abandoned slave, his bones broken, symbolized the fate of anyone who violated the treaty. Some slaves might also be sacrificed to give a dead chief's soul some company on its journey into the next world.

In other ways, African slavery was more flexible and benign than the system Europeans would soon establish in the New World. Over a generation or two, slaves could often earn or be granted their freedom, and free people and slaves sometimes intermarried. Nonetheless, the fact that trading in human beings existed in any form turned out to be catastrophic for Africa, for when Europeans showed up, ready to buy endless shiploads of slaves, they found African chiefs willing to sell.

Soon enough, the slave-buyers came. They arrived in small numbers at first, but then in a flood unleashed by events across the Atlantic. In 1500, only nine years after the first Europeans arrived at Mbanza Kongo, a Portuguese expedition was blown off course and came upon Brazil. Within a few decades, the Western Hemisphere became a huge, lucrative, nearly insatiable market for African slaves. They were put to work by the millions in Brazil's mines and on its coffee plantations, as well as on the Caribbean islands where other European powers quickly began using the lush, fertile land to grow sugar.

In the Kingdom of the Kongo, the Portuguese forgot the search for Prester John. Slaving fever seized them. Men sent out from Lisbon to be masons or teachers at Mbanza Kongo soon made far more money by herding convoys of chained Africans to the coast and selling them to the captains of slave-carrying caravels.

The lust for slave profits engulfed even some of the priests, who abandoned their preaching, took black women as concubines, kept slaves themselves, and sold their students and converts into slavery. The priests who strayed from the fold stuck to their faith in one way, however; after the Reformation they tried to ensure that none of their human goods ended up in Protestant hands. It was surely not right, said one, "for persons baptized in the Catholic church to be sold to peoples who are enemies of their faith."

A village near Diogo Cão's stone pillar on the south shore of the Congo River estuary became a slave port, from which more than five thousand slaves a year were being shipped across the Atlantic by the 1530s. By the next century, fifteen thousand slaves a year were exported from the Kingdom of the Kongo as a whole. Traders kept careful records of their booty. One surviving inventory from this region lists "68 head" of slaves by name, physical defects, and cash value, starting with the men, who were worth the most money, and ending with: "Child, name unknown as she is dying and cannot speak, male without value, and a small girl Callenbo, no value because she is dying; one small girl Cantunbe, no value because she is dying."

Many of the slaves shipped to the Americas from the great river's mouth came from the Kingdom of the Kongo itself; many others were captured by African slave-dealers who ranged more than seven hundred miles into the interior, buying slaves from local chiefs and headmen. Forced-marched to the coast, their necks locked into wooden yokes, the slaves were rarely given enough food, and because caravans usually traveled in the dry season, they often drank stagnant water. The trails to the slave ports were soon strewn with bleaching bones.

Once they were properly baptized, clothed in leftover burlap cargo wrappings, and chained together in ships' holds, most slaves from this region were sent to Brazil, the nearest part of the New World. Starting in the 1600s, however, a growing demand tempted many ship captains to make the longer voyage to the British colonies in North America. Roughly one of every four slaves imported to work the cotton and tobacco plantations of the American South began his or her journey across the Atlantic from equatorial Africa, including the Kongo kingdom. The KiKongo language, spoken around the Congo River's mouth, is one of the African tongues whose traces linguists have found in the Gullah dialect spoken by black Americans today on the coastal islands of South Carolina and Georgia.

When the Atlantic slave trade began decimating the Kongo, that nation was under the reign of a ManiKongo named Nzinga Mbemba Affonso, who had gained the throne in 1506 and ruled as Affonso I for nearly forty years. Affonso's life spanned a crucial period. When he was born, no one in the kingdom knew that Europeans existed. When he died, his entire realm was threatened by the slave-selling fever they had caused. He was a man of tragic self-awareness, and he left his mark. Some three hundred years later, a missionary said, "A native of the Kongo knows the name of three kings: that of the present one, that of his predecessor, and that of Affonso."

He was a provincial chief in his early thirties when the Portuguese first arrived at Mbanza Kongo, in 1491. A convert to Christianity, he took on the name Affonso and some Portuguese advisers, and studied for ten years with the priests at Mbanza Kongo. One wrote to the king of Portugal that Affonso "knows better than us the prophets, the Gospel of our Savior Jesus Christ, all the lives of the saints and all that has to do with our holy mother Church. If Your Highness saw him, You would be astonished. He speaks so well and with such assurance that it always seems to me that the Holy Spirit speaks through his mouth. My Lord, he does nothing but study; many times he falls asleep over his books and many times he forgets to eat or drink because he is speaking of our Savior." It is hard to tell how much of this glowing portrait was inspired by the priest's attempt to impress the Portuguese king and how much by Affonso's attempt to impress the priest.

In the language of a later age, King Affonso I was a modernizer. He urgently tried to acquire European learning, weapons, and goods in order to strengthen his rule and fortify it against the destabilizing force of the white arrival. Having noticed the Portuguese appetite for copper, for example, he traded it for European products that would help him buy the submission of outlying provinces. Clearly a man of unusual intelligence, Affonso tried to do something as difficult in his time as in ours: to be a *selective* modernizer. He was an enthusiast for the church, for the written word, for European medicine, and for woodworking, masonry, and other skills to be learned from Portuguese craftsmen. But when his fellow king in Lisbon sent an envoy to urge the adoption of Portugal's legal code and court protocol, Affonso wasn't interested. And he tried hard to keep out prospectors, fearing total takeover of his land if Europeans found the gold and silver they coveted.

Because virtually everything we know about this part of Africa for the next several hundred years comes to us from its white conquerors, King Affonso I provides something rare and valuable: an African voice. Indeed, his is one of the very few central African voices that we can hear at all before the twentieth century. He used his fluency in Portuguese to dictate a remarkable series of letters to two successive Portuguese kings, the first known documents composed by a black African in any European language. Several dozen of the letters survive, above his signature, with its regal flourish of double underlinings. Their tone is the formal one of monarch to monarch, usually beginning "Most high and powerful prince and king my brother . . ." But we can hear not just a king speaking; we hear a human being, one who is aghast to see his people taken away in ever greater numbers on slave ships.

Affonso was no abolitionist. Like most African rulers of his time and later, he owned slaves, and at least once he sent some as a present to his "brother" king in Lisbon, along with leopard skins, parrots, and copper anklets. But this traditional exchange of gifts among kings seemed greatly different to Affonso from having tens of thousands of his previously free subjects taken across the sea in chains. Listen to him as he writes King João III of Portugal in 1526:

> Each day the traders are kidnapping our people — children of this country, sons of our nobles and vassals, even people of our own family. . . . This corruption and depravity are so widespread that our land is entirely depopulated. . . . We need in this kingdom only priests and schoolteachers, and no merchandise, unless it is wine and flour for Mass. . . . It is our wish that this kingdom not be a place for the trade or transport of slaves.

Later the same year:

> Many of our subjects eagerly lust after Portuguese merchandise that your subjects have brought into our domains. To satisfy this inordinate appetite, they seize many of our black free subjects. . . . They sell them . . . after having taken these prisoners [to the coast] secretly or at night. . . . As soon as the captives are in the hands of white men they are branded with a red-hot iron.

Again and again Affonso speaks about the twin themes of the slave trade and the alluring array of cloth, tools, jewelry, and other knickknacks that the Portuguese traders used to buy their human cargoes:

> These goods exert such a great attraction over simple and igno-rant people that they believe in them and forget their belief in God. . . . My Lord, a monstrous greed pushes our subjects, even Christians, to seize members of their own families, and of ours, to do business by selling them as captives.

While begging the Portuguese king to send him teachers, pharmacists, and doctors instead of traders, Affonso admits that the flood of material goods threatened his authority. His people "can now procure, in much greater quantity than we can, the things we formerly used to keep them obedient to us and content." Affonso's lament was prescient; this was not the last time that lust for Europe's great cornucopia of goods undermined traditional ways of life elsewhere.

The Portuguese kings showed no sympathy. King João III replied: "You . . . tell me that you want no slave-trading in your domains, because this trade is depopulating your country. . . . The Portuguese there, on the contrary, tell me how vast the Congo is, and how it is so thickly populated that it seems as if no slave has ever left."

Affonso pleaded with his fellow sovereigns as one Christian with another, complete with the prejudices of the day. Of the priests turned slave-traders, he wrote:

> In this kingdom, faith is as fragile as glass because of the bad
> examples of the men who come to teach here, because the lusts
> of the world and lure of wealth have turned them away from the
> truth. Just as the Jews crucified the Son of God because of covet-
> ousness, my brother, so today He is again crucified.

Several times Affonso sent his appeals for an end to the slave trade directly to the Pope in Rome, but the Portuguese detained his emissaries to the Vatican as they stepped off the boat in Lisbon.

Affonso's despair reached its depth in 1539, near the end of his life, when he heard that ten of his young nephews, grandsons, and other relatives who had been sent to Portugal for a religious education had disappeared en route. "We don't know whether they are dead or alive," he wrote in desperation, "nor how they might have died, nor what news we can give of them to their fathers and mothers." We can imagine the king's horror at being unable to guarantee the safety even of his own family. Portuguese traders and sea captains along the long route back to Europe sidetracked many a cargo between the Kongo kingdom and Lisbon; these youngsters, it turned out, ended up in Brazil as slaves.

His hatred for the overseas slave trade and his vigilance against its erosion of his authority won Affonso the enmity of some of the Portuguese merchants living in his capital. A group of eight made an attempt on his life as he was attending Mass on Easter Sunday in 1540. He escaped with only a bullet hole in the fringe of his royal robe, but one of his nobles was killed and two others wounded.

After Affonso's death, the power of the Kongo state gradually diminished as provincial and village chiefs, themselves growing rich on slave sales, no longer gave much allegiance to the court at Mbanza Kongo. By the end of the 1500s, other European countries had joined in the slave trade; British, French, and Dutch vessels roamed the African coast, looking for human cargo. In 1665, the army of the weakened Kingdom of the Kongo fought a battle with the Portuguese. It was defeated, and the ManiKongo was beheaded. Internal strife further depleted the kingdom, whose territory was all taken over by European colonies by the late 1800s.

Except for Affonso's letters, the written record of these times still shows them entirely through white men's eyes. How did the Europeans, beginning with Diogo Cão and his three ships with faded red crosses on their sails, appear to the people living at the great river's mouth? To see with their eyes, we must turn to the myths and legends that have filtered down over the centuries. At first, Africans apparently saw the white sailors not as men but as *vumbi* — ancestral ghosts — since the Kongo people believed that a person's skin changed to the color of chalk when he passed into the land of the dead. And it was obvious that this was where these menacing white *vumbi* had come from, for people on the shore saw first the tips of an approaching ship's masts, then its superstructure, then its hull. Clearly the ship had carried its passengers up from their homes beneath the surface of the earth. Here is how the Portuguese arrival was recounted by Mukunzo Kioko, a twentieth-century oral historian of the Pende people:

> Our fathers were living comfortably. . . . They had cattle and crops; they had salt marshes and banana trees.
>
> Suddenly they saw a big boat rising out of the great ocean. This boat had wings all of white, sparkling like knives.
>
> White men came out of the water and spoke words which no one understood.
>
> Our ancestors took fright; they said that these were *vumbi,* spirits returned from the dead.
>
> They pushed them back into the ocean with volleys of arrows.

But the *vumbi* spat fire with a noise of thunder. Many men were killed. Our ancestors fled.

The chiefs and wise men said that these *vumbi* were the former possessors of the land. . . .

From that time to our days now, the whites have brought us nothing but wars and miseries.

The trans–Atlantic slave trade seemed further confirmation that Europeans had come from the land of the dead, for after they took their shiploads of slaves out to sea, the captives never returned. Just as Europeans would be long obsessed with African cannibalism, so Africans imagined Europeans practicing the same thing. The whites were thought to turn their captives' flesh into salt meat, their brains into cheese, and their blood into the red wine Europeans drank. African bones were burned, and the gray ash became gunpowder. The huge, smoking copper cooking kettles that could be seen on sailing vessels were, it was believed, where all these deadly transformations began. The death tolls on the packed slave ships that sailed west from the Congo coast rose higher still when some slaves refused to eat the food they were given, believing that they would be eating those who had sailed before them.

As the years passed, new myths arose to explain the mysterious objects the strangers brought from the land of the dead. A nineteenth-century missionary recorded, for example, an African explanation of what happened when captains descended into the holds of their ships to fetch trading goods like cloth. The Africans believed that these goods came not from the ship itself but from a hole that led into the ocean. Sea sprites weave this cloth in an "oceanic factory, and, whenever we need cloth, the captain . . . goes to this hole and rings a bell." The sea sprites hand him up their cloth, and the captain "then throws in, as payment, a few dead bodies of black people he has bought from those bad native traders who have bewitched their people and sold them to the white men." The myth was not so far from reality. For what was slavery in the American South, after all, but a system for transforming the labor of black bodies, via cotton plantations, into cloth?

※※※※※

Because African middlemen brought captives directly to their ships, Portuguese traders seldom ventured far from the coast. For nearly four centuries, in fact, after Diogo Cão came upon the Congo River, Europeans did not know where the river came from. It pours some 1.4 million cubic feet of water per second into the ocean; only the Amazon carries more water. Besides its enormous size and unknown course, the Congo posed another puzzle. Seamen noticed that its flow, compared with that of other tropical rivers, fluctuated relatively little during the year. Rivers such as the Amazon and the Ganges had phases of extremely high water and low water, depending on whether the land they drained was experiencing the rainy or the dry season. What made the Congo different?

The reason several centuries' worth of visitors failed to explore the Congo's source was that they couldn't sail upstream. Anyone who tried found that the river turned into a gorge, at the head of which were impassable rapids.

Much of the Congo River basin, we now know, lies on a plateau in the African interior. From the western rim of this plateau, nearly a thousand feet high, the river descends to sea level in a mere 220 miles. During this tumultuous descent, the river squeezes through narrow canyons, boils up in waves 40 feet high, and tumbles over 32 separate cataracts. So great is the drop and the volume of water that these 220 miles have as much hydroelectric potential as all the lakes and rivers of the United States combined.

For any sailor bold enough to get out of his ship and walk, the land route around the rapids wound uphill through rough, rocky country feared for its treacherous cliffs and ravines and for malaria and the other diseases to which Europeans had no immunity. Only with enormous difficulty did some Capuchin missionaries twice manage to get briefly inland as far as the top of the great rapids. A Portuguese expedition that tried to repeat this trek never returned. By the beginning of the nineteenth century, Europeans still knew nothing about the interior of central Africa or about where the river began.

In 1816, a British expedition, led by Captain James K. Tuckey of the Royal Navy, set off to find the Congo's origins. His two ships carried a wonderfully odd assortment of people: Royal Marines, carpenters, blacksmiths, a surgeon, a gardener from the royal gardens at Kew, a botanist, and an anatomist. The anatomist was directed, among other things, to make a careful study of the hippopotamus and to "preserve in spirits and if possible in triplicate, the organ of hearing of this animal." A Mr. Cranch was entered on the ship's log as Collector of Objects of Natural History; another expedition member was simply listed as Volunteer and Observant Gentleman.

When he arrived at the Congo's mouth, Tuckey counted eight slave ships from various nations at anchor, awaiting their cargoes. He sailed his own ships as far up the river as he could and then set off to skirt the thunderous rapids overland. But he and his exhausted men grew discouraged by endless "scrambling up the sides of almost perpendicular hills, and over great masses of quartz." These came to be called the Crystal Mountains. The river was a mass of foaming rapids and enormous whirlpools. At a rare calm stretch Tuckey observed, rather provincially, that "the scenery was beautiful and not inferior to any on the banks of the Thames." One by one, the Englishmen began to suffer from an unknown illness, most likely yellow fever, and after about 150 miles, Tuckey lost heart. His party turned around, and he died shortly after getting back to his ship. By the time the shaken survivors of the expedition made their way back to England, twenty-one of the fifty-four men who had set out were dead. The source of the Congo River and the secret of its steady flow was still a mystery. For Europeans, Africa remained the supplier of valuable raw materials — human bodies and elephant tusks. But otherwise they saw the continent as faceless, blank, empty, a place on the map waiting to be explored, one ever more frequently described by the phrase that says more about the seer than the seen: the Dark Continent.

I

WALKING INTO FIRE

"I SHALL NOT GIVE UP
THE CHASE"

O N JANUARY 28, 1841, a quarter-century after Tuckey's failed
expedition, the man who would spectacularly accomplish what
Tuckey tried to do was born in the small Welsh market town of Denbigh.
He was entered on the birth register of St. Hilary's Church as "John
Rowlands, Bastard" — an epithet that was to mark the boy for the rest of
his life, a life obsessively devoted to living down a sense of shame. Young
John was the first of five illegitimate children born to Betsy Parry, a
housemaid. His father may have been John Rowlands, a local drunkard
who died of *delirium tremens,* or a prominent and married lawyer named
James Vaughan Horne, or a boyfriend of Betsy Parry's in London, where
she had been working.

After giving birth, Betsy Parry departed from Denbigh in disgrace,
leaving her baby behind in the home of his two uncles and his maternal
grandfather, a man who believed a boy needed a "sound whipping" if he
misbehaved. When John was five, his grandfather died, and the uncles
immediately got rid of their unwanted nephew by paying a local family
half a crown a week to take him in. When the family asked for more
money, the uncles refused. One day the foster family told young John that
their son Dick would take him to visit his "Aunt Mary" in another
village:

> The way seemed interminable and tedious. . . . At last Dick set
> me down from his shoulders before an immense stone building,
> and, passing through tall iron gates, he pulled at a bell, which I

could hear clanging noisily in the distant interior. A sombre-faced stranger appeared at the door, who, despite my remonstrances, seized me by the hand and drew me within, while Dick tried to sooth my fears with glib promises that he was only going to bring Aunt Mary to me. The door closed on him and, with the echoing sound, I experienced for the first time the awful feeling of utter desolateness.

Six-year-old John Rowlands was now an inmate of the St. Asaph Union Workhouse.

Records of life at St. Asaph's are generally covered by a veil of Victorian euphemism, but a local newspaper complained that the master of the workhouse was an alcoholic who took "indecent liberties" with women on his staff. An investigative commission that visited the workhouse in 1847, about the time John Rowlands arrived, reported that male adults "took part in every possible vice," and that children slept two to a bed, an older child with a younger, resulting in their starting "to practice and understand things they should not." For the rest of his life, John Rowlands would show a fear of sexual intimacy in any form.

Whatever John may have endured or seen in the workhouse dormitory, in its schoolroom he thrived. For his achievements he won a prize Bible from the local bishop. He was fascinated by geography. He had an unusual ability to mimic someone else's handwriting after studying it for a few minutes. His own penmanship was strikingly graceful; his youthful signature was stylish and forward-leaning, with the stems and tails of the letters sweeping dramatically far above and below the line. It was as if, through his handwriting, he were trying to pull himself out of disgrace and turn the script of his life from one of poverty to one of elegance.

One evening, when John was twelve, his supervisor "came up to me during the dinner-hour, when all the inmates were assembled, and, pointing out a tall woman with an oval face, and a great coil of dark hair behind her head, asked me if I recognized her.

"'No, sir,' I replied.

"'What, do you not know your own mother?'

"I started, with a burning face, and directed a shy glance at her, and perceived she was regarding me with a look of cool, critical scrutiny. I had expected to feel a gush of tenderness towards her, but her expression was so chilling that the valves of my heart closed as with a snap."

Adding to his shock was the fact that his mother had brought two new illegitimate children to St. Asaph's with her, a boy and a girl. Some weeks later, she left the workhouse. For John, it was the latest in a chain of abandonments.

At fifteen, John left St. Asaph's and stayed with a succession of relatives, all of whom seemed queasy about sheltering a poorhouse cousin. At seventeen, while he was living with an uncle in Liverpool and working as a butcher's delivery boy, he feared he was about to be turned out once more. One day he delivered some meat to an American merchant ship at the docks, the *Windermere*. The captain eyed this short but sturdy-looking young man and asked, "How would you like to sail in this ship?"

In February 1859, after a seven-week voyage, the *Windermere* landed in New Orleans, where the young newcomer jumped ship. He long remembered the city's fascinating array of smells: tar, brine, green coffee, rum, and molasses. Roaming the streets in search of work, on the porch of a warehouse he spied a middle-aged man in a stovepipe hat, a cotton broker, as it turned out, and approached him: "Do you want a boy, sir?"

The cotton broker, impressed by John's only reference, the prize Bible with the bishop's inscription, took on the Welsh teenager as an employee. Soon after, young John Rowlands, now living in the New World, decided to give himself a new name. The procedure was gradual. In the 1860 New Orleans census, he is listed as "J. Rolling." A woman who knew him at this time remembered him as John Rollins: "smart as a whip, and much given to bragging, big talk and telling stories." Within a few years, however, he began using the first and last name of the merchant who had given him his job. He continued to experiment with the middle names, using Morley, Morelake, and Moreland before finally settling on Morton. And so the boy who had entered the St. Asaph Union Workhouse as John Rowlands became the man who would soon be known worldwide as Henry Morton Stanley.

Stanley gave himself not only a new name; he tried for the rest of his life to give himself a new biography. The man who would become the most famous explorer of his time, renowned for his accurate observations of African wildlife and terrain, was a world-class obfuscator when it came to his early life. In his autobiography, for example, he tells of leaving the Welsh workhouse in melodramatic terms: he leaped over a garden wall and escaped, he claims, after leading a class rebellion against a cruel supervisor named James Francis, who had viciously brutalized the entire senior class. "'Never again,' I shouted, marvelling at my own audacity. The words had scarcely escaped me ere I found myself swung upwards into the air by the collar of my jacket and flung into a nerveless heap on the bench. Then the passionate brute pummelled me in the stomach until I fell backward, gasping for breath. Again I was lifted, and dashed on the bench with a shock that almost broke my spine." Stanley was then a vigorous, healthy fifteen-year-old and would not have been an easy victim for Francis, a former coal miner who had lost one hand in a mining accident. Other students later recalled no mutiny, much less one led by Stanley; they remembered Francis as a gentle man and Stanley as a teacher's pet, often given favors and encouragement and put in charge of the class when Francis was away. Workhouse records show Stanley leaving not as a runaway but to live at his uncle's while going to school.

Equally fanciful is Stanley's account of his time in New Orleans. He lived, he says, at the home of the benevolent cotton broker, Henry Stanley, and his saintly, fragile wife. When a yellow fever epidemic struck the city, she sickened and died, in a bed curtained with white muslin, but at the moment of death "she opened her mild eyes, and spoke words as from afar: 'Be a good boy. God bless you!'"

Soon after, her sorrowing widower clasped his young tenant and employee to his breast and declared that "in future *you are to bear my name.*" What followed, Stanley claims, were two idyllic years of traveling on business with the man he refers to as "my father." They took river boats up and down the Mississippi, walking the decks together, reading aloud to each other, and talking about the Bible. But sadly, in 1861, Stanley's generous adoptive father followed his beloved wife into the next world. "For the first time I understood the sharpness of the pang which pierces the soul when a loved one lies with folded hands icy cold in the eternal sleep. As I contemplated the body I vexed myself with asking, Had my conduct been as perfect as I then wished it had been? Had I failed in aught? Had I esteemed him as he deserved?"

A poignant story — except that records show that both the elder Stanleys did not die until 1878, seventeen years later. Although they did adopt two children, both were girls. According to city directories and census reports, young Stanley lived not in their home but in a series of boarding houses. And Stanley the merchant had an angry quarrel and permanent rupture with his employee, after which he asked that the young man's name never again be mentioned in his presence.

Stanley's wishful description of his youth clearly owes something to his contemporary Charles Dickens, similarly fond of deathbed scenes, saintly women, and wealthy benefactors. It also owes much to Stanley's feeling that his real life was so embedded in disgrace that he would have to invent whatever self he presented to the world. Not only did he make up events in his autobiography, but he created journal entries about a dramatic shipwreck and other adventures that never happened. Sometimes an episode in his African travels appears in strikingly different form in his journal, in letters, in the newspaper articles he sent home, and in the books he wrote after each trip. Psychohistorians have had a feast.

One of the more revealing episodes Stanley describes or invents took place soon after he arrived in New Orleans, when he was sharing a bed in a boarding house with Dick Heaton, another young man who had come over from Liverpool as a deckhand. "He was so modest he would not retire by candle-light, and . . . when he got into bed he lay on the verge of it, far removed from contact with me. When I rose in the morning I found that he was not undressed." One day Stanley awoke and, looking at Dick Heaton asleep at his side, was "amazed to see what I took to be two tumours on his breast. . . . I sat up . . . and cried out . . . 'I know! I know! Dick, you are a girl.'" That evening Dick, who by then had confessed to being Alice, was gone. "She was never seen, or heard of, by me again; but I have hoped ever since that Fate was as propitious to her, as I think it was wise, in separating two young and simple creatures who might have been led, through excess of sentiment, into folly."

Like his Dickensian deathbed scene, this has an echo of legend — of the girl who disguises herself as a boy so that she can enlist as a soldier or run away to sea. Whether real or made up, the episode's emotional message is the same: Stanley's horror at the idea of finding himself so close to a woman.

When the American Civil War began, Stanley joined the Confederate Army, and in April 1862 went into combat with his regiment of Arkansas Volunteers at the battle of Shiloh, in Tennessee. On the second day of fighting he was surrounded by half a dozen Union soldiers and soon afterward found himself in a crowded, typhus-ridden prisoner-of-war camp outside Chicago. The only way out of this miserable place, he discovered, was to enlist in the Union Army, which he promptly did, only to fall ill with dysentery and receive a medical discharge. After working his way back and forth across the Atlantic as a sailor, in 1864 he enlisted in the Union Navy. His fine handwriting got him a post as ship's clerk on the frigate *Minnesota*. When the ship bombarded a Confederate fort in North Carolina, Stanley became one of the few people to see combat on both sides of the Civil War.

The *Minnesota* returned to port in early 1865, and the restless Stanley deserted. Now the pace of his movements accelerates. It is as if he has no more patience for confining, regulated institutions like the workhouse, a merchant ship, or the military. He goes first to St. Louis, signs on as a free-lance contributor to a local newspaper, and sends back a series of florid dispatches from ever farther west: Denver, Salt Lake City, San Francisco. He writes disapprovingly of "debauchery and dissipation" and the "whirlpool of sin" of the Western frontier towns.

After an adventure-seeking trip to Turkey, Stanley returned to the American West, and his career as a newspaperman took off. For most of 1867 he covered the Indian Wars, sending dispatches not only to St. Louis but to East Coast papers as well. It did not matter that the long, hopeless struggle of the southern Plains Indians against the invaders of their land was almost at an end, that the expedition Stanley accompanied saw little combat, or that most of the year was devoted to peace negotiations; Stanley's editors wanted war reporting about dramatic battles, and this he gave them: "The Indian War has at last been fairly inaugurated. . . . the Indians, true to their promises, true to their bloody instincts, to their savage hatred of the white race, to the lessons instilled in their bosoms by their progenitors, are on the warpath."

These dispatches caught the eye of James Gordon Bennett, Jr., the flamboyant, hard-driving publisher of the *New York Herald*. He hired Stanley to cover an exotic little war that promised to sell many newspapers: a punitive expedition the British government was organizing against the Emperor of Abyssinia. At Suez, on his way to the war, Stanley bribed the chief telegraph clerk to make sure that when correspondents' reports arrived from the front, his would be the first cabled home. His foresight paid off, and his glowing account of how the British won the war's only significant battle was the first to reach the world. In a grand stroke of luck, the trans-Mediterranean telegraph cable broke just after Stanley's stories were sent off. The dispatches of his exasperated rivals, and even the British army's official reports, had to travel part of the way to Europe by ship. In a Cairo hotel, in June 1868, Stanley savored his scoop and the news that he had been named a permanent roving foreign correspondent for the *Herald*. He was twenty-seven years old.

⁂

Now based in London, Stanley could hear around him the first rumblings of what would before long become known as the Scramble for Africa. In a Europe confidently entering the industrial age, brimming with the sense of power given it by the railroad and the oceangoing steamship, there now arose a new type of hero: the African explorer. To those who had lived in Africa for millennia, of course, "there was nothing to discover, we were here all the time," as a future African statesman would put it. But to nineteenth-century Europeans, celebrating an explorer for "discovering" some new corner of Africa was, psychologically, a prelude to feeling that the continent was theirs for the taking.

In a Europe ever more tightly knit by the telegraph, the lecture circuit, and widely circulating daily newspapers, African explorers became some of the first international celebrity figures, their fame crossing national boundaries like that of today's champion athletes and movie stars. From Africa's east coast, the Englishmen Richard Burton and John Speke made a bold journey to the interior to find Lake Tanganyika, the longest freshwater lake in the world, and Lake Victoria, the continent's largest body of water, and capped their adventure with a spectacle the public always enjoys from celebrities, a bitter public falling-out. From Africa's west coast, the Frenchman Paul Belloni Du Chaillu brought back the skins and skeletons of gorillas, and told riveted audiences how the great hairy beasts abducted women to their jungle lairs for purposes too vile to be spoken of.

Underlying much of Europe's excitement was the hope that Africa would be a source of raw materials to feed the Industrial Revolution, just as the search for raw materials — slaves — for the colonial plantation economy had driven most of Europe's earlier dealings with Africa. Expectations quickened dramatically after prospectors discovered diamonds in South Africa in 1867 and gold some two decades later. But Europeans liked to think of themselves as having higher motives. The British, in particular, fervently believed in bringing "civilisation" and Christianity to the natives; they were curious about what lay in the continent's unknown interior; and they were filled with righteousness about combating slavery.

Britain, of course, had only a dubious right to the high moral view of slavery. British ships had long dominated the slave trade, and only in 1838 had slavery's vestiges been abolished in the British Empire. But the English quickly forgot all this, just as they forgot that there had been slave revolts in the West Indies and that economic factors had hastened slavery's end by making it less profitable. In their opinion, slavery had come to an end throughout most of the world for one reason only: British virtue. When London's Albert Memorial was built in 1872, one of its statues showed a young black African, naked except for some leaves over his loins. The memorial's inaugural handbook explained that he was a "representative of the uncivilised races" listening to a European woman's teaching, and that the "broken chains at his feet refer to the part taken by Great Britain in the emancipation of slaves."

Significantly, most British and French antislavery fervor in the 1860s was directed not at Spain and Portugal, which allowed slavery in their colonies, or at Brazil, with its millions of slaves. Instead, righteous denunciations poured down on a distant, weak, and safely nonwhite target: the so-called Arab slave-traders raiding Africa from the east. In the slave markets of Zanzibar, traders sold their human booty to Arab plantation owners on the island itself, and to other buyers in Persia, Madagascar, and the various sultanates and principalities of the Arabian peninsula. For Europeans, here was an ideal target for disapproval: one "uncivilised" race enslaving another.

Arab was a misnomer; Afro-Arab would have been more accurate. Although their captives often ended up in the Arab world, the traders on the African mainland were largely Swahili-speaking Africans from territory that today is Kenya and Tanzania. Many had adopted Arab dress and Islam, but only some of them were of even partly Arab descent. Nonetheless, from Edinburgh to Rome, indignant books and speeches and sermons denounced the vicious "Arab" slavers — and with them, by implication, the idea that any part of Africa might be colonized by someone other than Europeans.

All these European impulses toward Africa — antislavery zeal, the search for raw materials, Christian evangelism, and sheer curiosity — were embodied in one man, David Livingstone. Physician, prospector, missionary, explorer, and at one point even a British consul, he wandered across Africa for three decades, starting in the early 1840s. He searched for the source of the Nile, denounced slavery, found Victoria Falls, looked for minerals, and preached the gospel. As the first white man to cross the continent from coast to coast,* he became a national hero in England.

In 1866, Livingstone set off on another long expedition, looking for slave-traders, potential Christians, the Nile, or anything else that might

---

* Unfortunately for the apostles of European civilization, the first recorded crossing of central Africa, unacknowledged by Stanley and almost all the other white explorers, had been made half a century earlier by two mulatto slave traders, Pedro Baptista and Anastasio José. Theirs was also the first round trip.

need discovering. Years passed, and he did not return. As people began to wonder about his fate, *New York Herald* publisher James Gordon Bennett saw a great opportunity. In 1869, or so went the story Stanley would tell, Stanley received an urgent telegram from Bennett, his boss: COME TO PARIS ON IMPORTANT BUSINESS. A journalist, Stanley wrote with the self-importance that had now become part of his public persona, is "like a gladiator in the arena. . . . Any flinching, any cowardice, and he is lost. The gladiator meets the sword that is sharpened for his bosom — the . . . roving correspondent meets the command that may send him to his doom." He dashed to Paris to meet his publisher at the Grand Hotel. There, a dramatic conversation about Livingstone climaxed with Bennett's saying, "I mean that you shall go, and find him wherever you may hear that he is, and to get what news you can of him, and perhaps . . . the old man may be in want: — take enough with you to help him should he require it . . . do what you think best — BUT FIND LIVINGSTONE!"

This scene provided a splendid introduction for Stanley's first book, *How I Found Livingstone,* and it made Bennett, to whom the volume is dedicated, appear the far-sighted initiator of the great adventure. But nothing like this conversation seems to have happened. The pages of Stanley's journal for the dates around the alleged meeting with Bennett have been torn out, and in fact Stanley did not even begin looking for Livingstone until well over a year later.

However inflated, Stanley's story of Bennett's dramatic summons to Paris sold plenty of books, and to Stanley that mattered. He was after more than fame as an explorer; his melodramatic flair made him, as one historian has remarked, "the progenitor of all the subsequent professional travel writers." His articles, books, and speaking tours brought him greater riches than any other travel writer of his time, and probably of the next century as well. With every step he took in Africa, Stanley planned how to tell the story once he got home. In a twentieth-century way, he was always sculpting the details of his own celebrity.

To leave no clues for possible competitors in the search for Livingstone, Stanley carefully spread the word, as he headed for Africa, that he was planning to explore the Rufiji River. He first went to Zanzibar to recruit porters to carry his supplies, and from there wrote a stream of letters to Katie Gough-Roberts, a young woman in his home town of Denbigh. Theirs had been a brief, stiff, nervous courtship, punctuated by Stanley's many departures for journalistic assignments, but in his letters he poured out his heart to her, confessing the painful secret of his illegitimate birth. Stanley planned to marry her on his return from finding Livingstone.

At last, in the spring of 1871, accompanied by a dog named Omar and porters, armed guards, an interpreter, cooks, a guide carrying the American flag, and two British sailors — some 190 men in all, the largest African exploring expedition to date — Stanley marched inland from the east coast in search of Livingstone, who by now had not been seen by any European for five years. "Wherever he is," Stanley declared to his New York newspaper readers, "be sure I shall not give up the chase. If alive, you shall hear what he has to say; if dead I will find and bring his bones to you."

Stanley had to trek for more than eight months before he found the explorer and was able to utter his famous "Dr. Livingstone, I presume?" The long search was shaped into legend by his stream of dispatches and Bennett's realization that his newspaper had one of the great human-interest scoops of the century. Because Stanley was the only source of information about the search (his two white companions died during the expedition, and no one ever bothered to interview the surviving porters), the legend remained heroic. There were the months of arduous marching, the terrible swamps, the evil "Arab" slave-traders, the mysterious deadly diseases, the perilous attacks by crocodiles, and finally Stanley's triumphant discovery of the gentle Dr. Livingstone.

Livingstone was haloed in Stanley's prose, for he was the noble father figure the younger man had long been looking for and, to some extent, had actually found. According to Stanley, the experienced sage and the bold young hero became fast friends as they explored together for several months. (They sailed around the northern end of Lake Tanganyika, hoping to find the Nile flowing out, but to their disappointment found only another river flowing in.) The older man passed on his wisdom to the younger before they sadly bade each other farewell and parted forever. Conveniently for Stanley, Livingstone remained in Africa and died soon afterward, before he could come home to share the spotlight or to tell the story at all differently. Stanley cannily sprinkled his tale with picturesque chiefs, exotic sultans, and faithful servants, and he introduced it with the sweeping generalizations that allowed his readers to feel at home in an unfamiliar world: "The Arab never changes"; "The Banyan is a born trader"; "For the half-castes I have great contempt."

Unlike the uncombative and paternalistic Livingstone, who traveled without a huge retinue of heavily armed followers, Stanley was a harsh and brutal taskmaster. "The blacks give an immense amount of trouble; they are too ungrateful to suit my fancy," he wrote while on the journey. Although they are softened by successive revisions, his writings show him given to explosive rage. He drove his men up hills and through swamps without letup. "When mud and wet sapped the physical energy of the lazily-inclined, a dog-whip became their backs, restoring them to a sound — sometimes to an extravagant — activity." Only half a dozen years earlier Stanley had deserted from the U.S. Navy, but now he noted with satisfaction how "the incorrigible deserters . . . were well flogged and chained." People in the villages that the expedition marched through may well have mistaken it for another slave caravan.

Like many whites who would follow him, Stanley saw Africa as essentially empty. "Unpeopled country," he called it. "What a settlement one could have in this valley! See, it is broad enough to support a large population. Fancy a church spire rising where that tamarind rears its dark crown of foliage, and think how well a score or two of pretty cottages would look instead of those thorn clumps and gum trees!" And again: "There are plenty of . . . Pilgrim Fathers among the Anglo-Saxon race yet, and when America is filled up with their descendants, who shall say that Africa . . . shall not be their next resting place?"

To him and to his public, Stanley's future was now firmly linked to Africa. On his return to Europe, the French press compared his finding Livingstone to Hannibal's and Napoleon's crossing the Alps. Even more aptly, given Stanley's boasts about shooting anyone who got in his way, General William Tecumseh Sherman met the explorer for breakfast in Paris and likened Stanley's trip to his own scorched-earth march to the sea.

The British were more hostile. The Royal Geographical Society had belatedly sent an expedition to find Livingstone, and its members had been appalled to cross paths with Stanley in Africa just as he was triumphantly boarding a ship to return home. Between the lines of huffy statements from the society's officials was their exasperation that their native son had been found by someone who was neither a proper explorer nor a proper Englishman, but a "penny-a-liner," writing for the American yellow press. Furthermore, some in England noticed, Stanley's American accent tended to change to a Welsh one whenever he got excited. The rumors about his Welsh birth and illegitimacy worried Stanley deeply, because, writing for a jingoistic and anti-British New York newspaper, he was vigorously claiming to be American born and bred.

(He sometimes implied that he came from New York; sometimes from St. Louis. Mark Twain sent congratulations to his "fellow Missourian" for finding Livingstone.)

Stanley, quick to feel rejected, especially by upper-crust Englishmen, now found himself rejected also by his fiancée. During his travels, he discovered, Katie Gough-Roberts had married an architect named Bradshaw. Stanley was desperate to retrieve the letters he had sent her, particularly the one in which he had told her about his origins. But when he wrote to ask for them, she refused to give them back except in person. At a lecture he gave in Manchester, she and her husband were in the audience. Afterward, she came to the house where he was staying and asked the butler to tell him she had the letter with her. Stanley sent the butler back to the door to collect it; once again she refused to hand it over to anyone but Stanley. He would not go to the door, and she departed, letter in hand. His hurt pride remained like an open wound. Before long he would once again seek solace in Africa.

2

THE FOX CROSSES
THE STREAM

WHEN WORD that Stanley had found Livingstone flashed over the
telegraph wires in the spring of 1872, one person who followed
such news with avid interest was a tall, august thirty-seven-year-old man
with a spade-shaped beard, living in the rambling château of Laeken on a
low hill on the outskirts of Brussels.

Seven years earlier, on the death of his father, Leopold II had inherited the distinctive title by which his country's monarchs were known,
King of the Belgians. Belgium itself was barely older than its young
monarch. After spells of Spanish, Austrian, French, and Dutch rule, it
had only become independent in 1830, following a revolt against Holland. Any respectable country of course needed a king, and the infant
nation had gone looking for one, finally settling on a German prince,
related to the British royal family, who had taken the Belgian throne as
Leopold I.

The small nation was an uneasy amalgam of speakers of French and
speakers of Flemish, as the Dutch spoken in Belgium's northern half was
then called. In his father's court, the future Leopold II spoke French and
German from childhood and soon became fluent in English. However,
although he tossed a few phrases of it into speeches now and then, he
never bothered to learn Flemish, spoken by more than half his subjects. In
this snobbery Leopold was not alone, for at this time his country's bitter
language division marked class as well as region. Even in the north,
business people and professionals tended to speak French and to look

down on the impoverished Flemish-speaking farmworkers and factory laborers.

The marriage of Leopold's parents had been a loveless one of political convenience. Their older son was a gangling child who seemed ill at ease in the world, and his parents clearly preferred his younger brother and sister. When he was fourteen, Leopold's mother wrote to him, "I was very disturbed to see in the Colonel's report that you had again been so lazy and that your exercises had been so bad and careless. This was not what you promised me, and I hope you will make some effort to do your homework better. Your father was as disturbed as I by this last report." The young heir took little interest in his studies, with the notable exception of geography. From the age of ten on, he was given military training; by fifteen, he held the rank of lieutenant in the Belgian Army, at sixteen captain, at eighteen major, at nineteen colonel, and by the time he was twenty he was a major general. A formal portrait painted in his late teens shows him with sword, crimson sash, and medals. The awkward young Leopold's body is pencil-thin; his gold epaulettes seem too big for his shoulders; his head too big for his torso.

If Leopold wanted to see his father, he had to apply for an audience. When the father had something to tell the son, he communicated it through one of his secretaries. It was in this cold atmosphere, as a teenager in his father's court, that Leopold first learned to assemble a network of people who hoped to win his favor. Court officials proved eager to befriend the future monarch, to show him documents, to teach him how the government worked, to satisfy his passion for maps and for information about far corners of the world.

Even though there was little affection between father and son, the old king was a shrewd observer. "Leopold is subtle and sly," he told one of his ministers. "He never takes a chance. The other day . . . I watched a fox which wanted to cross a stream unobserved: first of all he dipped a paw carefully to see how deep it was, and then, with a thousand precautions, very slowly made his way across. That is Leopold's way!" Leopold would not always be cautious; at times he would overreach himself or reveal too much about what prey he was after. But there was something fox-like about the manner in which this constitutional monarch of a small, increasingly democratic country became the totalitarian ruler of a vast empire on another continent. Stealth and dissembling would be his trusted devices, just as the fox relies on these qualities to survive in a world of hunters and larger beasts.

In 1853, when Leopold turned eighteen, his father took him to Vienna and, eager for ties with the Austro-Hungarian Empire, betrothed him to an eligible young Hapsburg, Archduchess Marie-Henriette.

No match could have been more disastrous. The sixteen-year-old bride was best known for her passion for horses and for a most unroyal raucous laugh. Leopold had a distinct tendency to fall off horses and no visible sense of humor. He was an ungainly, haughty young man whom his first cousin Queen Victoria of England thought "very odd" and in the habit of "saying disagreeable things to people." Then known as the Duke of Brabant, Leopold had a pedantic obsession with trade matters, which baffled everyone. In Vienna, one lady observed that this puzzling engagement was "between a stable-boy and a nun, and by nun I mean the Duke of Brabant."

Leopold and Marie-Henriette loathed each other at first sight, feelings that apparently never changed. Everything possible went wrong with the wedding. Leopold got scarlet fever. The train bringing the royal entourage to a carefully timed elaborate welcoming ceremony for Marie-Henriette at the Belgian border was half an hour late, because a teenage railway telegraph operator had left his post to listen to a band concert celebrating the day. Marie-Henriette's barnyard laugh startled town hall receptions all over Belgium. On their honeymoon in Venice, she wept in public when Leopold would not let her ride in a gondola for which boatmen and musicians had already been hired. Leopold went for days at a time without speaking to her. "If God hears my prayers," she wrote to a friend a month after the wedding, "I shall not go on living much longer."

Like many young couples of the day, the newlyweds apparently found sex a frightening mystery. Like few others, however, they were enlightened about it by the woman who gave her name to the age. When they paid a visit to Cousin Victoria in England, the queen delicately expressed some doubt, in a letter to Leopold's father, as to whether the marriage had been consummated. Taking Marie-Henriette aside, she explained what was expected of her, as did her husband, Prince Albert, with the eighteen-year-old future king. This may have been the first time anyone had bothered to do so, for when Marie-Henriette became pregnant, several years later, Leopold wrote to Albert that "the wise and practical advice you gave me . . . has now borne fruit." But the marriage remained miserable. Marie-Henriette fled the royal château of Laeken to go horseback riding for most of each day. Leopold was to find respite from his frustrations on a wider stage.

When he thought about the throne that would be his, he was openly exasperated. *"Petit pays, petits gens"* (small country, small people), he once said of Belgium. The country, less than half the size of West Virginia, lay between Napoleon III's much grander France and the fast-rising empire of Germany. The young heir acted peeved and impatient. The country he was to inherit seemed too small to hold him.

His eyes turned abroad. Even before he was twenty, Leopold, pen and notebook in hand, visited the Balkans, Constantinople, the Aegean, and Egypt, traveling in style on British and Turkish warships, and, returning home, gave tedious speeches on Belgium's potential role in world trade. Everywhere he went, he looked for imperial opportunities. He got the Khedive of Egypt to promise to form a joint steamship company connecting Alexandria with Antwerp. He tried to buy lakes in the Nile delta so that he could drain them and claim the land as a colony. He wrote, "One could purchase a small kingdom in Abyssinia for 30,000 francs. . . . If instead of talking so much about neutrality Parliament looked after our commerce, Belgium would become one of the richest countries in the world."

In the nineteenth century, as is true today, Seville was a magnificent array of fountains and walled gardens, of red-tile roofs and white-stucco walls and windows covered by wrought-iron grillwork, of orange and lemon and palm trees. Threading through the Spanish city were narrow cobblestone streets filled with visitors come to look at one of the largest Gothic cathedrals in Europe.

When the twenty-seven-year-old Leopold arrived in Seville, in March 1862, his purpose was not to see the cathedral or the famous mosaics and courtyards of the brightly tiled Alcázar palace. Instead, he spent a full month in the Casa Lonja, or Old Exchange Building, a massive, square structure opposite the cathedral.

For two centuries Seville was the port through which colonial gold, silver, and other riches had flowed back to Spain; some eighty years before Leopold's visit, King Carlos III had ordered that there be gathered in this building, from throughout the country, all decrees, government and court records, correspondence, maps and architectural drawings, having to do with the Spanish conquest of the Americas. Collected under one roof, these eighty-six million handwritten pages, among them the supply manifest for one of Columbus's ships, have made the General Archive of the Indies one of the great repositories of the world. Indifferent to his schoolwork as a boy, with no interest whatever in art, music, or literature, Leopold was nonetheless a dedicated scholar when it came to one subject, profits. During the month he spent in Seville, he wrote home to a friend, "I am very busy here going through the Indies archives and calculating the profit which Spain made then and makes now out of her colonies." The man whose future empire would be intertwined with the twentieth-century multinational corporation began by studying the records of the conquistadors.

The research whetted his appetite and made him restless. He claimed that his doctors had prescribed long cruises in hot climates, and, escaping his miserable home life, he headed farther afield. In 1864, now twenty-nine and more obsessed with colonies than ever, he set off to see the British possessions of Ceylon, India, and Burma. He also visited the East Indian islands owned, to his irritation, by Belgium's next-door neighbor, Holland, whose small size had not prevented it from acquiring lucrative colonies.

The future king's interest in the Dutch East Indies was stimulated by a curious two-volume treatise called *Java; or, How to Manage a Colony.* Fascinated by the book, Leopold began corresponding with the author, an English lawyer aptly named J. W. B. Money. Money had been impressed by the coffee, sugar, indigo, and tobacco plantations of Java, whose profits had paid for railroads and canals back in Holland. Judging from Leopold's later actions, we can guess which features of the book might have caught his eye. Money described, for example, a monopoly trading concession given to a private company, one of whose major shareholders was the Dutch king. To stimulate production, Dutch plantation owners paid bonuses to supervisors on Java in relation to the size of the crop harvested. And finally Money noted that the huge Dutch profits from Java depended on forced labor. Leopold agreed, remarking that forced labor was "the only way to civilize and uplift these indolent and corrupt peoples of the Far East."

Few Belgians shared Leopold's dreams of colonies. They were deterred by practical considerations — such as their country's lack of a merchant fleet or navy — that seemed petty to him. When he returned from one of his trips he presented to the finance minister, a vocal opponent of colonialism, a gift: a piece of marble from the ruins of the Acropolis, with a locket holding Leopold's portrait, around which was the legend *Il faut à la Belgique une colonie* (Belgium must have a colony).

Where was it to be found? Throughout his twenties, he scoured the world. He wrote to an aide:

> I am specially interested in the Argentine Province of Entre Rios and the very small island of Martin Garcia at the confluence of the Uruguay and the Parana. Who owns this island? Could one buy it, and establish there a free port under the moral protection of the King of the Belgians? . . . Nothing would be easier than to become the owner of lands in the Argentine states three or four times as big as Belgium.

He invested in the Suez Canal Company. He asked an aide to try to acquire Fiji, because one should not "let such a fine prey escape." He looked into railways in Brazil and into leasing territory on the island of Formosa.

Leopold's letters and memos, forever badgering someone about acquiring a colony, seem to be in the voice of a person starved for love as a child and now filled with an obsessive desire for an emotional substitute, the way someone becomes embroiled in an endless dispute with a brother or sister over an inheritance, or with a neighbor over a property boundary. The urge for more can become insatiable, and its apparent fulfillment seems only to exacerbate that early sense of deprivation and to stimulate the need to acquire still more.

During the nineteenth-century European drive for possessions in Africa and Asia, people justified colonialism in various ways, claiming that it Christianized the heathen or civilized the savage races or brought everyone the miraculous benefits of free trade. Now, with Africa, a new rationalization had emerged: smashing the "Arab" slave trade. At this early stage of his career, however, the future Leopold II did not try to cloak his ambitions with such rhetoric. For him, colonies existed for one purpose: to make him and his country rich. "Belgium doesn't exploit the world," he complained to one of his advisers. "It's a taste we have got to make her learn."

Leopold did not care whether the colonial wealth he wanted came from the precious metals sought by the Spaniards in South America, from agriculture, or — as would turn out to be the case — from a raw material whose potential was as yet undreamed of. What mattered was the size of the profit. His drive for colonies, however, was shaped by a desire not only for money but for power. In western Europe, after all, times were fast changing, and a king's role was not as enjoyable as it once had been. Most annoying to him was that in Belgium, as in surrounding countries, royal authority was gradually giving way to that of an elected parliament. Someone once tried to compliment Leopold by saying that he would make "an excellent president of a republic." Scornfully, he turned to his faithful court physician, Jules Thiriar, and asked, "What would you say, Doctor, if someone greeted you as 'a great veterinarian'?" The ruler of a colony would have no parliament to worry about.

After ascending the throne, in 1865, Leopold was even more restless than before. A French marshal who saw him at a reception in Paris in 1867 thought him conspicuous "by his great height, his great nose, and his great beard; with his sword, which banged his legs, he looked like a functionary who had put on his uniform without knowing how to wear it." Everyone was struck by the nose. "It is such a nose," Disraeli wrote, "as a young prince has in a fairy tale, who has been banned by a malignant fairy."

At home, life went from bad to worse. In 1869, the king's nine-year-old son fell into a pond, caught pneumonia, and died. At the funeral, for the only time in his life, Leopold broke down in public, collapsing to his knees beside the coffin and sobbing uncontrollably. He had the presence of mind, however, to ask Parliament to pass a law requiring the state to pay the expenses of the royal funeral.

What made the loss of his only son especially devastating was the king's firm belief that thrones and royal property were for men only. In the course of their marriage, however, Queen Marie-Henriette gave birth to three daughters, Louise, Stephanie, and Clementine, but to no more sons. When the last daughter, Clementine, was born, according to her sister Louise, "the King was furious and thenceforth refused to have anything to do with his admirable wife." From the beginning, she wrote, "the King paid little attention to me or my sisters." Leopold unsuccessfully tried to have himself made an exception to a Belgian law requiring assets to be bequeathed to one's children.

Marie-Henriette found solace with her beloved horses, which she trained herself. Princess Louise once watched as, obeying the queen's commands, a horse entered the château of Laeken, climbed the staircase to the queen's rooms, and descended again. Marie-Henriette befriended the minister of war, and at maneuvers, to the astonishment of military attachés, he sometimes invited her to lead cavalry charges.

Still lacking a colony to rule, Leopold focused on building projects at home. He had a taste for monuments, great parks, broad boulevards, and grand palaces. Soon after taking the throne he began what turned out to be a lifelong program of renovations at Laeken. Through purchases and expropriations, he enlarged the grounds of the royal estate severalfold. When one local resident refused to move, Leopold ordered an earth embankment built around the reluctant landowner's estate. Among the new buildings at Laeken was a vast string of greenhouses. When they were finally finished, a person could walk for more than a kilometer through them, the château, and connecting passageways, without going outdoors. In later years, when the king was showing his nephew, Prince Albert, some work in progress, Albert said, "Uncle, this is going to become a little Versailles!" Leopold replied, "Little?"

⚜

If Leopold were a figure in fiction, his creator might, at this point in the story, introduce a foil, a minor character whose fate would sound an ominous warning about where dreams of empire can lead. But Leopold already had such a character in his life, more appropriate to the role than one a novelist could have invented. It was his sister.

The Belgian royal family, always eager to form alliances with the Hapsburgs, had married off Leopold's younger sister Charlotte to Archduke Maximilian, brother of the Emperor of Austria-Hungary. In 1864, Maximilian and his wife, her name appropriately changed to Carlota, were installed by Napoleon III of France as the figurehead Emperor and Empress of Mexico, where Napoleon was maneuvering to establish a French-aligned regime. Leopold enthusiastically supported his sister's venture into empire-building. As Maximilian and Carlota set off for their new dominion, the European public cheered the handsome young couple, who were portrayed as following in the footsteps of the conquistadors. Most Mexicans, understandably, wanted no such rulers imposed on them, and they rose in rebellion. The nascent empire collapsed, and in June 1867 rebels captured and executed Maximilian. His death was inglorious but not inelegant: he shook hands with the members of the firing squad, handed them all gold pieces, pointed to his heart, and said, "*Muchachos,* aim well."

The previous year, Carlota had returned to Europe to plead for support for her husband's failing regime. Napoleon III was unwilling to back up his Mexican ambitions with the necessary military force, so Carlota went to Rome to beg for help from the Pope. On the way she began behaving strangely. Modern psychiatry would doubtless have a more precise diagnosis, but the language of her day seems more appropriate: Carlota went mad. She became convinced that an organ grinder on the street was a Mexican colonel in disguise, and that spies of every sort were trying to poison her. As a precaution she ate only oranges and nuts, checking the peels and shells for signs of tampering. She made her coachman stop at Rome's Trevi fountain so that she could fill a crystal pitcher with water certain not to be poisoned. In her hotel suite she kept a small charcoal stove and, tied to table legs, several chickens, to be slaughtered and cooked only in her sight. With her obedient staff in despair, her rooms slowly filled with feathers and chicken droppings.

Flushed and weeping, Carlota burst in on the Pope one morning as he was finishing breakfast, dipped her fingers in his hot chocolate, and licked them hungrily, crying, "This at least is not poisoned. Everything they gave me is drugged, and I am starving, literally starving!" A cardinal and the commander of the Papal Guards maneuvered her out of the room, whereupon Carlota gave the guards' commander a list of her staff members who should be arrested for treachery.

Carlota's aides sent an urgent telegram to Leopold in Brussels. Since he did not want his sister rattling around Europe in this condition, he installed her and her keepers in a succession of Belgian châteaux, safely out of public sight. She was never to appear in the wider world again. For fear of unhinging her further, no one dared tell her for some months of Maximilian's execution; when they finally did, Carlota refused to believe them. She continued to send him letters and presents, believing that he would soon become Emperor of France, Spain, and Portugal.

The collapse, in so short a time, of his sister's and brother-in-law's empire did not dampen Leopold's enthusiasm for one of his own. All around him he saw the stirrings of a new age of colonialism; this was the era in which the future South African politician and diamond magnate Cecil Rhodes would say, "I would annex the planets if I could." In 1875, Leopold tried to buy the Philippines from Spain but was once again frustrated. "For the moment, neither the Spanish nor the Portuguese nor the Dutch are inclined to sell," he wrote to one of his officials that year, and then added, "I intend to find out discreetly if there's anything to be done in Africa."

In the mid-1870s, sub-Saharan Africa was a logical place for an aspiring colonialist to look. The British and the Boers controlled South Africa, and an enfeebled Portugal claimed most of what used to be the Kingdom of the Kongo, as well as Mozambique on the east coast. Along Africa's great western bulge, Portugal, Spain, Britain, and France owned a few islands and small pockets of territory. Otherwise, about 80 percent of the entire land area of Africa was still under indigenous rulers. It was ripe for conquest — or, as Leopold was now learning to say, for protection.

Leopold carefully combed the *Proceedings of the Royal Geographical Society* for information about the continent and closely followed the treks of white explorers. He amassed a big file of notes, in nearly illegible hand-writing. When the Scottish explorer Verney Lovett Cameron, about to become the first European to cross Africa from east to west, was reported in 1875 to be running out of money, Leopold swiftly offered a contribution of 100,000 francs. The money was not needed, it turned out, but the king's gesture declared him a patron of African exploration.

Henry Morton Stanley at this time was in the midst of another expedition in Africa. He and his usual huge caravan of guards and porters had set off in 1874 from the east coast to the interior, heading for the biggest blank space on the map, the equatorial heart of the continent, where no European had yet been. On the way, he planned to map several of the great east African lakes and then push on to a large river, west of them, which might be the start of the Nile or the Congo. While he was still near the coast, messengers brought back Stanley's newspaper dispatches; then nothing more was heard from him.

Livingstone, Stanley, and the other explorers, Leopold saw, had succeeded in stirring Europeans by their descriptions of the "Arab" slave-traders leading sad caravans of chained captives to Africa's east coast. As king of a small country with no public interest in colonies, he recognized that a colonial push of his own would require a strong humanitarian veneer. Curbing the slave trade, moral uplift, and the advancement of science were the aims he would talk about, not profits. In 1876, he began planning a step to establish his image as a philanthropist and advance his African ambitions: he would host a conference of explorers and geographers.

He sent a trusted aide to Berlin to recruit German participants while he himself slipped across the English Channel to London, settling into a suite at Claridges. By this time, he was far from being the awkward, naive youngster who had visited Queen Victoria on his honeymoon, more than twenty years earlier. As we watch him now moving about London, for the first time in his life he seems polished and cosmopolitan, at ease and quietly purposeful. He moves mainly in a world of men, but he remembers the names of their wives and children, and always asks about them warmly. His frustrations are concealed, his raw lust for colonies moderated by the knowledge that he must depend on subterfuge and flattery. He pays a visit to dear Cousin Victoria at Balmoral Castle in Scotland, dines twice with her son, the Prince of Wales, and visits eminent geographers and military men. Shrewdly, he also goes to lunch with Baroness Angela Burdett-Coutts, a well-known patron of missionaries. Most important, he meets the explorer Cameron, recently returned from crossing Africa, and grills him about his travels. To his delight, Leopold finds that the British have little interest in the great swath of territory Cameron has just explored. Most of it is believed to be the basin of the Congo River, although Cameron himself traveled far south of the river, and like everyone else in Europe still has no clear idea of its course. This is the land that now becomes the object of the king's desires.

In September 1876, Leopold's Geographical Conference convened in Brussels. In the orders he gave to subordinates, no detail of protocol, however minute, escaped his attention: "The names must be spelled just as I have written them. G.C.B. means Grand Cross of Bath. F.R.G.S. means Fellow of the Royal Geographical Society. K.C.B. means Knight Commander of the Bath. . . . These letters must be written after the names." He sent a Belgian ship across the Channel to Dover for the British guests, and had a special express train bring them the rest of the way. He issued orders that all those coming to the conference should be waved across the Belgian frontier without customs formalities. Representatives, who came from all the major European countries, were appropriately greeted by Leopold in English, French, or German.

Among the thirteen Belgians and twenty-four foreign guests were famous explorers, like France's Marquis de Compiègne, who had gone up the Ogowe River in Gabon, and Germany's Gerhard Rohlfs, who had had himself circumcised so that he could pass for a Muslim while trekking to remote parts of the Sahara; geographers, like Baron Ferdinand von Rich-thofen, the president of the Berlin Geographical Society; humanitarians, like Sir Thomas Fowell Buxton, president of Britain's Anti-Slavery Soci-ety, and Sir John Kennaway, president of the Church Missionary Society; business executives, like William Mackinnon of the British India Line; and military men, like Rear Admiral Sir Leopold Heath of England, who had headed the Royal Navy's Indian Ocean antislavery patrol, and Vice Admiral Baron de la Roncière-le-Noury, president of the Paris Geo-graphical Society. Never in the nineteenth century had so many eminent Europeans in the field of exploration gathered in one spot, and the guests were delighted to become acquainted with one another in the luxurious surroundings of the Royal Palace. Almost the only notable European concerned with Africa who was not there was Stanley, whose work the conference acknowledged with a formal resolution. He was, everyone hoped, still alive somewhere in the middle of the continent. There had been no news of him for months.

Leopold knew that even the wealthy and well-born would be de-lighted to live in a palace. The only complication was that the Royal Palace, in downtown Brussels, was really the king's office; the royal fam-ily's home was the suburban château of Laeken. And so the Royal Palace's staff quarters and offices were hastily converted to guest bedrooms. To make room for the visitors, some servants slept in linen closets, and desks, books, and filing cabinets were moved to the basement or the stables. On the opening day, dazzled conference participants filed up a new baroque grand staircase of white marble to be received by Leopold in a throne room illuminated by seven thousand candles. The king awarded the Cross of Leopold to everyone he had invited. "I have a suite of magnificent apartments to myself — all crimson damask and gold," Major General Sir Henry Rawlinson of the Royal Geographical Society wrote to his wife the first night. "Everything is red, even the Ink and the Ammunition [toilet paper]!"

Leopold's welcoming speech was a masterpiece. It clothed the whole enterprise in noble rhetoric, staked out his own role in what was to come, and guaranteed his plans a stamp of approval by the group he was hosting.

To open to civilization the only part of our globe which it has not yet penetrated, to pierce the darkness which hangs over entire peoples, is, I dare say, a crusade worthy of this century of progress. . . . It seemed to me that Belgium, a centrally located and neutral country, would be a suitable place for such a meeting. . . . Need I say that in bringing you to Brussels I was guided by no egotism? No, gentlemen, Belgium may be a small country, but she is happy and satisfied with her fate; I have no other ambition than to serve her well.

He ended by naming the specific tasks he hoped the conference would accomplish, among them deciding on the "location of routes to be successively opened into the interior, of hospitable, scientific, and pacification bases to be set up as a means of abolishing the slave trade, establishing peace among the chiefs, and procuring them just and impartial arbitration."

Between sumptuous banquets, those attending the conference pulled out their maps and marked points in the blank space of central Africa for such "hospitable, scientific, and pacification bases." Each one, the high-minded guests decided, would be staffed by a half-dozen or so unarmed Europeans — scientists, linguists, and artisans who would teach practical skills to the natives. Every post would contain laboratories for studying local soil, weather, fauna, and flora, and would be well stocked with supplies for explorers: maps, trading goods, spare clothing, tools to repair scientific instruments, an infirmary with all the latest medicines.

Chairing the conference — Leopold stayed modestly in the background — was the Russian geographer Pyotr Semenov. In honor of Semenov's daring exploration of the Tyan Shan Mountains of Central Asia, the tsar had granted him the right to add Tyan-Shansky to his name. Semenov, however, knew next to nothing about Africa — which suited Leopold perfectly. He was easily able to maneuver Semenov so that the chain of bases endorsed by the conference would stretch across the unclaimed territory of the Congo River basin that interested Leopold most. The British participants had wanted some of these posts nearer to British possessions.

Before the guests dispersed to their respective countries, they voted to establish the International African Association. Leopold magnanimously volunteered space in Brussels for the organization's headquarters. There were to be national committees of the association set up in all the participating countries, as well as an international committee. Leopold was elected by acclamation as the international committee's first chairman. Self-effacingly, he said that he would serve for one year only so that the chairmanship could rotate among people from different countries. He presented each guest with a gilt-framed portrait of himself in dress uniform, and the awed dignitaries and explorers headed home.

The new body was welcomed throughout Europe. Prominent citizens, from the Rothschilds to Viscount Ferdinand de Lesseps, the builder of the Suez Canal, hastened to send contributions. The national committees, which sounded impressive, were to be headed by grand dukes, princes, and other royals, but most of them never got off the ground. The international committee did meet once in the following year, reelected Leopold as chairman, despite his earlier pledge not to serve again, and then evaporated.

Nonetheless, Leopold had, foxlike, gone a step forward. He had learned from his many attempts to buy a colony that none was for sale; he would have to conquer it. Doing this openly, however, was certain to upset both the Belgian people and the major powers of Europe. If he was to seize anything in Africa, he could do so only if he convinced everyone that his interest was purely altruistic. In this aim, thanks to the International African Association, he succeeded brilliantly. Viscount de Lesseps, for one, declared Leopold's plans "the greatest humanitarian work of this time."

If we take a step back and look at Leopold at this moment we can imagine him the political equivalent of an ambitious theatrical producer. He has organizational talent and the public's good will, as proven by his successful Geographical Conference. He has a special kind of capital: the great public relations power of the throne itself. He has a script: the dream of a colony that had been running through his head since he was a teenager. But he has as yet no stage, no cast. One day in September 1877, however, while the king-producer is planning his next move, a bulletin in the London *Daily Telegraph* from a small town on the west coast of Africa announces some remarkable news. It is just the opening Leopold has been waiting for. Stage and star have appeared, and the play can begin.

3

THE MAGNIFICENT CAKE

T HE TOWN of Boma lay on the Congo River's north shore, about fifty miles in from the Atlantic Ocean. Besides its African inhabitants, sixteen whites lived there, most of them Portuguese — rough, hardbitten men used to wielding the whip and the gun — who ran a few small trading posts. Like Europeans for several centuries before them, these traders had never trekked inland through the forbidding jumble of rocks lining the great river on the tumultuous 220 miles of intermittent rapids that carried it down to sea level.

On August 5, 1877, an hour after sunset, four bedraggled black men walked out of the bush at Boma. They had come from a village some two days' walk inland and were carrying a letter addressed "To any Gentleman who speaks English at Embomma."

> Dear Sir:
>
> I have arrived at this place from Zanzibar with 115 souls, men, women, and children. We are now in a state of imminent starvation . . . but if your supplies arrive in time, I may be able to reach Embomma within four days . . . better than all would [be] ten or fifteen man-loads of rice or grain. . . . The supplies must arrive within two days, or I may have a fearful time of it among the dying. . . . Yours sincerely, H.M. Stanley, Commanding Anglo-American Expedition for Exploration of Africa.

At dawn the next day the traders sent Stanley porters carrying potatoes, fish, rice, and canned food. They realized instantly what the letter meant: Stanley had crossed the entire African continent, from east to west. But unlike Verney Lovett Cameron, the only European to do this before him, he had emerged at the Congo's mouth. He must therefore have followed the river itself, becoming the first white man to chart its course and to solve the mystery of where it came from.

Resupplied just in time, Stanley and the haggard survivors of his expedition slowly walked the rest of the way to Boma. Since leaving Zanzibar, just off the east coast, they had covered a zigzag course of more than seven thousand miles and had been traveling for more than two and a half years.

A Welshman masquerading as a native-born United States citizen, Stanley was both the Anglo and the American of his Anglo-American Expedition. The name, however, acknowledged that this trip, far more expensive and ambitious than his search for Livingstone, was financed both by James Gordon Bennett's *New York Herald* and Edward Levy-Lawson's London *Daily Telegraph*. Stanley's dispatches appeared in both papers, and he bestowed the names of their owners on his route across Africa: Mount Gordon-Bennett, the Gordon-Bennett River, the Levy Hills, Mount Lawson. He left his own name on Stanley Falls in the center of the continent and on a spot about a thousand miles downstream, at the head of the rapids, where the Congo River widened into a lake. He claimed that naming the latter was the idea of his second-in-command, Frank Pocock, who "cried out, 'Why . . . this signal expanse we shall call Stanley Pool!'" Pocock was not able to confirm this; he drowned in the river soon after christening, or not christening, this portion of it.

On the eve of his formidable trans-African journey, Stanley had once again fallen in love, this time with Alice Pike, a seventeen-year-old American heiress. Falling for a flighty teenager half his age just before leaving for three years was not the most likely path to wedded bliss, which may have been just what attracted Stanley, who remained fearful of women. He and Alice agreed to marry on his return, signed a marriage pact, and fixed the date of the wedding.

It was after his new love that Stanley named the expedition's key means of transport. The *Lady Alice* was a forty-foot boat of Spanish cedar, divided into five sections. When the sections were fastened together, the boat could be rowed along African lakes and rivers; when they were separated and slung from poles, they could be carried overland by teams of porters for hundreds of miles.

Stanley was always uncomfortable with anyone whose talents might outshine his own. From the twelve hundred men who applied to join the expedition, some of them highly experienced travelers, he chose three unsuitable companions: a pair of sailor-fishermen, the brothers Frank and Edward Pocock, and a young hotel clerk named Frederick Barker. Edward Pocock's main skill seems to have been playing the bugle. None of the three had had any experience exploring.

When the four white men marched westward into the interior at the head of the Anglo-American Expedition, they led a group close to double the size of Stanley's expedition to find Livingstone — 356 people all told. Forty-six were women and children, for some of the senior Africans had been granted the privilege of taking along their families. This miniature army carried more than sixteen thousand pounds of arms, equipment, and goods that could be traded for food along the way. On the march the column stretched for half a mile, a distance so long that halts had to be signaled by Edward Pocock's bugle.

The bugle calls were appropriate; for Stanley, continual combat was always part of exploring. He never bothered to count the dead that the expedition left behind it, but the number must have been in the hundreds. Stanley's party carried the latest rifles and an elephant gun with exploding bullets; the unlucky people they fought had spears, bows and arrows, or, at best, ancient muskets bought from slave-traders. "We have attacked and destroyed 28 large towns and three or four score villages," he wrote in his journal. Most of the fighting took place on lakes and rivers, with the explorer and his men flying the British and American flags and firing from the *Lady Alice* and dugout canoes. The thin-skinned Stanley was remarkably frank about his tendency to take any show of hostility as a deadly insult. It is almost as if vengeance were the force driving him across the continent. As he piloted the *Lady Alice* toward a spot on Lake Tanganyika, for instance, "the beach was crowded with infuriates and mockers . . . we perceived we were followed by several canoes in some of which we saw spears shaken at us . . . I opened on them with the Winchester Repeating Rifle. Six shots and four deaths were sufficient to quiet the mocking."

In the early months of the journey, Stanley was able to describe such skirmishes in newspaper stories carried by messengers to Africa's east coast, where they were relayed to England by sea and telegraph. There, they stirred a storm of outrage from humanitarian groups like the Aborigines Protection Society and the Anti-Slavery Society. Stanley "shoots negroes as if they were monkeys," commented the explorer and writer Richard Burton. The British foreign secretary, however, seemed far more upset that this brash writer for the popular press, who claimed to be an American, was flying the Union Jack. He sent Stanley a pompous message declaring that such display was not authorized.

To the *New York Herald*'s vehemently anti-British publisher James Gordon Bennett, Jr., the controversy brought nothing but delight. He lashed out enthusiastically at Stanley's critics as "the howling dervishes of civilization . . . safe in London . . . the philanthropists . . . [whose] impractical view is that a leader . . . should permit his men to be slaughtered by the natives and should be slaughtered himself and let discovery go to the dogs, but should never pull a trigger against this species of human vermin."

Among the achievements of this first stage of his travels, Stanley claimed, was telling the Emperor of Uganda about the Ten Commandments and converting him to Christianity. However, a French officer who happened to be visiting Uganda at this time later said that Stanley convinced the emperor only by telling him that Christians had eleven commandments. The eleventh was: "Honor and respect kings, for they are the envoys of God."

After months of carrying heavy loads, many of the expedition's porters mutinied, pilfered supplies, and fled. Again and again, Stanley dealt out swift punishment: "The murderer of Membé . . ." he wrote in his diary, "was sentenced to 200 lashes . . . the two drunkards to 100 lashes each, and to be kept in chains for 6 months." Later, he wrote of his porters, "They are faithless, lying, thievish, indolent knaves, who only teach a man to despise himself for his folly in attempting a grand work with such miserable slaves."

With his fiancée, Alice Pike, he took a different tone, writing on his first Christmas of the expedition: "How your kind woman's heart would pity me and mine. . . . The camp is in the extreme of misery and the people appear as if they were making up their minds to commit suicide or to sit still inert until death relieves them." Always carrying her photograph with him, wrapped safely in oilskin, Stanley marked on his map an Alice Island and the Lady Alice Rapids.

"I do love dancing so much. . . ." Alice wrote to him. "I would rather go to an opera . . . than a party. . . . Almost every evening some fellows come in — I get awfully tired of them. . . . I have the most horrid sore finger all blistered from playing the harp. I am getting along quite well with it, only I never practice." She apparently had little idea of where Stanley was, or that letters from him, if they could be delivered at all, had to be carried through the bush for months. "You never write to me any more," she complained, "and I just want to know why??? I am real angry with Central Africa."

In the book he later wrote about this expedition, *Through the Dark Continent,* Stanley followed several rules he would use in books to come: stretch the account to two volumes (a total of 960 pages in this case); use "dark" in the title (*In Darkest Africa* and *My Dark Companions and Their Strange Stories* would follow); and employ every possible medium for telling the story. There are before-and-after photographs of the author showing his hair turned white by the journey; "extracts from my diary" (when compared with Stanley's actual journal, they turn out to be nothing of the sort); an elaborate foldout map marked with the route of the trip; more than a hundred drawings — of battles, dramatic meetings, a canoe being sucked into a whirlpool; floor plans of African houses; street plans of villages; lists of supplies. A cornucopia of diagrams shows everything from the lineages of African kings to the shapes of different canoe paddles. Stanley shrewdly sensed that his readers' ignorance of Africa would make them all the more fascinated by endless mundane details, such as a chart of prices showing that a chicken cost one bead necklace at Abaddi, while six chickens cost twelve yards of cloth in Ugogo. Readers got their money's worth. Pre-electronic though they were, Stanley's books were multimedia productions.

To read Stanley today is to see how much his traveling was an act of appropriation. He is forever measuring and tabulating things: temperature, miles traveled, lake depths, latitude, longitude, and altitude (which he calculated by measuring the temperature at which water boiled). Specially trusted porters carried fragile loads of thermometers, barometers, watches, compasses, and pedometers. It is almost as if he were a surveyor, mapping the continent he crossed for its prospective owners.

It is the second half of Stanley's journey which turns it into an epic feat of exploration. From Lake Tanganyika, where he had found Livingstone several years earlier, he and his diminished band of porters, including some rebellious ones who start the trip in chains, trek westward into the interior for some weeks, until they reach a large river, known locally as the Lualaba. No European explorer has ever gone downstream beyond this point, and no one knows where the Lualaba leads. Livingstone had thought it was the long-sought source of the Nile, since the Lualaba here flows north, straight toward Egypt.

Stanley, however, is sure the Lualaba is far too big to be the beginning of the Nile; for a time he thinks it might be the Niger, whose outlet, like the Nile's, is far to the north. Then, descending the river, he becomes increasingly convinced that it is the Congo. But he is not certain, for the estuary where the Congo empties into the Atlantic, half a continent away, is *south* of the point where his celestial bearings show him to be, on the shore of the northward-flowing Lualaba. On European maps, everything in between is blank.

According to Stanley, he stands on the banks of the mysterious river and addresses his assembled followers:

"Into whichever sea this great river empties, there shall we follow it. . . . On your lives depends my own; if I risk yours, I risk mine. As a father looks after his children, I will look after you. . . . Therefore, my children, make up your minds as I have made up mine, that, as we are now in the very middle of this continent, and it would be just as bad to return as to go on, we shall continue our journey, that we shall toil on, and on, by this river and no other, to the salt sea."

Frank Pocock, the faithful deputy, asks, "Before we finally depart, sir, do you really believe, in your inmost soul, that we shall succeed?"

To which Stanley replies: "Believe? Yes, I do believe that we shall all emerge into light again some time. It is true that our prospects are as dark as this night. . . . I believe [this river] will prove to be the Congo; if the Congo, then there must be many cataracts . . . whether the Congo, the Niger, or the Nile, I am prepared. . . . *Believe?* I see us gliding down by tower and town, and my mind will not permit a shadow of doubt. Good-night, my boy! Good-night! and may happy dreams of the sea, and ships, and pleasure, and comfort, and success attend you in your sleep!"

Did Stanley really stand on the riverbank and speak words even re-motely like these? We will never know, because none of the other three white men on the expedition survived. Long before Frank Pocock drowned, Fred Barker died of "aguish fits" so severe that "his blood seemed to stagnate in its veins" until "the congealed blood would not run, and . . . the poor young man was dead." Edward Pocock became delirious. "I sprang to him," Stanley claims, "— only in time, however, to see him take his last gasp."

If the Lualaba was going to turn out to be the Congo, Stanley knew, the river had to somewhere make a 180–degree curve. As he and his expedition floated down it, or at the beginning sometimes marched alongside it, he frequently measured his latitude and longitude. For several hundred miles, the river mystifyingly continued to flow north. But at last it began to make a wide counterclockwise arc to the west, ending up flowing southwest toward its fearsome cataracts and the Atlantic.

Stanley's journey solved another geographical mystery. The Congo begins and ends below the equator, but the top part of its great half-circle lies above the equator. In central Africa, the equator is the rough dividing line between the dry and rainy seasons: when it is one above the line, it is the other below. Therefore, whatever the time of year, part of the Congo's course passes through land being drenched with rain and part through dry country. This explained why, over the course of a year, the Congo's flow varied much less than that of other tropical rivers.

The gigantic, steadily widening river, Stanley found, was a rich source of food for the people living near it. Since his time, scientists have counted more than five hundred species of fish in the river. These feed on an array of insects, on each other, and on fruit and leaves that fall into the water, especially during flood seasons, when the river rises above its banks and sheets of water sweep through the bordering forests and grasslands.

It is frustrating that the only African voices we hear are those recorded by Stanley himself. Every once in a while he does note or imagine such a voice, as if he had paused to take a quick, half-guilty glance in the mirror. Here is one such glance from his journal of September 12, 1876, which was, coincidentally, the very day that dignitaries in evening dress filed up the Royal Palace's marble staircase for the opening of King Leopold II's Geographical Conference in Brussels:

> The White man in the opinion of the Waguhha:
> "How can he be a good man who comes for no trade, whose feet you never see, who always goes covered with clothes, unlike all other people? No, there is something very mysterious about him, perhaps wicked, perhaps he is a magician, at any rate it is better to leave him alone and not disturb him."

Stanley's bloody progress down the river became part of local oral history, sometimes taking on the elements of legend, for the range and accuracy of his rifles seemed supernatural to those who had never seen such weapons. A traveler some years later heard one such account:

> The chief of the strangers was covered with cloth, and his face was white, and it shone like sun-light on the river. . . . The stranger chief had only one eye. . . . It was in the middle of his forehead. . . . When the Basoko went out on the river in their war-canoes to fight and capture the strangers, they cried: "Meat! meat!" for they intended eating their bodies, but they were not to be captured, and they killed many of the Basoko with sticks, which sent forth thunder and lightning. They spoke words in a strange tongue. They . . . drifted on down the river and passed the strong Basoko with jeers.

This Basoko image of Stanley as one-eyed could be a memory, filtered through many retellings, of seeing him squinting through a telescope or a rifle's sights. It also strangely echoes the image of the one-eyed creatures some medieval European geographers imagined Africans to be. We know from a later scrap of oral tradition that Europeans were often believed to have hoofs; not having seen shoes before, some Africans along the river thought them part of white anatomy.

Several hundred miles downstream from his starting point, Stanley had to portage around rapids, which he named Stanley Falls. After that, there were no more natural obstacles to his progress for a thousand miles, to Stanley Pool. It was clear sailing for the *Lady Alice* and the fleet of about two dozen canoes the expedition had bought or stolen from people living along the riverbank.

Stanley and his Zanzibari porters and soldiers watched in awe as the river grew in size, becoming at times so wide they could barely see across it. Its expanse was sprinkled with some four thousand islands, many of them inhabited. In the languages spoken along its banks it was known not as the Congo but, because of its many tributaries, as the Nzadi or Nzere,* meaning "the river that swallows all rivers." Stanley did not

---

* Curiously, it was a Portuguese corruption of this word, Zaire, that Congo dictator Mobutu Sese Seko picked when he renamed his country in 1971.

venture up these side rivers, but as he passed one after another, each hundreds of yards across, he was impressed by their size. As well he might have been. Just one of the Congo's tributaries, the Kasai, carries as much water as the Volga and is half again as long as the Rhine. Another, the Ubangi, is even longer. Steamboats on this network, Stanley immediately saw, could travel long distances. It was as if he had found the equivalent of thousands of miles of railroad track, already laid. "The Power possessing the Congo . . ." he wrote, "would absorb to itself the trade of the whole of the enormous basin behind. This river is and will be the grand highway of commerce to West Central Africa."

The last leg of Stanley's extraordinary journey proved by far the hardest. At the head of the 220-mile final stretch of rapids, where the river bulged out to make Stanley Pool, the explorer's easy floating came to an end. He was prepared to portage around rapids and waterfalls, but what he did not realize was how much of the river's rush to the sea was through rock gorges that compressed the water into fast-moving, unnavigable chutes of white foam.

He grew steadily more dismayed. In many places the current, he estimated by timing tree trunks that floated past, was thirty miles an hour.

> Take a strip of sea blown over by a hurricane . . . and a pretty accurate conception of its leaping waves may be obtained. . . . There was first a rush down into the bottom of an immense trough, and then, by its sheer force, the enormous volume would lift itself upward steeply until, gathering itself into a ridge, it suddenly hurled itself 20 or 30 feet straight upward, before rolling down into another trough. . . . The base of either bank, consisting of a long line of piled boulders of massive size, was buried in the tempestuous surf. The roar was tremendous and deafening. I can only compare it to the thunder of an express train through a rock tunnel.

Hoping, usually in vain, for calm stretches of river between such rapids, the explorer ignored the advice of local Africans and for an almost fatally long time did not abandon the *Lady Alice* and his dugout canoes. It was particularly agonizing to move the canoes overland, for they could not be taken apart and carried like the *Lady Alice*. The largest canoe was fifty-four feet long and weighed three tons. The men had to cut and pile brush along a rough path, then drag the canoes forward. Sometimes they built tracks of logs and used other logs crosswise as rollers. It took thirty-seven days to go one stretch of thirty-four miles. Again and again the jagged Crystal Mountains threw up barriers; at one point the weary and emaciated men had to pull the boats up twelve hundred feet, then along three miles of relatively level ground, then down again. The rainy season arrived, with downpours that lasted five or six hours a day.

The perpetual noise of the rapids grew ever more oppressive. Men fainted from hunger. Stanley's last pair of boots disintegrated. One of his best men lost his mind and raced off into the bush, carrying only a parrot. Finally, after wasting months dragging the now-useless boats, the expedition abandoned them entirely. In Stanley's diary, as he despairingly records one death, mass desertion, or mutiny after another, his elegant handwriting becomes almost illegible and his prose incoherent. Altogether, it took him and his starving, disease-ridden band four and a half months to travel overland the 250 miles from Stanley Pool to the seaport of Boma.

The explorer was vague and contradictory in his numbers, but the death toll among the expedition's members was overwhelming. Many succumbed to festering wounds, dysentery, smallpox, or typhus, all exacerbated by spells of near-starvation. Stanley would not allow porters ill with smallpox to stay behind and convalesce, or even to walk off into the forest to die; he made them carry their loads until they dropped. And he drove himself almost as hard as he did his men; on the journey he lost more than sixty pounds. Several times the expedition ran perilously short of water; it endured snake and hippo attacks, spear grass, worms that bored into the soles of porters' feet, and paths that led over knife-sharp rocks. By the time the survivors reached Boma, they were numb with exhaustion, suffering from what today we would call posttraumatic stress syndrome. Several soon died of no apparent cause, waiting to sail home.

"What means have I to convey my heart's load of love to you," Stanley had written Alice Pike from the middle of the continent, "but this letter which must go through a thousand miles of savages, exposed to all dangers of flood and fire and battle until it reaches the sea? . . . Grant then that my love towards you is unchanged, that you are in my dream, my stay and my hope, and my beacon, and believe that I shall still cherish you in this light until I meet you."

When he brought his remaining porters and soldiers by sea back to their jumping-off point in Zanzibar, Stanley had a shock. Amid two years' worth of mail waiting for him was a newspaper clipping eighteen months old, announcing that Alice Pike had married an Ohio railway heir named

Albert Barney. Stanley fell into a deep depression and never saw her again.*

In public statements after his trip, Stanley made the usual condemnations of the "Arab" slave trade, called for missionaries to come to Africa, fulminated about the way Africans went about in "the general indecency of their nakedness," and proclaimed that the aim of his journey was "to flash a torch of light across the western half of the Dark Continent." But business was never far from his mind. After leaving one district where he had been plagued by desertions and a flood, he wrote in his journal, "A farewell to it . . . until some generous and opulent philanthropist shall permit me or some other to lead a force for the suppression of this stumbling block to commerce with Central Africa."

The opulent philanthropist was waiting.

In fact, the philanthropist was elated. For several months before Stanley emerged at Boma, Leopold had eagerly scanned the *Times of London* daily for news of his fate. At one point he wrote to an aide, "The first thing on the agenda . . . seems to me to check again if Stanley has reached the Lualaba." As soon as Stanley reappeared, the king sent him a telegram of congratulations.

Now Leopold could read the long *Daily Telegraph* articles Stanley wrote about his journey, as well as the voluminous press reports on the accolades and banquets the explorer received in Cape Town, Cairo, and his other stops on his way back to England. A joint resolution congratulating him came from both houses of the United States Congress, and fellow explorers hailed his descent of the Congo as the century's greatest feat of exploration. Leopold was now certain that this vast territory in the middle of Africa, miraculously still unclaimed by any European power, could become the colony he craved. At last his long-dreamed-of production could reach the stage, and Stanley would be its star.

The king instructed his minister in London to keep him *au courant*

---

* The explorer never knew that, as she watched his fame grow, the new Mrs. Barney spent much of her life regretting that she had not become Mrs. Stanley. Long after his death, in a highly romanticized unpublished novel-memoir, she claimed credit for his great Congo journey: "She made it possible for him. Without her spirit animating him, he would never have accomplished it, not even had the desire to penetrate those abysmal darknesses again. . . . 'Lady Alice' had conquered Africa!"

regarding news about Stanley. Behind the elegant smokescreen of his International African Association, Leopold was maneuvering with great subtlety. Be discreet, he told the envoy: "I'm sure if I quite openly charged Stanley with the task of taking possession in my name of some part of Africa, the English will stop me. If I ask their advice, they'll stop me just the same. So I think I'll just give Stanley some job of exploration which would offend no one, and will give us the bases and headquarters which we can take over later on." Above all, Leopold told his man in London, "I do not want to risk . . . losing a fine chance to secure for ourselves a slice of this magnificent African cake."

Firing off telegrams, Leopold mapped a plan to intercept Stanley on his way home and lure him to Brussels. In Alexandria, where the explorer stopped for a few days, the king arranged for someone to plant the idea with Stanley while he was the guest of honor at a dinner on board a yacht carrying former U.S. President Ulysses S. Grant. Then, for the next step in his courtship, Leopold turned for help to an American friend in Brussels, General Henry Shelton Sanford. It was a brilliant choice: with Stanley so eagerly passing himself off as American, who better to appeal to him than a high-born countryman?

General Sanford was eager to take on this glamorous mission for Leopold. Born to a wealthy Connecticut family, he had been appointed by Abraham Lincoln as American minister to Belgium, and had stayed on after his eight-year tenure ended. He and his wife, a famous beauty much younger than he, entertained lavishly at their turreted, three-story country house outside Brussels. With his stovepipe hat, gold-headed cane, pince-nez, and handsome chestnut mustache and beard, Sanford was a familiar figure in the city's highest social circles. He had never been a soldier, however; the "General," as well as the sword and blue-and-gold uniform he wore for some years, were rewards for his having given a battery of cannon to an infantry regiment during the Civil War.

Sanford had invested in American railroads and Western real estate and in huge citrus orchards and other enterprises in Florida, giving the town that sprang up to house their workers the name of Sanford.* But, as with

---

* Sanford, Florida, had a brief moment of notoriety three quarters of a century later, when its police chief, evoking an ordinance banning interracial sports on city property, ordered Jackie Robinson off the field in the middle of a spring-training exhibition game.

his military rank, Sanford's prowess as a financier was less than met the eye. He had the elegance of someone who had grown up with a fortune but not the shrewdness needed to make one, and he lost money on everything he touched. He never recovered the large sums he put into a series of odd patents — for a wool loom, a new type of whiskey still, and a little box designed to lubricate railroad car axles with water instead of oil. A silver mine in Nevada and a zinc mine in Arkansas proved disastrous. A Minnesota railroad went bankrupt. His cotton crop at a South Carolina plantation was devoured by caterpillars.

As Sanford saw his inherited fortune draining away, his connections at the Belgian court loomed larger for him. He even named one of his sons Leopold. Always a shrewd judge of people, the king understood what royal patronage would mean to Sanford, and he flattered him ceaselessly, knowing that someday he could use him. When Sanford failed in one of many fruitless efforts to win another American diplomatic post, Leopold's aide Baron Jules Greindl wrote to him, "The King is pleased that you will continue to reside among us where everyone loves and appreciates you." Like many Americans, Sanford had a fondness for royalty and Leopold valued him, he felt, in a way that his own country did not.

In January 1878, Leopold secretly dispatched Sanford and Greindl to intercept Stanley in France, where the explorer, still on his way to London, was due for another round of medals and banqueting. At the Marseilles railway station, the envoys caught up with Stanley, who was thin, ill, and exhausted, and followed him to Paris, where they formally offered him a job with the International African Association. He turned down their invitation but clearly was gratified. Always anxious about his reception in the upper reaches of society, Stanley never forgot that courtiers of the King of the Belgians — a baron and a general, no less — had sought him out on his return to Europe.

From France, Stanley at last headed home to London and a hero's welcome. Despite his claiming to be American, his heart was still in England. It was the Union Jack, he said at one banquet or white-tie dinner party after another, that ought to fly over the territory crossed by the great river. Stanley's hopes for British interest in the Congo basin rose when the Prince of Wales came to hear him talk, but all he said to the explorer afterward was that Stanley was wearing his medals in the wrong order. Already much of the world's map was filled with British dominions, colonies, and protectorates of one sort or another; with a recession at home and their hands full with various colonial crises and rebellions overseas, few Britons seemed interested in a new territory whose main transportation route was blocked by notorious cataracts.

"I do not understand Englishmen at all," Stanley wrote. "Either they suspect me of some self-interest, or they do not believe me. . . . For the relief of Livingstone I was called an impostor; for the crossing of Africa I was called a pirate." Nor was there enthusiasm in the United States for Congo colonization. James Gordon Bennett, Jr., in New York, now wanted to send Stanley off in search of the North Pole.

Leopold continued to press his suit. He had his minister in London invite Stanley to lunch. He sent Sanford across the Channel to talk to the explorer again. And he made sure that Stanley heard a few hints about his possibly making a deal with another explorer instead. Leopold knew his man. Five months after returning to Europe, Stanley accepted an invitation to visit Belgium.

4

"THE TREATIES MUST GRANT US EVERYTHING"

O N JUNE 10, 1878, a steamer carried Henry Morton Stanley across
the English Channel to his first meeting with the King of the
Belgians. We do not know what Leopold was doing as he waited for the
explorer in his office at the Royal Palace, his patient months of wooing
about to bear fruit. But it would not be unreasonable to imagine that this
geographer-king once again looked at his maps.

Such a look would have confirmed that only in Africa could Leopold
hope to achieve his dream of seizing a colony, especially one immensely
larger than Belgium. There was no more unclaimed territory in the
Americas, and Maximilian and Carlota's disastrous adventure in Mexico
was a reminder of what could happen if one tried to take control of an
independent country there. Nor were there blank spaces in Asia: the
Russian Empire stretched all the way to the Pacific, the French had taken
Indochina, the Dutch the East Indies, and most of the rest of southern
Asia, from Aden to Singapore, was colored with the British Empire's pink.
Only Africa remained.

Stanley had followed the Congo River for some fifteen hundred miles.
He had obviously not seen all of it, though, because when he first reached
it, far upstream, it was already nearly a mile wide. Full exploration would
take many years, but after eagerly devouring Stanley's newspaper articles,
Leopold had a rough idea of what the explorer had found.

Eventually the statistics would be known. The Congo River drains
more than 1.3 million square miles, an area larger than India. It has an
estimated one sixth of the world's hydroelectric potential. Most impor-

tant of all, for a nineteenth-century empire-builder, the river and its fan-shaped web of tributaries constitute more than seven thousand miles of interconnecting waterways, a built-in transportation grid rivaled by few places on earth. Once disassembled steamboats could be transported around the great rapids and onto that network, they would find wood to burn in their boilers growing right at dockside; most of the navigable rivers ran through the fast-growing rain forest that covered half the basin.

Of the people who lived in the Congo basin, Europeans still knew little. When not drawing a bead on them through his gun sights, Stanley had been interested in them mainly as a source of supplies, people with whom he could trade trinkets or cloth for food. But he had made two important discoveries about the area's inhabitants. One was that they were no military threat: his nearly three dozen battles showed their spears and arrows and decrepit muskets to be no match for his new, breech-loading Snider rifles. His other discovery was that, along the crucial transportation artery of the Congo River, there was no single all-powerful state that had to be subdued. Further exploring along the river's tributaries would find several large kingdoms, but centuries of slave-hunting raids from both the east and west African coasts had severely weakened most of them. Many of the peoples of the Congo basin were small in population. As the next round of exploration would soon show, there were more than two hundred different ethnic groups speaking more than four hundred languages and dialects. With the potential opposition so fragmented, conquest would be relatively easy.

On the day in 1878 when he sat down for his long-anticipated meeting with Stanley, Leopold was forty-three. With the pedantic awkwardness of his youth far behind him, he had learned to play the royal role superbly. Although the thirty-seven-year-old Stanley was a head shorter than the king and uneasy about his rudimentary French, he too had come into his own. The ne'er-do-well naval deserter of a mere thirteen years earlier was now a best-selling author, recognized as one of the greatest of living explorers. His stern, mustachioed face appeared in magazines everywhere beneath a Stanley Cap, his own invention. It had a high crown surrounded by ventilation holes, a brim over the eyes, and a havelock, a cloth to keep the sun off ears and neck. To our eyes the cap looks like a cross between that of a Foreign Legionnaire and a doorman — which, in a way, summed up Stanley's personality: one part titan of rugged force and mountain-moving confidence; the other a vulnerable, illegitimate son of the working class, anxiously struggling for the approval of the powerful.

In photographs each part seems visible: the explorer's eyes carry both a fierce determination and a woundedness.

At this first meeting, Leopold immediately put Stanley at ease in fluent English. The men who met each other that June day at the Royal Palace each represented a class type that would become familiar. The commanders of the ground troops in the great African land grab, the whites who led soldiers into the bush, directed the rifle and machine-gun fire and wielded the surveyors' instruments, who braved malaria, dysentery, and typhoid, were often, like Stanley, from the lower or lower middle class in their home countries. For them, Africa was a chance to gain upward mobility toward wealth and glory. But those who made the greatest fortunes from the Scramble for Africa, like Leopold, were often men who had fortunes to begin with.

Although he had lived a pampered life in yachts and palaces, Leopold was, of the two, the wiser in the ways of the world. He had taken the measure of Stanley's ambition, of his immense capacity for hard work, of his craving for constant flattery, and of his need for a sponsor. Stanley, still smarting from British lack of interest in the Congo, was delighted to meet a monarch who admired what he had done and wanted him to do more.

After that meeting, Stanley traveled about Europe for the rest of 1878, promoting *Through the Dark Continent,* meeting members of the new Stanley Club in Paris, and receiving honors everywhere. Leopold sent messages and emissaries after him, to keep his man on the hook. Before the year was out, the two had agreed on the terms of Stanley's return to the Congo, this time working for the king. Stanley's contract ran for five years; he would be paid 25,000 francs a year for time spent in Europe and 50,000 francs (roughly $250,000 in today's dollars) a year for time spent in Africa. And, of course, Leopold would fund the expeditionary force to accompany him.

They agreed that Stanley would first set up a base near the river's mouth and then construct a road around the rapids, through the rugged Crystal Mountains — a precursor to a railway. Over this road porters would carry several steamboats broken down into small pieces, which Stanley would later assemble and use to travel upstream, building a chain of trading stations along the thousand-mile navigable main stretch of the Congo River. Afterward, he could write a book about his experiences — but Leopold would have the right to edit it.

Of the riches Leopold hoped to find in the Congo, the one that gleamed most brightly in his imagination was ivory. European and American merchants were already eagerly buying African ivory in the markets of Zanzibar. Because it could be easily carved, ivory in the nineteenth century was a more rare and expensive version of what plastic is today, with the added cachet of having an exotic origin — a cachet that grew greater with the public idolization of African explorers. Ivory from elephant tusks was shaped into knife handles, billiard balls, combs, fans, napkin rings, piano and organ keys, chess pieces, crucifixes, snuffboxes, brooches, and statuettes. In a faint echo of its original use to the elephant, it was made into false teeth. Despite the long distances ivory had to be carried from the elephant ranges far inland, it was attractive to dealers all the way along the line because, like drugs or precious metals, it had high value and low bulk. The hundred pounds of ivory in an average pair of African elephant tusks could make hundreds of piano keys or thousands of false teeth. Ivory dealers preferred African elephant tusks to Indian, and the elephants of equatorial Africa, which included the Congo basin, tended to have the largest tusks of all. Stanley had found ivory so plentiful that it was used for doorposts in African homes.

For the moment, such riches lay at least several years in Leopold's future, for first Stanley had to build his road. He left nothing out of the detailed budget he prepared for the king: small boats, wooden buildings in pieces, rope, tools, African porters, and European supervisors. Among the latter were two young Englishmen who, in the tradition of Stanley's inept subordinates, had never been out of the country. Having hired neophytes, he could later rail about their inexperience: "I have had no friend on any expedition, no one who could possibly be my companion, on an equal footing, except while with Livingstone. . . . How can he who has witnessed many wars hope to be understood by one whose most shocking sight has been a nose-bleed?"

Stanley was savvy enough to demand his money from Leopold in advance because, despite a plethora of contracts, whom he was working for remained foggy: was it the king himself, the king's International African Association, which seemed to be withering away, or a new and somewhat secretive body called the Committee for Studies of the Upper Congo? The committee's stockholders officially were a small group of Dutch and British businessmen and a Belgian banker — who, in fact, was quietly holding a large block of shares as Leopold's proxy. A trusted henchman of the king's, Colonel Maximilien Strauch, was the committee's president.

Ambitious as his and Stanley's plans were, Leopold was intent that they be seen as nothing more than philanthropy. The contracts Stanley made his European staff sign forbade them to divulge anything about the real purpose of their work. "Only scientific explorations are intended," Leopold assured a journalist. To anyone who questioned further, he could point to a clause in the committee's charter that explicitly prohibited it from pursuing political ends. The king wanted to protect himself against the widespread feeling in Belgium that, for a small country, a colony would be a money-losing extravagance. He also wanted to do nothing to alert any potential rivals for this appetizing slice of the African cake, especially France, which was starting to show interest.

In February 1879, slipping on board a steamship under the name M. Henri, Stanley set off again for Africa. Behind him in Europe, another story was unfolding. A Dutch company that had been a key shareholder in the Committee for Studies of the Upper Congo went bankrupt, its chief reportedly fleeing to New York and going to work as a horse-cab driver. Leopold did not mind; he used the shock of the Dutch company's collapse to offer, in effect, a buy-out of the committee's other stockholders. They gratefully accepted, and the committee legally ceased to exist before the end of the year. But as a smokescreen it was still useful, and the king continued to refer to the committee as if it were functioning and as if its former shareholders, and not he alone, were funding Stanley and making decisions. Stanley himself did not find out about the committee's demise until more than a year after the fact.

To obfuscate things still further and give his African operations a name that could serve for a political entity, the master impresario created another new cover organization, the International Association of the Congo. This was calculated to sound confusingly similar to the moribund "philanthropic" International African Association of crown princes and explorers. "Care must be taken not to let it be obvious that the Association of the Congo and the African Association are two different things," Leopold instructed one of his aides. "The public doesn't grasp that." Adding to the public's confusion, the new International Association of the Congo, like the defunct Committee for Studies of the Upper Congo, used the flag of the International African Association, which had been adopted with much fanfare at that group's first and last meeting — a gold star on a blue background, intended to symbolize a blaze of hope in the proverbial African darkness.

Even before making his deal with Stanley, Leopold had begun reaching for his slice of the African cake from the other side of the table, by financing an attempt to reach the Congo basin from Africa's east coast. Three more such expeditions, all well-publicized but inept, followed. One of them included four baggage-carrying Indian elephants with the suitably exotic names Sundergrund, Naderbux, Sosankalli, and Pulmalla. The elephants, it turned out, required fifty laborers with axes and machetes to precede them, clearing trees and branches so that they and their loads could pass through.* But before dropping heavily and prematurely dead of various ailments, the elephants proved a journalist's dream. The European readers who followed each stage of the animals' unhappy journey failed to realize that the real story lay on Africa's other coast, where Stanley was quietly working on his road around the Congo River rapids.

Almost imperceptibly, the name *Congo* now began to refer not just to a river but to an entire territory. When the public finally did start paying attention to the new colony-in-the-making, the king reached new heights as an illusionist. He or one of his stagehands managed to open the curtains on a completely different set each time, depending on the audience. Henry Shelton Sanford, a board member of Leopold's venture in its incarnation as the International African Association, made it sound almost like Travelers Aid. In New York, on a 1879 trip to tend to his money-losing investments, Sanford gave a speech saying that the king's aim was "to found a chain of posts or hospices, both hospitable and scientific, which should serve as means of information and aid to travellers . . . and ultimately, by their humanizing influences, to secure the abolition of the traffic in slaves." His new International Association of the Congo, Leopold insisted in a piece he wrote and managed to get published, over the byline "from a Belgian correspondent," in the London *Times,* was a sort of "Society of the Red Cross; it has been formed with the noble aim of rendering lasting and disinterested services to the cause of progress." When talking to the more military-minded Germans, Leopold nimbly changed the scenery and likened his men in the Congo to the knights of the Crusades. Almost everyone was fooled. Baroness Burdett-Coutts, the British patron of missionaries, gave him a donation of 50,000 francs for his humanitarian endeavors. In the United States, one

---

* Even getting the elephants to land proved a near-disaster. The ship that brought them from India lowered them over the side in slings, but instead of swimming obediently to the beach, the elephants tried to climb back on board. When the ship's boats attempted to tow them toward shore, the elephants started to pull the boats out to sea.

writer declared Leopold's great work "enough to make an American believe in Kings forever."

Meanwhile, Leopold sent word that Stanley was to lay the groundwork in the Congo for a "confederation of free negro republics," black tribes whose president would live in Europe and rule under the guidance of the Belgian king. This particular illusion, echoing the idea of a union of states, was likely to appeal to an American audience. To Europeans, on the other hand, the king talked about free cities. "Bremen, Lübeck, Hamburg were free cities for a long time," one of his aides wrote. "Why would there not be some in the Congo?" Those backstage, however, knew that in either case the free was merely a prop to be removed as soon as the curtains closed. As one of Leopold's subordinates bluntly wrote to Stanley: "There is no question of granting the slightest political power to negroes. That would be absurd. The white men, heads of the stations, retain all the powers."

For five years, Stanley was Leopold's man in the Congo. The explorer's combative energy was now directed mainly against the territory's forbidding landscape, not its people. His crews of workmen carved a rough track, more a trail than a road, around the big rapids, using existing paths in some areas, in others cutting through brush and forest, filling in gullies, and throwing log bridges over ravines. Then they moved more than fifty tons of supplies and equipment up the trail. Draft animals like horses and oxen could not survive the Congo's climate and diseases, so supplies traveled mostly on porters' heads.

After two years of trail building, pulling, and hauling, two small steamboats were reassembled at the top of the rapids and puffed their way up the river to land parties that set up more bases on its banks. Names left no doubt whose colony this would be. The station established at the top of the big rapids, within earshot of their thunder, and featuring a heavily fortified blockhouse and a vegetable garden, was christened Leopoldville. Above it rose Leopold Hill. Soon maps showed Lake Leopold II and the Leopold River. One of the later-arriving steamboats, which would briefly be piloted by the Congo's most famous ship's officer, would be the *Roi des Belges* (King of the Belgians).

Stanley was a harsh taskmaster. "The best punishment is that of irons," he explained in one of his letters to Brussels, "because without wounding, disfiguring, or torturing the body, it inflicts shame and discomfort."

(Whites were not put in irons, of course; only blacks.) Illness and other dangers were even more deadly than Stanley's wrath. In the first year alone, six Europeans and twenty-two Africans under his command died, including one eaten by a crocodile.

For the first time we are at last able to see Stanley in Africa through eyes not his own. A steamboat engineer named Paul Nève fell sick and wrote home:

> Mr. Stanley has taken great care of me during these bad days . . .
> the sort of care a blacksmith applies to repair an implement that
> is most essential and that has broken down through too rough
> usage . . . teeth clenched in anger, he smites it again and again on
> the anvil, wondering whether he will have to scrap it or whether
> he will yet be able to use it as before.

Nève died several weeks later.

Stanley himself might not have minded the blacksmith analogy. "Every cordial-faced aborigine whom I meet . . ." he wrote, "I look upon . . . with much of the same regard that an agriculturist views his strong-limbed child; he is a future recruit to the ranks of soldier-laborers." It was during this period, when he was pushing his men so hard, that Stanley became known by the Africans who worked for him as Bula Matadi or Bula Matari, "Breakstones." Stanley himself preferred the grander translation "Breaker of Rocks," and claimed that it was bestowed on him when he taught awed Africans how to use a sledgehammer and when they saw giant boulders dynamited as he built the trail through the Crystal Mountains

In Stanley's account of his labors, he snorts at Africans, who are lazy by definition, and at whites who are "weak-minded." He preaches "the gospel of enterprise," declaring that "the European middleman who has his home in Europe but has his heart in Africa is the man who is wanted. . . . They are the missionaries of commerce, adapted for nowhere so well as for the Congo basin, where are so many idle hands." And nowhere does he wax as passionate as when his moneymaking instincts and his Victorian prudery intersect. Getting the "clothesless and over-tattooed" Africans out of their "unabashed nudity" and into European clothes is his continuing obsession:

I foresaw a brilliant future of Africa, if by any miracle of good-
fortune I could persuade the dark millions of the interior to cast
off their fabrics of grass clothing and don . . . second-hand costumes. . . . See what a ready market lies here for old clothes! The
garments shed by the military heroes of Europe, of the club
lackeys, of the liveried servants of modern Pharaohs, the frock-
coats of a lawyer, merchant, or a Rothschild; or perhaps the grave
garb of these my publishers, might find people of the rank of
Congo chieftainship to wear them.

As Stanley shuttled back and forth on foot through the rugged, humid
countryside, supervising construction, he carefully kept up his personal
appearance, shaving and putting blacking on his mustache each day. During this sojourn, as during all his time in Africa, his sturdy, compact frame
survived the diseases that sent so many European visitors to early graves.
Several times he was delirious with fever and twice came near death. One
bout of malaria, he wrote, reduced his weight to a hundred pounds, and
he grew too weak to speak or raise his arms. For two weeks he lay in his
tent, convinced that the end was near, then summoned his sun-helmeted
European officers and African workers to give his last instructions, to say
goodbye, and to make — so he claimed — one last profession of loyalty:
"Tell the King . . . that I am sorry not to have been able to carry out to a
finish the mission he entrusted to me."

He recovered, but some months later fell sick again and, brought
downriver, was carried ashore at Leopoldville unconscious. In 1882,
barely able to walk, he went back to Europe to recuperate, traveling on a
slow Portuguese steamer. On this ship, he fulminated, "underbred" second-class passengers were allowed onto the first-class deck, where they
"expectorated, smoked, and sprawled in the most socialistic manner."
Worse yet was an invasion by third-class "females, and half a score of
half-naked white children."

At last he was rescued from these indignities by the ship's arrival in
Europe. Doctors warned Stanley that it might be fatal for him to return
to the Congo, but Leopold insisted: there was still much to be done. Not
only did the king want his colony secured; he also wanted the explorer
out of the way for a few more years because, always a loose cannon in
public, Stanley continued to talk openly about his hopes for a *British*
Congo. Leopold turned on the royal charm. "Surely, Mr. Stanley," he said,

"you cannot think of leaving me now, just when I most need you?" Simultaneously fighting a painful relapse of illness and firing off orders for an array of new equipment and supplies, Stanley returned to the Congo after only two months.

With the great prize almost within his grasp, Leopold wanted as much land in the Congo as possible, and he wanted it *now*. His instructions and letters to Stanley all through these years pulsate with his lust for territory.

> I take advantage of a safe opportunity to send you a few lines in my bad English. . . . It is indispensable you should purchase . . . as much land as you will be able to obtain, and that you should place successively under . . . suzerainty . . . as soon as possible and without losing one minute, all the chiefs from the mouth of the Congo to the Stanley Falls. . . . If you let me know you are going to execute these instructions without delay I will send you more people and more material. Perhaps Chinese coolies.

Although piously assuring the British minister in Brussels that his venture in Africa "had no commercial character; it did not carry on trade," Leopold had already written to Stanley, "I am desirous to see you purchase all the ivory which is to be found on the Congo, and let Colonel Strauch know the goods which he has to forward you in order to pay for it and when. I also recommend you to establish barriers and tolls on the parts of the road you have opened. It is but fair and in accordance with the custom of every country."

Leopold and Stanley knew that other Europeans were beginning to nose around the basin. Their chief worry was the French explorer and naval officer Count Pierre Savorgnan de Brazza, who had landed on the coast north of the Congo River and headed inland. One day while he was still building his trail around the rapids, Stanley was startled to have the courtly Frenchman, in a white helmet and blue navy coat, show up at his tent. A still greater shock awaited him at Stanley Pool, where he found that de Brazza had signed a treaty with a chief ceding to France a strip of the northern shoreline. De Brazza had left a sergeant in command of an outpost there, flying the French flag.

Stanley was a man who brooked no rivals, and over the next few years he and de Brazza carried on a loud feud. Stanley claimed the French explorer's treaty was based on trickery; his rival called Stanley a warrior who was no friend to the Africans. The Paris press loved it. While Leopold schemed with Stanley about how to outfox de Brazza, behind Stanley's back the king invited the Frenchman to Brussels, gave him the Order of Leopold, and tried unsuccessfully to hire him.

The comings and goings of Stanley and de Brazza began to arouse interest elsewhere. Doddering Portugal resurrected its old claim to the land surrounding the Congo River's mouth. Britain, worried by French interest in the Congo, backed the Portuguese. Leopold felt he had no time to waste.

Stanley, under pressure, drove his men harder. He exploded at white subordinates who were drinking too much or who had let weeds grow around their river stations. "These people had already given me more trouble than all the African tribes put together. They had inspired such disgust in me that I would rather be condemned to be a boot-black all my life than to be a dry-nurse to beings who had no . . . claim to manhood." Despite his own brief and inglorious career on opposite sides of the American Civil War, Stanley was at heart a military man. He liked order and discipline and was a terrifying but effective commander. By now he had amassed a powerful private army, equipped with a thousand quick-firing rifles, a dozen small Krupp cannon, and four machine guns. Among his Zanzibari soldiers there was a Swahili saying: *Bunduki sultani ya bara bara* (The gun is the sultan of the hinterland).

Meanwhile, Leopold had hired an Oxford scholar, Sir Travers Twiss, to provide a learned legal opinion backing the right of private companies to act as if they were sovereign countries when making treaties with native chiefs. Stanley was under instructions to lead his well-armed forces up and down the river and do just that. "The treaties must be as brief as possible," Leopold ordered, "and in a couple of articles must grant us everything."

They did. By the time Stanley and his officers were done, the blue flag with the gold star fluttered over the villages and territories, Stanley claimed, of more than 450 Congo basin chiefs. The texts varied, but many of the treaties gave the king a complete trading monopoly, even as he placated European and American questioners by insisting that he was opening up Africa to free trade. More important, chiefs signed over their land to Leopold, and they did so for almost nothing. At Isangila, near the big rapids, Stanley recorded, he was able to buy land for a station by paying some chiefs with "an ample supply of fine clothes, flunkey coats, and tinsel-braided uniforms, with a rich assortment of divers marketable wares . . . not omitting a couple of bottles of gin." The conquerors of

Africa, like those of the American West, were finding alcohol as effective as the machine gun.

The very word *treaty* is a euphemism, for many chiefs had no idea what they were signing. Few had seen the written word before, and they were being asked to mark their X's to documents in a foreign language and in legalese. The idea of a treaty of friendship between two clans or villages was familiar; the idea of signing over one's land to someone on the other side of the ocean was inconceivable. Did the chiefs of Ngombi and Mafela, for example, have any idea of what they agreed to on April 1, 1884? In return for "one piece of cloth per month to each of the under-signed chiefs, besides present of cloth in hand," they promised to "freely of their own accord, for themselves and their heirs and successors for ever . . . give up to the said Association the sovereignty and all sovereign and governing rights to all their territories . . . and to assist by labour or otherwise, any works, improvements or expeditions which the said Association shall cause at any time to be carried out in any part of these territories. . . . All roads and waterways running through this country, the right of collecting tolls on the same, and all game, fishing, mining and forest rights, are to be the absolute property of the said Association."

By labour or otherwise. Stanley's pieces of cloth bought not just land, but manpower. It was an even worse trade than the Indians made for Manhattan.

What kind of societies existed in this land that, unknown to most of its inhabitants, Stanley was busily staking out for the King of the Belgians? There is no simple answer, for what would turn out to be the Congo's borders, if superimposed on the map of Europe, would stretch from Zürich to Moscow to central Turkey. It was as large as the entire United States east of the Mississippi. Although mostly rain forest and savanna, it also embraced volcanic hills and mountains covered with snow and glaciers, some of whose peaks reached higher than the Alps.

The peoples of this vast territory were as diverse as the land. They ranged from citizens of large, organizationally sophisticated kingdoms to the Pygmies of the Ituri rain forest, who lived in small bands with no chiefs and no formal structure of government. The kingdoms, with large towns as their capitals, tended to be in the savanna, where long-distance travel was easier. In the rain forest, where paths had to be hacked through thick, rapidly growing foliage, communities were generally far smaller.

These forest-dwellers were sometimes seminomads: if a group of Pygmies, for instance, killed an elephant, that site became a temporary settlement for a week or two of feasting, since it was easier to move a village than a dead elephant.

Although some Congo peoples, like the Pygmies, were admirably peaceful, it would be a mistake to see most of them as paragons of primeval innocence. Many practiced slavery and ritual cannibalism and were as likely to make war on other clans or ethnic groups as people anywhere on earth. And traditional warfare in this part of Africa, where a severed head or hand was sometimes proof of an enemy killed in battle, was as harsh as warfare elsewhere. In some areas of the Congo all women were maimed, as still happens today, by forced clitoridectomies, a practice no less brutal for being a cultural initiation rite.

Like many indigenous peoples, inhabitants of the Congo basin had learned to live in balance with their environment. Some groups practiced what was, in effect, birth control, where couples had to abstain from sex before the men left on a hunting expedition, for example, or as long as the woman was breast-feeding a baby. Substances found in certain leaves and bark could induce miscarriages or had contraceptive properties. All these means of population control, incidentally, were strikingly similar to those which had evolved in another great rain forest an ocean away, the Amazon basin.

Most striking about the traditional societies of the Congo was their remarkable artwork: baskets, mats, pottery, copper and ironwork, and, above all, woodcarving. It would be two decades before Europeans really noticed this art. Its discovery then had a strong influence on Braque, Matisse, and Picasso — who subsequently kept African art objects in his studio until his death. Cubism was new only for Europeans, for it was partly inspired by specific pieces of African art, some of them from the Pende and Songye peoples, who live in the basin of the Kasai River, one of the Congo's major tributaries.

It is easy to see the distinctive brilliance that so entranced Picasso and his colleagues at their first encounter with this art at an exhibit in Paris in 1907. In these central African sculptures some body parts are exaggerated, some shrunken; eyes project, cheeks sink, mouths disappear, torsos become elongated; eye sockets expand to cover almost the entire face; the human face and figure are broken apart and formed again in new ways and proportions that had previously lain beyond the sight of traditional European realism.

The art sprang from cultures that had, among other things, a looser sense than Islam or Christianity of the boundaries between our world and the next, as well as of those between the world of humans and the world of beasts. Among the Bolia people of the Congo, for example, a king was chosen by a council of elders; by ancestors, who appeared to him in a dream; and finally by wild animals, who signaled their assent by roaring during a night when the royal candidate was left at a particular spot in the rain forest. Perhaps it was the fluidity of these boundaries that granted central Africa's artists a freedom those in Europe had not yet discovered.

※

In June 1884, his work for Leopold done and a sheaf of treaties in his baggage, Stanley sailed home to Europe. He grumbled a bit about his employer's greed; the king, he complained, had the "enormous voracity to swallow a million of square miles with a gullet that will not take in a herring." But it was Stanley who made the big swallow possible.

As he settled in England to write his usual thousand-page two-volume account of his travels, Stanley found around him a Europe that had awakened to Africa. The Scramble had begun. The treaty de Brazza had made at Stanley Pool would soon lead to a French colony on the northwest bank of the Congo River. In Germany, Chancellor Otto von Bismarck wanted colonies in Africa. The British, the outsiders with the most substantial foothold on the continent, were beginning to worry about competitors.

Leopold was certain that none of these larger powers would be eager to recognize the one-man colony Stanley had staked out for him. Diplomatic recognition, however, is partly a matter of precedent. Once one major country recognizes another's existence, other nations are likely to fall into line. If no major European country would take this crucial first step, Leopold decided, he would look elsewhere. Unnoticed on his home continent, the king had already quietly begun making a dazzling end-run around Europe entirely.

5

FROM FLORIDA
TO BERLIN

A N UNUSUALLY late spring snowfall lay thick on the White House lawn as President Chester A. Arthur, wearing a high silk hat, boarded a private car lent to him by the Pennsylvania Railroad and headed south for a vacation. High blood pressure and other complaints had left him tired, he told his staff, and he wanted a good rest in Florida. Traveling with the president as he left Washington, on April 5, 1883, were the secretary of the navy, Arthur's valet, his personal secretary, and his French chef, whom a journalist on the train described as "a gentleman with a well-developed waist . . . evidently a good feeder." A friend of the president's was also on board, and several of his late wife's cousins joined the party as the train rolled south. After Petersburg, Virginia, as the private car moved onto the tracks of a new railroad, a gray-bearded conductor provoked great hilarity by walking into the car, counting the passengers, and trying to collect $47.50 in fares. A telegram ordering him to let the presidential party travel for free was waiting at the next stop.

In Jacksonville, Florida, the president and his entourage were greeted by a twenty-one-gun salute. They then boarded a paddlewheel steamer and headed up the winding St. Johns River, lined with cypress trees and flocks of herons and cranes. More friends and relatives joined the sociable president along the way, and fireworks shot up from the banks of the river. The following day, the steamer tied up at a spot some thirty-five miles from today's Disney World, where the party climbed into carriages to visit the elegant mansion of the Belair orange plantation. They tasted different varieties of the plantation's prize oranges, and the secretary of the navy climbed a tree to pick some that particularly caught his eye. In the evening, the presidential entourage watched a song-and-dance perform-ance, with banjo music, by a troupe of six local black boys.

One of the more forgettable of American presidents, Chester A. Arthur was an amiable man whose highest job, only a few years earlier, had been as collector of customs revenue for the port of New York — a position he had been forced to leave amid charges of corruption and mismanage-ment. Soon after this, Arthur's ties to the powerful New York State Re-publican machine won him nomination as candidate for vice president. To near-universal dismay, he had entered the White House when Presi-dent James A. Garfield died from an assassin's bullet. A good storyteller and man about town, fond of whiskey, cigars, and expensive clothes, the dapper, sideburned Arthur is perhaps best remembered for saying, "I may be president of the United States, but my private life is nobody's damned business." On this trip to Florida, however, his private life fitted very nicely into someone else's business. The owner of the Belair orange plantation was General Henry Shelton Sanford, the man who had helped Leopold recruit Stanley.

Sanford did not bother to leave his home in Belgium to be in Florida for the president's visit. With the self-assurance of the very rich, he played host in absentia. He made sure that the president and his party were greeted by his personal agent, and that they got the best rooms at the Sanford House hotel, which stood on a lakeshore fringed with palm trees in the town of Sanford. When the president and his guests were not out catching bass, trout, and catfish, or shooting alligators, or exploring the area by steamboat, the Sanford House was where they stayed for the better part of a week. There is no record of who paid the hotel bill, but most likely, as with the rail journey south, it was not the president.

Ironically, the huge Sanford orange plantation the Washington visitors admired was proving as disastrous a venture as Sanford's other invest-ments. Some Swedish contract laborers found the working conditions too harsh and tried to leave as stowaways on a steamboat. A slaughter-house Sanford invested in had a capacity fifty times larger than what the local market could consume and went bankrupt. A 540-foot wharf with a warehouse at the end of it that he ordered built was washed away by a flood. The manager of one of the hotels in Sanford absconded while owing him money. Foremen failed to put up fences, and wandering cattle nibbled at the orange trees. But if everything Sanford touched as a businessman turned to dust, as an accomplice of Leopold he was a grand success.

Sanford was a long-time supporter of President Arthur's Republican Party. For two years, he had been corresponding with Arthur and other high United States officials about Leopold's plans for the Congo. Now, after the president's trip to Florida, confident that Arthur would pay attention, he pressed his case with more letters. Seven months later, Leopold sent Sanford across the Atlantic to make use of his convenient connection to the White House. The man who had once been American minister to Belgium was now the Belgian king's personal envoy to Washington.

Sanford carried with him to Washington a special code for telegraphing news to Brussels: *Constance* meant "negotiations proceeding satisfactorily; success expected"; *Achille* referred to Stanley, *Eugénie* to France, *Alice* to the United States, *Joseph* to "sovereign rights," and *Émile* to the key target, the president. *Bonheur* (happiness) meant "agreement signed today." The agreement Leopold wanted was one that gave full American diplomatic recognition of his claim to the Congo.

Sanford also carried a letter to the president from the king, which he himself had carefully edited and translated. "Entire territories ceded by Sovereign Chiefs have been constituted by us into independent States," Leopold declared, a claim that would have startled Stanley, then finishing up his work on the Congo River. From Arthur, Leopold asked only "the official announcement that the Government of the United States . . . [will] treat as a friendly flag . . . the blue standard with the golden star which now floats over 17 stations, many territories, 7 steamers engaged in the civilizing work of the Association and over a population of several millions."

On November 29, 1883, only two days after his ship arrived in New York and he had boarded the overnight train for Washington, Sanford was received by President Arthur at the White House. Leopold's great work of civilization, he told the president and everyone else he met in Washington, was much like the generous work the United States itself had done in Liberia, where, starting in 1820, freed American slaves had moved to what soon became an independent African country. This was a shrewdly chosen example, since it had not been the United States government that had resettled ex-slaves in Liberia, but a private society like Leopold's International Association of the Congo.

Like all the actors in Leopold's highly professional cast, Sanford relied on just the right props. He claimed, for example, that Leopold's treaties with Congo chiefs were similar to those which the Puritan clergyman Roger Williams, famed for his belief in Indian rights, had made in Rhode Island in the 1600s — and Sanford just happened to have copies of those treaties with him. Furthermore, in his letter to President Arthur, Leopold promised that American citizens would be free to buy land in the Congo and that American goods would be free of customs duties there. In support of these promises, Sanford had with him a sample copy of one of Leopold's treaties with a Congo chief. The copy, however, had been altered in Brussels to omit all mention of the monopoly on trade ceded to Leopold, an alteration that deceived not only Arthur but also Sanford, an ardent free-trader who wanted the Congo open to American businessmen like himself.

In Washington, Sanford claimed that Leopold's civilizing influence would counter the practices of the dreadful "Arab" slave-traders. And weren't these "independent States" under the association's generous protection really a sort of United States of the Congo? Not to mention that, as Sanford wrote to Secretary of State Frederick Frelinghuysen (Stanley was still vigorously passing himself off as born and bred in the United States), the Congo "was discovered by an American." Only a week after Sanford arrived in Washington, the president cheerfully incorporated into his annual message to Congress, only slightly rewritten, text that Sanford had drafted for him about Leopold's high-minded work in the Congo:

> The rich and populous valley of the Kongo is being opened by a society called the International African Association, of which the King of the Belgians is the president. . . . Large tracts of territory have been ceded to the Association by native chiefs, roads have been opened, steamboats have been placed on the river and the nuclei of states established . . . under one flag which offers freedom to commerce and prohibits the slave trade. The objects of the society are philanthropic. It does not aim at permanent political control, but seeks the neutrality of the valley.

Leopold was delighted to hear his own propaganda coming so readily from the president's mouth. His aide Colonel Maximilien Strauch cabled Sanford: ENCHANTED WITH ÉMILE.

Sanford next went to work on Congress. He rented a house at 1925 G Street, a few blocks from the White House, telegraphed for his wife and chef to come over from Belgium, and began wining and dining senators, representatives, and Cabinet members. It was Sanford's finest hour, for the affable personality that made him both a *bon vivant* and a poor business-man served him wonderfully as a lobbyist. He had an excellent wine cellar, and he was called "the gastronomic diplomat," waging a "gastro-nomic campaign." "What a charming dinner that was at your house and in such a queenly presence too," one visitor wrote to him. Secretary of State Frelinghuysen was a frequent guest; President Arthur and members of Congress and the Cabinet found themselves receiving boxes of Florida oranges.

As he was winning congressional support for Leopold's claim to the Congo, Sanford discovered an unexpected ally. Senator John Tyler Mor-gan of Alabama, a former Confederate brigadier general, was chairman of the Senate Foreign Relations Committee. Like most white Southern politicians of the era, he was frightened by the specter of millions of freed slaves and their descendants harboring threatening dreams of equal-ity. The fierce-looking, mustachioed senator, small in stature but loud in bluster, thundered ominously about the dangers of "enforced negro rule," as blacks were "foisted into . . . white families," where they might inflict "a worse fate than death upon an innocent woman." Morgan fretted for years over the "problem" of this growing black population. His solution, endorsed by many, was simple: send them back to Africa!

Always urging a "general exodus" of Southern blacks, at various times in his long career Morgan also advocated sending them to Hawaii, to Cuba, and to the Philippines — which, perhaps because the islands were so far away, he claimed were a "native home of the negro." But Africa was always first choice. To Morgan, Leopold's new state seemed heaven-sent. Wouldn't this territory require manpower to develop? And wouldn't the Congolese be eager to trade with the United States if the Americans they met had the same skin color? And couldn't the Congo become a market for the South's cotton surplus? Africa, he later said on the Senate floor, "was prepared for the negro as certainly as the Garden of Eden was prepared for Adam and Eve. . . . In the Congo basin we find the best type of the negro race, and the American negro . . . can find here the field for his efforts."*

Sanford completely agreed. Although he was born in Connecticut, once he invested in the South he quickly assimilated the send-them-back-to-Africa feelings of white businessmen there. The Congo could serve, he had said, as "an outlet . . . for the enterprise and ambition of our colored people in more congenial fields than politics." To the end of his life he would promote this new "Canaan for our modern Israelites," which could be "the ground to draw the gathering electricity from that black cloud spreading over the Southern states." Sanford and Morgan hit it off splendidly, and Morgan, too, began receiving crates of Florida oranges.

In early 1884, Morgan introduced a Senate resolution in support of Leopold's Congo claims, first sending a rough draft to Sanford. Like any lobbyist given the chance, Sanford reached for more. To Morgan's reference to land "drained by the Congo River" he added the words "its tributaries and adjacent rivers," a phrase that could be interpreted as meaning all of central Africa. The Senate toned this down, soon passing a modified version of Morgan's resolution. It also issued a thousand copies of a long report on the Congo under Morgan's name, mainly written by Sanford. "It may be safely asserted," the report declared, "that no barbarous people have ever so readily adopted the fostering care of benevolent enterprise as have the tribes of the Congo, and never was there a more honest and practical effort made to . . . secure their welfare."

Knowing how carefully President Arthur's Republicans listened to business, Sanford got the New York Chamber of Commerce to pass a resolution endorsing U.S. recognition of Leopold's association. Favorable accounts of the king's philanthropic work began appearing in major American newspapers, stimulated, in the fashion of the day, by quiet payments from Sanford. Sanford's multilayered campaign was probably the most sophisticated piece of Washington lobbying on behalf of a foreign ruler in the nineteenth century, and on April 22, 1884, it bore

---

* Morgan gave this speech in support of a bill providing federal funds for the transportation costs of Southern blacks emigrating abroad. In response, an African-American convention in Chicago passed a resolution urging federal funds for the emigration of Southern whites, Senator Morgan in particular.

fruit. The secretary of state declared that the United States of America recognized King Leopold II's claim to the Congo. It was the first country to do so.

Leopold knew he owed this great coup to Sanford, and knew also that what mattered more than money to the "General" was royal praise. He invited to breakfast Sanford's wife, Gertrude, who had returned to Belgium. "I cannot begin to tell you," she wrote to her husband afterward, "of all the flattering things the King said about you. . . . My dear *nothing* could have been more flattering to you or tender to me than were both the King and Queen."

During his adroit Washington lobbying, Sanford had passed around documents that thoroughly jumbled the names of the International Association of the Congo, entirely controlled by Leopold, and the International African Association, at this point defunct but still vaguely remembered as a philanthropic society of famous explorers, crown princes, and grand dukes. Everyone was left pleasantly confused. In his official statement of recognition, Secretary of State Frelinghuysen actually managed to use both names in the same sentence:

> The Government of the United States announces its sympathy with and approval of the humane and benevolent purposes of the International Association of the Congo, administering, as it does, the interests of the Free States there established, and will order the officers of the United States, both on land and sea, to recognize the flag of the International African Association as the flag of a friendly Government.

Like most such official documents, this one rapidly disappeared into bureaucrats' filing cabinets. But it was later transformed, in a curious way that no one seems to have noticed. When this very statement was reprinted the following year in Stanley's best-selling *The Congo and the Founding of Its Free State: A Story of Work and Exploration,* which was translated into many languages and read all over the world, the wording was different. The key change was that it referred only to Leopold's wholly-owned International Association of the Congo. The editor who made the change was most likely the king himself, who carefully corrected Stanley's manuscript, chapter by chapter. Long before Stalin, who also edited writers' manuscripts with his own hand, Leopold knew the uses of rewriting history.

✿✿✿✿

"The recognition of the United States was the birth unto new life of the Association," wrote Stanley, and he was right. Meanwhile, as Sanford was preparing to return in triumph to Belgium, Leopold closed a similar deal in France. As in Washington, the king had his own man in Paris, a well-connected art dealer named Arthur Stevens. He negotiated directly with Premier Jules Ferry while Leopold paid a large monthly stipend to a journalist from the influential *Le Temps* to ensure a stream of sympathetic articles about his activities in the Congo.

The French did not feel threatened by tiny Belgium or by the vast size of Leopold's claims. Their main fear was that when the king ran out of money — as they were sure he would — in his expensive plan to build a railway around the rapids, he might sell the whole territory to their main colonial rival, England. After all, hadn't Stanley repeatedly pressed for a British Congo?

Leopold calculated that Stanley's impulsive Anglophile fusillades might now actually be helping him. "It is my judgment," the king had confided to Colonel Strauch some months earlier, after one such salvo from Stanley, "that we should not try to make a correction. It does no harm for Paris to fear that a British protectorate could be established in the Congo." To allay the French anxiety, Leopold offered a remedy. If France would respect his claim, he would give the country *droit de préférence* over the Congo — what real estate lawyers today call a right of first refusal. The French, relieved, quickly agreed. Confident that Leopold's planned railway would bankrupt him and that he would then have to sell them the land, they thought they were getting an excellent deal.

The Americans had been so charmed by Sanford's bonhomie that they had not bothered to specify the exact borders of the distant territory they were implicitly recognizing as Leopold's. France, on the other hand, was willing to draw these boundaries on a map, where they included most of the Congo River basin.

Leopold had used the words "independent States" in writing to President Arthur. But in his pronouncements over the next few months this became "State." As for the association, that "was a purely temporary body and would disappear when its work was completed," said a Belgian journalist in 1884, explaining the king's thinking. By such sleight of hand, the entity that came to be recognized by a lengthening list of countries over the following year gradually changed from a federation of states under the benevolent protection of a charitable society to one colony ruled by one man.

Leopold found that the hardest nut to crack was Chancellor Bismarck of Germany. At first, the king's greed got him in trouble. Besides the Congo basin, he wrote to Bismarck, he was claiming vaguely defined areas "abandoned by Egypt, where the slave-trade continues to flourish. To allow these [provinces] to be incorporated into and administered by a new State would be the best way to get at the root of the trouble and eradicate it." Bismarck, no fool, scribbled a comment in the margin beside this passage: "Swindle." Beside a passage about a confederation of free states, he put "Fantasies." When Leopold wrote that the precise frontiers of the new state or states would be defined later, Bismarck said to an aide, "His Majesty displays the pretensions and naïve selfishness of an Italian who considers that his charm and good looks will enable him to get away with anything."

In the end, though, Leopold outsmarted even the Iron Chancellor, once again by working through the perfect intermediary. Gerson Bleichröder, Bismarck's banker, the financier of the St. Gotthard Tunnel under the Alps and many other projects, was a man of much behind-the-scenes influence in Berlin. The king had met him some years earlier at the fashionable Belgian beach resort of Ostend and had identified him as someone he could make use of. Bleichröder quietly bought good will for Leopold by conveying a 40,000-franc royal contribution to Berlin's Africa Society. He reported to Brussels on the latest doings at court in the city, and eventually he brought his friend the chancellor around to accepting Leopold's claim to the Congo. In return, Bleichröder received some banking business from advisers to Leopold and the chance to invest in the Congo himself. A woman pianist, thought to be a romantic interest of his, was invited to give a recital at the Belgian court, where she was presented with a medal by Leopold.

The king's negotiations with Bismarck reached a climax soon after Stanley returned to Europe in the summer of 1884. For five days the explorer was the guest of Leopold, now on holiday at Ostend's Royal Chalet, a sprawling seaside villa studded with turrets and towers. The king brought in a special cook to make Stanley a traditional English breakfast each morning, and the two men talked far into the night. Just as Stanley was about to leave came a message from Bismarck with questions about the boundaries of the new Congo state, so Stanley remained for a few hours to draw them in on a large map on the wall of the king's study. Bismarck let himself be convinced that it was better for the Congo to go to the king of weak little Belgium, and be open to German traders, than go to protection-minded France or Portugal or to powerful England. In return for guarantees of freedom of trade in the Congo (like everyone else, Bismarck did not know the full text of Leopold's treaties with the chiefs), he agreed to recognize the new state.

In Europe, the thirst for African land had become nearly palpable. There were some conflicting claims to be resolved, and clearly some ground rules were needed for further division of the African cake. Bismarck offered to host a diplomatic conference in Berlin to discuss some of these issues. To Leopold, the conference was one more opportunity to tighten his grip on the Congo.

On November 15, 1884, representatives of the powers of Europe assembled at a large, horseshoe-shaped table overlooking the garden of Bismarck's yellow-brick official residence on the Wilhelmstrasse. The ministers and plenipotentiaries in formal attire who took their seats beneath the room's vaulted ceiling and sparkling chandelier included counts, barons, colonels, and a vizier from the Ottoman Empire. Bismarck, wearing scarlet court dress, welcomed them in French, the diplomatic *lingua franca,* and seated before a large map of Africa, the delegates got to work.

More than anyone, Stanley had ignited the great African land rush, but even he felt uneasy about the greed in the air. It reminded him, he said, of how "my black followers used to rush with gleaming knives for slaughtered game during our travels." The Berlin Conference was the ultimate expression of an age whose newfound enthusiasm for democracy had clear limits, and slaughtered game had no vote. Even John Stuart Mill, the great philosopher of human freedom, had written, in *On Liberty,* "Despotism is a legitimate mode of government in dealing with barbarians, provided the end be their improvement." Not a single African was at the table in Berlin.

With his embryonic state already recognized by the United States and Germany, and with his friendly right-of-first-refusal deal made with France, Leopold was in a strong position. His International Association of the Congo was not a government — in fact, conference delegates

seemed confused as to just what it was — so it was not officially represented at Berlin. But Leopold had no problem staying abreast of what
went on at the conference. To begin with, keeping a close ear to the
ground in the German capital was his friend Bleichröder, who was host
to the delegates at an elegant dinner. Further, the king had ties with no
fewer than three of the national delegations.

First, the Belgian representatives were his trusted underlings; one of
them was appointed secretary of the meeting. Second, Leopold was unusually well informed about confidential matters in the British Foreign
Office, because the foreign secretary's personal assistant owed a large sum
of money to a businessman friend of the king's who had been one of his
original co-investors in sending Stanley to the Congo. In addition, a legal
adviser to the British delegation was Sir Travers Twiss, who had recently
consulted for Leopold about his treaties with the Congo chiefs. Finally,
who was appointed as one of two American delegates to the conference?
None other than Henry Shelton Sanford, who sent Leopold informative
dispatches almost daily. And who was "technical adviser" to the American
delegation, even as he remained on Leopold's payroll? Henry Morton
Stanley. Between sessions of the conference, Leopold sent Sanford to Paris
and Stanley to London on diplomatic lobbying missions.

Although his role at Berlin was mainly as a figurehead for Leopold's
Congo ambitions, Stanley was lionized by everyone and had a splendid
time. "This evening I had the honour of dining with Prince Bismarck
and his family," he wrote in his journal. "The prince is a great man, a kind
father, and excellently simple with his family. . . . The Prince asked many
questions about Africa and proved to me that in a large way he understood the condition of that continent very well." Bismarck, acquiring the
beginnings of a substantial African empire for Germany, was glad to have
the famous explorer stimulate German interest in the continent. He
arranged for Stanley a round of banquets and lectures in Cologne, Frank-
furt, and Wiesbaden.

In snowy Berlin, almost none of the conference participants except
Stanley had seen more of Africa than the drawings of its scenery on the
menus for Bismarck's banquets. So when anyone seemed unclear about
why Leopold's claim was so grand, Stanley could speak with the authority of someone who had just spent five years in the Congo for the king.
Early on, reported one diplomat, Stanley went to the big map of Africa
"and immediately engrossed the interest of every delegate, by a vivid
description of the features of the Congo basin; and finally of the [adja-

cent] country necessary to go with it under the same *régime* to secure the utmost freedom of communication."

Telegrams zipped back and forth between Berlin and Brussels, where Leopold was following every move. Contrary to myth, the Berlin Conference did not partition Africa; the spoils were too large, and it would take many more treaties to divide them all. But by resolving some conflicting claims, the conference (and a separate pact the king negotiated with France) did help Leopold in one important way: the king, France, and Portugal each got land near the Congo River's mouth, but Leopold got what he most wanted, the seaport of Matadi on the lower stretch of the river and the land he needed to build a railway from there around the rapids to Stanley Pool.

More important to Leopold was the web of bilateral agreements he made with other countries during and after the conference, recognizing his colony-in-the-making and marking out its boundaries. When talking to the British, for instance, he hinted that if he didn't get all the land he had in mind, he would leave Africa completely, which would mean, under his right-of-first-refusal deal, that he would sell the Congo to France. The bluff worked, and England gave in.

Europeans were still used to thinking of Africa's wealth mainly in terms of its coastline, and there was remarkably little conflict over ceding to Leopold the vast spaces he wanted in the interior. A major reason he was able to get his hands on so much is that other countries thought that they were giving their approval to a sort of international colony — under the auspices of the King of the Belgians, to be sure, but open to traders from all of Europe. In addition to perfunctory nods in favor of freedom of navigation, arbitration of differences, Christian missionaries, and the like, the major agreement that came out of Berlin was that a huge swath of central Africa, including Leopold's territory in the Congo basin, would be a free-trade zone.

The conference ended in February 1885, with signatures on an agreement and a final round of speechmaking. No one benefited more than the man who had not been there, King Leopold II. At the mention of his name during the signing ceremony, the audience rose and applauded. In his closing speech to the delegates, Chancellor Bismarck said, "The new Congo state is destined to be one of the most important executors of the work we intend to do, and I express my best wishes for its speedy development, and for the realization of the noble aspirations of its illustrious creator." Two months later, like a delayed exclamation mark at the end of Bismarck's speech, a United States Navy vessel, the *Lancaster*, appeared at the mouth of the Congo River and fired a twenty-one-gun salute in honor of the blue flag with the gold star.

※

Most Belgians had paid little attention to their king's flurry of African diplomacy, but once it was over they began to realize, with surprise, that his new colony was bigger than England, France, Germany, Spain, and Italy combined. It was one thirteenth of the African continent, more than seventy-six times the size of Belgium itself.

To make clear the distinction between his two roles, the King of the Belgians at first considered calling himself "Emperor of the Congo"; he also toyed with the idea of outfitting loyal chiefs with uniforms modeled on those of the famous red-clad Beefeaters at the Tower of London. Then he decided to be merely the Congo's "King-Sovereign." In later years, Leopold several times referred to himself — more accurately, for his main interest in the territory was in extracting every possible penny of wealth — as the Congo's "proprietor." His power as king-sovereign of the colony was shared in no way with the Belgian government, whose Cabinet ministers were as surprised as anyone when they opened their newspapers to find that the Congo had promulgated a new law or signed a new international treaty.

Even though the entity officially recognized by the Berlin Conference and various governments had been the International African Association or the International Association of the Congo (or, in the case of the befuddled U.S. State Department, both), Leopold decided on yet another change of name. The pretense that there was a philanthropic "Association" involved in the Congo was allowed to evaporate. All that remained unchanged was the blue flag with the gold star. By royal decree, on May 29, 1885, the king named his new, privately controlled country the État Indépendant du Congo, the Congo Free State. Soon there was a national anthem, "Towards the Future." At last, at age fifty, Leopold had the colony he had long dreamed of.

6

UNDER THE
YACHT CLUB FLAG

WHILE HIS POWER overseas was on the rise, at home Leopold's family life grew worse. He increasingly found refuge in the beds of various mistresses, one of whom Belgians promptly nicknamed "Queen of the Congo." In April 1885, only six weeks after his diplomatic triumph at Berlin, the king was named in a British courtroom as one of the clients of a high-class "disorderly house" prosecuted at the urging of the London Committee for the Suppression of the Continental Traffic in English Girls. Leopold had paid £800 a month, a former servant of the house testified, for a steady supply of young women, some of whom were ten to fifteen years old and guaranteed to be virgins. A Paris newspaper reported rumors that Leopold had secretly crossed to England in his yacht and paid a royal sum to the house's madam to be sure his name was not mentioned again. More likely, what made the case close with unusual speed was that the Prince of Wales was said to be another of the establishment's customers. The British home secretary sent a special observer to the court, apparently a veiled message to all concerned that the less said, the better. After pleading guilty, the madam of the house got off with a remarkably light fine.

When she was seventeen, Leopold married off his eldest daughter, Louise, to a much older Austro-Hungarian prince. After citywide festivities, the couple's wedding night at Laeken was so traumatic that Louise fled into the château gardens in her nightgown and had to be retrieved by a servant and lectured on wifely duty by her mother. Some years later, she got caught up in a tangle of bad debts and an adulterous romance with a cavalry officer. After the officer fought a duel with her husband, Austrian authorities jailed him and gave Louise the choice of going back to her husband or entering an insane asylum. She chose the asylum, and Leopold refused to speak to her again. Afraid of further embarrassment, he urged that she be guarded more closely. At last the cavalry officer was released from jail and dramatically rescued Louise from custody, only to die not long afterward. For the rest of her unhappy life, Louise bought clothes in the same obsessional way in which her father tried to buy countries, a compulsion that ate up her share of the royal fortune and more. Her exasperated creditors finally managed to seize and auction off a portion of her wardrobe: sixty-eight veils, ninety hats, twenty-seven evening gowns, twenty-one silk or velvet cloaks, and fifty-eight umbrellas and parasols.

Nor was Leopold a better father to his middle daughter, Stephanie. When she was only sixteen, he betrothed her to black-bearded Crown Prince Rudolph of Austria-Hungary so that she would one day become the empress. Leopold particularly envied the Hapsburgs because, unlike him, they were little encumbered by parliaments and constitutions. However, in what proved to be an omen of things to come, Rudolph, arriving in Brussels to meet Stephanie for the first time, brought his current mistress with him.

The king's main relief from domestic misery was his new colony. The Congo, later recalled Louise, "was the one topic of conversation around me." And compared to his household, for Leopold things in the Congo ran more smoothly. Just as he had found the perfect political moment to acquire his new territory, so he found himself at the right technological moment to consolidate his grip on it. As he prepared to develop the enormous colony, he found a number of tools at his disposal that had not been available to empire builders of earlier times. The tools were crucial, for they would soon allow a few thousand white men working for the king to dominate some twenty million Africans.

To begin with, there was weaponry. The primitive muzzle-loaders which were the best arms that most Congolese could obtain were little better than the muskets of George Washington's army. Starting in the late 1860s, however, Europeans could rely on breech-loading rifles, which had just shown their deadly power on the battlefields of the American Civil War. These shot much farther and more accurately, and, instead of needing loose gunpowder, which was useless in the rain, they used quick-loading waterproof brass cartridges.

An even more decisive advance quickly followed: the repeating rifle, which could fire a dozen or more shots without being reloaded. Soon after came the machine gun. As the poet Hilaire Belloc wrote:

> *Whatever happens, we have got*
> *The Maxim Gun, and they have not.*

Another tool that allowed Europeans to seize virtually all of tropical Africa in the two decades that followed the Berlin Conference was medical knowledge. Midcentury explorers had blamed malaria on everything from "marshy exhalations" to sleeping in the moonlight, but, whatever its cause, they learned that quinine was a useful defense. Around the turn of the century malaria and hematuria became better understood; researchers also mastered yellow fever and other diseases, and the awesomely high death rate for Europeans in the African tropics began to drop.

Finally, because of the Congo's unusual geography, one tool was even more important to Leopold than to other imperialists, and we have already seen it in action: the steamboat. It was known to Congo Africans as "the house that walks on water," or, after its sound, as *kutu-kutu*. The steamboat was an instrument of colonization throughout the nineteenth century, serving everyone from the British on the Ganges in India to the Russians on the Ob and Irtysh in Siberia. Congo steamboats included both sidewheelers and sternwheelers; all had awnings against the tropical sun. Usually they were long and narrow, with the shallow draft needed to clear the innumerable sandbars on the main river and its tributaries. Sometimes wire netting hung from the awning to protect the captain and helmsman from arrows.

By now, steam had also largely replaced sail on the high seas, making the long voyage from Europe down the coast of Africa far swifter and closer to a fixed schedule. These steamships carried the next wave of Leopold's agents to Africa. By the end of 1889, there were 430 whites working in the Congo: traders, soldiers, missionaries, and administrators of the king's embryonic state. Fewer than half of them were Belgians, for Leopold's homeland still showed little interest in its king's new possession. Significantly, almost all Leopold's agents in the Congo were officers on extended leave from the Belgian or other European armies.

Staff in place and tools in hand, Leopold set out to build the infrastructure necessary to exploit his colony. A rudimentary Congo transportation system was the first item on his agenda; without it, the territory's riches, whatever they might turn out to be, could not be brought to the sea except on foot. In 1887, a party of surveyors began to chart the route for a railroad to skirt the notorious 220 miles of rapids. Mosquitoes, heat, fever, and the rocky landscape laced with deep ravines took a severe toll, and it was three years before workers could start laying tracks.

As such work began getting under way, a Congo state bureaucracy grew in Belgium as well as in the colony itself. Henry Shelton Sanford tried to get himself a job as a top colonial executive in Brussels, writing hopefully to his wife, "There is just the sort of work I would like, with both reputation & money to gain & the satisfaction of doing good. . . . I think I will . . . propose a plan of operations, and offer my services." His hopes were in vain, for Leopold knew that Sanford's ability to give sumptuous Washington dinner parties was not matched by talent as an administrator or by the ruthlessness the king would require. Instead, Leopold gave Sanford permission to gather ivory and other products in the Congo, and the promise of help (not followed through on, as it turned out) in the form of porters, buildings, and steamboat transportation. But the Sanford Exploring Expedition, as the venture was euphemistically called, soon went the way of Sanford's other businesses. As usual, he tried to manage everything from Belgium, where mounting debts forced him to sell off some of his art collection and move to a smaller château. Meanwhile, his man in charge in the Congo took to drink, while steamboat boilers rusted on the trailside.

Leopold was a far better businessman than Sanford, but he too began to find himself under financial pressure. He had inherited a sizable fortune, yet by the late 1880s, explorers, steamboats, mercenaries, armaments, and other Congo expenses had burned up almost all of it. All these expenses, however, would continue — even increase — if he hoped to turn a profit in exploiting the territory. Where was the money to come from? Getting it from the Belgian government would be difficult, because a clause in the country's constitution had required parliamentary approval for Leopold to become monarch of another state. To obtain this approval, he had to promise that the Congo would never be a financial drain on Belgium. He had convinced skeptical legislators that he had sufficient funds to develop the territory, even though this was not true.

From 1885 to 1890, the king spent much of his time looking for money. For a while, he was able to borrow from bankers, but in time even his main creditors, the Rothschilds, would not lend him more. Hundreds of his letters from this period show an obsessive concern with money. He lost weight and sleep; his ministers thought he looked gray and distracted. He was known for his enormous appetite (he often ordered a new entrée after finishing a big meal, and at a Paris restaurant once ate two entire roast pheasants), and in a bid for public sympathy and funds he let it be known that to economize he was eating one less course daily at lunch. One day Queen Marie-Henriette cried out, "Leopold, you're going to ruin us with your Congo!"

The king raised some money through selling bonds, although far less than he had hoped. He wrote to the Pope, urging the Catholic Church to buy Congo bonds to encourage the spread of Christ's word. To the railway and a few other projects, he was able to attract private investors, but on terms that diminished his own share of what he was sure would be vast profits. He decided that the only solution to his financial crisis was a massive loan. Given his already heavy burden of debt, the most likely source for such a loan was the Belgian Parliament. As time passed, Leopold hoped, legislators would forget his earlier promises, so he waited before approaching Parliament. And as he waited, he worked, once again, on burnishing his reputation as a philanthropist and humanitarian.

※

People in Europe continued to feel indignant over the "Arab" slave-traders based on Zanzibar and Africa's east coast. The slavers were indeed, it must be said, spreading a wide swath of terror through much of east and central Africa, and the slaves they captured continued to be sold all along the northeast shore of the Indian Ocean and the Persian Gulf. But European righteousness over the issue was more intertwined than ever with a growing desire for African colonies. Conveniently, the slave-traders were mostly Muslim, which allowed Europeans to feel still more virtuous about their ambitions. Leopold won much praise for his patronage of Christian missionaries in his new colony; he so impressed people with his vigorous denunciations of the slave trade that he was elected honorary president of the Aborigines Protection Society, a venerable British human rights organization.

To the king's great satisfaction, Brussels was chosen as the location, for eight months of intermittent meetings starting in November 1889, for an Anti-Slavery Conference of the major powers. The "humanitarian" king happily entertained the delegates, in whose meeting room at the Belgian Foreign Ministry a forked slave-yoke was on display. "It is hard work," the senior British representative reported back to the Foreign Office; "all the dinners, receptions and balls." For diplomatic reasons, Turkey had to be included in the Anti-Slavery Conference, even though slavery was legal there. Its delegate roared with laughter when speakers denounced the Islamic harem as a stimulus to the slave trade.

For the diplomats, the conference was a long party. Their conference room looked out on a fashionable downtown street, and one official recalled of Count von Kevenhuller, the Austro-Hungarian representative: "Upon the appearance of each woman's hat, he got up and rushed to the window as if moved by a spring. And each time it was the occasion for great joy. Finally, for fear that he would miss a chance for his favorite sport, people from one end of the green-covered table to the other called out to alert him to the approach of a new pretty woman."

The Anti-Slavery Conference was a boon to Leopold, for the delegates paused from ogling the passersby long enough to approve some plans the king proposed for fighting the slave-traders — plans that, it happened, bore a striking resemblance to those for the expensive transportation infrastructure he was hoping to build in the Congo. The king described the need for fortified posts, roads, railways, and steamboats, all of which would support columns of troops pursuing the slavers. He grandly offered the services of the new Congo state toward this noble end, and asked in return only that the conference authorize him to levy import duties to finance the attack on slavery. The powers eventually agreed, in effect amending in Leopold's favor the Berlin agreement, which had guaranteed free trade.

Henry Shelton Sanford, who attended the Anti-Slavery Conference as an American delegate, was horrified. Six years earlier he had won United States recognition for Leopold's Congo in exchange for his own signature on an agreement promising free trade; here was Leopold suddenly asking for customs duties. His naïve admiration shattered, Sanford felt that the king had betrayed him. Troubled by gout and insomnia, his chestnut beard now turning gray, and his face showing the effects of age and financial worries, Sanford was a different man from the glamorous top-hatted envoy of half a dozen years before. He died the year after the conference ended, bitterly disillusioned with Leopold and deeply in debt. His Congo investments came to nothing, and the only sign that remained of him there was a six-ton steamboat called the *Général Sanford*.

While the conference was still in session, Leopold invited Stanley to Belgium for a week. Stanley spoke to the delegates, and Leopold presented him with the Grand Cross of the Congo, arranged a banquet and a gala opera performance in his honor, and put him up in the gilt and scarlet rooms at the Royal Palace normally reserved for visiting royalty. In return, Stanley praised his host to the Belgians in a speech:

> What does the greatness of a monarch consist in? If it is the extent of his territory, then the Emperor of Russia is the greatest of all. If it is the splendour and power of military organiza-tion, then William II [of Germany] takes first place. But if royal greatness consists in the wisdom and goodness of a sovereign leading his people with the solicitude of a shepherd watching over his flock, then the greatest sovereign is your own.

Leopold was using Stanley as a modern American president might bring a famous movie star on the campaign trail. Stanley's visit to Brussels was a key part of a carefully planned public relations campaign to mark the twenty-fifth year of the king's reign. Leopold also gave a garden party for twenty-five hundred members of the Belgian elite at Laeken, and opened for the awed partygoers the château's enormous new glass-domed greenhouses, whose exotic array of plants and trees constituted the largest private botanical collection in the world. Even the Brussels stock exchange, whose members had long been reluctant to put up money for the king's African projects, now gave a big reception in his honor, decorating the exchange hall with African spears and one of the more unusual flower arrangements on record, a mass of foliage sprouting four hundred elephant tusks.

Leopold's campaign was directed toward one goal: money. As his efforts neared a climax, he struck a deal with important members of the Cabinet, who were beginning to realize that the king's African possession might someday be quite valuable. If Parliament gave him the loan he wanted, Leopold declared, he would leave the Congo to Belgium in his will. And so, when this generous monarch, known as an antislavery crusader, praised by the famous explorer Stanley, fêted by his loyal subjects, at last asked Parliament for a loan of twenty-five million francs (some $125 million in today's money) to support the philanthropic work he was doing in the Congo, he got it. Interest-free.

Perhaps nowhere does Leopold's breathtaking arrogance show so clearly as in the curious document where he blithely bequeaths one of his countries to the other.

> We, Leopold II, King of the Belgians, Sovereign of the État
> Indépendant du Congo, wishing to secure for Our beloved fa-
> therland the fruits of the work which, for many long years, We
> have been pursuing on the African continent . . . declare, by these
> presents, to bequeath and transmit, after Our death, to Belgium,
> all Our sovereign rights over l'État Indépendant du Congo.

There was one added twist. When the king made public his will, it was
backdated, so that his bequest looked like an act of generosity instead of
part of a financial bargain.

For Henry Morton Stanley, the five years preceding his red-carpet 1890
visit to Brussels had not been easy. From the time the Berlin Conference
ended in 1885, Leopold had been wondering what to do with Stanley. To
ensure that the explorer would not go to work for the British, he kept
him on retainer as a consultant. What the king needed now, however, was
not explorers but surveyors, mining engineers, railway builders, steamboat
captains, soldiers, and administrators. Years earlier, Leopold had promised
to appoint Stanley director general of the future Congo state. Then,
however, in return for recognition of his Congo by the French (who
resented Stanley for outexploring and belittling their man de Brazza), he
had quietly promised them that he would never again employ Stanley in
the Congo. In everything but public relations, the restless Stanley was
now of little use to the king. Leopold, a Belgian prime minister once
remarked, "treats men as we use lemons, when he has squeezed them dry
he throws away the peel."

Stanley guessed that Leopold had made a secret deal with the French,
and, as so often in his life, felt hurt. His African travel equipment was
packed and ready, but there was no mission to go on. He didn't need the
money he received from being on Leopold's payroll; he was earning far
greater sums from his lectures and books. Nonetheless, he maintained
his starstruck loyalty to the king, even when Leopold continued to put
him off by saying, as Stanley complained in an 1886 letter, "We do not
know exactly when we shall need you, but we shall let you know, my dear
Mr. Stanley, in ample time to prepare."

As always, when he hoped to leave for Africa, Stanley thought about
marriage, even though, as he confessed despairingly, "the fact is, I can't
talk to women." For more than a year, he carried on another of his shy,

clumsy courtships, this time with a London high society painter named Dorothy Tennant. She painted Greek nymphs, London street urchins, and Stanley's own portrait. It seemed an appropriate match, for she was as stiff and ill at ease with men as Stanley was with women. At the age of thirty-four she still shared a bedroom with her mother and addressed her diary to her long-dead father. Stanley confided to Tennant the unhappy story of his abandonment by Alice Pike and then proposed to her. But she turned him down. Once again rejected, he was convinced that Dorothy Tennant held his class origins against him. "That woman entrapped me with her gush," he wrote to a friend, "and her fulsome adulations, her knickknacks inscribed with 'Remember Me,' her sweet scented notes."

While Stanley was suffering through this experience, Leopold's ambitions had grown. His desire for colonies inflamed, he was now dreaming of the valley of the Nile. "My dear minister," he once said to the Belgian prime minister, who was trying to talk him out of this fantasy, "Do you consider worth nothing the glory of being a Pharaoh?" Compared with this, he insisted, the Congo was "prosaic." But of the Nile he exclaimed, "It is my panache, and I will never give it up!" In 1886, an opportunity appeared that promised Leopold, all in one swoop, the chance to advance his Nile dreams, to see Stanley put to work again, and to consolidate his hold on the Congo.

The Sudan, through which the upper branches of the Nile flowed, was under joint Anglo-Egyptian rule. But distances were vast and control loose. Members of a rebel Muslim fundamentalist movement, the Mahdists, staged a rebellion in the mid-1880s, killing the British governor general and rebuffing the British forces sent against them. England was shocked, but the country had too many colonial wars under way elsewhere and decided, for the moment, not to fight this one. The rebels pushed to the south, where, holding out against them, was the governor of the Sudan's southernmost province. Most conveniently for Leopold, it bordered on the Congo.

The governor, Emin Pasha, asked for help from Europe; one of his letters was published in the *Times*, and a movement arose to send a private expedition to support him. The *Times* said it would be an "errand of mercy and of peril — to rescue Emin Pasha . . . who is surrounded by savage and hostile tribes and cut off from the reach and resources of civilisation." Fueled by anti-Islamic fervor, the plan won a large following. The British were further outraged with the Mahdists when their leader demanded that Queen Victoria come to the Sudan, submit to his rule, and convert to Islam.

Now the British had not only Muslim villains, but, in Emin, a white hero. For despite his title (*emin* means "the faithful one"), the beleaguered pasha was a slight, short German Jew, originally named Eduard Schnitzer. In photographs, Emin's unmistakably European face, adorned with thick spectacles and topped with a red fez, looks like that of a nearsighted delegate to a Shriners' convention. A physician by training, the pasha was a brilliant linguist and an eccentric; besides trying to govern his province, heal the sick, and hold out against the Mahdist rebels, he was painstakingly gathering specimens of plant and animal life and assembling a collection of stuffed birds for the British Museum.

Plans for the relief expedition took shape, and donations poured in. The food merchants Fortnum and Mason contributed cases of delicacies; the inventor Hiram Maxim sent the very latest model of his machine gun; also destined for Emin was a new dress uniform. And to lead the Emin Pasha Relief Expedition, who was a more suitable choice than Henry Morton Stanley? The explorer eagerly accepted the invitation. He was particularly delighted by the Maxim gun, which he tried out at its maker's home, satisfying himself that it really could shoot the advertised six hundred rounds per minute. The new gun, Stanley said, would be "of valuable service in helping civilisation to overcome barbarism."

When Stanley asked Leopold to release him from the consulting contract so that he could lead the expedition, the king agreed — on two conditions. First, instead of traveling to Emin by the shorter, easier route leading from the east African coast through German and British highland territory, the expedition was to go through Leopold's Congo, which would require its crossing the unexplored Ituri rain forest. Second, once Stanley found Emin Pasha, he would ask him to remain the governor of his province — but as a province of the Congo state.

Leopold would thus get not only an unknown corner of his territory explored and perhaps enlarged; he would have it all done at other people's expense. The financing for the venture came from sources ranging from the Royal Geographical Society to British traders interested in Emin's rumored stash of £60,000 worth of ivory to press barons who knew that a new Stanley expedition would sell newspapers. As he departed in early 1887, the explorer adroitly juggled the demands of his many sponsors. A surprised witness who later came upon Stanley and his huge force marching around the lower rapids of the Congo River noticed that the standard-bearer at the head of the column was carrying — at the request of *New York Herald* publisher James Gordon Bennett, Jr. — the flag of the New York Yacht Club.

Stanley's usual two-volume thousand-page best-seller turned out to be only one of many books subsequently written about the Emin Pasha Relief Expedition. (In recruiting his officers, Stanley made each one sign a contract promising that no book he wrote would appear until six months after Stanley's "official" account.) But other than benefiting the press and the publishing industry, the expedition proved a disaster for almost everyone involved, except, perhaps, for the New York Yacht Club, which at least had its banner borne across a continent.

Stanley threw his usual temper tantrums. Four times he fired his personal manservant and four times took him back. He had screaming matches with his white officers — several of whom later painted a highly unglamorous picture of Stanley. "The slightest little thing," one wrote, "is sufficient to work him into a frenzy of rage." He compounded the problems of Henry Sanford's collapsing Congo business venture by commandeering its partly built steamboat as a barge for his troops and returning it several months later badly damaged. Most important, he made the strategic mistake of dividing his eight hundred soldiers, porters, and camp followers into two columns so that he, with a smaller, faster-moving force, would reach Emin Pasha and accomplish the dramatic, headline-catching rescue more quickly.

As always, Stanley bungled his choice of subordinates. The officer he left in charge of the rear column, Major Edmund Barttelot, promptly lost his mind. He sent Stanley's personal baggage down the river. He dispatched another officer on a bizarre three-thousand-mile three-month round trip to the nearest telegraph station to send a senseless telegram to England. He next decided that he was being poisoned, and saw traitors on all sides. He had one of them given three hundred lashes (which proved fatal). He jabbed at Africans with a steel-tipped cane, ordered several dozen people put in chains, and bit a village woman. An African shot and killed Barttelot before he could do more.

Stanley, meanwhile, slogged through the rain forest at the head of the vanguard column, sentencing a deserter to be hanged and ordering numerous floggings, some of which he administered himself. Supply snafus meant that much of the time his porters and soldiers were near starvation. To those unfortunate enough to live in its path, the expedition felt like an invading army, for it sometimes held women and children hostage until local chiefs supplied food. One of Stanley's officers wrote in his diary, "We finished our last plantain to-day . . . the natives do not trade, or offer to, in the least. As a last resource we must catch some more of their women." When it seemed that they might be attacked, another recalled, "Stanley gave the order to burn all the villages round." Another described the slaughter as casually as if it were a hunt:

> It was most interesting, lying in the bush watching the natives quietly at their day's work. Some women . . . were making banana flour by pounding up dried bananas. Men we could see building huts and engaged in other work, boys and girls running about, singing. . . . I opened the game by shooting one chap through the chest. He fell like a stone. . . . Immediately a volley was poured into the village.

One member of the expedition packed the severed head of an African in a box of salt and sent it to London to be stuffed and mounted by his Piccadilly taxidermist.

Of the 389 men in Stanley's vanguard, more than half died as they hacked their way with machetes through the Ituri rain forest, sometimes making only four hundred yards' progress a day. When they ran out of food, they roasted ants. They climbed over giant tree roots and had to pitch camp on swampy ground in the midst of tropical downpours, one of which lasted seventeen hours without interruption. Men deserted, got lost in the jungle, drowned, or succumbed to tetanus, dysentery, and gangrenous ulcers. Others were killed by the arrows and poisoned-stake traps of forest-dwellers terrified by these armed, starving strangers rampaging through their territory.

By the time they finally reached Emin, Stanley and his surviving men were hungry and exhausted. Because most of the supplies were hundreds of miles behind them with the rear column and its mad commander, the explorer could offer the diminutive pasha little except some ammunition, fan mail, several bottles of champagne, and the new dress uniform — which turned out to be much too large. In fact, it was Stanley who had to ask Emin for supplies. The pasha met them, Stanley wrote, in "a clean suit of snowy cotton drilling, well-ironed and of perfect fit," his face showing "not a trace . . . of ill-health or anxiety; it rather indicated good condition of body and peace of mind." Emin, still happily gathering specimens for the British Museum, politely declined Leopold's proposal to join his province to the new Congo state. Most embarrassing of all to the bedraggled vanguard of the Emin Pasha Relief Expedition, the rebel threat had eased since Emin's letters of several years earlier, and he turned out not to be eager for relief.

Stanley greatly feared returning home without Emin. The pasha wrote in his diary, "For him everything depends on whether he is able to take me along, for only then . . . would his expedition be regarded as totally successful. . . . He would rather perish than leave without me!" Stanley did at last succeed in persuading the reluctant pasha to head back to Europe with him, in part because the very arrival of the Relief Expedition's large trigger-happy force stirred up the Mahdist rebels all over again. So Stanley and Emin and their followers trekked for several months to the east African coast, reaching the sea at a small German post in today's Tanzania.

A German battery fired an artillery salute in their honor, and officials gave the two of them a banquet at the local officers' mess. A naval band played; Stanley, Emin, and a German major gave speeches. "The wines were choice and well-selected and iced," writes Stanley. Then the near-sighted Emin, who had been moving up and down the banquet table, chatting with the guests and drinking champagne, stepped through a second-floor window that he apparently thought opened on a veranda. It didn't. He fell to the street and was knocked unconscious. He had to remain in a local German hospital for two months, and Stanley was unable to bring him back to Europe in triumph. Most embarrassing of all for Stanley was that Emin Pasha, once he recovered, went to work neither for his British rescuers nor for Leopold, but for the Germans.

For some months after Stanley's return in 1890, a controversy boiled in England over the loss of more than half the expedition's men and over the atrocities committed under his command. One weekly lampooned him:

> *And when the heat of Afric's sun*
> *Grew quite too enervating,*
> *Some bloodshed with the Maxim gun*
> *Was most exhilarating!*

The Emin Pasha Relief Expedition had indeed been brutal. But those who condemned it were unaware that, compared with the bloodshed beginning just then in central Africa, it was only a sideshow.

7

THE FIRST HERETIC

L EOPOLD'S WILL treated the Congo as if it were just a piece of uninhabited real estate to be disposed of by its owner. In this the king was no different from other Europeans of his age, explorers, journalists, and empire-builders alike, who talked of Africa as if it were without Africans: an expanse of empty space waiting to be filled by the cities and railway lines constructed through the magic of European industry.

To see Africa instead as a continent of coherent societies, each with its own culture and history, took a leap of empathy, a leap that few, if any, of the early European or American visitors to the Congo were able to make. To do so would have meant seeing Leopold's regime not as progress, not as civilization, but as a theft of land and freedom. For the first time, however, a visitor now arrives in the Congo who sees the colony around him with such eyes. Let us catch up with him at a station on the banks of the Congo River, on the muggy mid-July day in 1890 when he first puts his feelings on paper.

There are now a number of Leopold's stations on the river network, each a combination of military base and collecting point for ivory. Typically, a few buildings with thatched roofs and shady verandas, sheltered by palm trees, provide sleeping quarters for white officials. From a pole flies the blue flag with the gold star. Some food comes from banana trees, a garden growing manioc and other vegetables, and pens for chickens, goats, or pigs. A wooden blockhouse with rifle ports atop a small man-made hillock provides defense; often there is a stockade as well. Elephant tusks lie in a shed or in the open, guarded by armed sentries and awaiting transport to the coast. African dugout canoes are drawn up on the river-bank beside piles of wood cut in short lengths for steamboat boilers. One of the most important stations is a thousand miles upstream from Leopoldville at Stanley Falls, the upper limit of navigation on the main stretch of the Congo River.

At the Stanley Falls station on this July day, a forty-year-old man sits down in a white-hot blaze of anger. In a graceful, energetic hand, he begins writing. Perhaps he sits outside, his back against a palm trunk; perhaps he borrows the desk of the station clerk. As we can see in the handful of stiff, formal portrait photos we have of him, his hair is cropped short; his mustache tapers to long tips; he wears a bowtie and a high, white, starched collar. Maybe it is too hot for the collar and tie this day on the riverbank, but maybe not: some visitors dress formally in the Congo at all times.

The document that flows from the man's pen over the next day or two is a milestone in the literature of human rights and of investigative journalism. It is entitled *An Open Letter to His Serene Majesty Leopold II, King of the Belgians and Sovereign of the Independent State of Congo, by Colonel the Honorable Geo. W. Williams, of the United States of America.*

George Washington Williams was indeed an American. He was not, however, a colonel, a claim that was to cause him problems later. And he was black. Largely because of that, he has long been ignored. Among the eager throng of visitors drawn to the Congo as Leopold began to exploit it, Williams became the first great dissenter. And like many travelers who find themselves in a moral inferno, he had begun in search of something he hoped would be more like paradise.

Williams had come to the Congo over a route that seems almost as if it had taken him through several different lives. Born in Pennsylvania in 1849, he had only scanty schooling, and in 1864 he enlisted — semiliterate, underage, and with an assumed name — in the 41st U.S. Colored Troops of the Union Army. He fought in several battles during the drive on Richmond and Petersburg in the closing months of the war and was wounded in combat.

Afterward, like some other Civil War veterans in search of work, he enlisted in the army of the Republic of Mexico, which was fighting to overthrow King Leopold II's ambitious but unlucky brother-in-law, Emperor Maximilian. When he returned home, with no job skills except soldiering, Williams reenlisted in the U.S. Army and passed the better part of a year with a cavalry regiment fighting the Plains Indians. Sometime during the second half of 1867, when they both spent time at various army posts in Kansas, Williams's path may have crossed that of a young newspaper correspondent, Henry Morton Stanley.

After leaving the army the next year, Williams studied briefly at Howard University, which, when he mentioned it in later years, sometimes came out sounding like Harvard University. Later in his life, he also claimed a doctoral degree he had never earned. He was a brilliant student, however, and, moving on to the Newton Theological Institution, outside Boston, managed to compress a three-year graduate theology curriculum into two. In letters he wrote just after his army days, barely a word is spelled correctly, and the sentences are painfully garbled. But a few years later he could compose fluently in the rolling cadences of the nineteenth-century pulpit. A speech he gave when he graduated from Newton in 1874 sounded the theme that would lead him to the Congo sixteen years later:

> For nearly three centuries Africa has been robbed of her sable sons. . . . The Negro of this country can turn to his Saxon brothers, and say, as Joseph said to his brethren, who wickedly sold him, ". . . we, after learning your arts and sciences, might return to Egypt and deliver the rest of our brethren who are yet in the house of bondage." That day will come!

Williams had already begun writing and speaking about a bondage closer to home — the position of American blacks, enduring the long post–Civil War backlash of lynchings and Ku Klux Klan violence, and the return of white supremacist rule throughout the South. As a veteran, he was especially angry that so few hopes of the war that ended slavery had been realized.

The year he graduated from the seminary, Williams married and became pastor of the Twelfth Baptist Church, the major black congregation in Boston. In this job, as in others to come, he did not stay long. His life seems to have been infused with restlessness, for although he had considerable success in each new profession he took up, he seldom remained in it.

After only a year as a minister, he moved to Washington, D.C., and founded a national black newspaper, the *Commoner*. The first issue proudly printed congratulatory letters from the famous Abolitionists Frederick Douglass and William Lloyd Garrison, but the paper soon folded, and Williams returned to the ministry, this time in Cincinnati. He became a columnist for a local newspaper and once again started a paper of his own. Then, in another abrupt turn, he resigned his pulpit, studied law, and apprenticed himself to a lawyer. In 1879, at the age of thirty, he was elected the first black member of the Ohio state legislature, where he raised hackles by trying to win repeal of a law banning interracial marriages. He left the legislature after only one term.

In his next career, Williams made a much greater mark, and by the time he again moved on, he left something substantial and lasting behind him. It was a massive book, *History of the Negro Race in America from 1619 to 1880. Negroes as Slaves, as Soldiers, and as Citizens, together with a preliminary consideration of the Unity of the Human Family and historical Sketch of Africa and an Account of the Negro Governments of Sierra Leone and Liberia*. Published in two volumes, in 1882 and 1883, the book took its readers from early African kingdoms all the way through the Civil War and Reconstruction.

Williams was a pioneer among American historians in the use of nontraditional sources. He sensed what most academics only began to acknowledge nearly a hundred years later: that in writing the history of powerless people, drawing on conventional, published sources is far from enough. While traveling around the country, Williams did look through innumerable libraries, but he did much more. He wrote a letter to a national black newspaper asking readers to send him "minutes of any colored church organization" and other such documents. He wrote to General William Tecumseh Sherman, asking his opinion of his black troops. He interviewed fellow Civil War veterans. And when his 1092-page book appeared, it was widely and favorably reviewed. Several decades earlier, wrote the *New York Times*, patronizing but impressed, "it would have been very generally doubted if one of that race could be the author of a work requiring so much native ability." W.E.B. Du Bois would later call Williams "the greatest historian of the race."

Williams began to travel the lecture circuit, addressing veterans' groups, fraternal organizations, and church congregations, black and white. He seemed to have a speech for any occasion, from Fourth of July celebrations to a meeting of the Philomathian Literary Society of Washington, and he soon signed up with the leading lecture agent of the day, James B.

Pond, one of whose clients was Stanley. He managed to meet everyone from Henry Wadsworth Longfellow to Presidents Grover Cleveland and Rutherford B. Hayes; and many who met him came away with a positive impression of the earnest young man. Less impressed were many black Americans, who thought Williams too quick to turn his back on them in his eagerness to consort with the high and mighty.

Despite his successes, money flowed through Williams's fingers, and he left a string of angry creditors behind him. He continued to pour his immense energy into a variety of projects. He wrote a second book, about the experience of black soldiers in the Civil War. He went to New Mexico in search of land for a possible settlement of black farmers. He fired off articles for newspapers. He worked as a lawyer for the Cape Cod Canal Company. He wrote a play about the slave trade. He threw himself into the work of Union veterans' organizations, receiving the honorary title of colonel from the most important of them, the Grand Army of the Republic. He testified before Congress in favor of a monument to black Civil War veterans. He was nominated as minister to Haiti by President Chester A. Arthur, for whom he had campaigned. But Arthur left office, and political enemies circulated rumors about Williams's debts, so the appointment did not take effect.

Once when Williams was meeting with Arthur at the White House, someone else had chosen the same time to see the president: Henry Shelton Sanford, then lobbying in Washington for United States recognition of Leopold's Congo. The president introduced his two visitors to each other. In the embryonic Congo state that Sanford described, Williams saw a chance to pursue the dream he had first mentioned in his seminary graduation speech. He wrote to one of Leopold's aides, proposing to recruit black Americans to work in the Congo. In Africa, surely, there would be the chance for pioneering and advancement then denied blacks in the United States. He also submitted a statement to the Senate Committee on Foreign Relations urging recognition of the International Association of the Congo and added the Congo to his list of lecture topics.

In 1889, Williams won an assignment to write a series of articles from Europe for a press syndicate. He also tried but failed to be appointed an American delegate to the Anti-Slavery Conference in Brussels; nonetheless, he passed himself off as a delegate when he visited London. Brussels, he found, was a city filled with Europeans trying to outdo each other in condemning slavery, and in this atmosphere the young American son of a freed slave made a good impression. Yet despite his impressive list of achievements, Williams could not resist embellishing it:

> Colonel Williams [reported the newspaper *L'Indépendance Belge*], who won his rank during the Civil War . . . has written at least five or six works about Negroes. . . . He was the first person to propose official recognition of the Congo state by the United States and was allowed, to this end, to give a major speech to the Senate Committee on Foreign Relations in Washington which was crowned with complete success.

The first newspaper piece Williams sent home from Belgium was an interview with Leopold, whom he described as "a pleasant and entertaining conversationalist. His hair and full beard were carefully trimmed and liberally sprinkled with gray. His features were strong and clear cut and keen; and his eyes, bright and quick, flashed with intelligent interest from behind a pair of eyeglasses."

When Williams asked what the king expected in return for all the money he had spent developing the Congo, Leopold replied, "What I do there is done as a Christian duty to the poor African; and I do not wish to have one franc back of all the money I have expended." On this first meeting, Williams, like many others, was dazzled by the man whom he called "one of the noblest sovereigns in the world; an emperor whose highest ambition is to serve the cause of Christian civilization, and to promote the best interests of his subjects, ruling in wisdom, mercy, and justice."

Leopold clearly saw that the way to charm this particular visitor was to offer a sympathetic ear to his projects, for in the same article Williams reported that the king "proved himself a good listener." What he listened to, apparently, was Williams's long-cherished plan to put black Americans to work in Africa. Williams struck an agreement with a Belgian company to sign up forty skilled artisans and take them to work in the Congo, and also made plans to write a book about the territory. When he returned to the United States, however, and gave his recruitment pitch at a black college in Virginia, he found a skeptical audience with many questions about life in Africa that he could not answer. At that point he postponed the recruiting plan and decided to go first to the Congo and gather material for his book.

That presented him with the job of raising the money for steamship tickets, food, supplies, and porters for the long trek around the rapids. The main patron he pursued was the American railroad baron Collis P. Huntington, who was a minor investor in the planned Congo railway. Williams sought him out and followed the visit with a stream of flattering letters, which eventually produced a small subsidy for his African travels.

In December 1889, Williams met President Benjamin Harrison at the White House. It is not clear that Harrison did more than wish him a good trip to Africa, but, as was often the case in his life, Williams later used this meeting with a man of power to imply that he was carrying out an important confidential mission for him.

As Williams prepared for his trip, dropping references to his connection with the president and Huntington, Leopold and his aides grew suspicious that he might be covertly serving American businessmen intent on moving into the territory. When Williams passed through Brussels on the way to the Congo, he later said:

> every possible influence was exerted to turn me aside from my mission. An officer of the King's Household was dispatched to me for the purpose of persuading me not to visit the Congo. He dwelt upon the deadly character of the climate during the rainy seasons, the perils and hardships of travelling by caravans, and the heavy expenses of the voyage. . . . After this the King sent for me [and] said . . . that it was difficult to travel in the country, and more difficult to obtain wholesome food for white men; that he hoped I would postpone my visit to the Congo for at least five years; and that all necessary information would be furnished me in *Brussels*. In reply I told His Majesty that I was going to the Congo *now*, and would start within a few days.

Between January 1890 and the beginning of the following year, Williams sailed around the entire African continent, periodically sending Huntington urgent requests for more money. He managed to meet everyone from the vice president of the Boers' Transvaal Republic to the Sultan of Zanzibar to the Khedive of Egypt, as well as to receive an honorary membership in Zanzibar's English Club and to deliver a lecture at Cairo's Khedival Geographical Society. But his most important visit was to the Congo, where he spent six months, proceeding on foot around the lower rapids and by steamer up the great river, with many stops, all the way to Stanley Falls.

❦

Traveling the river by steamboat at this time was a matter of progressing perhaps thirty miles a day, sometimes fewer when heading upstream. Each day the boat stopped in the late afternoon, sometimes docking at a state post or mission station, but more often being moored to the riverbank for the night. The captain posted sentries and sent a crew of black woodcutters to chop down trees as fuel for the following day's run. One traveler described the typical scene:

> At dusk huge fires were lit, and by the blaze of these the men cut up the logs into small chunks, three or four feet in length. . . . It was a . . . sight attended with . . . the thud, thud of the axes, the crash of the falling trees, then the firelight scene, with the scraping of the saw . . . the blocks were . . . then tossed from hand to hand till they were all loaded on to the steamer.

European or American passengers slept in cabins on board, usually on the upper deck; the woodcutters slept on shore on the ground. At dawn, a whistle blast brought the crew back on board or into canoes or a barge towed by the boat, and the paddlewheel at the stern slowly pushed the boat upstream.

Making his way up the river in these slow stages, Williams had ample time to take in the Africa he had long dreamed of. A keen observer and experienced interviewer, he had the ability — as rare among journalists as it is among historians — to be uninfluenced by what others had already written. And in the villages and state posts and mission stations along the banks of the river, he found not the benignly ruled colony described by Stanley and others, but what he called "the Siberia of the African Continent." His impressions were distilled in the remarkable document he wrote at Stanley Falls, when he could contain his rage no longer.

At the beginning of his *Open Letter* to the king, Williams is respectful: "Good and Great Friend, I have the honour to submit for your majesty's consideration some reflections respecting the Independent State of Congo, based upon a careful study." By the second paragraph, though, he is referring Leopold to a higher authority, the "King of Kings." And God, it is clear, is *not* pleased by what he sees happening in the Congo.

The *Open Letter* is the work of a man who seems doubly horrified: first by what he has seen, and second by "how thoroughly I have been disenchanted, disappointed and disheartened" after "all the praisefull [sic] things I have spoken and written of the Congo country, State and Sovereign." Almost immediately, Williams gets down to business, assuming the tone of one of his many professions, that of a lawyer:

"Every charge which I am about to bring against your Majesty's personal Government in the Congo has been carefully investigated; a list of competent and veracious witnesses, documents, letters, official records and data has been faithfully prepared." The documents would be kept "until such time as an International Commission can be created with power to send for persons and papers, to administer oaths, and attest the truth or falsity of these charges." It is easy to imagine Leopold's fury on finding himself addressed in this prosecutorial voice by a foreigner, by someone he had tried to dissuade from going to the Congo in the first place, and, no less, by a black man.

If it were printed as this book is, the *Open Letter* would run to only about a dozen pages. Yet in that short space Williams anticipated almost all the major charges that would be made by the international Congo protest movement of more than a decade later. Although by 1890 scattered criticism of Leopold's Congo state had been published in Europe, most of it focused on the king's discrimination against foreign traders. Williams's concern was human rights, and his was the first comprehensive, systematic indictment of Leopold's colonial regime written by anyone. Here are his main accusations:

- Stanley and his white assistants had used a variety of tricks, such as fooling Africans into thinking that whites had supernatural powers, to get Congo chiefs to sign their land over to Leopold. For example: "A number of electric batteries had been purchased in London, and when attached to the arm under the coat, communicated with a band of ribbon which passed over the palm of the white brother's hand, and when he gave the black brother a cordial grasp of the hand the black brother was greatly surprised to find his white brother so strong, that he nearly knocked him off his feet. . . . When the native inquired about the disparity of strength between himself and his white brother, he was told that the white man could pull up trees and perform the most prodigious feats of strength." Another trick was to use a magnifying glass to light a cigar, after which "the white man explained his intimate relation to the sun, and declared that if he were to request him to burn up his black brother's village it would be done." In another ruse, a white man would ostentatiously load a gun but covertly slip the bullet up his sleeve. He would then hand the gun to a black chief, step off a distance, and ask the chief to take aim and shoot; the white man, unharmed, would bend over and retrieve the bullet from his shoe. "By such means . . . and a few boxes of gin, whole villages have been signed away to your Majesty." Land purchased in this way, Williams wrote, was "territory to which your Majesty has no more legal claim, than I have to be the Commander-in-Chief of the Belgian army."

- Far from being a great hero, Stanley had been a tyrant. His "name produces a shudder among this simple folk when mentioned; they remember his broken promises, his copious profanity, his hot temper, his heavy blows, his severe and rigorous measures, by which they were mulcted of their lands." (Note Williams's assumption, so unimaginable to his white contemporaries, that Africans had a right to African land.) Of the hundreds of Europeans and Americans who traveled to the Congo in the state's early years, Williams is the only one on record as questioning Africans about their personal experience of Stanley.

- Leopold's establishment of military bases along the river had caused a wave of death and destruction, because the African soldiers who manned them were expected to feed themselves. "These piratical, buccaneering posts compel the natives to furnish them with fish, goats, fowls, and vegetables at the mouths of their muskets; and whenever the natives refuse . . . white officers come with an expeditionary force and burn away the homes of the natives."

- "Your Majesty's Government is excessively cruel to its prisoners, condemning them, for the slightest offenses, to the chain gang. . . . Often these ox-chains eat into the necks of the prisoners and produce sores about which the flies circle, aggravating the running wound."

- Leopold's claim that his new state was providing wise government and public services was a fraud. There were no schools and no hospitals except for a few sheds "not fit to be occupied by a horse." Virtually none of the colony's officials knew any African language. "The

Courts of your Majesty's Government are abortive, unjust, partial and delinquent." (Here, as elsewhere, Williams provided a vivid example: a white servant of the governor-general went unpunished for stealing wine while black servants were falsely accused and beaten.)

- White traders and state officials were kidnapping African women and using them as concubines.
- White officers were shooting villagers, sometimes to capture their women, sometimes to intimidate the survivors into working as forced laborers, and sometimes for sport. "Two Belgian Army officers saw, from the deck of their steamer, a native in a canoe some distance away. . . . The officers made a wager of £5 that they could hit the native with their rifles. Three shots were fired and the native fell dead, pierced through the head."
- Instead of Leopold's being the noble antislavery crusader he portrayed himself as, "Your Majesty's Government is engaged in the slave-trade, wholesale and retail. It buys and sells and steals slaves. Your Majesty's Government gives £3 per head for able-bodied slaves for military service. . . . The labour force at the stations of your Majesty's Government in the Upper River is composed of slaves of all ages and both sexes."

Williams was not done. Three months after writing the *Open Letter,* he produced *A Report upon the Congo-State and Country to the President of the Republic of the United States of America.* President Harrison probably had no more expected to hear from him than Leopold had. In writing to the president, Williams repeated his charges, adding that the United States had a special responsibility toward the Congo, because it had "introduced this African Government into the sisterhood of States." As in the *Open Letter,* he supported the charges with personal examples. "At Stanley-Falls slaves were offered to me in broad day-light; and at night I discovered canoe loads of slaves, bound strongly together." Williams called for this "oppressive and cruel Government" to be replaced by a new regime that would be "local, not European; international, not national; just, not cruel."

Whether Williams was calling for self-government or for international trusteeship, it would be many years before anyone else from Europe or the United States would do the same. In a letter Williams wrote to the American secretary of state, he used a phrase that seems plucked from the

Nuremberg trials of more than half a century later. Leopold's Congo state, Williams wrote, was guilty of "crimes against humanity."

◎◎◎◎◎

The *Open Letter* was printed as a pamphlet, and before the end of 1890, while its author was still completing his circuit of Africa, it was distributed widely in both Europe and the United States. It is not clear who arranged for the distribution, but it was probably a Dutch trading company, the Nieuwe Afrikaansche Handels Vennootschap, which had trading posts in the Congo and owned the steamboat, the *Holland,* on which Williams traveled. Company officials were angry that Leopold was aggressively shutting out foreign traders from his new colony, saving the lucrative supplies of ivory for himself and his business partners. But Williams did not allow the company to shape his message: the *Open Letter* mentions the issue of free trade only briefly, and far down on the list of accusations.

After the *Open Letter* was published, the *New York Herald,* which had sent Stanley to Africa, devoted a full column to it under the headline, THE ADMINISTRATION OF THE AFRICAN FREE STATE DECLARED BY AN AMERICAN CITIZEN TO BE BARBAROUS — INVESTIGATION DEMANDED. The article quoted Stanley, who called the *Open Letter* "a deliberate attempt at blackmail." What was more ominous for Williams was that Collis P. Huntington, his benefactor, thought him grossly unfair to the king, who was "solicitous of the best welfare of the natives of that country."

A furious Leopold told the British minister in Brussels not to believe Williams. "Colonel Williams may be all the King says he is," the envoy reported to his home office, "but I suspect there is a good deal of disagreeable truth in his pamphlets." In his memoirs, one of Leopold's advisers recalls an urgent meeting held to discuss what to do about *"le pamphlet Williams,"* of which the Paris press was making *"un vrai scandale."*

Leopold and his aides quickly orchestrated a counterattack. The *Journal de Bruxelles* asked, "First of all, who is Mr. Williams? This man is not a United States colonel." In subsequent articles the paper referred to him as "the so-called 'Colonel'," "the pseudo colonel," "an unbalanced negro," and "Mr. Williams, who is not a colonel." (The Belgian press, of course, had never questioned the rank of "General" Henry Shelton Sanford.) *Le Mouvement Géographique,* a newspaper closely tied to Leopold's Congo venture, also attacked Williams and pointed out that, though

112

Congo natives did not always receive full justice, neither did the American Indians.

Other Belgian newspapers, however, took Williams's accusations seriously. "With commercial speculation dominant in the Congo, a personal, absolute and uncontrolled regime, whose chief autocrat has never set foot in the country he is governing, is fatally bound to produce the majority of grave deeds pointed out by the American traveler," wrote the liberal *La Réforme*. "We are not inclined to accept as gospel truth everything the Congolese administration wishes to offer in its own defense," declared *Le Courrier de Bruxelles*. Papers in other countries also picked up the story, reporting Williams's allegations and sometimes printing long excerpts.

By June 1891, the furor reached the Belgian Parliament, where several deputies and the prime minister rose to speak in the king's defense. Some weeks later, the État Indépendant du Congo issued a forty-five-page report signed by its top administrators. It was clearly aimed, the British legation in Brussels reported to London, at "refuting the accusations brought by Colonel Williams and others."

Williams, in the meantime, had completed his circuit of Africa and was in Egypt, where he had fallen seriously ill with tuberculosis. As usual, he was out of money. With his customary air of being on urgent business for the powerful, he somehow persuaded the British minister in Cairo, Sir Evelyn Baring, to dispatch a physician to take care of him. Down to his last £14, he sent desperate pleas for money to Huntington. When he recovered some strength, he wangled free passage to England on a British steamer. On board he met a young Englishwoman who had been a governess in a British family in India, and by the time they arrived in Britain, the two were engaged. Williams settled in London, despite problems over his debts incurred there on a previous visit. But his tuberculosis grew worse. His fiancée and her mother took him to Blackpool, where they hoped the sea air would cure him so that he could resume working on his book about Leopold's Congo.

Their hopes were in vain. Early on the morning of August 2, 1891, tended by his fiancée, her mother, a minister, and a doctor, George Washington Williams died. He was forty-one years old. In Belgium, *Le Mouvement Géographique* noted his death with satisfaction, comparing him with those who had burned the temple at Delphi. "His early death," writes a modern diplomatic historian, S.J.S. Cookey, ". . . saved the Congo government from what might have been an embarrassingly formidable opponent." He was buried in Blackpool in an unmarked grave. Not until

1975 did his grave acquire a proper tombstone — arranged by his biographer, the historian John Hope Franklin.

Only after the funeral, apparently, did Williams's British fiancée learn that he had abandoned a wife and a fifteen-year-old son in the United States. In this deception and other ways, from his neglect of debts to his vaunting a nonexistent doctoral degree, there was something of the hustler about him. But, in a sense, this was the flip side of the extraordinary boldness that enabled him to defy a king, his officials, and the entire racial order of the day. By contrast, for example, there was George Grenfell, a veteran British missionary whom Williams visited on the Congo River. He too had seen firsthand the full range of abuses, including Leopold's state employees buying chained slaves, but, he wrote home within a few days of meeting Williams, he did not feel he could "publicly question the action of the State." And whatever Williams's elaboration of his own résumé, virtually everything he wrote about the Congo would later be corroborated — abundantly — by others.

Williams's *Open Letter* was a cry of outrage that came from the heart. It gained him nothing. It lost him his patron, Huntington. It guaranteed that he could never work, as he had hoped, to bring American blacks to the Congo. It brought him none of the money he always needed, and in the few months he had left before his life ended in a foreign beach resort, it earned him little but calumny. By the time he went to the Congo in 1890, close to a thousand Europeans and Americans had visited the territory or worked there. Williams was the only one to speak out fully and passionately and repeatedly about what others denied or ignored. The years to come would make his words ever more prophetic.

8

WHERE THERE AREN'T NO
TEN COMMANDMENTS

LEOPOLD established the capital of his new Congo state at the port
town of Boma, just upriver from the Atlantic, where Stanley had
finished his epic trans-African trek in 1877. As the 1890s began, Boma
was complete with a narrow-gauge trolley — a steam engine pulling a
couple of cars — that linked the bustling docks and trading-company
warehouses to a cooler plateau above. There stood the government offices
and houses for the Europeans who worked in them. Boma also boasted
a Catholic church made of iron, a hospital for Europeans, a post office, a
military base whose cannon fired a salute to any newly arriving VIP, and a
two-story hotel. Three times a day — at 6 A.M., 11:45, and 6:30 P.M. —
about seventy-five white officials took the trolley down the hill and
through a plantation of banana trees for meals in the hotel dining room.
The only European who ate elsewhere was the governor general, who
took his meals in his dignified Victorian mansion, complete with a cupola,
French windows, and covered porches. Every year, the king's birthday was
celebrated with such events as a ceremonial review of troops, a target-
shooting contest, and a concert by a Catholic black children's choir.

Despite his impressive mansion, guarded by African sentries with blue
uniforms and red fezes, the Congo's governor general had far less power
than did a British, French, or German colonial governor. More than any
other colony in Africa, the Congo was administered directly from
Europe. The real headquarters of the État Indépendant du Congo were
not in Boma but in suites of offices in Brussels, one on the grounds of the
Royal Palace, the others next door or across the street. All the Congo's

high- and middle-level administrators were picked and promoted by the king himself, and a mini-cabinet of three or four Belgians at the top, in Brussels, reported to Leopold directly.

His one-man rule over this huge territory was in striking contrast to Leopold's ever more limited power at home. Once, in his later years, while he was talking in his study with several Cabinet ministers, his nephew and heir apparent, Prince Albert, opened a window, and a draft blew some papers onto the floor. Leopold ordered Albert to pick them up. "Let him do it," the king said to one of the ministers, who had hastily offered to do so instead. "A future constitutional monarch must learn to stoop." But in the Congo there was no stooping; Leopold's power was absolute.

At the lowest level, the king's rule over his colony was carried out by white men in charge of districts and river stations throughout the vast territory; some of them were not visited by steamboats for months at a time. Far in the interior, practice often lagged behind theory, but on paper, at least, even the humblest station chief was allotted a bottle of red wine per day and a plentiful supply of English marmalade, Danish butter, canned meats, soups and condiments, and *foie gras* and other pâtés from Fischer's of Strasbourg.

For these functionaries there was a plethora of medals, whose grades reflected the burgeoning hierarchy of imperial rule. For holders of the Order of the African Star, for instance, there were six classes, ranging from *grands-croix* and *commandeurs* down to mere *médaillés.* The Royal Order of the Lion, created by Leopold to "recognize merit and acknowledge services rendered to Us," also had six classes. For African chiefs who collaborated with the regime, there was a special medal — bronze, silver, or gold-plated, depending on the degree of "service" rendered. It bore Leopold's profile on one side and, on the other, the Congo state coat of arms and the words LOYALTY AND DEVOTION.

The white officials in Leopold's Congo were usually single men, many of whom took on one or more African concubines. But by the turn of the century a few officials began to bring their wives, and some of those who didn't turned to an enterprising British matchmaking agency that supplied mail-order brides from Europe.

Photographs of remote Congo posts from the 1890s generally show the same pattern. From the long shadows, it appears to be late afternoon. The two or three white men in the picture wear suits and ties and elongated sun helmets, like a London bobby's cap in white. They are

Leopold as a young man.

Henry Morton Stanley,
in the "Stanley Cap" he
designed for exploring
in the tropics.

Henry Shelton Sanford, the wealthy Connecticut aristocrat who successfully lobbied the United States into recognizing Leopold's claim to the Congo.

Form No. 1.

THE WESTERN UNION TELEGRAPH COMPANY.

This Company TRANSMITS and DELIVERS messages only on conditions limiting its liability, which have been assented to by the sender of the following message.
Errors can be guarded against only by repeating a message back to the sending station for comparison, and the company will not hold itself liable for errors or delays in transmission or delivery of Unrepeated Messages, beyond the amount of tolls paid thereon, nor in any case where the claim is not presented in writing within sixty days after sending the message.
This is an UNREPEATED MESSAGE, and is delivered by request of the sender, under the conditions named above.
THOS. T. ECKERT, General Manager.   NORVIN GREEN, President.

NUMBER   SENT BY   REC'D BY   CHECK

59 my   14g   5   21   alleah 4 ex

Received at   NEW ORLEANS.   1255 —   Pm DEC. 8 1883.

Dated Brussels Via Washington y Via Charleston SC

To Gen Sanford   St Charles Hotel no

Enchanted with Emile Before beginning
negotiations please wire what you know
about dispositions of Senate will

Williams

Coded telegram from Brussels congratulating Sanford on his Washington lobbying. "Emile" was President Chester A. Arthur, who had just praised Leopold in a speech to Congress. "William" was Leopold's top Congo aide, Colonel Maximilien Strauch.

King Leopold II.

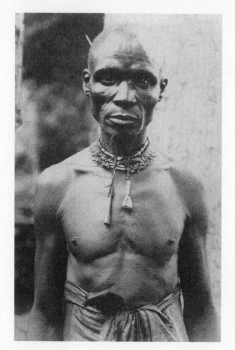

Twa Mwe, a Kwango chief. Indigenous leaders often faced the choice of supplying their people as rubber slaves or being held hostage or killed.

The British missionary steamboat *Goodwill*, typical of craft on the river network in the 1890s.

George Washington Williams, a lawyer, journalist, minister, and historian, wrote the first full exposé of Leopold's reign of terror in the Congo.

An ivory gathering post in the Congo, c. 1890. Elephant tusks, bought from Africans for a pittance or confiscated at gunpoint, fetched high prices in Europe as raw material for everything from false teeth to piano keys.

Joseph Conrad.

One prototype for Conrad's Mr. Kurtz: Léon Rom. This swashbuckling officer was known for displaying a row of severed African heads around his garden. He also wrote a book on African customs, painted portraits and landscapes, and collected butterflies.

BELOW: Rom (with rifle) after a hunt.

Another Kurtz prototype: Guillaume Van Kerckhoven, who cheerfully told a fellow traveler that he paid his black soldiers "5 brass rods (2½ d.) per human head they brought him during the course of any military operations he conducted. He said it was to stimulate their prowess in the face of the enemy."

E. D. Morel.

BELOW: The docks at Antwerp, where the young E. D. Morel's suspicions about Congo slave labor were awakened.

Sir Roger Casement, British consul, activist witness to Congo atrocities, and Irish patriot.

Hezekiah Andrew Shanu. Although awarded medals for his service to the regime, he secretly turned against it, sent important evidence to the reformers abroad, and was driven to suicide by Leopold's officials when they discovered this.

Reverend William H. Sheppard, Presbyterian missionary, explorer, and the first outsider to visit the capital of the Kuba kingdom. Sheppard's writings documenting the brutality of the Congo state made him the object of a lawsuit and trial.

Nsala, of the district of Wala, looking at the severed hand and foot of his five-year-old daughter, Boali, a victim of the Anglo-Belgian India Rubber Company (A.B.I.R.) militia.

BELOW: British missionaries with men holding hands severed from victims named Bolenge and Lingomo by A.B.I.R. militiamen, 1904.

Two youths of the Equator district. The hands of Mola, seated, have been destroyed by gangrene after being tied too tightly by soldiers. The right hand of Yoka, standing, was cut off by soldiers wanting to claim him as killed.

BELOW: The *chicotte* in use. Note the pile of chain at lower left.

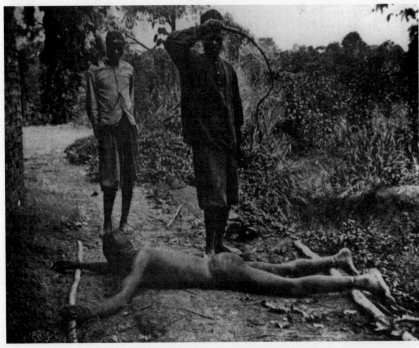

Women hostages, held under guard in order to force their husbands to go into the rain forest to gather wild rubber.

The village of Baringa. The chief is seated on the stool at center; his house is at right. Cooking smoke rises through the roofs of other houses.

BELOW: Baringa after it was razed to make way for a rubber plantation. When wild rubber supplies ran low, the regime ordered more rubber trees planted. It was often cheaper to use an existing clearing, like that of a village, than to cut down the forest.

..GREAT..
CONGO DEMONSTRATION.

THE
Protest of Christian England
.AT THE..
ROYAL ALBERT HALL
..ON..
Friday, November 19, 1909,
AT **7.30** P.M.

Chairman: HIS GRACE
THE ARCHBISHOP OF CANTERBURY.

SPEAKERS:

The Right Rev. **THE LORD BISHOP OF LONDON,**

Rev. Dr. JOHN CLIFFORD, M.A.

The Right Rev. **THE LORD BISHOP OF OXFORD,**

Rev. J. SCOTT LIDGETT, M.A., D.D.

Rev. C. SILVESTER HORNE, M.A.

Supported by

The Lord Bishops of Rochester, Birmingham, Manchester, Carlisle, Ely, Newcastle, St. Asaph, Truro, Wakefield, Exeter, Gloucester, Lichfield, Liverpool, Durham;

Dr. CAMPBELL MORGAN, Rev. J. E. RATTENBURY, Dr. MONRO GIBSON, Rev. D. J. HILEY, Rev. SILAS K. HOCKING, Rev. J. H. SHAKESPEARE, Rev. J. D. JONES, Rev. GEO. HOOPER, Rev. THOMAS YATES, Prof. A. E. GARVIE, Dr. HORTON, Rev. F. B. MEYER.

RESERVED SEATS, *Price 5/. 2/6 and 1/.*

FREE RESERVED SEAT TICKETS may be obtained (by enclosing 1d. Stamp) from TRAVERS BUXTON, Esq. Hon. Treasurer, 51, Denison House, Vauxhall Bridge Road, S.W., who will gladly welcome offers of financial assistance.

THE ALBERT HALL is Ten minutes' walk from either of the following Stations HIGH STREET KENSINGTON, SOUTH KENSINGTON, (both on the District Railway.)

BUSES from all parts of London pass the Door.

This cartoon appeared in Germany, accompanied by some doggerel about Leopold's zest for cutting off both black heads and bond coupons.

Congo reformers often pointed to the Berlin agreement of 1885, one of many broken promises regarding the treatment of Africans.

THE APPEAL.

"IN THE NAME OF ALMIGHTY GOD.—All the Powers exercising sovereign rights, or having influence in the said territories undertake to watch over the preservation of the native races, and the amelioration of the moral and material conditions of their existence."

Article VI. The Act of Berlin. 1885.

EXPERT OPINION.

LEOPOLD. "SILLY FUSS THEY'RE MAKING ABOUT THESE SO-CALLED ATROCITIES IN MY CONGO PROPERTY."
ABDUL. "ONLY *TALK*, MY DEAR BOY. THEY WON'T *DO* ANYTHING. THEY NEVER TOUCHED *ME!*"

Punch, 1905: One of a number of cartoons where Leopold compares notes with the sultan of Turkey, also condemned for his massacres (of Armenians).

IN THE RUBBER COILS.

SCENE—*The Congo "Free" State.*

THE GUILT OF DELAY.

CONGO SLAVE-DRIVER. "*I'M ALL RIGHT. THEY'RE STILL TALKING.*"

Punch, 1906.   *Punch,* 1909.

seated on wicker chairs, a dog at their feet, in front of a tent or simple thatched-roofed building, smiling. Behind them stand their unsmiling African servants, holding some emblem of their status: a serving tray, a towel draped over an arm, a bottle ready to pour. Wine glasses or tea cups rest on a table, symbols of the comforts of home. The white men are always dressed in white.

Underpinning such scenes were a number of royal decrees from Brussels. The first and most important had been issued on the very day in 1885 that the existence of the Congo state was formally proclaimed; it declared that all "vacant land" was the property of the state. There was no definition of what made land vacant. All over the world, of course, land that *looks* vacant has often been deliberately left to lie fallow while crops are planted somewhere else — especially in the tropics, where heavy rainfalls leach nutrients out of the soil.

Leopold was after whatever could be quickly harvested. In that sense, he treated both vacant and nonvacant land as his property, claiming a right to all its products. He made no distinction between the tusks of an elephant roaming wild or villagers' vegetables that could feed his soldiers; it was all his.

He did not, however, have the resources to exploit the entire territory, so another set of decrees carved parts of the Congo into several giant blocks, whose "vacant land" was leased out for long periods as concessions to private companies. These concession companies had shareholders — largely, though not entirely Belgian — and interlocking directorates that included many high Congo state officials. But in each of them the state — which in effect meant Leopold himself — usually kept 50 percent of the shares. In setting up this structure, Leopold was like the manager of a venture capital syndicate today. He had essentially found a way to attract other people's capital to his investment schemes while he retained half the proceeds. In the end, what with various taxes and fees the companies paid the state, it came to more than half.

Unlike a venture capitalist in the marketplace, however, the king deployed troops and government officials as well as investment funds. He used them ruthlessly to shut out of the territory most businesses in which he did not have a piece of the action. The Dutch trading firm on whose steamboat Williams had traveled found itself facing stiff competition for ivory from Congo state officials who stopped its boats, in one case with gunfire. Once, according to a history of the company, "a state of siege was proclaimed for a certain region which made it closed territory for traders. When the state of siege was lifted, all the ivory had disappeared."

The king, meanwhile, continued to claim that making a profit was the farthest thing from his mind. "I thank you for having done justice yesterday to the calumnies spread by enemies of the Congo state, to the accusation of secrecy and the spirit of gain," he wrote to the prime minister after a parliamentary debate in 1891. "The Congo state is certainly not a business. If it gathers ivory on certain of its lands, that is only to lessen its deficit."

And if Africans were made to help out in the ivory-gathering, why that too, Heaven forbid, was not to make a profit, but to rescue these benighted people from their indolence. Talk of the lazy native accompanied the entire European land grab in Africa, just as it had been used to justify the conquest of the Americas. To an American reporter, Leopold once declared, "In dealing with a race composed of cannibals for thousands of years it is necessary to use methods which will best shake their idleness and make them realize the sanctity of work."

As the 1890s began, the work whose sanctity Leopold prized most highly was seizing all the ivory that could be found. Congo state officials and their African auxiliaries swept through the country on ivory raids, shooting elephants, buying tusks from villagers for a pittance, or simply confiscating them. Congo peoples had been hunting elephants for centuries, but now they were forbidden to sell or deliver ivory to anyone other than an agent of Leopold. A draconian refinement of the ivory-gathering method, which set the pattern for much that was to come, was a commission structure the king imposed in 1890, whereby his agents in the field got a cut of the ivory's market value — but on a sliding scale. For ivory purchased in Africa at eight francs per kilo, an agent received 6 percent of the vastly higher European market price. But the commission climbed, in stages, to 10 percent for ivory bought at four francs per kilo. The European agents thus had a powerful incentive to force Africans — if necessary, at gunpoint — to accept extremely low prices.

Almost none of these Belgian francs actually reached any Congolese elephant hunters. They received only small amounts of cloth, beads, and the like, or the brass rods that the state decreed as the territory's main currency. For Africans, transactions in money were not allowed. Money in free circulation might undermine what was essentially a command economy.

The commands were above all for labor. At the beginning, the state most wanted porters. Like Stanley, any official who ventured away from the river system and into the bush — to collect ivory, set up new posts, put down a rebellion — needed long columns of porters to carry everything from machine-gun ammunition to all that red wine and pâté. These tens of thousands of porters were usually paid for their work, if only sometimes the food necessary to keep them going, but most of them were conscripts. Even children were put to work: one observer noted seven- to nine-year-olds each carrying a load of twenty-two pounds.

"A file of poor devils, chained by the neck, carried my trunks and boxes toward the dock," a Congo state official notes matter-of-factly in his memoirs. At the next stop on his journey more porters were needed for an overland trip: "There were about a hundred of them, trembling and fearful before the overseer, who strolled by whirling a whip. For each stocky and broad-backed fellow, how many were skeletons dried up like mummies, their skin worn out . . . seamed with deep scars, covered with suppurating wounds. . . . No matter, they were all up to the job."

Porters were needed most at the points where the river system was blocked by rapids, particularly — until the railroad was built — for the three-week trek between the port town of Matadi and Stanley Pool. This was the pipeline up which supplies passed to the interior and down which ivory and other riches were carried to the sea. Moving dismantled steamboats to the upper section of the river was the most labor-intensive job of all: one steamboat could comprise three thousand porter loads. Here is how Edmond Picard, a Belgian senator, described a caravan of porters he saw on the route around the big rapids in 1896:

> Unceasingly we meet these porters . . . black, miserable, with only a horribly filthy loin-cloth for clothing, frizzy and bare head supporting the load — box, bale, ivory tusk . . . barrel; most of them sickly, drooping under a burden increased by tiredness and insufficient food — a handful of rice and some stinking dried fish; pitiful walking caryatids, beasts of burden with thin monkey legs, with drawn features, eyes fixed and round from preoccupation with keeping their balance and from the daze of exhaustion. They come and go like this by the thousands . . . requisitioned by the State armed with its powerful militia, handed over by chiefs whose slaves they are and who make off with their salaries, trotting with bent knees, belly forward, an arm raised to steady the

load, the other leaning on a long walking-stick, dusty and sweaty, insects spreading out across the mountains and valleys their many files and their task of Sisyphus, dying along the road or, the journey over, heading off to die from overwork in their villages.

The death toll was particularly high among porters forced to carry loads long distances. Of the three hundred porters conscripted in 1891 by District Commissioner Paul Lemarinel for a forced march of more than six hundred miles to set up a new post, not one returned.

Stanislas Lefranc, a devout Catholic and monarchist, was a Belgian prosecutor who had come to the Congo to work as a magistrate. Early one Sunday morning in Leopoldville, he heard the sound of many children screaming desperately.

On tracing the howls to their source, Lefranc found "some thirty urchins, of whom several were seven or eight years old, lined up and waiting their turn, watching, terrified, their companions being flogged. Most of the urchins, in a paroxysm of grief . . . kicked so frightfully that the soldiers ordered to hold them by the hands and feet had to lift them off the ground. . . . 25 times the whip slashed down on each of the children." The evening before, Lefranc learned, several children had laughed in the presence of a white man, who then ordered that all the servant boys in town be given fifty lashes. The second installment of twenty-five lashes was due at six o'clock the next morning. Lefranc managed to get these stopped, but was told not to make any more protests that interfered with discipline.

Lefranc was seeing in use a central tool of Leopold's Congo, which in the minds of the territory's people, soon became as closely identified with white rule as the steamboat or the rifle. It was the *chicotte* — a whip of raw, sun-dried hippopotamus hide, cut into a long sharp-edged corkscrew strip. Usually the *chicotte* was applied to the victim's bare buttocks. Its blows would leave permanent scars; more than twenty-five strokes could mean unconsciousness; and a hundred or more — not an uncommon punishment — were often fatal.

Lefranc was to see many more *chicotte* beatings, although his descriptions of them, in pamphlets and newspaper articles he published in Belgium, provoked little reaction.

The station chief selects the victims. . . . Trembling, haggard, they lie face down on the ground . . . two of their companions, sometimes four, seize them by the feet and hands, and remove their cotton drawers. . . . Each time that the torturer lifts up the *chicotte,* a reddish stripe appears on the skin of the pitiful victims, who, however firmly held, gasp in frightful contortions. . . . At the first blows the unhappy victims let out horrible cries which soon become faint groans. . . . In a refinement of evil, some officers, and I've witnessed this, demand that when the sufferer gets up, panting, he must graciously give the military salute.

The open horror Lefranc expressed succeeded only in earning him a reputation as an oddball or troublemaker. He "shows an astonishing ignorance of things which he ought to know because of his work. A mediocre agent," the acting governor general wrote in a personnel evaluation. In an attempt to quiet his complaints, Lefranc wrote, officials ordered that executions at his post be carried out in a new location instead of next to his house.

Except for Lefranc, few Europeans working for the regime left records of their shock at the sight of officially sanctioned terror. The white men who passed through the territory as military officers, steamboat captains, or state or concession company officials generally accepted the use of the *chicotte* as unthinkingly as hundreds of thousands of other men in uniform would accept their assignments, a half-century later, to staff the Nazi and Soviet concentration camps. "Monsters exist," wrote Primo Levi of his experience at Auschwitz. "But they are too few in number to be truly dangerous. More dangerous are . . . the functionaries ready to believe and to act without asking questions."

What made it possible for the functionaries in the Congo to so blithely watch the *chicotte* in action and, as we shall see, to deal out pain and death in other ways as well? To begin with, of course, was race. To Europeans, Africans were inferior beings: lazy, uncivilized, little better than animals. In fact, the most common way they were put to work was, like animals, as beasts of burden. In any system of terror, the functionaries must first of all see the victims as less than human, and Victorian ideas about race provided such a foundation.

Then, of course, the terror in the Congo was sanctioned by the authorities. For a white man to rebel meant challenging the system that provided your livelihood. Everyone around you was participating. By going along with the system, you were paid, promoted, awarded medals. So men who would have been appalled to see someone using a *chicotte* on the streets of Brussels or Paris or Stockholm accepted the act, in this different setting, as normal. We can hear the echo of this thinking, in another context, half a century later: "To tell the truth," said Franz Stangl of the mass killings that took place when he was commandant of the Nazi death camps of Sobibor and Treblinka, "one did become used to it."

In such a regime, one thing that often helps functionaries "become used to it" is a slight, symbolic distance — irrelevant to the victim — between an official in charge and the physical act of terror itself. That symbolic distance was frequently cited in self-defense by Nazis put on trial after World War II. Dr. Johann Paul Kremer, for example, an SS physician who liked to do his pathology research on human tissue that was still fresh, explained:

> The patient was put on the dissecting table while he was still alive. I then approached the table and put several questions to the man as to such details which pertained to my researches. . . . When I had collected my information the orderly approached the patient and killed him with an injection in the vicinity of the heart. . . . I myself never made any lethal injections.

I myself never made any lethal injections. Although some whites in the Congo enjoyed wielding the *chicotte,* most put a similar symbolic distance between themselves and the dreaded instrument. "At first I . . . took upon myself the responsibility of meting out punishment to those whose conduct during the previous day seemed to warrant such treatment," recalled Raoul de Premorel, who worked for a company operating in the Kasai River basin. "Soon . . . I found it desirable to assign the execution of sentences to others under my direction. The best plan seemed to be to have each *capita* [African foreman] administer the punishment for his own gang."

And so the bulk of *chicotte* blows were inflicted by Africans on the bodies of other Africans. This, for the conquerors, served a further purpose. It created a class of foremen from among the conquered, like the *kapos* in the Nazi concentration camps and the *predurki,* or trusties, in the

Soviet gulag. Just as terrorizing people is part of conquest, so is forcing someone else to administer the terror.*

Finally, when terror is the unquestioned order of the day, wielding it efficiently is regarded as a manly virtue, the way soldiers value calmness in battle. This is the ultimate in "becoming used to it." Here, for instance, a station chief named Georges Bricusse describes in his diary a hanging he ordered in 1895 of a man who had stolen a rifle:

> The gallows is set up. The rope is attached, too high. They lift up the nigger and put the noose around him. The rope twists for a few moments, then *crack,* the man is wriggling on the ground. A shot in the back of the neck and the game is up. It didn't make the least impression on me this time!! And to think that the first time I saw the *chicotte* administered, I was pale with fright. Africa has some use after all. I could now walk into fire as if to a wedding.

The framework of control that Leopold extended across his enormous realm was military. After all, without armed force, you cannot make men leave their homes and families and carry sixty-five-pound loads for weeks or months. The king was particularly happy to run his own army in Africa, since in Belgium he was forever at loggerheads with legislators who did not share his passion for building great forts, spending more money on the army, and instituting the draft.

Leopold had made use of African mercenaries ever since sending Stanley to stake out his claim from 1879 to 1884. In 1888 he formally organized them into the Force Publique, an army for his new state. Over the next dozen years, it grew to more than nineteen thousand officers and men, the most powerful army in central Africa. By the late 1890s, it consumed more than half the state's budget. At once counterguerrilla troops, an army of occupation, and a corporate labor police force, it was

---

* If the underlings' allegiance is unreliable, sometimes the conquerors take precautions. When eighteen mutinous black soldiers were executed in Boma in 1900, a photographer recorded the scene: the condemned rebels are tied to stakes and a firing squad of loyal black troops has just fired a salvo. But in case the loyalists waver, the entire white male population of Boma is standing in a long row at right angles to both groups, each sun-helmeted white man with a rifle at the ready.

divided mainly into small garrisons — typically, several dozen black soldiers under one or two white officers, on a riverbank. The initial handful of military posts quickly grew to 183 by 1900, and to 313 by 1908.

The Force Publique had its hands full. Many of the king's new subjects belonged to warrior peoples who fought back. More than a dozen different ethnic groups staged major rebellions against Leopold's rule. The Yaka people fought the whites for more than ten years before they were subdued, in 1906. The Chokwe fought for twenty years, inflicting heavy casualties on Leopold's soldiers. The Boa and the Budja mobilized more than five thousand men to fight a guerrilla war from deep within the rain forest. Just as Americans used the word *pacification* in Vietnam seventy years later, so the Force Publique's military expeditions were officially called *reconnaissances pacifiques.*

The history of central Africa before the European arrival was as filled with wars and conquests as Europe's own, and even during Leopold's rule not all the Congo's violence was between colonizer and colonized. Because so many Congo peoples had earlier fought among themselves, the Force Publique was often able to ally itself with one ethnic group to defeat another. But sooner or later the first group found itself subdued as well. With their forces stretched thin over a huge territory, Leopold's commanders made clever use of this shifting pattern of alliances. In the end, though, their superior firepower guaranteed victory — and a history written by the victors.

Yet sometimes, even through those records, we can glimpse the determination of those who resisted the king. In Katanga in the far south, warriors from the Sanga people were led by a chief named Mulume Niama. Though the state troops were armed with artillery, his forces put up a stiff fight, killing one officer and wounding three soldiers. They then took refuge in a large chalk cave called Tshamakele. The Force Publique commander ordered his men to light fires at the three entrances to the cave to smoke the rebels out, and after a week he sent an emissary to negotiate Mulume Niama's surrender. The chief and his men refused. Soldiers lit the fires again and blocked the cave for three months. When the troops finally entered it, they found 178 bodies. Fearful of leaving any sign of a martyrs' grave, the Force Publique soldiers triggered landslides to obliterate all traces of the existence of the Tshamakele cave and of the bodies of Mulume Niama and his men.

Another rebellion took place along the caravan route around the lower Congo rapids. A notorious state agent, a Belgian named Eugène

Rommel, built a station there to procure porters for the three-week trek from Matadi to Stanley Pool, a job for which the state needed fifty thousand men a year by the mid-1890s. Unlike the Protestant missionaries and some private traders, who hired the porters they used on this route and negotiated wages with them, the Congo state — at Leopold's specific order — used forced labor. Rommel named his station Baka Baka, which means "capture, capture."

A local chief named Nzansu led an uprising, ambushing and killing Rommel on December 5, 1893, and burning his station to the ground. The rebels also burned and pillaged two other nearby state posts, where they killed two white officials and wounded several more. However, Nzansu spared Mukimbungu, a Swedish mission on the caravan route. He even gave the missionaries some supplies he had found abandoned on the trail and returned some goods his men had taken from the mission station. One of the missionaries, Karl Teodor Andersson, wrote to his church members back in Sweden:

> If our friends of the Mission at home are worried for our safety here as a result of letters and newspaper reports about the unrest in these parts, I wish to reassure them. . . . The leader of the rebels, Chief Nzansu of Kasi, has let us know that he does not wish harm to any one of us as we have always shown that we are friends of the black people. But to the men of the State he has sworn death. And anyone who knows of the conditions out here cannot feel surprised.

This rebellion particularly alarmed the state because it completely stopped traffic on the crucial caravan route to Stanley Pool. To crush the rebels, the authorities sent out a force of fifteen white officers and two hundred black soldiers. Another Swedish missionary, C. N. Börrisson, wrote home a few weeks later, "The rebels have not fled . . . but have assembled in the leader's village, which they are defending unto death although their other villages have been burned."

Börrisson goes on to speak powerfully for the rebels whose own voices we cannot hear:

> A man sows what he reaps. In reality, the state is the true source of these uprisings. It is strange that people who claim to be civilized think they can treat their fellow man — even though he is of a

different color — any which way. . . . Without a doubt one of
the most disreputable [of the officials] is the late Mr. Rommel.
One should not speak ill of the dead but I must simply mention some smaller matters to prove that the unrest has been
justified. . . . He imprisoned women when the people refused
to transport [supplies] and to sell him goods below market
prices. . . . He was not ashamed to come by our station and
abduct our school girls . . . and treat them in despicable ways.
One Sunday morning brother Andersson and I went to a neighboring village and helped release three poor women whom his
soldiers had imprisoned because one of them had asked for the
return of a stone jug which had been taken from her. . . .

But what happens to all of the women who are taken prisoner? Some are set free . . . when their husbands have done all
they can to regain the one who is dearest to them. Others are
forced to work in the fields and also to work as prostitutes. . . .
Our most respected men here . . . have told us with tears in their
eyes and much vexation in their hearts that they had recently
seen a group of seven hundred women chained together and
transported [to the coast on steamboats]. "And," they said,
"whether they cut off our heads or that of a chicken it is all the
same to them. . . ."

So can anyone feel truly surprised that the discontent has
finally come to the surface? Nzansu, the leader of the uprising,
and [Rommel's] assassin, only wanted to become the Engelbrekt
of the Congo and the Gustaf Wasa of his people. His followers are
as loyal to him as Swedes were to their leaders in those times.

The missionary's comparison was to two Swedish patriots of the fifteenth
and sixteenth centuries, noblemen who led rebellions of Swedish peas-
ants against harsh foreign kings. Wasa was successful and was himself
elected King of Sweden. Nzansu was less fortunate. He and his warriors
fought on against Leopold's Force Publique for eight months, and, despite
several scorched-earth expeditions sent against them, continued to fight
sporadically for five more years. There seems to be no record of
Nzansu's fate.

All the commissioned officers and some sergeants of the Force Publique were white, mostly Belgian, but from other countries as well. Their own armies were usually happy to give them leave to gain a few years' combat experience. All the ordinary soldiers were black. Mercenaries from Zanzibar and the British West African colonies in the army's first few years were soon outnumbered by soldiers from the Congo itself, most of whom were conscripts. Even those who volunteered often did so because, as one soldier explained to a European visitor, he preferred "to be with the hunters rather than with the hunted." Ill paid, ill fed, and flogged with the *chicotte* for the slightest offense, many tried to desert, and in the early days officers had to spend much of their time capturing them. Then, to guard against desertions, the state began sending new conscripts far from their home districts. As a soldier finishing your seven-year term, you might then face a journey of several hundred to a thousand miles to get home. Sometimes even then you would not be allowed to go.

The soldiers' frustrations frequently boiled over into mutinies, large and small. The first big one erupted at the military base at Luluabourg in the south-central savanna country in 1895. The base commander, Mathieu Pelzer, was a notorious bully who used his fists on those under him and routinely ordered soldiers given 125 lashes with the *chicotte*. When his African concubine slept with another man, he ordered her killed. At one point Pelzer ordered a soldier punished, but before the man wielding the *chicotte* could begin, a sergeant named Kandolo went up to him and snatched the whip out of his hands. When rebellion against Pelzer broke out shortly afterward, it was led by angry black noncommissioned officers with Kandolo at their head.

Soldiers attacked and wounded Pelzer, who fled into the bush and hid. But the rebels tracked him down and killed him. Under Kandolo, dressed in white and riding on a bull, they set off for other Force Publique posts, gathering supporters among the black soldiers and killing several European officers. For more than half a year, the rebels controlled most of the Kasai region. In the bush, they split into small groups, spreading out over a broad area and successfully evading or fighting off a long series of heavily armed expeditions sent against them. A year later, worried Force Publique officers estimated that there were still four hundred to five hundred rebels at large, recruiting new members and allying themselves with local chiefs against the state. Altogether, suppressing the revolt cost the Force Publique the lives of several hundred black soldiers and porters and fifteen white officers or NCOs. One was an American, Lieutenant Lindsay Burke, a twenty-six-year-old native of New Orleans, who had been in Africa less than a year. He marched into an ambush and died, along with twenty-seven of his men, in early 1897. The rebel leader Kandolo was fatally wounded in battle, but two corporals who played a major role in the revolt, Yamba-Yamba and Kimpuki, fought on as guerrilla leaders; they were killed, still fighting, in 1908, thirteen years after the uprising began.

At the other end of the country, in the far northeast, a great mutiny broke out in 1897 among three thousand soldiers and an equal number of porters and auxiliaries. The men, who had been forced to march for months through forests and swamps in a renewed reach by Leopold toward the headwaters of the Nile, finally had enough. The fighting went on for three years, as column after column of loyalist Force Publique troops fought the rebels over some six hundred miles of forest and savanna along the chain of lakes on the Congo's eastern border. Beneath their own red-and-white flag, rebels from different ethnic groups fought together, maintained military discipline, and staged ambushes to replenish their supplies of weapons and ammunition. Sympathetic chiefs gave them support, including warnings by talking drum of approaching troops. Even the Force Publique's official history acknowledges that in battle "the rebels displayed a courage worthy of a better cause."

More than two years after the revolt began, the rebels were able to muster twenty-five hundred soldiers to attack a heavily fortified position. One contingent of loyalist Force Publique mercenaries was reduced from three hundred men to three during the campaign. The rebels were still fighting in 1900, when two thousand of them finally withdrew across the frontier into German territory, today's Rwanda and Burundi, where they gave up their arms in return for the right to settle.

This prolonged mutiny is the sole case in the history of Leopold's Congo where we have an eyewitness account of what it was like behind rebel lines. In April 1897, these insurgents captured a French priest, Father Auguste Achte, who unintentionally walked into their hands, assuming that the "immense camp" he had come upon must be that of a Force Publique expedition. Finding himself instead among some two thousand rebels, whose leaders were wearing captured gold-braided officers' uniforms and pistols, Achte was terrified, certain that he was going to die. Some of the mutineers did rough him up and tell him they had sworn to kill all white people. But the leaders of the group argued them down, making a distinction between those whites who worked for the hated Congo state and those who did not. Mulamba, the chief of this group of rebels, reported Achte, told the priest that they were sparing his life because "I had no rifle, I taught God's word, I took care of sick natives, and (the decisive argument) I had never hit a black." The rebels had reached this conclusion after interrogating a dozen young Africans to whom the priest was giving religious instruction.

To Father Achte's surprise, the rebels eventually slaughtered a goat, fed him, brewed him a cup of coffee, and presented him with a gift of ivory to compensate for those of his goods they had confiscated, "so you won't write in Europe that we stole from you." After several days, he was released. The rebels told him they had killed their Belgian officers because the officers treated them like animals, they hadn't been paid for months, and soldiers and chiefs alike were flogged or hung for the slightest offense. They spoke of one white officer who shot sixty soldiers in a single day because they refused to work on a Sunday, and of another who "with his own hands poured salt and pepper on the bloody wounds made by the *chicotte* and ordered the sick from his post thrown alive into the Lualaba River."

"For three years I built up a hatred against the Belgians in my heart, and choked it back," Mulamba said to Achte. "When I saw Dhanis [Baron Francis Dhanis, the Force Publique commander in the area] face to face with my rebelling countrymen, I trembled with happiness: it was the moment of deliverance and vengeance." Other rebels told Achte that they had chosen Mulamba as their king and two others as his deputies, and that they wanted to set up an independent state free of white rule. This uprising and the other Force Publique rebellions were more than mutinies of disgruntled soldiers; they were precursors of the anticolonial guerrilla wars that shook central and southern Africa starting in the 1960s.

⁂

While Leopold grandly issued edicts banning the slave trade, virtually no visitors except George Washington Williams stated the obvious: not only the porters but even the soldiers of the Force Publique were, in effect, slaves. Moreover, under a system personally approved by the king, white state agents were paid a bonus according to the number of men they turned over to the Force Publique. Sometimes agents bought men from collaborating chiefs, who delivered their human goods in chains. (In one transaction, recorded in a district commissioner's notes, twenty-five francs per person was the price received for a half-dozen teenagers delivered by two chiefs from Bongata in 1892.) Congo state officials were paid an extra bonus for "reduction in recruiting expenses" — a thinly veiled invitation to save the state money by kidnapping these men directly instead of paying chiefs for them.

Always, however, the slave system was bedecked with euphemisms, used even by officers in the field. "Two boats . . . just arrived with Sergeant Lens and 25 volunteers from Engwettra in chains; two men drowned trying to escape," wrote one officer, Louis Rousseau, in his monthly report for October 1892. Indeed, some three quarters of such "volunteers" died before they could even be delivered to Force Publique posts, a worried senior official wrote the same year. Among the solutions to the problem of this "wastage" he recommended were faster transport and lightweight steel chains instead of heavy iron ones. Documents from this time repeatedly show Congo state officials ordering additional supplies of chain. One officer noted the problem of files of conscripts crossing narrow log bridges over jungle streams: when *"libérés* [liberated men] chained by the neck cross a bridge, if one falls off, he pulls the whole file off and it disappears."

White officers who bargained with village chiefs to acquire "volunteer" soldiers and porters were sometimes dealing with the same sources that had supplied the east coast Afro-Arab slave-traders. The most powerful of these Zanzibar-based slavers was the handsome, bearded, strongly built Hamed bin Muhammed el Murjebi, popularly known as Tippu Tip. His nickname was said to have come from the sound of the slave-traders' principal instrument, the musket.

Tippu Tip was a shrewd, resourceful man who made a fortune in ivory as well as slaves, businesses he was able to expand dramatically, thanks to Stanley's discovery of the route of the upper Congo River.* Leopold knew that Tippu Tip's power and administrative acumen had made him

---

* Tippu Tip had supplied porters to Stanley, who had known enough not to ask too many questions about why they were sometimes in chains. On two of Stanley's expeditions, Tippu Tip and his entourage came along for part of the way. One reason the explorer's ill-fated Emin Pasha rescue operation drew such criticism in Europe was that at one point Stanley imperiously commandeered a missionary steamboat to transport his forces up the Congo River. The aghast men of God saw their boat carry off part of an expedition that included Tippu Tip and his thirty-five wives and concubines.

almost the de facto ruler of the eastern Congo. In 1887, the king asked him to serve as governor of the colony's eastern province, with its capital at Stanley Falls, and Tippu Tip accepted; several relatives occupied posts under him. At this early stage, with Leopold's military forces spread thin, the bargain offered something to both men. (The king also contracted to buy the freedom of several thousand of Tippu Tip's slaves, but one condition of their freedom, these "liberated" slaves and many others quickly discovered, was a seven-year enlistment term in the Force Publique.) Although Leopold managed for most of his life to be all things to all people, the spectacle of this antislavery crusader doing so much business with Africa's most prominent slave-dealer helped spur the first murmurings against the king in Europe.

Eventually the two men parted ways. Ambitious white state officials in the eastern Congo, without the approval of their superiors in Brussels, then fought several victorious battles against some of the Afro-Arab warlords in the region, fighting that after the fact was converted into a noble campaign against the dastardly "Arab" slave-dealers. Colonial-heroic literature elevated it to a central place in the period's official mythology, echoes of which can be heard in Belgium to this day. However, over the years Congo military forces spilled far more blood in fighting innumerable uprisings by Africans, including the rebels from their own ranks. Furthermore, as soon as the rogue campaign against the slavers was over, Leopold put many of them back in place as state officials.

What was it like to be captured and enslaved by the Congo's white conquerors? In one rare instance we can hear an African voice describe the experience. It was recorded by an American Swahili-speaking state agent, Edgar Canisius, who found himself unexpectedly moved by the story told to him by "a woman of great intelligence, named Ilanga." Later, when he met the officer and soldiers who had captured her, he concluded that she had indeed spoken the truth. The events she describes took place in the eastern part of the territory, near Nyangwe, the town where Stanley had first seen the giant river that turned out to be the Congo. Here, as recorded by Canisius, is Ilanga's story:

> Our village is called Waniendo, after our chief Niendo. . . . It is a
> large village near a small stream, and surrounded by large fields of
> *mohago* (cassava) and *muhindu* (maize) and other foods, for we all

worked hard at our plantations, and always had plenty to eat. . . . We never had war in our country, and the men had not many arms except knives. . . .

We were all busy in the fields hoeing our plantations, for it was the rainy season, and the weeds sprang quickly up, when a runner came to the village saying that a large band of men was coming, that they all wore red caps and blue cloth, and carried guns and long knives, and that many white men were with them, the chief of whom was Kibalanga [the African name for a Force Publique officer named Oscar Michaux, who once received a Sword of Honor from Leopold's own hands]. Niendo at once called all the chief men to his house, while the drums were beaten to summon the people to the village. A long consultation was held, and finally we were all told to go quietly to the fields and bring in ground-nuts, plantains, and cassava for the warriors who were coming, and goats and fowls for the white men. The women all went with baskets and filled them, and then put them in the road. . . . Niendo thought that, by giving presents of much food, he would induce the strangers to pass on without harming us. And so it proved. . . .

When the white men and their warriors had gone, we went again to our work, and were hoping that they would not return; but this they did in a very short time. As before, we brought in great heaps of food; but this time Kibalanga did not move away directly, but camped near our village, and his soldiers came and stole all our fowls and goats and tore up our cassava; but we did not mind that as long as they did not harm us. The next morning . . . soon after the sun rose over the hill, a large band of soldiers came into the village, and we all went into the houses and sat down. We were not long seated when the soldiers came rushing in shouting, and threatening Niendo with their guns. They rushed into the houses and dragged the people out. Three or four came to our house and caught hold of me, also my husband Oleka and my sister Katinga. We were dragged into the road, and were tied together with cords about our necks, so that we could not escape. We were all crying, for now we knew that we were to be taken away to be slaves. The soldiers beat us with the iron sticks from their guns, and compelled us to march to the camp of Kibalanga, who ordered the women to be tied up separately, ten to each cord, and the men in the same way. When we were all collected — and there were many from other villages whom we now saw, and many from Waniendo — the soldiers brought baskets of food for us to carry, in some of which was smoked human flesh. . . .

We then set off marching very quickly. My sister Katinga had her baby in her arms, and was not compelled to carry a basket; but my husband Oleka was made to carry a goat. We marched until the afternoon, when we camped near a stream, where we were glad to drink, for we were much athirst. We had nothing to eat, for the soldiers would give us nothing. . . . The next day we continued the march, and when we camped at noon were given some maize and plantains, which were gathered near a village from which the people had run away. So it continued each day until the fifth day, when the soldiers took my sister's baby and threw it in the grass, leaving it to die, and made her carry some cooking pots which they found in the deserted village. On the sixth day we became very weak from lack of food and from constant marching and sleeping in the damp grass, and my husband, who marched behind us with the goat, could not stand up longer, and so he sat down beside the path and refused to walk more. The soldiers beat him, but still he refused to move. Then one of them struck him on the head with the end of his gun, and he fell upon the ground. One of the soldiers caught the goat, while two or three others stuck the long knives they put on the ends of their guns into my husband. I saw the blood spurt out, and then saw him no more, for we passed over the brow of a hill and he was out of sight. Many of the young men were killed the same way, and many babies thrown into the grass to die. . . . After marching ten days we came to the great water . . . and were taken in canoes across to the white men's town at Nyangwe.

Even children were not spared the rigors of Leopold's regime. "I believe we must set up three children's colonies," the king wrote on April 27, 1890. "One in the Upper Congo near the equator, specifically military, with clergy for religious instruction and for vocational education. One at Leopoldville under clergy with a soldier for military training. One at

Boma like that at Leo. . . . The aim of these colonies is above all to furnish us with soldiers. We thus have to build three big barracks at Boma, Leo, and near the equator . . . each capable of housing 1500 children and administrative personnel." Following up on Leopold's orders, the governor general six weeks later directed his district commissioners "from now on to gather the most male children possible" for the three state colonies.

As the years passed, many more children's colonies were established by Catholic missionaries. Unlike the Congo's Protestant missionaries, who were foreigners and beyond Leopold's control, the Catholics were mostly Belgian and loyal supporters of the king and his regime. (One Belgian order, the Scheut fathers, even named a mission station after a director of one of the big concession companies.) Leopold subsidized the Catholics lavishly and sometimes used this financial power to deploy priests, almost as if they were soldiers, to areas where he wanted to strengthen his influence.

The children taken in by these missionaries were, theoretically, "orphans." But in most intact, indigenous African societies, with their strong sense of extended family and clan ties, the concept of orphanhood in the European sense did not exist. To the extent that these children literally were orphans, it was frequently because their parents had been killed by the Force Publique. In the wake of their deadly raids throughout the territory, soldiers often collected survivors, both adults and children, and brought them to the Catholic missionaries.

> Monsieur Devos furnished us with five prisoners, tied by the neck, to dig up clay for brick-making, as well as 25 laborers from Ibembo for gathering wood [a Catholic priest reported to his superior in 1899]. . . . Since the last convoy of children from Buta, 25 others have arrived. . . . From time to time we have baptized some of the littler ones, in case of danger of their dying. . . . On July 1st we celebrated the national day of the État Indépendant du Congo. At 8 o'clock, with all our children and a flag in front, we were at the bottom of the stairway carved out of the cliff to welcome Commandant Devos and his soldiers. Returning to the mission, the children marched in front, the soldiers following. . . . During Mass . . . at the moment of the elevation of the host, "present arms!" was sounded by bugles.

The children's colonies were usually ruled by the *chicotte* and the chain. There were many mutinies. If they survived their kidnapping, transport, and schooling, most of the male graduates of the state colonies became soldiers, just as Leopold had ordered. These state colonies were the only state-funded schools for Africans in Leopold's Congo.

Among the traumatized and malnourished children packed into both the state and Catholic colonies, disease was rife and the death rate high, often over 50 percent. Thousands more children perished during the long journeys to get there. Of one column of 108 boys on a forced march to the state colony at Boma in 1892–1893, only sixty-two made it to their destination; eight of them died within the following few weeks. The mother superior of one Catholic colony for girls wrote to a high Congo state official in 1895, "Several of the little girls were so sickly on their arrival that . . . our good sisters couldn't save them, but all had the happiness of receiving Holy Baptism; they are now little angels in Heaven who are praying for our great king."

❦

Despite such prayers, back home the great king was having more domestic troubles. For one thing, his hopes of seeing his daughter Stephanie become Empress of Austria-Hungary ended in disaster. Her husband, Crown Prince Rudolph, turned out to be an alcoholic and a morphine addict. One day in 1889 he and his mistress were found dead in a hunting lodge, an apparent double suicide — although for years rumors swirled that he had been murdered by political enemies. In any event, Stephanie could never become empress. Leopold rushed to Vienna, where the Belgian Cabinet sent him its condolences. The king, then in the midst of his campaign to raise Congo development funds, replied: "We thank you for your kind expressions regarding the disaster which has befallen us. We know the feelings of the ministers, and count upon their sympathy in the terrible trials which God has laid upon us. Do whatever you can to help Monsieur Van Neuss [the Congo state administrator general for finance] to place some more shares on the market; this would be most agreeable to me. Once more, I thank you."

The widowed Stephanie later married a Hungarian count whose blood was not royal enough for Leopold; the king referred to his son-in-law as "that shepherd." As with her sister Louise, Leopold refused to speak to Stephanie again.

Besides his disobedient daughters to fret over, the king had his mad sister Carlota, confined to her château on the outskirts of Brussels, apparently believing she was still Empress of Mexico. Her bridal dress, faded flowers, and a feathered Mexican idol hung on her wall. She was reported to spend her days talking to a life-size doll dressed in imperial robes. Rumors of her delusions provided endless reams of copy to tabloid editors all over Europe. Once when her château caught fire, Carlota was said to have leaned over a parapet and shouted at the flames, "That is forbidden! That is forbidden!"

Family problems could not, however, sap Leopold's energy in the slightest. It was as if he took for granted that this aspect of his life would be miserable, and he lived for other things, above all for his role as King-Sovereign of the Congo. And as he looked around himself in the 1890s, he could see previously uninterested Belgians beginning to share his dreams of conquest and glory. Steeped in the racial imagery of the time, these fantasies trickled even into stories for schoolboys. One contained this glorification of a young Belgian lieutenant martyred for the imperial cause in suppressing the 1897 mutiny:

> The situation was desperate. All seemed lost. But brave De Le Court sprang into the breach.
>
> Together with two other Belgian officers and the remnants of their platoons, he immobilized the black demons who had rushed into the pursuit of the column. . . . Sinister black heads seemed to emerge from every corner, grinding their white teeth. . . .
>
> He fell. . . . He understood the supreme moment of death had come. . . . Smiling, disdainful, sublime, thinking of his King, of his Flag . . . he looked for the last time upon the screaming horde of black demons. . . .
>
> Thus Charles De Le Court died in the fullness of youth in the face of the enemy.

These were years when, to the distress of many a young male European, Europe was at peace. For a young man looking for battle, especially battle against a poorly armed enemy, the Congo was the place to go. For a white man, the Congo was also a place to get rich and to wield power. As a district commissioner, you might be running a district as big as all of Holland or Belgium. As a station chief, you might be a hundred miles away from the next white official; you could levy whatever taxes you chose in labor, ivory, or anything else, collect them however you wanted, and impose whatever punishments you liked. If you got carried away, the penalty, if any, was a slap on the wrist. A station chief at Manyanga, on the big rapids, who beat two of his personal servants to death in 1890 was only fined five hundred francs. What mattered was keeping the ivory flowing back to Belgium. The more you sent, the more you earned. "*Vive le Congo,* there is nothing like it!" one young officer wrote to his family in 1894, "We have liberty, independence, and life with wide horizons. Here you are free and not a mere slave of society. . . . Here one is everything! Warrior, diplomat, *trader!!* Why not!" For such people, just as for the humbly born Stanley, the Congo offered a chance for a great rise in status. Someone fated for a life as a small-town bank clerk or plumber in Europe could instead become a warlord, ivory merchant, big game hunter, and possessor of a harem.

Léon Rom, for example, was born in the provincial Belgian town of Mons. He enlisted in the army at the age of sixteen, but did not have enough education to become an officer. He then worked as a book-keeper with a firm of customs brokers, but quickly tired of that. He came to the Congo in search of adventure in 1886, at the age of twenty-five. At a time when there were only a few hundred white men in the entire territory, his progress was rapid. Rom soon found himself district com-missioner at Matadi, and in that capacity presided over the first civil marriage ceremony of a white couple in the Congo state. He next served briefly as a judge. With so few whites running the vast colony, there was no clear line between civilian and military functions, and Rom was soon put to work training black troops for the Force Publique. The pay was good, too; once promoted to captain, he earned 50 percent more than a colonel in the Belgian Army back home.

Acquiring various medals, Rom won some glory for an episode in a battle against the "Arabs" when he brashly entered an enemy fort to negotiate surrender terms. According to one account: "Rom spontane-ously volunteered. . . . He left unarmed, accompanied only by an inter-preter and, from the spot assigned as a rendezvous, saw all the Arab troops massed behind their ramparts, their rifles at the ready. An emissary, with the sultan's Koran as a safe-conduct, invited him to enter the fortress. In spite of the apprehensions of the interpreter, who smelled a trap, Rom penetrated resolutely into the enemy camp. After two hours of negotia-tions, he left this lair, carrying an Arab flag as proof of surrender." Rom's own description is even more dramatic: he prevails over the shifty Arabs only because of his *"attitude décidée,"* while the terrified, trembling interpreter says, "Master, they're going to kill you!" Whether accepting this surrender was anything that risky to begin with, we do not know. One of the benefits of service as a Force Publique officer was that the nearest journalist was usually thousands of miles away, so you and a few friends could largely shape the record of your exploits.

Rom's upward mobility lay in more than just military rank; it also had intellectual trappings. Each time he returned to Europe he brought with him many butterfly specimens and in time was elected a member of the Entomological Society of Belgium. Honors like this, as well as his officer's sword and his cap with the Congo state star on it, were a far cry from the life of a provincial bookkeeper.

Beneath the eagerly repeated stories of wealth and glory to be found by young white men in the Congo usually lay something else: the sly hint that you could leave your bourgeois morality back in Europe. (As we shall see, this would be the case for Léon Rom.) For Europeans of the day, colonies all over the world offered a convenient escape. Kipling wrote:

> *Ship me somewheres east of Suez,*
> *where the best is like the worst,*
> *Where there aren't no Ten Commandments,*
> *an' a man can raise a thirst.*

In the Congo the Ten Commandments were practiced even less than in most colonies. Belgium was small, the Congo was huge, and the white death rate in the African tropics was still notoriously high. (Authorities tried hard to keep such figures secret, but before 1895 fully a third of white Congo state agents died there; some of the others died of the effects of disease after returning to Europe.) And so in order to find enough men to staff his far-flung network of river posts in malaria-ridden territory, Leopold had to recruit not just Belgians like Léon Rom, but young white men from throughout Europe, attracting them by such get-rich-quick incentives as the lucrative commission structure for acquiring ivory. Many who came out to work in the Congo were like the mercenaries who joined the French Foreign Legion or the fortune hunters who flocked to the two great gold rushes of the day, in South Africa and the Klondike. With its opportunities for both combat and riches, to

Europeans the Congo was a gold rush and the Foreign Legion combined.

This first wave of Leopold's agents included many hard-bitten men fleeing marital troubles, bankruptcy, or alcoholism. A popular song sums up the mood of the time. One official describes in his memoirs how, newly arrived in the Congo, he was kept awake all night by drunken agents singing it endlessly in the bar of his seedy seaport hotel. The first verse runs:

> *Y en a qui font la mauvais' tête*
>   *A leurs parents;*
> *Qui font les dett', qui font la bête,*
>   *Inutil'ment:*
> *Qui, un beau soir, de leur maîtresse*
>   *Ont plein le dos.*
> *Ils fich' le camp, plein de tristesse*
> *Pour le Congo. . . .*

(There're those who blow up at their families,
Who run up debts, who play the fool in vain,
Who one fine evening are fed up with their girls.
They take off, full of sorrow, for the Congo. . . .)

Africans in the Congo, meanwhile, were singing very different songs. A missionary transcribed this one:

> *O mother, how unfortunate we are! . . .*
> *But the sun will kill the white man,*
> *But the moon will kill the white man,*
> *But the sorcerer will kill the white man,*
> *But the tiger will kill the white man,*
> *But the crocodile will kill the white man,*
> *But the elephant will kill the white man,*
> *But the river will kill the white man.*

9

MEETING MR. KURTZ

A T THE BEGINNING of August 1890, several weeks after he wrote his
furious *Open Letter* to King Leopold II, George Washington Williams finished the long return journey down the Congo River to the
station of Kinshasa, on Stanley Pool. Either in the waters of the pool or
when docked on the riverbank at Kinshasa, Williams's steamboat crossed
paths with a boat that was at the start of its voyage upstream, the *Roi des
Belges,* a long, boxy sternwheeler with a funnel and pilot house on its
top deck. Had Williams managed to catch a glimpse of the other boat's
crew, he would have seen a stocky, black-bearded officer with eyes that
look, in the photographs we have, as if they were permanently narrowed
against the tropical sun. Newly arrived in the Congo, the young officer
would be at the captain's side for the entire trip upstream, learning the
river in preparation for taking command of a steamer himself.

The apprentice officer was in many ways typical of the whites who
came to the Congo at this time: an unmarried young man, in need of a
job, who had a yen for adventure and some troubles in his past. Konrad
Korzeniowski, born in Poland, had grown up with an image of Africa
based on the hazy allure of the unknown: "When nine years old or
thereabouts . . . while looking at a map of Africa of the time and putting
my finger on the blank space then representing the unsolved mystery of
that continent, I said to myself . . . 'When I grow up I shall *go there.*'" In
his youth, partly spent in France, he had problems with debts, dabbled, he
claimed, in gunrunning, and made a suicide attempt. He then spent more
than a decade as a ship's officer in the British merchant marine, learning

English along the way, although never losing his strong Polish accent. In early 1890, Korzeniowski was looking in vain for a master's berth at sea. While job-hunting in London, a city filled with talk of Stanley's just-completed Emin Pasha expedition, he began thinking again of the exotic land of his childhood fantasies. He went to Brussels, applied for work on the Congo River, and returned to Belgium for his final job interview just as Stanley was finishing his gala visit to the city.

In conversations before he took up his new job, the thirty-two-year-old Korzeniowski showed that, like almost everyone in Europe, he believed Leopold's mission in Africa was a noble and "civilizing" one. He then said goodbye to his relatives and sailed for the Congo on the ship that carried the first batch of rails and ties for the new railway. Like other white men heading for the interior, he first had to make the long trek from Matadi around the rapids, along with a caravan of black porters. Once he reached the river at last, he filled his diary with the notes of a businesslike seaman, making long entries about shoals, refueling points, and other items not included on the primitive navigational charts available. It would be almost a decade before the aspiring steamship captain managed to get down on paper the other features of the Congo not shown on the map, and by that time, of course, the world would know him as Joseph Conrad.

He spent some six months in the Congo altogether, carrying with him the partly written manuscript of his first novel, *Almayer's Folly*. The thousand-mile apprenticeship trip upriver, from Stanley Pool to Stanley Falls, took only four weeks, a fast voyage for the time. Sandbars, rocks, and shallow water made navigation tricky, especially far up the river in the dry season, which it then was. "The subdued thundering mutter of the Stanley Falls hung in the heavy night air of the last navigable reach of the Upper Congo . . ." he later wrote, "and I said to myself with awe, 'This is the very spot of my boyish boast.' . . . What an end to the idealized realities of a boy's daydreams!"

At Stanley Falls, both Conrad and the steamer's captain fell ill. Conrad recovered sooner, and on the first part of the return trip downriver — going with the current, the boat traveled almost twice as fast as earlier — he was in command of the *Roi des Belges*. But a few weeks after the voyage ended, he canceled his contract and began the long journey back to Europe.

Several bitter disappointments punctured Conrad's dreams. At the start, he hit it off badly with an official of the company he was working for, which meant that he would not gain command of a steamer after all. Then, after coming downstream, he got sick again, with malaria and dysentery, and had to convalesce at an American Baptist mission station on Stanley Pool, in the care of a Scotch missionary doctor. He remained so weak that he had to be carried back to the coast and never fully recovered his health. Finally, he was so horrified by the greed and brutality among white men he saw in the Congo that his view of human nature was permanently changed. Until he spent his six months in Africa, he once told his friend the critic Edward Garnett, he had had "not a thought in his head."

After brooding about his Congo experience for eight years, Conrad transformed it into *Heart of Darkness,* probably the most widely reprinted short novel in English. The nautical jottings in his ship's officer's notebook — "Lulonga Passage. . . . NbyE to NNE. On the Port Side: Snags. Soundings in fathoms: 2, 2, 2, 1, 1, 2, 2, 2, 2" — now become prose unsurpassed by any of the other literary travelers to the Congo over the years:

> Going up that river was like travelling back to the earliest beginnings of the world, when vegetation rioted on the earth and the big trees were kings. An empty stream, a great silence, an impenetrable forest. The air was warm, thick, heavy, sluggish. There was no joy in the brilliance of sunshine. The long stretches of the waterway ran on, deserted, into the gloom of overshadowed distances. On silvery sandbanks hippos and alligators sunned themselves side by side. The broadening waters flowed through a mob of wooded islands. You lost your way on that river as you would in a desert and butted all day long against shoals trying to find the channel till you thought yourself bewitched and cut off for ever from everything you had known.

Marlow, the narrator of *Heart of Darkness* and Conrad's alter ego, is hired by an ivory-trading company to sail a steamboat up an unnamed river whose shape on the map resembles "an immense snake uncoiled, with its head in the sea, its body at rest curving afar over a vast country and its tail lost in the depths of the land." His destination is a post where the company's brilliant, ambitious star agent, Mr. Kurtz, is stationed. Kurtz has collected legendary quantities of ivory, but, Marlow learns along the way, is also rumored to have sunk into unspecified savagery. Marlow's steamer survives an attack by blacks and picks up a load of ivory and the ill Kurtz; Kurtz, talking of his grandiose plans, dies on board as they travel downstream.

Sketched with only a few bold strokes, Kurtz's image has nonetheless remained in the memories of millions of readers: the lone white agent far up the great river, with his dreams of grandeur, his great store of precious ivory, and his fiefdom carved out of the African jungle. Perhaps more than anything, we remember Marlow, on the steamboat, looking through binoculars at what he thinks are ornamental knobs atop the fenceposts in front of Kurtz's house — and then finding that each is "black, dried, sunken, with closed eyelids — a head that seemed to sleep at the top of that pole, and with the shrunken dry lips showing a narrow white line of the teeth."

High school teachers and college professors who have discussed this book in thousands of classrooms over the years tend to do so in terms of Freud, Jung, and Nietzsche; of classical myth, Victorian innocence, and original sin; of postmodernism, postcolonialism, and poststructuralism. European and American readers, not comfortable acknowledging the genocidal scale of the killing in Africa at the turn of the century, have cast *Heart of Darkness* loose from its historical moorings. We read it as a parable for all times and places, not as a book about one time and place. Two of the three times the story was filmed, most notably in Francis Ford Coppola's *Apocalypse Now*, it was not even set in Africa. But Conrad himself wrote, "*Heart of Darkness* is experience . . . pushed a little (and only very little) beyond the actual facts of the case." Whatever the rich levels of meaning the book has as literature, for our purposes what is notable is how precise and detailed a description it is of "the actual facts of the case": King Leopold's Congo in 1890, just as the exploitation of the territory was getting under way in earnest.

In the novel Marlow, as Conrad had done, begins his trip with the long walk around the rapids: "A slight clinking behind me made me turn my head. Six black men advanced in a file toiling up the path. They walked erect and slow, balancing small baskets full of earth on their heads, and the clink kept time with their footsteps. . . . I could see every rib, the joints of their limbs were like knots in a rope, each had an iron collar on his neck and all were connected together with a chain whose bights swung between them, rhythmically clinking." These were the laborers starting work on Leopold's railway.

A few pages later, Marlow describes a spot where some starving railway workers had crawled away to die. Farther along the trail, he sees "now and then a carrier dead in harness, at rest in the long grass near the path, with an empty water-gourd and his long staff lying by his side," and notes the mysterious "body of a middle-aged negro, with a bullet-hole in the forehead." This is simply a record of what Conrad himself saw on his walk around the rapids to Stanley Pool. In his diary entry for July 3, 1890, he noted: "Met an off[ic]er of the State inspecting; a few minutes afterwards saw at a camp[in]g place the dead body of a Backongo. Shot? Horrid smell." The following day: "Saw another dead body lying by the path in an attitude of meditative repose." And on July 29: "On the road today passed a skeleton tied up to a post."

During the hike around the rapids, Marlow also describes how people had fled to avoid being conscripted as porters: "The population had cleared out a long time ago. Well if a lot of mysterious niggers armed with all kinds of fearful weapons suddenly took to travelling on the road [in England] between Deal and Gravesend catching the yokels right and left to carry heavy loads for them, I fancy every farm and cottage thereabouts would get empty very soon. . . . I passed through several abandoned villages." This, too, was what Conrad himself saw. The porters of the caravan the novelist was with came close to mutiny during the trip. Only three and a half years later a fierce uprising would break out along this very route, as Chief Nzansu and his men fought their long, doomed battle against the Force Publique.

In describing the caravans of porters that walked this trail, Marlow gives a crisp summary of the Leopoldian economy: "a stream of . . . rubbishy cottons, beads, and brass-wire set into the depths of darkness and in return came a precious trickle of ivory." In 1890, this was still the colony's most prized commodity. "The word 'ivory' rang in the air, was whispered, was sighed. You would think they were praying to it," says Marlow. He even mentions Leopold's commission system for agents: "The only real feeling was a desire to get appointed to a trading-post where ivory was to be had, so that they could earn percentages."

Conrad stayed true to life when creating the charismatic, murderous figure at the center of his novel, perhaps the twentieth century's most famous literary villain. Mr. Kurtz was clearly inspired by several real people, among them Georges Antoine Klein, a French agent for an ivory-gathering firm at Stanley Falls. Klein, mortally ill, died on shipboard, as Kurtz does in the novel, while Conrad was piloting the *Roi des Belges* down the river. Another model closer to Kurtz in character was Major

Edmund Barttelot, the man whom Stanley left in charge of the rear column on the Emin Pasha expedition. It was Barttelot, remember, who went mad, began biting, whipping, and killing people, and was finally murdered. Yet another Kurtz prototype was a Belgian, Arthur Hodister, famed for his harem of African women and for gathering huge amounts of ivory. Hodister eventually muscled in too aggressively on the territory of local Afro-Arab warlords and ivory-traders, who captured and beheaded him.

However, Conrad's legion of biographers and critics have almost entirely ignored the man who resembles Kurtz most closely of all. And he is someone we have already met, the swashbuckling Captain Léon Rom of the Force Publique. It is from Rom that Conrad may have taken the signal feature of his villain: the collection of African heads surrounding Kurtz's house.

The "Inner Station" of *Heart of Darkness,* the place Marlow looks at through his binoculars only to find Kurtz's collection of the shrunken heads of African "rebels," is loosely based on Stanley Falls. In 1895, five years after Conrad visited this post, Léon Rom was station chief there. A British explorer-journalist who passed through Stanley Falls that year described the aftermath of a punitive military expedition against some African rebels: "Many women and children were taken, and twenty-one heads were brought to the falls, and have been used by Captain Rom as a decoration round a flower-bed in front of his house!" If Conrad missed this account, which appeared in the widely read *Century Magazine,* he almost certainly noticed when *The Saturday Review,* a magazine he admired and read faithfully, repeated the story in its issue of December 17, 1898. That date was within a few days of when Conrad began writing *Heart of Darkness.*

Furthermore, in the Congo, Rom and Conrad may have met.

On August 2, 1890, Conrad, accompanied by another white man and a caravan of porters, finished his month-long trek inland from the coast. Five miles before his caravan reached the village of Kinshasa on Stanley Pool, where the *Roi des Belges* was waiting, it had to pass through the neighboring post of Leopoldville. These two collections of thatch-roofed buildings were only an hour and a half's walk apart. (They soon grew and merged into one city, called Leopoldville by the Belgians and Kinshasa today.) When Conrad's caravan, trudging along a path near the riverbank, passed through Leopoldville, the station chief there was Léon Rom. Conrad made no entry in his diary on August 2, and Rom's notebook, which in a calligraphic hand faithfully records any raid or campaign that could win him another medal, mentions no expeditions away from Leopold-ville at that time. If Rom was on hand, he would certainly have greeted a caravan with European newcomers, for there were only a few dozen white men at Leopoldville and Kinshasa, and new ones did not arrive every day. What, if anything, spoken or unspoken, passed between Rom and Conrad we will never know. Rom's collection of twenty-one African heads lay in a different place and a different time, half a decade in the future, but when Conrad read about Rom in December 1898, it is possi-ble that he made the connection to a young officer he had met in the Congo.

Heart of Darkness is one of the most scathing indictments of imperialism in all literature, but its author, curiously, thought himself an ardent impe-rialist where England was concerned. Conrad fully recognized Leopold's rape of the Congo for what it was: "The horror! The horror!" his charac-ter Kurtz says on his deathbed. And Conrad's stand-in, Marlow, muses on how "the conquest of the earth, which mostly means the taking it away from those who have a different complexion or slightly flatter noses than ourselves, is not a pretty thing when you look into it too much." Yet in almost the same breath, Marlow talks about how the British territories colored red on a world map were "good to see at any time because one knows that some real work is done in there"; British colonialists were "bearers of a spark from the sacred fire." Marlow was speaking for Con-rad, whose love of his adoptive country knew no bounds: Conrad felt that "liberty . . . can only be found under the English flag all over the world." And at the very time he was denouncing the European lust for African riches in his novel, he was an investor in a gold mine near Johannesburg.

Conrad was a man of his time and place in other ways as well. He was partly a prisoner of what Mark Twain, in a different context, called "the white man's notion that he is less savage than the other savages." *Heart of Darkness* has come in for some justified pummeling in recent years be-cause of its portrayal of black characters, who say no more than a few words. In fact, they don't speak at all: they grunt; they chant; they produce a "drone of weird incantations" and "a wild and passionate uproar"; they spout "strings of amazing words that resembled no sounds of human language . . . like the responses of some satanic litany." The true message of the book, the Nigerian novelist Chinua Achebe has argued, is: "Keep away from Africa, or else! Mr. Kurtz . . . should have heeded that warning and the prowling horror in his heart would have kept its place, chained to its lair. But he foolishly exposed himself to the wild irresistible allure of the jungle and lo! the darkness found him out."

However laden it is with Victorian racism, *Heart of Darkness* remains the greatest portrait in fiction of Europeans in the Scramble for Africa. When Marlow says goodbye to his aunt before heading to his new job, "she talked about 'weaning those ignorant millions from their horrid ways,' till, upon my word, she made me quite uncomfortable. I ventured to hint that the Company was run for profit."* Conrad's white men go about their rape of the continent in the belief that they are uplifting the natives, bringing civilization, serving "the noble cause."

All these illusions are embodied in the character of Kurtz. He is both a murderous head collector and an intellectual, "an emissary of . . . science and progress." He is a painter, the creator of "a small sketch in oils" of a woman carrying a torch that Marlow finds at the Central Station. And he is a poet and journalist, the author of, among other works, a seventeen-page report — "vibrating with eloquence . . . a beautiful piece of writing" — to the International Society for the Suppression of Savage Customs. At the end of this report, filled with lofty sentiments, Kurtz scrawls in a shaky hand: "Exterminate all the brutes!"

In Kurtz's intellectual pretensions, Conrad caught one telling feature of the white penetration of the Congo, where conquest by pen and ink so often confirmed the conquest by rifle and machine gun. Ever since Stanley shot his way down the Congo River and then promptly wrote a two-volume best-seller, ivory collectors, soldiers, and explorers had tried to imitate him — in books, and in thousands of articles for the geographical society journals and magazines about colonial exploration that were as popular in the late nineteenth century as the *National Geographic*

---

* The biggest profiteer, King Leopold II, does not appear in *Heart of Darkness,* although he does in *The Inheritors,* the lesser novel that Conrad later co-authored with Ford Madox Ford. One of its central characters is the heavily bearded Duc de Mersch, who controls the Greenland Protectorate. The duc's Society for the Regeneration of the Arctic Regions is dedicated to uplifting the benighted Eskimos by bringing them a railway, proper clothes, and other benefits of civilization. The duc has invested in an English newspaper in an attempt to buy favorable press coverage of his "philanthropic" activities. "We have," he says, "protected the natives, have kept their higher interests ever present in our minds." The Greenland of the novel is rich in oil and gold.

is in the United States today. It was as if the act of putting Africa on paper were the ultimate proof of the superiority of European civilization. This aspect of Kurtz is yet another reason to suspect that, in creating him, Conrad was partly inspired by Léon Rom. Rom, we saw, was a budding entomologist. He was also a painter; when not collecting butterflies or human heads, he did portraits and landscapes, of which five survive in a Belgian museum today. Most interesting of all, he was a writer.

In 1899, Rom, by then back in Belgium, published a book of his own. *Le Nègre du Congo* is an odd little volume — jaunty, arrogant, and sweepingly superficial. Short chapters cover "Le Nègre en général," the black woman, food, pets, native medicine, and so on. Rom was an enthusiastic hunter who jubilantly posed for one photo atop a dead elephant, and his chapter on hunting is as long as those on Congolese religious beliefs, death rituals, and chiefly succession combined.

The voice we hear in Rom's book is very much like the voice in which we might imagine Mr. Kurtz writing his report to the International Society for the Suppression of Savage Customs. Of *la race noire,* Rom says, "The product of a mindless state, its feelings are coarse, its passions rough, its instincts brutish, and, in addition, it is proud and vain. The black man's principal occupation, and that to which he dedicates the greatest part of his existence, consists of stretching out on a mat in the warm rays of the sun, like a crocodile on the sand. . . . The black man has no idea of time, and, questioned on that subject by a European, he generally responds with something stupid."

There is much more in this vein. When Rom describes, for example, the Congolese conscripted to work as porters, he says they enjoyed themselves splendidly. As a caravan sets off in the morning, the porters all bustle noisily about, each one eagerly wanting "to succeed in finding a place in line of his choice, for example beside a friend with whom he can trade dreams of the previous night or elaborate the menu, more or less varied and delicious, of the meal they will have at the next stop."

At some point while he was in the Congo, Rom must have begun planning his book. Did Rom, finding that Conrad spoke perfect French, confide in him his literary dreams? Did Conrad see one of Rom's paintings on the wall at Leopoldville, just as Marlow sees one of Kurtz's? Or was it sheer coincidence that the real head-collector Rom and the imaginary head-collector Kurtz were both painters and writers? We will never know.

There are several other tantalizing parallels between Léon Rom and

Mr. Kurtz. In the novel, Kurtz succeeds in "getting himself adored" by the Africans of the Inner Station: chiefs crawl on the ground before him, the people obey him with slavish devotion, and a beautiful black woman apparently is his concubine. In 1895, a disapproving Force Publique lieutenant confided to his diary a strikingly similar situation involving a fellow officer:

> He makes his agents *starve* while he gives lots of food to the black women of his harem (for he wants to act like a great Arab chief). . . . Finally, he got into his dress uniform at his house, brought together his women, picked up some piece of paper and pretended to read to them that the king had named him the big chief and that the other whites of the station were only small fry. . . . He gave fifty lashes to a poor little negress because she wouldn't be his mistress, then he *gave* her to a soldier.

What is significant is how the diarist introduces his account of the officer: "This man wants to play the role of a second Rom."

Finally, the murderousness of Kurtz seems to echo one other detail about Rom. When Rom was station chief at Stanley Falls, the governor general sent a report back to Brussels about some agents who "have the reputation of having killed masses of people for petty reasons." He mentions Rom's notorious flower bed ringed with human heads, and then adds: "He kept a gallows permanently erected in front of the station!"

We do not know whether Rom was already acting out any of these dreams of power, murder, and glory when Conrad passed through Leopoldville in 1890 or whether he only talked of them. Whatever the case, the moral landscape of *Heart of Darkness* and the shadowy figure at its center are the creations not just of a novelist but of an open-eyed observer who caught the spirit of a time and place with piercing accuracy.

10

THE WOOD THAT WEEPS

I T WAS RAINING in London on July 12, 1890, but the crowd gathered outside Westminster Abbey anyway, ignoring the downpour. Thousands of people surged back and forth on the slick pavement, trying to glimpse the dignitaries who stepped out of carriages and filed into the cathedral between lines of policemen: former Prime Minister Gladstone, the speaker of the House of Commons, the lord chancellor, assorted dukes and princes, bejeweled women and bemedaled generals. The rich and famous filled the abbey, even standing in the aisles.

Finally, a carriage pulled up and the man everyone was waiting for eased himself out, ill, pale, leaning on a walking stick. Henry Morton Stanley was about to do something more daunting for him than any of his African adventures. He was getting married.

The bride, Dorothy Tennant, was the eccentric, high-society portrait painter who had previously rejected him. While the explorer had been plodding through the jungle in search of Emin Pasha, Tennant had changed her mind. On his return to England, she had begun sending Stanley startlingly passionate letters. "Suppose a wild, uncultivated tract of land and suppose that one day this land is ploughed up and sown with corn. If the field could speak it might say: 'I have never borne corn, I do not bear corn, I shall never bear corn.' And yet all the while the wheat lies hidden in its bosom. . . . My love is a flame which will never die, it began so small a spark you could not see it light, now it burns like the altar flame."

To the altar it was. The news spread, the price of Tennant's paintings soared, the congratulations poured in from around the world. Queen Victoria gave Tennant a locket with thirty-eight diamonds, and Thomas Edison sent one of his new phonograph machines. From Brussels, Leopold dispatched his representative, the Count d'Aarche, to be best man.

On the day itself, Stanley was painfully ill with gastritis, an inflammation of the stomach lining. He had suffered from it before, but its recurrence now was probably not by chance. He tottered up the aisle of Westminster Abbey but had to sit in an armchair for part of the ceremony. After the wedding, he was helped into the couple's carriage. Protected by a mounted police escort, it headed off through a shouting and jostling crowd that almost blocked its passage. During the reception, Stanley lay on a couch in a separate, darkened room, in agony. The illness continued into the honeymoon.

At war in Stanley all his life were the craving for acceptance and the fear of intimacy. The fear was so strong, believes the explorer's most thorough biographer, Frank McLynn, that Stanley's marriage was never consummated. The evidence is mainly circumstantial. Dorothy Stanley did not produce children, and clearly, despite her letters, had powerful neuroses of her own. In a most unromantic decision, Stanley insisted that his young male assistant come along on the couple's honeymoon in Switzerland. Finally, Stanley's diary of the honeymoon period has several passages inked out, apparently by his wife after his death. The end of one such entry, however, is legible: "I do not regard it wifely, to procure these pleasures, at the cost of making me feel like a monkey in a cage." Stanley's fear of women was so great, McLynn concludes, that "when he was finally called upon to satisfy a wife, Stanley in effect broke down and confessed that he considered sex for the beasts."

Whether this inference is right or wrong, the inhibitions that caused Stanley so much pain are a reminder that the explorers and soldiers who carried out the European seizure of Africa were often not the bold, bluff, hardy men of legend, but restless, unhappy, driven men, in flight from something in their past or in themselves. The economic explanations of imperial expansion — the search for raw materials, labor, and markets — are all valid, but there was psychological fuel as well.

Stanley's marriage marked the end of his exploring; he now devoted his time to being famous. Having reached the upper class at last, he became something of a caricature of its attitudes. He traveled about the world giving lectures and after-dinner speeches, receiving honorary degrees, inaugurating railroads, and granting interviews. He fulminated against sloth, socialism, immorality, "general mediocrity," labor unions, Irish nationalism, the eight-hour working day, women journalists, and American hotel servants ("untrained, undisciplined, loutish and ill-bred"). He received a knighthood and was elected to Parliament. When he made a speaking tour of the United States and Canada, he again took along his young assistant; his wife took her mother. Doubly chaperoned, the Stanleys traveled across the continent in royal style in a private railroad car complete with grand piano. The car was named the *Henry M. Stanley.*

Only two years after Stanley hobbled down the cathedral aisle, another man accomplished a remarkable feat of exploration in the Congo. Unlike Stanley's journeys, his was respectful and nonviolent. But William Sheppard seldom shows up in the annals of exploration, because he doesn't fit the conventional image of the white explorer in Africa. To begin with, he wasn't white.

Paradoxically, what allowed Sheppard, a black American, to go to the Congo at all was partly the work of the white supremacist Alabama Senator John Tyler Morgan, who had helped engineer United States recognition of Leopold's Congo in the hope that American blacks would emigrate there. Morgan and his fellow send-them-back-to-Africa enthusiasts had long envisaged, as a first step, dispatching black American missionaries to the continent. They would be a beachhead, Morgan hoped, for millions of American blacks to follow, the sooner the better. As early as 1865 — the year white Southerners lost all hope of keeping blacks in their place as slaves — the General Assembly of the Southern Presbyterian Church had voted to begin recruiting "missionaries from among the African race on this continent, who may bear the Gospel of the grace of God to the homes of their ancestors."

It was some years after the Civil War before such plans could take effect. For one thing, the Southern Presbyterians, whose enthusiasm for slavery had made them split off from Presbyterians in the North, not surprisingly had few black members. Nonetheless, the back-to-Africa plans of white racist diehards like Morgan in part overlapped with the interests of some African Americans. Although few were interested in moving to Africa permanently, George Washington Williams was not the only black American of his time who wanted to work there. The Reverend William Sheppard had the same ambition, and probably for the same unspoken reason: this might be a way to escape the humiliating barriers of segregation.

Born in Virginia in 1865, Sheppard had gone to the state's Hampton Institute, one of the few higher educational institutions for blacks in the South. After further study at the Colored Theological Seminary in Tuscaloosa, Alabama, he worked as a Presbyterian minister in Montgomery and Atlanta, where he acquired a reputation for energy, zest, and physical courage. At one point, he saved someone from drowning; at another, he ran up three flights of stairs in a burning house to rescue a woman and got burned in the process. In the late 1880s, Sheppard began petitioning the Southern Presbyterian Church to send him to Africa as a missionary.

For two years the Presbyterians put Sheppard on hold: church authorities wouldn't let him go to Africa unless a white man was available to be his superior. At last, with encouragement from Senator Morgan himself, an aspiring white missionary appeared — the Reverend Samuel Lapsley, a year younger than Sheppard and the son of Morgan's former law partner. Although one was the descendant of slaves and the other of slave-owners, the two young clerics hit it off well and set out together for the Congo. On the way, with introductions from Morgan and Henry Shelton Sanford, Lapsley met President Benjamin Harrison in Washington and King Leopold II in Brussels. Sheppard, being black, was not included in these audiences. Sanford insisted that Lapsley get a silk top hat for his trip to the Royal Palace to meet Leopold, and the king charmed Lapsley as much as he did other visitors.

In May 1890, Sheppard and Lapsley arrived in the Congo, and for some weeks stayed at a mission station just outside Matadi. As the two of them assembled porters and supplies for the trip around the lower Congo River rapids, someone else doing the same thing on the streets of this small hillside town was Joseph Conrad. He and his caravan began walking up the trail to Stanley Pool eleven days after the Americans.

Having conferred with experienced missionaries at Stanley Pool and upriver, Lapsley and Sheppard decided to establish the first Southern Presbyterian mission far up the Kasai River. Sheppard went off into the bush for several weeks to recruit African helpers; Lapsley stayed at an American mission station in Leopoldville, where he again crossed paths with Conrad. (The novelist may have braved not just malaria and dysentery, but also some evangelizing. Conrad, Lapsley wrote home, "is sick in a room at the other end of the court. As I sit . . . I look across the fruit and palm trees right into his window. He is a gentlemanly fellow. An English Testament on his table furnishes a handle I hope to use on him.")

Once they completed their preparations, the two young missionaries headed up the Kasai. The letters Lapsley sent home during these months ring with an admiration for Sheppard that would have been nearly impossible for a white man to voice for a black back home. "The Bateke think there is nobody like 'Mundéle Ndom,' the black white man, as they call Sheppard. . . . His temper is bright and even — really a man of unusual graces and strong points of character. So I am thankful to God for Sheppard." He describes Sheppard as a "born trader. . . . I let him do most of the buying," and speaks admiringly of Sheppard's physical hardiness and his skill at hunting, of his coping with storms that threatened to blow away their tents, and of Sheppard's pulling himself fifteen feet down an anchor chain underwater to loosen the snagged anchor. Sheppard once shot a hippo, jumped into the water to tie a rope around it, and narrowly escaped a crocodile who also had an eye on the hippo. The black man was supposed to be the junior partner in the mission, but as one reads Lapsley's letters, one is reminded of James Barrie's play *The Admirable Crichton,* in which a yacht full of upper-class Britons is shipwrecked on an island, and the resourceful butler becomes the leader.

William Sheppard was the first black American missionary in the Congo. As we listen to him in the book, letters, and magazine articles he writes over the next two decades, and in speeches given to rapt audiences at Hampton and elsewhere while he is on leave, we hear someone strikingly different from almost all the Americans and Europeans who have been to Africa before him. He is, to be sure, a Christian evangelist, and remains one for the twenty years he works in Africa. He occasionally expresses the customary condescension toward "the dense darkness of heathenism" and the "wild, naked savages, bowing down to idols, filled with superstition and sin." But his tone is usually far different. "I always wanted to live in Africa," Sheppard writes to a friend back in the United States; "I felt that I would be happy, and so I am." He eagerly absorbs his new surroundings along the Kasai River: "We immediately began to study their language by pointing at objects and writing down the names they gave us." He acquires pet parrots and a small black monkey jokingly named Tippu Tip, after the Afro-Arab slave-trader. His voice, stronger and more confident, becomes that of a man who feels, in a way that is perhaps, politically and religiously, too risky for him to fully explore, that he has come home. He rejoices at being among "my people" in "the country of my forefathers."

In early 1892, Lapsley had to go to Boma, the capital, on mission business, and left Sheppard alone for some months on the Kasai. When Sheppard joyfully met the steamer he thought was bringing Lapsley back, to his shock he found a letter from another missionary:

> Dear Bro. Sheppard:
> You will be surprised and grieved to know that your friend and comrade, Rev. S. N. Lapsley, while here at the coast was taken down with bilious hematuric fever, and on the 26th of March died."

The Southern Presbyterians, embarrassed to find themselves with a black man in de facto command of their new Congo mission, dispatched more white Presbyterians to the Congo. By the time they arrived, Sheppard had had several years' experience in the territory, and had become, according to a Belgian trader, very popular "among the BaKuba whose language he alone speaks of all the Europeans."

Sheppard continued to thrive. He loved to hunt and was famous for his charismatic oratory and strength. He rode what he cheerfully claimed was the first bicycle in central Africa. His *joi de vivre* seems to have made him liked by almost everyone, black and white. It may be a measure of his popularity that when, later in his life, he strayed from his marriage and fathered a son with a village woman, the transgression did not end his career in the church. The boy, called Shapit, as the Africans called his father, eventually ended up running the mission printing press.

Unlike other missionaries, generally a pretty somber-looking lot, in photographs Sheppard seems to be enjoying himself, whether posing with game he has shot or jubilantly displaying a giant dead snake or strumming a banjo. Tall and husky, he stands among a group of black warriors with spears and shields, holding a spear himself. Or, with a rifle, he grins broadly, a row of men with bows and arrows arrayed beside him. Again and again, Sheppard strikes a distinctive pose. He is wearing a white sun helmet, white shirt, white tie, white linen suit, even white canvas shoes. His chest is thrust out, his hands confidently on his hips, and, amid a group of Africans, his smile is warm and proud and almost proprietary. He has the distinct look of a football coach showing off a winning team.

The area where Sheppard was working bordered on the homeland of the Kuba people. The Kuba are among Africa's greatest artists, working in masks, sculpture, textiles, and elaborately carved tools; Sheppard's collection of Kuba art, much of which ended up at his alma mater in Virginia, was the first significant one acquired by an outsider. He made ethnographic notes on the Kuba and other peoples of the Kasai region and recorded ancestral myths, rituals, and crop yields. Although he is frank to say when some practice — such as human sacrifice, or the killing of women as witches — appalls him, his writings show an empathetic, respectful curiosity about African customs radically different from the harsh, quick judgments of someone like Stanley. Sheppard was particularly impressed with the Kuba, who "make one feel that he has again entered a land of civilization. . . . Perhaps they got their civilization from the Egyptians — or the Egyptians got theirs from the Bakuba!" Sheppard was fascinated when he saw a Kuba ceremonial cup for drinking palm wine; carved on it was a face with features strikingly similar to those on ancient Egyptian artifacts. "The cup is made of mahogany," Sheppard wrote, "and the face on it seems to verify their tradition that many, many years ago they came from a far-away land."

Because of its location deep in the Congo's interior, the Kuba kingdom had been largely protected from the slave-raiders of both the east and west coasts. The Kuba valued their isolation and did all they could to keep outsiders at bay. Their homeland was within the boundaries of the territory Europe had recognized as Leopold's, but at this early stage of colony-building his sovereignty over more remote areas existed only on paper. For nearly a decade, Belgian traders had been trying to gain access to the Kuba kingdom and had been repeatedly turned away; gifts they sent to its king were returned.

Achieving something most anthropologists can only dream of, in 1892 Sheppard became the first foreigner to reach the town of Ifuca, seat of the court of the Kuba king, Kot aMbweeky II. The king had repeatedly threatened to behead anyone who helped strangers intrude, so no one dared give Sheppard directions. It took him and a small group of Africans three months to find their way to the capital, which they finally did by clandestinely following the trail of an ivory caravan. Sheppard was still dressed all in white, including white canvas shoes, and "what had been," he writes ruefully, his white linen suit.

The king angrily ordered Sheppard, his followers, and everyone who had helped them brought to court for beheading. Then he discovered that the intruder had dark skin and could speak some Kuba. This meant, the elders decided, that he was a reincarnated spirit. Furthermore, they announced that they knew just who he was: Bope Mekabe, a former king. According to Sheppard, nothing he could say about his greater king in heaven would convince them otherwise.*

This visit was one of the high points of Sheppard's life and provided a mine of information for later scholars, for the Kuba had one of central Africa's most sophisticated political systems. Sheppard remained at the Kuba court for four months, and, interested in all he saw, made notes about everything from court rituals to the workings of a royal police force that dealt with thefts and other crimes. Servants spread leopard skins for him to walk on whenever he approached the king, who sat on an ivory throne and wore a crown of beads and feathers.

"I grew very fond of the Bakuba. . . ." he writes. "They were the finest looking race I had seen in Africa, dignified, graceful, courageous, honest, with an open smiling countenance and really hospitable. Their knowledge of weaving, embroidery, wood carving and smelting was the highest in equatorial Africa." Sheppard attended an annual gathering of chiefs and headmen from the towns of the kingdom, where each in turn reported on births, deaths, harvests, and other events in his domain and did a ceremonial dance. The book he later wrote about his experiences in Africa is entitled *Presbyterian Pioneers in Congo,* but the distinctly un-Presbyterian Kuba run away with the story. His is a valuable, firsthand look at one of the last great African kingdoms unchanged by European influence. The Kuba creation myth, Sheppard reports, "says that their first people, man and woman, were let down from the skies by a rope, from which they untied themselves and the rope was drawn up."

Soon after this first visit to the Kuba, Sheppard headed back to the United States on leave. On the way he was invited to lecture at Exeter Hall in London. For his travels in the Kuba kingdom and his discovery of a lake Europeans had not known about, he was made a fellow of the Royal Geographical Society, the only Presbyterian missionary so honored. The society also named his discovery Lake Sheppard. In Washington, Sheppard presented President Grover Cleveland with a Kuba bamboo

---

* The noted anthropologist Jan Vansina has a different interpretation: Since the name Bope Mekabe is not in the Kuba royal genealogy, he suggests that the Kuba may have understood who Sheppard was, and were simply trying to flatter him into revealing the plans of other Europeans who wanted to enter the kingdom.

mat; on a later visit, he gave Theodore Roosevelt a pipe and a palm-fiber coverlet. On these trips home, Sheppard delivered innumerable speeches, at colleges, universities, and churches throughout the country, and his fervent preaching about Africa recruited more black missionaries for the Presbyterians. One of them, Lucy Gantt, a teacher and talented singer whom he had known while still a theology student, he married. To help staff what eventually became several mission stations, more white Presbyterians came to Africa as well, and a white man was always in charge. On the official rolls of the Southern Presbyterian mission society published in the United States, Sheppard and his new recruits always had "(colored)" or "(c.)" after their names. But in Africa itself he did not feel relegated to second-class citizenship: he called one of his children Maxamalinge, after a son of the Kuba king.

Not surprisingly, the Kuba were happy with their existing way of life, and, despite their friendliness toward Sheppard, showed little interest in Christianity. The mission station Sheppard ran among them made few converts. But Sheppard had become so well known back home for his discoveries that the Presbyterians were afraid of an adverse public reaction if they closed his mission to the Kuba and stationed him elsewhere.

The entire Kasai region, like the rest of the Congo, in time succumbed to the tightening grip of the Congo state. Some eight years after Sheppard's historic visit, Leopold's forces finally reached and looted the Kuba capital.

❦

The raid on the capital, like many other events in the Congo, was triggered by a discovery far away. One day a few years before William Sheppard first embarked for Africa, a veterinary surgeon with a majestic white beard was tinkering with his son's tricycle at his home in Belfast, Ireland. John Dunlop was trying to solve a problem that had bedeviled bicyclists for many years: how do you get a gentle ride without springs? Dunlop finally devised a practical way of making a long-sought solution, an inflatable rubber tire. In 1890 the Dunlop Company began making tires — setting off a bicycle craze and starting a new industry just in time, it turned out, for the coming of the automobile.

Europeans had known about rubber ever since Christopher Columbus noticed it in the West Indies. In the late 1700s, a British scientist gave the substance its English name when he noticed it could rub out pencil marks. The Scot Charles Macintosh contributed his name to the language in 1823 when he figured out a mass-production method for doing something long practiced by the Indians of the Americas: applying rubber to cloth to make it waterproof. Sixteen years later, the American inventor Charles Goodyear accidentally spilled sulfur into some hot rubber on his stove. He discovered that the resulting mixture did not turn stiff when cold or smelly and gooey when hot — major problems for those trying to make rubber boots or raincoats before then. But it was not until the early 1890s, half a decade after Dunlop fitted the pneumatic tire onto his son's tricycle wheel, that the worldwide rubber boom began. The industrial world rapidly developed an appetite not just for rubber tires, but for hoses, tubing, gaskets, and the like, and for rubber insulation for the telegraph, telephone, and electrical wiring now rapidly encompassing the globe. Suddenly factories could not get enough of the magical commodity, and its price rose throughout the 1890s. Nowhere did the boom have a more drastic impact on people's lives than in the equatorial rain forest, where wild rubber vines snaked high into the trees, that covered nearly half of King Leopold's Congo.

For Leopold, the rubber boom was a godsend. He had gone dangerously into debt with his Congo investments, but he now saw that the return would be more lucrative than he had ever imagined. The world did not lose its desire for ivory, but by the late 1890s wild rubber had far surpassed it as the main source of revenue from the Congo. His fortune assured, the king eagerly grilled functionaries returning from the Congo about rubber harvests; he devoured a constant stream of telegrams and reports from the territory, marking them up in the margins and passing them on to aides for action. His letters from this period are filled with numbers: commodity prices from world markets, interest rates on loans, quantities of rifles to be shipped to the Congo, tons of rubber to be shipped to Europe, and the exact dimensions of the triumphal arch in Brussels he was planning to build with his newfound profits. Reading the king's correspondence is like reading the letters of the CEO of a corporation that has just developed a profitable new product and is racing to take advantage of it before competitors can get their assembly lines going.

The competition Leopold worried about was from cultivated rubber, which comes not from a vine but a tree. Rubber trees, however, require much care and some years before they grow large enough to be tapped. The king voraciously demanded ever greater quantities of wild rubber from the Congo, because he knew that the price would drop once plantations of rubber trees in Latin America and Asia reached maturity.

This did indeed happen, but by then the Congo had had a wild-rubber boom nearly two decades long. During that time the search knew no bounds.

As with the men bringing in ivory, those supplying rubber to the Congo state and private companies were rewarded according to the amount they turned in. In 1903, one particularly "productive" agent received a commission eight times his annual salary. But the big money flowed directly back to Antwerp and Brussels, in the capital mostly to either side of the rue Bréderode, the small street that separated the back of the Royal Palace from several buildings holding offices of the Congo state and Congo business operations.

Even though Leopold's privately controlled state got half of concession-company profits, the king made vastly more money from the land the state exploited directly. But because the concession companies were not managed so secretly, we have better statistics from them. In 1897, for example, one of the companies, the Anglo-Belgian India Rubber and Exploration Company, or A.B.I.R., spent 1.35 francs per kilo to harvest rubber in the Congo and ship it to the company's headquarters at Antwerp — where it was sold for prices that sometimes reached 10 francs per kilo, a profit of more than 700 percent. By 1898, the price of A.B.I.R.'s stock was nearly thirty times what it had been six years earlier. Between 1890 and 1904, total Congo rubber earnings increased ninety-six times over. By the turn of the century, the État Indépendant du Congo had become, far and away, the most profitable colony in Africa. The profits came swiftly because, transportation costs aside, harvesting wild rubber required no cultivation, no fertilizers, no capital investment in expensive equipment. It required only labor.

How was this labor to be found? For the Congo's rulers, this posed a problem. They could not simply round up men, chain them together, and put them to work under the eye of an overseer with a *chicotte,* as they did with porters. To gather wild rubber, people must disperse widely through the rain forest and often climb trees.

Rubber is coagulated sap; the French word for it, *caoutchouc,* comes from a South American Indian word meaning "the wood that weeps." The wood that wept in the Congo was a long spongy vine of the *Landolphia* genus. Up to a foot thick at the base, a vine would twine upward around a tree to a hundred feet or more off the ground, where it could reach sunlight. There, branching, it might wind its way hundreds of feet through the upper limbs of another half-dozen trees. To gather the rubber, you had to slash the vine with a knife and hang a bucket or earthenware pot to collect the slow drip of thick, milky sap. You could make a small incision to tap the vine, or — officially forbidden but widely practiced — cut through it entirely, which produced more rubber but killed the vine. Once the vines near a village were drained dry, workers had to go ever deeper into the forest until, before long, most harvesters were traveling at least one or two days to find fresh vines. As the lengths of vine within reach of the ground were tapped dry, workers climbed high into the trees to reach sap. "We . . . passed a man on the road who had broken his back by falling from a tree while . . . tapping some vines," wrote one missionary. Furthermore, heavy tropical downpours during much of the year turned large areas of the rain forest, where the rubber vines grew, into swampland.

No payments of trinkets or brass wire were enough to make people stay in the flooded forest for days at a time to do work that was so arduous — and physically painful. A gatherer had to dry the syrup-like rubber so that it would coagulate, and often the only way to do so was to spread the substance on his arms, thighs, and chest. "The first few times it is not without pain that the man pulls it off the hairy parts of his body," Louis Chaltin, a Force Publique officer, confided to his journal in 1892. "The native doesn't like making rubber. He must be compelled to do it."

How was he to be compelled? A trickle of news and rumor gradually made its way to Europe. "An example of what is done was told me up the Ubangi [River]," the British vice consul reported in 1899. "This officer['s] . . . method . . . was to arrive in canoes at a village, the inhabitants of which invariably bolted on their arrival; the soldiers were then landed, and commenced looting, taking all the chickens, grain, etc., out of the houses; after this they attacked the natives until able to seize their women; these women were kept as hostages until the Chief of the district brought in the required number of kilogrammes of rubber. The rubber having been brought, the women were sold back to their owners for a couple of goats apiece, and so he continued from village to village until the requisite amount of rubber had been collected."

Sometimes the hostages were women, sometimes children, sometimes elders or chiefs. Every state or company post in the rubber areas had a stockade for hostages. If you were a male villager, resisting the order to gather rubber could mean death for your wife. She might die anyway, for in the stockades food was scarce and conditions were harsh. "The women taken during the last raid at Engwettra are causing me no end of trouble," wrote Force Publique officer Georges Bricusse in his diary on November 22, 1895. "All the soldiers want one. The sentries who are supposed to watch them unchain the prettiest ones and rape them."

Leopold, of course, never proclaimed hostage-taking as official policy; if anyone made such charges, authorities in Brussels indignantly denied them. But out in the field, far from prying eyes, the pretense was dropped. Instructions on taking hostages were even given in the semiofficial instruction book, the revealing *Manuel du Voyageur et du Résident au Congo,* a copy of which the administration gave to each agent and each state post. The manual's five volumes cover everything from keeping servants obedient to the proper firing of artillery salutes. Taking hostages was one more routine piece of work:

> In Africa taking prisoners is . . . an easy thing to do, for if the natives hide, they will not go far from their village and must come to look for food in the gardens which surround it. In watching these carefully, you will be certain of capturing people after a brief delay. . . . When you feel you have enough captives, you should choose among them an old person, preferably an old woman. Make her a present and send her to her chief to begin negotiations. The chief, wanting to see his people set free, will usually decide to send representatives.

Seldom does history offer us a chance to see such detailed instructions for those carrying out a regime of terror. The tips on hostage-taking are in the volume of the manual called *Practical Questions,* which was compiled by an editorial committee of about thirty people. One member — he worked on the book during a two-year period following his stint as the head-collecting station chief at Stanley Falls — was Léon Rom.

Hostage-taking set the Congo apart from most other forced-labor regimes. But in other ways it resembled them. As would be true decades later of the Soviet gulag, another slave labor system for harvesting raw materials, the Congo operated by quotas. In Siberia the quotas concerned cubic meters of timber cut or tons of gold ore mined by prisoners each day; in the Congo the quota was for kilos of rubber. In the A.B.I.R. concession company's rich territory just below the Congo River's great half-circle bend, for example, the normal quota assigned to each village was three to four kilos of dried rubber per adult male per fortnight — which essentially meant full-time labor for those men. Elsewhere, quotas were higher and might be raised as time went on. An official in the Mongala River basin in the far north, controlled by another concession company, the Société Anversoise du Commerce au Congo, estimated that to fill their quota, rubber gatherers had to spend twenty-four days a month in the forest, where they built crude cages to sleep in for protection — not always successful — against leopards.

To get at parts of the vine high off the ground, men frantic to get every possible drop of rubber would sometimes tear down the whole vine, slice it into sections, and squeeze the rubber out. Although the Congo state issued strict orders against killing the vines this way, it also applied the *chicotte* to men who didn't bring in enough rubber. The *chicotte* prevailed. One witness saw Africans who had to dig up roots in order to find enough rubber to meet their quotas.

The entire system was militarized. Force Publique garrisons were scattered everywhere, often supplying their firepower to the companies under contract. In addition, each company had its own militia force, euphemistically called "sentries." In military matters as in almost everything else, the companies operated as an extension of the Congo state, and when hostages had to be taken or a rebellious village subdued, company sentries and Force Publique soldiers often took to the field together.

Wherever rubber vines grew, the population was tightly controlled. Usually you had to get a permit from the state or company agent in order to visit a friend or relative in another village. In some areas, you were required to wear a numbered metal disk, attached to a cord around your neck, so that company agents could keep track of whether you had met your quota. Huge numbers of Africans were conscripted into this labor army: in 1906, the books of A.B.I.R. alone, responsible for only a small fraction of the Congo state's rubber production, listed forty-seven thousand rubber gatherers.

All along the rivers, columns of exhausted men, carrying baskets of lumpy gray rubber on their heads, sometimes walked twenty miles or more to assemble near the houses of European agents, who sat on their verandas and weighed the loads of rubber. At one collection point, a missionary counted four hundred men with baskets. After the sap was turned in, it was formed into rough slabs, each the size of a small suitcase, and left to dry in the sun. Then it was shipped downriver, on a barge or scow towed by a steamboat, the first stage of the long journey to Europe.

The state and the companies generally paid villagers for their rubber with a piece of cloth, beads, a few spoonfuls of salt, or a knife. These cost next to nothing, and the knives were essential tools for gathering more rubber. On at least one occasion, a chief who forced his people to gather rubber was paid in human beings. A legal dispute between two white officials near Stanley Falls put the following exchange on record in 1901. The witness being questioned was Liamba, chief of a village named Malinda:

> *Question:* Did M. Hottiaux [a company official] ever give you living women or children?
> *Answer:* Yes, he gave me six women and two men.
> *Question:* What for?
> *Answer:* In payment for rubber which I brought into the station, telling me I could eat them, or kill them, or use them as slaves — as I liked.

The rain forest bordering the Kasai River was rich in rubber, and William Sheppard and the other American Presbyterians there found themselves in the midst of a cataclysm. The Kasai was also the scene of some of the strongest resistance to Leopold's rule. Armed men of a chief allied with the regime rampaged through the region where Sheppard worked, plundering and burning more than a dozen villages. Floods of desperate refugees sought help at Sheppard's mission station.

In 1899 the reluctant Sheppard was ordered by his superiors to travel into the bush, at some risk to himself, to investigate the source of the fighting. There he found bloodstained ground, destroyed villages, and many bodies; the air was thick with the stench of rotting flesh. On the day he reached the marauders' camp, his eye was caught by a large number of objects being smoked. The chief "conducted us to a framework of sticks, under which was burning a slow fire, and there they were, the right hands, I counted them, 81 in all." The chief told Sheppard, "See! Here is our evidence. I always have to cut off the right hands of those we kill in order to show the State how many we have killed." He proudly showed

Sheppard some of the bodies the hands had come from. The smoking preserved the hands in the hot, moist climate, for it might be days or weeks before the chief could display them to the proper official and receive credit for his kills.

Sheppard had stumbled on one of the most grisly aspects of Leopold's rubber system. Like the hostage-taking, the severing of hands was deliberate policy, as even high officials would later admit. "During my time in the Congo I was the first commissioner of the Equator district," recalled Charles Lemaire after his retirement. "As soon as it was a question of rubber, I wrote to the government, 'To gather rubber in the district . . . one must cut off hands, noses and ears.'"

If a village refused to submit to the rubber regime, state or company troops or their allies sometimes shot everyone in sight, so that nearby villages would get the message. But on such occasions some European officers were mistrustful. For each cartridge issued to their soldiers they demanded proof that the bullet had been used to kill someone, not "wasted" in hunting or, worse yet, saved for possible use in a mutiny. The standard proof was the right hand from a corpse. Or occasionally not from a corpse. "Sometimes," said one officer to a missionary, soldiers "shot a cartridge at an animal in hunting; they then cut off a hand from a living man." In some military units there was even a "keeper of the hands"; his job was the smoking.

Sheppard was not the first foreign witness to see severed hands in the Congo, nor would he be the last. But the articles he wrote for missionary magazines about his grisly find were reprinted and quoted widely, both in Europe and the United States, and it is partly due to him that people overseas began to associate the Congo with severed hands. A half-dozen years after Sheppard's stark discovery, while attacking the expensive public works Leopold was building with his Congo profits, the socialist leader Émile Vandervelde would speak in the Belgian Parliament of "monumental arches which one will someday call the Arches of the Severed Hands." William Sheppard's outspokenness would eventually bring down the wrath of the authorities and one day Vandervelde, an attorney, would find himself defending Sheppard in a Congo courtroom. But that is getting ahead of our story.

As the rubber terror spread throughout the rain forest, it branded people with memories that remained raw for the rest of their lives. A Catholic priest who recorded oral histories half a century later quotes a man, Tswambe, speaking of a particularly hated state official named Léon

Fiévez, who terrorized a district along the river three hundred miles north of Stanley Pool:

> All the blacks saw this man as the Devil of the Equator. . . . From all the bodies killed in the field, you had to cut off the hands. He wanted to see the number of hands cut off by each soldier, who had to bring them in baskets. . . . A village which refused to provide rubber would be completely swept clean. As a young man, I saw [Fiévez's] soldier Molili, then guarding the village of Boyeka, take a big net, put ten arrested natives in it, attach big stones to the net, and make it tumble into the river. . . . Rubber caused these torments; that's why we no longer want to hear its name spoken. Soldiers made young men kill or rape their own mothers and sisters.

A Force Publique officer who passed through Fiévez's post in 1894 quotes Fiévez himself describing what he did when the surrounding villages failed to supply his troops with the fish and manioc he had demanded: "I made war against them. One example was enough: a hundred heads cut off, and there have been plenty of supplies at the station ever since. My goal is ultimately humanitarian. I killed a hundred people . . . but that allowed five hundred others to live."

With "humanitarian" ground rules that included cutting off hands and heads, sadists like Fiévez had a field day. The station chief at M'Bima used his revolver to shoot holes in Africans' ear lobes. Raoul de Premorel, an agent working along the Kasai River, enjoyed giving large doses of castor oil to people he considered malingerers. When villagers, in a desperate attempt to meet the weight quota, turned in rubber mixed with dirt or pebbles to the agent Albéric Detiège, he made them eat it. When two porters failed to use a designated latrine, a district commissioner, Jean Verdussen, ordered them paraded in front of troops, their faces rubbed with excrement.

As news of the white man's soldiers and their baskets of severed hands spread through the Congo, a myth gained credence with Africans that was a curious reversal of the white obsession with black cannibalism. The cans of corned beef seen in white men's houses, it was said, did not contain meat from the animals shown on the label; they contained chopped-up hands.

A SECRET SOCIETY
OF MURDERERS

O NCE WHEN Leopold and Kaiser Wilhelm II of Germany were watching a parade in Berlin, Leopold, grumbling about the erosion of royal authority, remarked to the kaiser, "There is really nothing left for us kings except money!" Rubber would soon bring Leopold money beyond imagining, but the Congo alone was never enough to satisfy him. Fantasizing an empire that would encompass the two legendary rivers of Africa, the Congo and the Nile, he imagined linking the rivers by a great railway, and in the early 1890s dispatched expeditions northeast from the Congo toward the Nile valley. One of these claimed the ancient copper mines of Bahr-el-Ghazal, taking care to claim the mines for Leopold personally while committing the Congo state to provide military protection.

The French finally blocked the king from further moves toward the Nile, but he was already dreaming of new colonies elsewhere. "I would like to make out of our little Belgium, with its six million people, the capital of an immense empire," he said. "The Netherlands, Spain, Portugal, are in a state of decadence and their colonies will one day or another come on to the market." He asked Prime Minister William Gladstone of England about the possibility of leasing Uganda.

Leopold was quick to embellish his imperial schemes with any humanitarian sentiment in the air. In 1896, he proposed to another surprised British prime minister, Lord Salisbury, that a Sudanese army under Congo state officers be used "for the purpose of invading and occupying

Armenia and so putting a stop to the massacres [of Armenians by the Turks] which were moving Europe so deeply." (Queen Victoria thought her cousin Leopold was becoming delusional.) When there was a crisis in Crete, he suggested that Congolese troops help restore order. After the United States won the Spanish-American War, he proposed that a corporation lease some of Spain's remaining territories, such as the Canary Islands in the Atlantic or the Carolines in the South Pacific. The corporation, he suggested, could be registered in a "neutral" state, such as, for example, the État Indépendant du Congo.

None of these dreams distracted Leopold from managing his main source of income. He kept the Congo's growing profitability as secret as possible, however, lest it stir up demands that he pay back the Belgian government's big loan. For as long as Leopold could get away with it, the Congo state did not publish a budget. When at last it did so, it presented revenue figures that grossly understated the state's real profits.

One advantage of controlling your own country is that you can issue bonds. This eventually was to become a source of revenue for Leopold almost equal to that of rubber. All told, the king issued bonds worth more than a hundred million francs, or roughly half a billion of today's dollars. Some bonds he sold; some he gave to favorites; some he kept for his personal portfolio; some he used in lieu of cash to pay for public works projects in Belgium. Since the bonds were for terms as long as ninety-nine years, Leopold knew that paying back the principal would be somebody else's problem. Supposedly the bond money was for development in the Congo, but little of it was ever spent there.

Leopold much preferred to spend it, and his Congo rubber profits, in Europe. For such a shrewd and ambitious man, he was notably unimaginative in his tastes, and used his vast new fortune in ways that would earn him a place less in the history books than in the guidebooks. A string of monuments, new palace wings, museums, and pavilions began going up all over Belgium. At his favorite seaside resort, Ostend, Leopold poured millions of francs into a promenade, several parks, and an elaborately turreted gallery (decorated with eighty-five thousand geraniums for its opening) for the racetrack he frequented. Rubber earnings also financed a golf course at nearby Klemskerke, a royal chalet at Raversijde, and endless renovations and the enlargement of the château of Laeken. Many of these riches Leopold officially gave to his country with much fanfare as a Royal Gift, although he continued to live in the castles and palaces in the same manner as he always had. His real purposes in bestowing the Royal Gift were to have the nation pay for the upkeep of these properties and to keep them out of the hands of his three daughters, to whom Belgian law required that he leave his personal possessions.

In 1895, Leopold turned sixty, and as he grew older he became a hypochondriac. Any aide who coughed risked banishment for several days. Always fearful of getting a cold, he wore a waterproof bag around his beard when he went outside in wet weather or swam in the sea. He demanded that the palace tablecloths be boiled daily to kill germs.

When not traveling, he lived mostly at Laeken. He rose early, had a cold shower, trimmed his great beard, received a massage, read the early morning mail, and ate a huge breakfast — a half-dozen poached eggs, a stack of toast, and an entire jar of marmalade. Then he spent much of the day walking around his beloved gardens and greenhouses, often reading mail and dictating answers while on the move; his secretaries had to learn to write while walking. Lunch lasted precisely half an hour; the king read newspapers and letters while eating and sometimes scribbled instructions in the margins of letters in nearly illegible handwriting that his staff spent anxious hours each day deciphering. Other family members at the table were expected to remain silent.

In the afternoon, he was driven to the Royal Palace in downtown Brussels to meet officials and visitors, then back to Laeken for the evening meal. The high point of his day was the arrival of the *Times of London*. Each afternoon a carefully wrapped copy of that morning's paper was tossed from the Ostend-Basel express as the train passed the private railway station, bearing the royal coat of arms, at Laeken. A footman ironed the paper — germs again — and the king read it in bed at night. (When the *Times* later joined his chorus of critics, Leopold angrily announced that he was stopping his subscription. But he secretly sent his valet to the Brussels railway station each day to buy him a copy.)

Perhaps Leopold liked the *Times* because it was a newspaper written not for a small country but for a powerful one. In any case, his lust for colonies still extended to all corners of the world. In 1897, he started to invest Congo state profits in a railway in China, eventually making big money on the deal. He saw that country as he had seen the "magnificent African cake," a feast to be consumed, and he was as ready as ever to invite himself to the table. Of the route he hoped to get for his railway line he said, "This is the spine of China; if they give it to me I'll also take some cutlets." He tried to arrange an exchange — Chinese laborers for the Congo; Congolese soldiers for China — that would give him a military foot in the door, like the other Western powers now maneuvering in the Far East. He bought several small parcels of land in China in the name of the État Indépendant du Congo. When Leopold sent a Congo state delegation — all Belgians, of course — for negotiations, the Chinese viceroy Li Hung-Chang feigned surprise: "Am I right in thinking that Africans are black?"

Back in the Congo, the rubber boom gave added urgency to the territory's major construction job: the narrow-gauge railway from Matadi to Stanley Pool, around the big rapids. This project required up to sixty thousand workers at one time. Although the line was only 241 miles long, and little more than half the width of American standard-gauge tracks, climate, disease, and terrain made it one of the more daunting railway construction projects in history. It took three years to build just the first fourteen miles. An early surveyor of this forbidding stretch of land described it as "a piling up of enormous stones which, in certain places, seem to have been thrown on top of each other by the hands of giants." The whole route required ninety-nine metal bridges, totaling more than twelve miles in length.

Construction workers were brought in from British and French territories in West Africa, from Hong Kong and Macao, and from the British West Indies. Leopold remained fascinated with the idea of using Chinese workers in the Congo. "What would it cost," he wrote to an aide, "to establish five big Chinese villages in the Congo? One in the North, another in the Northeast, one in the East, another in the South, and one between Matadi and Leopoldville. Two thousand Chinese to mark our frontiers, what would it cost?" The idea of five villages vanished, but Leopold's dream did cost the lives of many of the 540 Chinese brought to work on the railway in 1892. Three hundred of them died on the job or fled into the bush. Most of the latter were never seen again, although several were later found more than five hundred miles in the interior. They had walked toward the rising sun, trying to get to Africa's east coast and then home.

Several hundred laborers from the Caribbean island of Barbados had evidently been told they were being recruited for somewhere else; when their ship tied up at Boma in September 1892 and they realized they were in the Congo, they rebelled in fury. Soldiers fired at them, killing two and wounding many more; the rest were sent on to the railhead at Matadi the same day and put to work.

The railway was a modest engineering success and a major human disaster. Men succumbed to accidents, dysentery, smallpox, beriberi, and malaria, all exacerbated by bad food and relentless floggings by the two-hundred-man railway militia force. Engines ran off tracks; freight cars full of dynamite exploded, blowing to bits workers, black and white. Sometimes there were no shelters for the people to sleep in, and recalcitrant laborers were led to work in chains. The European construction foremen and engineers could cancel their contracts and go home, and a steady flow did so. The black and Asian workers could not. When bugles sounded in the morning, crowds of angry laborers laid at the feet of European supervisors the bodies of their comrades who had died during the night.

In a metaphor that is echoed elsewhere in Africa, local legend along the railway line has it that each tie cost one African life and each telegraph pole one European life. Even in the rosy official figures, the railway death toll was 132 whites and 1800 nonwhites. Some estimates, however, place the nonwhite toll close to 1800 a year in the first two years, which were the worst. Cemeteries dotted the rail line. Again and again workers tried to escape; three hundred men from Sierra Leone, brandishing hammers, shovels, and pickaxes, stormed the port of Matadi and tried to commandeer a ship at the dock to take them home. Club-wielding guards — themselves recruited from Zanzibar — forced them back. Other workers went on strike or fled to nearby Portuguese territory.

In 1898, eight years after construction started, the first short, stumpy steam engine, bedecked with flags, pulled two railway cars all the way up the narrow-gauge track from Matadi to Stanley Pool. A large tent decorated with flowers awaited its arrival; state officials, military men, officers of the railway, and a bishop all banqueted and drank to Leopold's health in champagne. The assembled VIPs ceremonially bolted the last rail, a cannon fired a twenty-one-gun salute, and all the steamboats in Stanley Pool blew their whistles. Officials erected a monument on the old caravan route that the rail line had replaced: three life-size metal figures of porters — one carrying a large box on his head, two collapsed in exhaustion beside him. The inscription read: THE RAILWAY FREED THEM FROM PORTERAGE. It said nothing about who made them become porters in the first place.

Although it included hairpin turns and steep grades that stretched a one-way trip to two days, the railway added enormously to the state's power and wealth. The more than eleven million pounds of rubber a year the Congo was producing by the turn of the century could now reach the sea from the steamboat docks of Stanley Pool without being carried for three weeks on men's heads. Rail cars going the other direction moved steamboats around the rapids in far larger pieces than porters could carry. Leopoldville quickly became the busiest river port in central Africa, home to steamers of up to five hundred tons. One sidewheeler on the river, the sixty-ton *Ville de Paris,* had begun life as an excursion boat on the Seine.

Except for those employed by the state or on projects like the railway, Leopold was wary of foreigners in the Congo. He was, however, saddled with one group of them, several hundred foreign Protestant missionaries like William Sheppard and his colleagues. Almost all had come from England, the United States, or Sweden, countries where Leopold hoped to curry favor. The missionaries had come to the Congo eager to evangelize, to fight polygamy, and to impart to Africans a Victorian sense of sin.* Before long, however, the rubber terror meant that missionaries had trouble finding bodies to clothe or souls to save. Frightened villagers would disappear into the jungle for weeks when they saw the smoke of an approaching steamboat on the horizon. One British missionary was asked repeatedly by Africans, "Has the Savior you tell us of any power to save us from the rubber trouble?" Unexpectedly, certainly without intending to take on such a role, the missionaries found themselves acting as observers on a battlefield, and Sheppard was by no means the only one who bore witness. In 1894, a Swedish missionary recorded a despairing Congolese song:

> *We are tired of living under this tyranny.*
> *We cannot endure that our women and children are taken away*
> *And dealt with by the white savages.*
> *We shall make war. . . .*

---

* A high state official visiting the Congo River town of Upoto recorded in astonishment in his diary that a British missionary wanted him to issue "a decree making the natives wear clothes(!?)."

We know that we shall die, but we want to die.
We want to die.

Due to the missionaries, from the mid-1890s on Leopold had to deal
with scattered protests, like Sheppard's articles, about severed hands and
slaughtered Africans. But the critics at first captured little attention, for
they were not as skilled at public relations as the king, who deployed his
formidable charm to neutralize them.

As a start, he encouraged mission society officials to talk with him
directly, personally urging one French clergyman to do this "instead of
having recourse to the press, which is always unpleasant *(toujours désagréable)*." Then he artfully used both promise and threat. While cultivat-
ing their leaders, he made sure to remind the mission societies of the
Congo state's ability to impose taxes or deny permission to build new
missions. The Southern Presbyterian mission where Sheppard worked
had endless trouble getting new land it wanted to build on.

A Swedish Baptist missionary, E. V. Sjöblom, was perhaps Leopold's
most forceful critic in the late 1890s, speaking to all who would listen and
publishing a detailed attack on the Congo's rubber terror in the Swedish
press in 1896, an attack that was picked up by newspapers in other
countries. At a public meeting in London the following year, Sjöblom
told how African Force Publique soldiers were rewarded for the number
of hands they collected. "[An] agent told me that he had himself seen a
State officer at one of the outposts pay a certain number of brass rods
(local currency) to the soldiers for a number of hands they had brought.
One of the soldiers told me . . . 'The Commissioner has promised us if
we have plenty of hands he will shorten our service. I have brought in
plenty of hands already, and I expect my time of service will soon be
finished.'" State officials threatened Sjöblom in the Congo itself and
quickly counterattacked in the Belgian and British press.

Another knowledgeable opponent of Leopold's was H. R. Fox
Bourne, secretary of the Aborigines Protection Society, a group that had
grown considerably wiser since it had elected Leopold its honorary president a decade earlier. The king himself reportedly paid a visit to the office
of the *Times* in London to try to persuade the newspaper not to run Fox
Bourne's articles.

Publicly, however, Leopold took the high road, pronouncing himself
deeply shocked at reports of misdeeds in his domain. Most accusations he
was able to survive with little damage, for they concerned atrocities

committed against Africans. But in 1895 he faced his first real trouble in Europe when a particularly brutal Congo state officer, as one shocked British journalist put it, *"dared to kill an Englishman."*

The victim was actually Irish: Charles Stokes, a colorful, flamboyant trader who had, as the British liked to say, gone native, marrying an African woman. Stokes's ivory trading competed with the lucrative monopoly Leopold was trying to establish in the eastern Congo. He was also accused of selling arms to the Afro-Arabs. A Force Publique expedition went looking for Stokes near the state's eastern border, found him, and hanged him on the spot. The London press thundered its outrage. There was also a wave of protest in Germany, for Stokes's home base was in German East Africa, and the Congo state was supposedly open to German traders. In a vain attempt to dampen the outcry, the Congo government admitted its mistake and made large indemnity payments to the British and German governments. But this was not the end of the matter. One German paper declared that if the Congo had so cavalierly executed a white man, think what it must do to the natives. The European press began paying more attention to news of Congo atrocities.

Leopold had to act. In 1896 he appointed the Commission for the Protection of the Natives: six prominent Congo missionaries, three of them Belgian Catholics, three foreign Protestants. The commission was greeted as a good thing everywhere in Europe, especially in England, where the king was most worried about criticism. "It is wholly to King Leopold's credit that he should have squarely faced the facts of the situation," said the *Manchester Guardian.*

Few people noticed that none of the commission members was based in any of the prime rubber areas where the atrocity reports were coming from; that the commissioners were scattered over more than a thousand miles; that the king had provided no money for them to travel to meetings; that one of the British members had previously advised his fellow missionaries against publishing any atrocity stories; that another had surveyed the Congo-Angola frontier for Leopold; and that the commission had no power whatever except to "inform" the Congo state authorities about abuses.

The commission met only twice, and each time, because of distance and expense, only three of the six members managed to attend. But for Leopold, the move was a public relations coup, and he cemented his triumph with visits to England, Germany, and Sweden in the summer of 1897. For the next few years Britons were distracted by the Boer War, and attacks on Leopold almost completely disappeared from the European press. The king's critics kept up sporadic fire, but no one seemed to heed them. They despaired of attracting much attention again.

Had there been approval ratings in Europe at the time, the closing years of the century would have found Leopold at his peak of favor, both abroad and at home. In Belgium, colonial chauvinism now began to bubble up in verse:

> Sur les plages où les entraîne
> La voix d'un sage Souverain,
> Nos soldats vont l'âme sereine,
> Affrontant un climat d'airain,
> De l'Africain briser la chaîne
> En domptant l'Arabe inhumain

> (On the beaches where a wise Sovereign's voice draws them,
> Our soldiers, hearts serene, brave the brazen climate
> To break the African's chain, and subdue the cruel Arab)

However, the sovereign's voice pushed rather than drew his soldiers to the beachheads, for, although the Congo was the dominating passion of his life, Leopold never went there.

Why should he have done so? The Congo in Leopold's mind was not the one of starving porters, raped hostages, emaciated rubber slaves, and severed hands. It was the empire of his dreams, with gigantic trees, exotic animals, and inhabitants grateful for his wise rule. Instead of going there, Leopold brought the Congo — *that* Congo, the theatrical production of his imagination — to himself. Red mahogany from it paneled the bedroom of his private railway car, animals from it appeared in Belgian zoos, and to the array of huge greenhouses at Laeken the king added a Congo Greenhouse (still full of palm trees today), topped with four glass cupolas and an octagonal dome bearing the star emblem of his private state.

From that serene, picturesque Congo stage setting of his fantasy, Leopold brought to himself even its people. In 1897, when a world's fair took place in Brussels, the most talked-about exhibit was on the outskirts of the city, at Tervuren. More than a million visitors came to see this celebration of the Congo. Items on display ranged from that great instrument of civilization so praised by Stanley (who twice visited the fair), the Maxim gun, to a large set of linen tapestries portraying Barbarism and

Civilization, Fetishism and Christianity, Polygamy and Family Life, Slavery and Freedom. The most extraordinary tableau, however, was a living one: 267 black men, women, and children imported from the Congo.*

With great fanfare they were brought by train to Brussels's Gare du Nord and then marched across the center of the city to take the tram for Tervuren. There, in a park, they were installed in three specially constructed villages: a river village, a forest village, and a "civilized" village. A pair of Pygmies rounded out the show. The "uncivilized" Africans of the first two villages used tools, drums, and cooking pots brought from home. They danced and paddled their dugout canoes around a pond. During the day they were on exhibit in "authentic" bamboo African huts with overhanging thatched roofs. European men hoping to see the fabled bare breasts of Africa went away disappointed, however, for the women were made to wear cotton dressing gowns while at the fair. Clothing, a local magazine observed, was, after all, "the first sign of civilization."

Leopold himself came to see the Congolese, his dream made flesh, and was introduced to one of their chiefs. Told that some of the Africans were suffering from indigestion because of snacks and candy given them by the public, he ordered up the equivalent of a don't-feed-the-animals sign. The placard said: THE BLACKS ARE FED BY THE ORGANIZING COMMITTEE. They were fed — and slept — in the royal stables.

The local press titillated its readers by speculating about whether the "uncivilized" Africans were dangerous. A reporter approached a circle of

---

* These were not the only indigenous people placed on exhibit at world's fairs and elsewhere around the turn of the century. Perhaps the most appalling case was that of Ota Benga, a Pygmy from the Congo, who was displayed in the monkey house of New York's Bronx Zoo in September 1906. An orangutan shared his space. Visitors ogled his teeth — filed, newspaper articles hinted, for devouring human flesh. To further this impression, zookeepers left a few bones scattered on the floor around him. A poem published in the *New York Times* declared that Ota Benga had been brought

> From his native land of darkness,
>   To the country of the free,
> In the interest of science
>   And of broad humanity

The promoter who staged this exhibit was a former Presbyterian missionary who abandoned his preaching for several business ventures. A delegation of black ministers finally rescued Ota Benga from the zoo. He remained in the United States and committed suicide ten years later.

them. "At the center, sitting on a log, was the chief, motionless and sacrosanct. The voice of a singer was first heard alone; then a chorus picked up a refrain, accompanied by hand claps and the banging of sticks on metal objects, and by a swaying motion of these crouching bodies. And what were the soloist and chorus singing about? The magnificent deeds of [Force Publique Captain Hubert] Lothaire, the great warrior." All was well.

The Africans of the "civilized" village included ninety Force Publique soldiers, some of whom made up a military band. The soldiers marched, the band played, and, near the end of their stay were guests at a banquet. A black sergeant rose and proposed a toast to King Leopold II. When the Africans sailed for home, a newspaper rhapsodized, "The soul of Belgium follows them, and, like the shield of Jupiter, protects them. May we always thus show the world an example of humanity!"

The ship that took the Congolese back to their homeland probably returned to Belgium with a cargo of rubber, for the riches of the Congo were now flowing to Europe on a regular schedule. Every few weeks, a fine new steamer, equipped with electric lights and refrigerators, arrived at Antwerp filled with rubber, ivory, and other products. The vessels belonged to a subsidiary of Elder Dempster, a Liverpool-based shipping line whose steamers had long plied the west coast of Africa. The firm had the contract for carrying all cargo to and from the Congo. For anybody curious about the Congo state, few jobs in Europe provided a better vantage point than a position with Elder Dempster. It was as if, in 1942 or 1943, somebody who began to wonder what was happening to the Jews had taken a job inside the headquarters of the Nazi railway system.

Elder Dempster needed someone to go to Belgium frequently to supervise the arrival and departure of ships on the Congo run. The company gave this task to a bright, hardworking young man on its staff, Edmund Dene Morel. Morel, then in his mid-twenties, was, conveniently, bilingual. His mother was English; his father had been a low-ranking French civil servant who died young, leaving no pension for his widow and small son. After a childhood on the edge of poverty, both in England and France, Morel had left school at fifteen to work in Paris to support his ailing mother. A few years later, he took a position as a clerk in Liverpool for Elder Dempster.

Unable at first to adequately support his mother and himself on his meager clerk's salary, the young Morel had also given French lessons for two shillings and sixpence an hour. Then he found a more satisfying sideline: writing free-lance articles on African trade issues for publications like the *Shipping Telegraph* and the *Liverpool Journal of Commerce*. These pieces reflected a businessman's view: they celebrated increases in cotton production and shipping tonnage and seldom questioned the prevailing dogmas of the day. Some praised Leopold's regime. "A great future is in store for the Congo," Morel wrote in one, "and . . . those vast territories secured to their country by the foresight of King Leopold II will one day prove a magnificent field for [Belgian] enterprise."

It was with such enthusiasm that, in the late 1890s, Morel began traveling back and forth across the English Channel as his company's liaison with officials of the Congo state. Here is how he later described the scene he saw once or twice a month:

> The quay at Antwerp; a steamer moored alongside; the musical chimes ringing from the old cathedral spire; the sound of the *Brabançonne* — the Belgian national anthem. On the quay and on the steamer's decks, a jostling, motley crowd. Military uniforms, the flutter of women's dresses. Ship's officers gliding to and fro. The hatches battening down. Steam getting up. Surrounded by groups of relatives or boon companions, passengers bound Congowards. Men, of whose fitness for residing and governing in tropical Africa even a novice would have doubts. Young mostly, and mostly of a poor type, undersized, pallid, wastrels. Some shaken with sobs; others stumbling in semi-intoxication. Many wearing broad tropical felts [hats] and with guns slung across their shoulders, proud possessors for the first time in their lives of either. Here and there an older bronzed individual — one who has obviously been through all this before. The faces of these, distinctly not good to look upon; scarred with brutality, with cruel and lustful eyes; faces from which one turns with an involuntary shudder of repulsion.

As Elder Dempster representative in Belgium, Morel dealt not just with business at the wharf, but with Leopold's top Congo executives. He later recalled how an episode in the office of the highest-ranking of them awakened his suspicions:

A room whose windows look out upon the back of the Royal Palace at Brussels. A gloomy room, thick-carpeted, heavy curtained: a room of oppressive shadows. In its centre a man, seated at a desk. A man thin to emaciation, with narrow, stooping shoulders; with receding forehead, high curved nose, large ears set far back: lantern jawed, cold eyed. A face in repose passively inhuman, bloodless, petrified, all sharp bones and gaunt cavities: the face of the then "Secretary of State" for the Congo Free State. . . . The physiognomy of the Secretary of State undergoes a remarkable and disconcerting transformation. It becomes affected by a sort of involuntary twitching. . . . It is the face of another man that looks at us. The mask of an impeccable officialdom peels off like a powdered glove from the hand. He leans forward and in rapid staccato accents complains that confidential information as to the last outward-bound steamer's cargo has been divulged to the Press. . . . The paragraph is pointed out. It looks innocent enough, being a list of the principal articles on board. But that list contains an enumeration of the cases of ball cartridges [rifle bullets], the cases of rifles and the boxes of percussion-cap guns [military muskets]. . . . That is the fault. That is the lapse from professional secrecy. As the enormity of the indiscretion is denounced, the speaker rises, the cadaverous cheeks flush, the voice trembles . . . the long bony hands saw the air. He will hear no excuses; allow no interruption. Again and again he repeats the words *secret professionnel* with passionate emphasis. His gestures are violent. . . . The youngest individual present leaves the room wondering why so large a quantity of material of war is required . . . why its export should be kept secret and why the Congo Government should be so greatly troubled at the "indiscretion."

At the dockside at Antwerp, Morel saw what the Elder Dempster ships were carrying. But he soon noticed that the records he carefully compiled for his employer did not conform with the trade statistics that the État Indépendant du Congo announced to the public. As he studied the discrepancies between the two sets of figures, he began to uncover an elaborate skein of fraud. Three discoveries shocked him:

The first was that the arms cargo sent to the Congo whose disclosure had so upset the secretary of state was not an exception; it was the rule:

"Elder Dempster steamers employed in the Congo trade had been regularly shipping for the past few years prodigious quantities of ball cartridge and thousands of rifles and cap-guns either consigned to the State itself or to sundry Belgian 'trading' Companies. . . . To what usage was this armament put?"

Morel's second discovery was that somebody was skimming handsome profits off the top. To the tune of tens of millions of today's dollars, "the amount of rubber and ivory brought home from the Congo in the Elder Dempster ships . . . greatly exceeded the amounts indicated in the Congo Government's returns. . . . Into whose pocket did the unavowed surplus go?"

His final discovery lay starkly before him on the docks, as he watched the ships being loaded and unloaded, and it was confirmed in Elder Dempster's records. There he found the most ominous message of all: "Of the imports going into the Congo something like 80% consisted of articles which were remote from trade purposes. Yet, the Congo was exporting increasing quantities of rubber and ivory for which, on the face of the import statistics, the natives were getting nothing or next to nothing. How, then, was this rubber and ivory being acquired? Certainly not by commercial dealing. Nothing was going in to pay for what was coming out."

Morel was right. We now know that the value of the rubber, ivory, and other riches coming to Europe each year on the Elder Dempster ships was roughly five times that of goods being shipped to the Congo that were destined for Africans. In return for the rubber and ivory, Morel knew, it was not possible that the Congo's Africans were being paid in money — which he knew they were not allowed to use — or in goods that came from elsewhere, for Elder Dempster had the cargo monopoly. Clearly, they were not being paid at all.

Later in life, E. D. Morel was to become good friends with Sir Arthur Conan Doyle, the creator of Sherlock Holmes. But the young Morel made a deduction more far-reaching than anything accomplished by Holmes. From what he saw at the wharf in Antwerp, and from studying his company's records in Liverpool, he deduced the existence — on another continent, thousands of miles away — of slavery.

"These figures told their own story. . . . Forced labour of a terrible and continuous kind could alone explain such unheard-of profits . . . forced labour in which the Congo Government was the immediate beneficiary; forced labour directed by the closest associates of the King himself. . . . I was giddy and appalled at the cumulative significance of my discoveries. It must be bad enough to stumble upon a murder. I had stumbled upon a secret society of murderers with a King for a croniman."

With this brilliant flash of recognition by an obscure shipping-company official, King Leopold II acquired his most formidable enemy.

II

A KING
AT BAY

12

DAVID AND GOLIATH

A T THE TIME E. D. Morel made his discoveries, most people in
Europe and the United States knew surprisingly little about
Leopold's apparatus of exploitation. Few Europeans who came home
from the Congo said much in public about the bloodshed they had
participated in. Except for George Washington Williams, almost ten years
earlier, journalists who went to the Congo usually copied Stanley in
celebrating the king's regime. (Twenty-six of them traveled there to marvel over the opening of the railway in 1898, for instance.) The foreign
missionaries, who had seen so many atrocities, had little media savvy or
political clout. Leopold's critics from British humanitarian societies were
easily dismissed by the public as relics of past battles like Abolitionism and
as people who were always upset about something in some obscure
corner of the world.

Morel would change all this. Until now, none of Leopold's opponents had had access to the facts and figures from the Congo administration in Europe that Morel had gleaned from his insider's position at Elder
Dempster. And until now none, except the prematurely dead Williams,
had had another quality Morel would soon exhibit: a rare skill at publiciz-
ing his message.

Having made his dramatic discoveries, Morel refused to remain quiet.
First, he confronted his boss, Sir Alfred Jones, head of the Elder Dempster
line, president of the Liverpool Chamber of Commerce — and honorary
consul in Liverpool of the Congo state. "He was not the easiest of men to
approach. He disliked having unpleasant facts brought to his notice. . . .

The next day he left for Brussels. Upon his return he preserved silence, as far as I was concerned, and I noted a marked coldness in his manner. . . . He told me he had seen the King and the King had promised him that reforms would be carried out, and that the Belgians were doing great things and must have time to set their African house in order."

Morel's employers were at great risk. If he made his information public and angered Leopold, the company could lose the lucrative Congo shipping contract. Now company officers did not know how to cope with this upstart junior functionary who was telling them that he had discovered something terrible about their best customer — and, worse, was demanding that they do something about it.

In Belgium, Morel found, abruptly "the atmosphere changed and in a hundred subtle ways it was intimated to me that my presence was unwelcome." He was cold-shouldered at Elder Dempster headquarters in Liverpool; then the company tried to silence him. It offered him a higher salary and a promotion to a post in some other country. When that didn't work, Jones offered him £200 a year to be an hour-a-day consultant, a thinly veiled attempt to buy him off. Morel again refused. In 1901, he quit his job and took up his pen full-time, filled with "determination to do my best to expose and destroy what I then knew to be a legalized infamy . . . accompanied by unimaginable barbarities and responsible for a vast destruction of human life."

Morel knew he had taken a momentous step. "I had launched the boat," he wrote, "and there could be no turning back." He was twenty-eight years old.

From Morel's hand there now flowed a torrent of attacks on Leopold. At first he went to work for a British newspaper dealing with Africa, but its editor limited what he could say about the Congo. So in 1903, with funding from various sources, including John Holt, a Liverpool businessman known for his integrity who was something of a mentor to Morel, he started his own publication. The *West African Mail,* "An Illustrated Weekly Journal Founded to Meet the Rapidly Growing Interest in West & Central African Questions," would be a forum where no one could censor him.

Morel was all of a piece: his thick handlebar mustache and tall, barrel-chested frame exuded forcefulness; his dark eyes blazed with indignation. The millions of words that would flow from his pen over the remainder of his life came in a handwriting that raced across the page in bold, forward-slanting lines, flattened by speed, as if they had no time to spare in reaching their destination.

In certain ways Morel is harder to fathom than some of the other figures of the Congo story. For example, it is easy to see how Stanley's painful poorhouse childhood may have fostered his cruel streak and the drive to place his mark on the world. The origin of the fiery passion for justice that fueled Morel is less evident. He spent his youth in the business world, not in the socialist movement that inspired many turn-of-the-century crusaders. As a young man, he was not active in any political party or social cause. Although he had some Quaker ancestors, he may have discovered them only later in life, for there is no record of his receiving Quaker teachings as a child. Formally, he was an unenthusiastic member of the Church of England, but at heart, like another great firebrand of Quaker ancestry, Thomas Paine, he had little use for any form of organized religion. From his campaign against King Leopold, he had nothing to gain, only a promising career at Elder Dempster to lose. He had a sick mother, a wife, and what would soon be a large family to support. In every way, he seemed an unlikely person to become the leader of a great moral crusade. His prodigious capacity for indignation seems to be something he was born with, as some people are born with great musical talent. After learning what he had in Brussels and Antwerp, he writes, "to have sat still . . . would have been temperamentally impossible."

It was this smoldering sense of outrage that led Morel to become, in short order, the greatest British investigative journalist of his time. Once he determined to find out all he could about the workings of the Congo and to reveal it to the world, he produced a huge, albeit sometimes repetitive, body of work on the subject: three full books and portions of two others, hundreds of articles for almost all the major British newspapers, plus many written in French for papers in France and Belgium, hundreds of letters to the editor, and several dozen pamphlets (he turned out six in one six-month stretch, one of them in French). He did all this while continuing to edit the *West African Mail* and to write much of it. Besides the articles under his byline, many columns by "Africanus" or "An Observer" seem the work of the editor himself. Before long, Morel was also editing a special monthly supplement to the newspaper, devoted solely to exposing injustice in the Congo. And despite the pace of his work, he found time for a hobby, collecting different species of moths.

Morel's writing combined controlled fury with meticulous accuracy.

Every detail in his books came from careful research, the evidence amassed as painstakingly as in a lawyer's brief. Over the years both admirers and enemies have searched his work for factual errors, with scant success. Even today, in almost any account of the rubber system in Leopold's Congo, if you trace statistics and quotations to their sources, many of them prove to have been first printed by Morel.

Although his soon became the most energetic voice in England directed against the Congo atrocities, it was not the only one. A few members of Parliament, especially Sir Charles Dilke, one of the most eloquent proponents of human rights in his day, spoke out strongly. Then there were the humanitarian groups like the Anti-Slavery Society and the Aborigines Protection Society; they preached a Christian humanitarianism, which, though it sounds somewhat paternalistic to our ears today, they applied to denouncing brutalities wherever they occurred, in England's colonies or elsewhere. Morel differed from them not only in his torrential energy but in his fervent belief that the Congo was a case apart, an entire state deliberately and systematically founded on slave labor. The humanitarians, Morel wrote, emphasized "the atrocious nature of the deeds committed, while my endeavor from the first was to show that given certain premises [Leopold's taking as his own the land and all its products] . . . those deeds must *of necessity* take place."

An important influence on Morel was the writer Mary Kingsley, who became a friend just before her death, in 1900. Kingsley's 1897 *Travels in West Africa* is both a high-spirited classic of travel writing and one of the first books by a European that treats Africans as human beings. She saw them not as "savages" in need of civilization, but as people living in coherent societies that were being torn apart by colonialists and missionaries who had no appreciation of African life.

Leopold's decree that "vacant" lands belonged to the state, as Morel came to see it, completely destroyed the traditional systems of communal ownership of land and its products. He had learned from Kingsley that most land in Africa traditionally belonged in common to one village, clan, or tribe. If it was not being used for crops, it was a hunting ground or a source of wood for building, iron for tools and weapons, or other materials.

Besides being theft, the seizure of the land left the Africans nothing to trade with, which was especially upsetting to Morel, who had a passionate faith in free trade. Like Kingsley, he was convinced that only free trade would humanely bring Africa into the modern age. In a way surprisingly conventional for such a firebrand, Morel assumed that what was good for the merchants of Liverpool was good for Africa. His belief is understandable, because several of his Liverpool businessmen friends were Quakers who took their business ethics seriously and who supported him unstintingly.

Morel now plunged ahead with books, speeches, articles, and pamphlets about the Congo. There was no question of his actually traveling there, for Leopold routinely banned unfriendly journalists. But this did not faze him. Once Morel had staked out his position as the best-informed, most outspoken critic of the Congo state, insiders knew that he was the man to come to if they had any revealing documents to leak. And the more he published, the more they leaked. His knack for getting inside information continually enraged Leopold and the men around him. As the king's well-burnished version of the Congo was put on display in world's fairs, greenhouses, and museums, a very different Congo began to be seen in the pages of the *West African Mail*.

When, for example, Leopold's spokesmen indignantly denied that there was any kidnapping of women to force their husbands to gather rubber, Morel reproduced the printed form in French where each agent of the A.B.I.R. concession company had to list "natives under bodily detention during the month of——, 1903." Across the page were columns to be filled in for each hostage: "Name," "Village," "Reason for arrest," "Starting date," "Ending date," "Observations." And there was no doubt why people were being held "under bodily detention"; he also printed an order from A.B.I.R. management instructing agents about the "up-keep and feeding of hostages."

Dissident state or company employees in the Congo could not easily write to Morel directly, for a *cabinet noir*, or censorship office, in Boma monitored their correspondence. But when these men came home, they brought documents. For years, one of Morel's secret sources was Raymond De Grez, a decorated Force Publique veteran, wounded in action several times, who quietly supplied Morel with a stream of inside information from a post in Brussels. Someone in the Belgian head office of a big Congo company — the one that had hired Joseph Conrad as a steamboat captain — apparently passed on to Morel a collection of letters from the company's agents in the Congo. And if any disillusioned Congo veteran came home and gave a newspaper interview, whether in Belgium or Germany, Sweden or Italy, Morel's contacts would send him a clipping, and he made sure that the critical information found its way into the

British press. He even taunted the Congo administration once by printing, in the original French, a long itemized list of confidential memoranda, letters, and other documents that someone had offered to sell him.

His campaign encouraged opposition to Leopold in Belgium, especially among the socialists in Parliament. And when damaging information surfaced in Belgian parliamentary debates, Morel quickly reprinted it for the much larger audience in England. One revealing item he published, for example, was a secret order to Congo state officials in the field about bonuses they would get for men conscripted into the Force Publique: "90 francs for every healthy and vigorous man considered fit for military service, and whose stature exceeds 1 metre 55 centimetres; 65 francs for every youth whose stature is at least 1 metre 35 centimetres; 15 francs per male child. The male children must be at least 1 metre 20 centimetres in height, and must be sufficiently strong to be able to support the fatigues of the road. . . . The bonus will only fall due when the men have been handed over to the headquarters of the various districts." The Congo's acting governor general added a warning to local officials that this order "must under no pretext be removed from your archives. You will convey to your subordinates such explanations as may be necessary in connection with this circular, *verbally.*" Morel gleefully included that warning as well.

From other material cited in Belgian parliamentary debates, Morel quoted a letter that a Force Publique officer, Lieutenant Édouard Tilkens, had written to his commander: "I expect a general uprising. I think I warned you of this, Major. . . . The motive is always the same. The natives are tired of . . . transport work, rubber collecting, furnishing livestock. . . . For three months I have been fighting, with ten days' rest. . . . I have 152 prisoners. For two years I have been making war in this country, always accompanied by forty or fifty *Albinis* [soldiers armed with Albini breech-loading rifles]. Yet I cannot say I have subjugated the people. . . . They prefer to die. . . . What can I do?"

Other vital sources of information were certain British, American, and Swedish missionaries. The Congo state censors couldn't read their letters, because they had their own steamboats and colleagues who could personally carry mail back to Europe. For years the missionaries had been helpless witnesses to *chicotte* whippings, Force Publique raids, burned villages, and the other aspects of rubber slavery in action. Suddenly, here was someone not only eager to publish their testimony, but to put it in the hands of the British Parliament. Morel barraged the missionaries with requests for more information. They gladly complied, and also began sending what turned out to be powerful tools for Morel's campaign: photographs — of devastated villages, severed hands, children with missing hands and feet.

The missionaries provided some of the most horrifying accounts Morel published. An American described seeing Congo state soldiers cut off someone's hand "while the poor heart beat strongly enough to shoot the blood from the cut arteries at a distance of fully four feet." A British Baptist described a Congo state official punishing some men for stealing rubber: "For this he had them tied up right in the sun to stakes for a day and a night. . . . They were naked and without food and water all day, and so great was their agony that their tongues were hanging out."

Sometimes missionaries sent Morel the names of the dead, and these, too, he published, like casualty lists in wartime. Nowhere else, of course, did these names ever appear in print:

```
 1. Bokangu . . . . Chief . . . Killed with blows with butt of gun
 2. Mangundwa . . . " . . . . .    "    "    "    "    "    "    "
 3. Ekunja . . . . . . . " . . . .    "    "    "    "    "    "    "
    . . . . . . . . . . . . . . . . .
21. Ekumba . . . . . Man . . . Shot
22. Monjangu . . . . . " . . . . .    "
23. Gili . . . . . . . Woman . .    "
24. Akaba . . . . . . Boy . . . .    "
```

Morel also exposed the web of deceptions, large and small, continually spun by Leopold and his allies. Little escaped him. For example, the king went to great lengths to cultivate Sir Hugh Gilzean Reid, a prominent British Baptist, newspaper owner, and former member of Parliament. Leopold invited Gilzean Reid to the Royal Palace several times, gave him the Order of Leopold, and made him a Knight Commander of the Order of the Crown. In return, Gilzean Reid led a delegation from the Baptist Missionary Society to Brussels in 1903. There, at a luncheon with the king and other prominent Belgians, the society presented a "memorial of thanks" voicing the hope that "the peoples of the Congo may ever have the advantage of just and upright rule." Morel swiftly pointed out in print that when Gilzean Read passed the news on to the London *Morning*

Post, he rewrote the Baptist message to express to the king the hope that "the peoples of the Congo State may realise increasingly the advantages of your enlightened rule."

Morel's attacks soon drew a response from the Royal Palace. One evening in London, Sir Alfred Jones, Morel's former boss, invited Morel to a dinner party. The two men's relations were, to say the least, strained, but at the meal all was smiles, and, Morel writes, "the wines were choice and copious." After dinner, Jones and the other guests retired, leaving Morel alone with a visiting Antwerp shipping executive named Aerts, who made it clear that he was acting as Leopold's representative.

After one last attempt to convince Morel that the king meant well and that reforms were in the offing, the visitor took, as Morel describes it, a different tack (the ellipsis is in the original):

> What were the Congo natives to me? Of what use this pursuit of an unrealisable ideal? I was a young man. I had a family — yes? I was running serious risks. And then, a delicately, very delicately veiled suggestion that my permanent interests would be better served if. . . . "A bribe?" Oh! dear, no, nothing so vulgar, so demeaning. But there were always means of arranging these things. Everything could be arranged with honour to all sides. It was a most entertaining interview, and lasted until a very late hour. "So nothing will shake your determination?" "I fear not." We parted with mutual smiles. But my companion, I thought, was a little ruffled. For my part I enjoyed myself most thoroughly.

One of the eyewitness attacks on Leopold's regime that Morel published consisted of several articles by an American, whose testimony, given at greater length in a 1903 book, was devastating [see pages 131–133 for one instance already cited]. On his latest tour of duty in the Congo, Edgar Canisius nominally had been a business agent of the Société Anversoise du Commerce au Congo, one of the big rubber concession companies, but in effect he was a counterguerrilla commander. When the thirty-four-year-old Canisius arrived at his post near the northwestern border of the Congo, at the start of 1900, the company had been harvesting rubber for several years, and vines were getting scarce. The gatherers of the Budja tribe, he writes, "became mere slaves to the company, for rubber-making occupied all their time, the victim having to search far and wide for the giant vines from which the sap is extracted. They were not even fed by their taskmasters, their only remuneration being merchandise or *mitakos* [pieces of brass wire] in ridiculously small quantities. . . . The natives bitterly bemoaned the scarcity of the rubber-producing lianas, and piteously begged to be allowed to perform other service than rubber-gathering."

Rebellious Budjas had killed thirty soldiers, and several punitive expeditions were sent against them. Canisius and two other white officers led one, accompanied by a force of fifty black troops and thirty porters. The column marched into villages abandoned by the fleeing Budjas and left scorched earth in its wake. "As our party moved through village after village. . . . A party of men had been detailed with torches to fire every hut. . . . As we progressed, a line of smoke hung over the jungle for many miles, announcing to the natives far and wide that civilization was dawning."

Porters carried the soldiers' supplies. "We . . . marched . . . through native clearings, where the trunks of large trees lay by hundreds across our path. Over these we had to climb, the trail seeming to lead to the top of every high ant-hill within range. The carriers had an especially hard time, for many of them were chained together by the neck. . . . They carried our boxes slung on poles, and when one fell he usually brought down all his companions on the same chain. Many of the poor wretches became so exhausted by this kind of marching that they could be urged forward only by blows from the butt-ends of the rifles. Some had their shoulders so chafed by the poles that they literally shrieked with pain."

From a military post far in the interior, Canisius's troops searched the jungle for rebels, and when they captured them, worked them to death: "All were compelled to carry heavy loads, each of which had previously required two men to transport . . . until they finally succumbed to starvation and smallpox."

As the fighting grew worse, the troops took to killing their prisoners, in one case thirty of them at a time. By the time the campaign was over, "we had undergone six weeks of painful marching and had killed over nine hundred natives, men, women, and children." The incentive, and the cause of the deaths, was the potential of "adding fully twenty tons of rubber to the monthly crop."

By 1903, after several years of hard work, Morel and his allies in Parliament and the humanitarian societies had succeeded in putting the "Congo Question" on the British public agenda more prominently than it had ever been. In May, following a major debate, the House of Commons unanimously passed a resolution urging that Congo "natives should be governed with humanity." The resolution also protested Leopold's failure to live up to his promises about free trade. Morel was proving a shrewd lobbyist. Behind the scenes he fed information to the speakers who supported the resolution; he would do so during many parliamentary debates on the Congo yet to come.

Leopold was alarmed. Britain was the superpower of the day and the most prominent colonial power in Africa. If it turned the full force of its influence against the Congo state, his profits would be at risk. Was a journalist like Morel capable of initiating this? Morel had been able to launch a barrage of criticism in print and to inspire a parliamentary resolution, but getting a reluctant British government to put pressure on a friendly monarch was surely something else. Leopold and his entourage were well aware of the difference: a Belgian newspaper editor had once shrewdly remarked that Lord Salisbury, the long-time British prime minister, "is not a man to care much about the fate of the blacks, any more than that of the Armenians or the Bulgarians."

Leopold's rule had been thoroughly exposed for what it was, but it remained in place. For the moment, he and Morel were at a stalemate. Neither knew that it would soon be broken by a man who, the very day after the British parliamentary debate ended, had embarked on a steamboat journey up the Congo River.

13

BREAKING INTO THE
THIEVES' KITCHEN

W HEN MOREL'S ALLIES in Parliament got the Congo protest resolution passed in May of 1903, the Foreign Office sent a telegram
to His Majesty's consul in the Congo, ordering him "to go to interior as
soon as possible, and to send reports soon."

The consul who received this telegram was an Irishman named Roger
Casement, a veteran of twenty years in Africa. The first time we catch a
glimpse of him in connection with the Congo, in fact, is in a photograph from some two decades earlier. It shows a group of four young
friends who went to work in the territory in the very early days of King
Leopold's regime. They wear coats, ties, and high, starched collars. Three
have bluff, hearty British faces, faces from a thousand other posed group
photos of army cadets or rugby players. But the fourth man, with a
handsome black beard, black hair, and heavy brows, has a quizzical tilt of
the head and a pensive look that sets him apart from the other three.
"Figure and face," wrote the Irish writer Stephen Gwynn, who knew
Casement only later, "he seemed to me one of the finest-looking creatures I had ever seen; and his countenance had charm and distinction and
a high chivalry. Knight errant he was."

It was back in 1883 that the nineteen-year-old Roger Casement first
made the long voyage out to the Congo, working, as it happened, as a
purser on an Elder Dempster ship. He returned the following year and
remained in the territory through the rest of the 1880s. He ran the supply
base for the ill-fated Sanford Exploring Expedition and worked for the

surveyors charting the course for the railway around the rapids. He became, he claimed, the first white man who ever swam across the crocodile-infested Inkisi River. When he served as the lay business manager of a Baptist mission station, he drew some gentle disapproval from his employer, who thought he didn't bargain hard enough at buying food. "He is very good to the natives, too good, too generous, too ready to give away. He would never make money as a trader."

When Stanley slogged through the Congo on his Emin Pasha Relief Expedition, Casement accompanied him for a week. "A good specimen of the capable Englishman," noted the explorer in his journal, not noticing that Casement was Irish. Casement was a better judge of Stanley, for although the explorer remained something of a hero to him, Casement recognized Stanley's sadistic streak. After seeing that Stanley's dog lacked a tail, he learned to his horror that Stanley had cut off the tail, cooked it, and fed it to the dog to eat.

Casement saw much more brutality on the part of other white men in Africa. It is hard to tell whether there was a particular moral turning point for him, as there would be for E. D. Morel when he made his discoveries in Antwerp and Brussels. One such moment for Casement may have been in 1887, when he traveled up the Congo River on a steamboat that also carried a Force Publique officer named Guillaume Van Kerckhoven. Van Kerckhoven was a hot-headed, notoriously aggressive commander with a rakish grin and waxed-tip mustache, one of whose expeditions even the Congo's governor general called "a hurricane which passed through the countryside leaving nothing but devastation behind it." Casement listened, aghast, as Van Kerckhoven cheerfully explained how he paid his black soldiers "5 brass rods (2½ d.) per human head they brought him during the course of any military operations he conducted. He said it was to stimulate their prowess in the face of the enemy."

In 1890, when Joseph Conrad arrived at Matadi, he jotted in his diary: "Made the acquaintance of Mr. Roger Casement, which I should consider as a great pleasure under any circumstances. . . . Thinks, speaks well, most intelligent and very sympathetic." The rough-and-ready Matadi, a hot, humid collection of corrugated sheet-iron buildings spread on a hillside overlooking the Congo River, was filled with drunken sailors, African prostitutes, and young European and American adventurers hoping to get rich quickly off the ivory boom. Both Casement and Conrad felt alienated from this gold rush atmosphere; they shared a room for some ten days while Conrad waited to go inland, and together visited nearby villages.

Everyone found Casement an impressive talker. "His greatest charm was his voice, which was very musical," a colleague remembered. "Casement doesn't talk to you," another person said. "He purrs at you." Talking or purring, Casement had a fund of stories that seems to have darkened Conrad's vision of colonialism in Africa. As he was leaving the Congo at the end of his six months there, Conrad saw Casement once more. The two men met again at a dinner in London, later in the decade, and according to Conrad, "went away from there together to the Sports club and talked there till 3 in the morning." The novelist wrote to a friend: "He could tell you things! Things I have tried to forget, things I never did know." One of those things — another possible source of Kurtz and his palisade of human skulls — may well have been the story about Van Kerckhoven, the collector of African heads.

In 1892, Roger Casement went to work for the British colonial administration in what is today Nigeria. He was developing an eye for injustice, however, even though he was employed by the leading colonial power of the day. His first recorded public protest, in an outraged letter he wrote in 1894 to the Aborigines Protection Society, was against a hanging. The twenty-seven victims were African conscript soldiers and their wives in the German colony of the Cameroons; the men had mutinied after the women were flogged. "I trust you may do something to raise a protesting voice in England," Casement wrote, "against the atrocious conduct of the Germans. Altho' the men were their soldiers we all on earth have a commission and a right to defend the weak against the strong, and to protest against brutality in any shape or form."

Casement soon transferred to the British consular service; after serving in several posts in southern Africa, in 1900 he was assigned to set up the first British consulate in the État Indépendant du Congo. When he passed through Brussels on his way to taking up the new job, King Leopold, with a keen eye for anyone in a position to help his cause, invited him to lunch. The lowly consul found himself eating at the Royal Palace with the King, Queen Marie-Henriette, their daughter Princess Clementine, and Prince Victor Napoleon of France.*

---

* The roster of those at lunch provides a picture of the current state of Leopold's family life. That the queen was there at all meant she was probably going to the opera or a

Leopold invited Casement to come again the next day, and he did so, listening to the king ramble on for an hour and a half about the civilizing, uplifting work he was doing in the Congo. Although Leopold granted that some of his agents might be guilty of excesses, Casement reported, the king also claimed that "it was impossible to have always the best men in Africa; and indeed the African climate seemed frequently to cause deterioration in the character." As ever, the king tried to make sure that if any damaging information turned up, he would be the first to hear. "His Majesty, in bidding me farewell," Casement wrote, "asked me to write him privately at any time, and to write frankly, should there be anything of interest I could, unofficially, advise him of." Unlike most visitors, Casement appears not to have been charmed by Leopold. He had already seen too much of the Congo.

At his post as consul, Casement remained fascinated by Africa, but it was a restless time in his life. He was approaching forty and seemed stuck in a backwater job that did not use his talents. The consular corps was the poor stepchild of the British diplomatic service. Beyond that, being responsible for the Congo was a far cry from being British consul in Paris or Berlin, a post far more likely to go to someone from a well-connected family in England than from a middle-class one in Ireland. Casement felt he was always at the bottom of the list. His everyday life was one long battle against leaky roofs, mosquitoes, dysentery, and the boredom of inglorious work — "sometimes being even compelled to rise from bed when ill, to listen to a drunken sailor's complaint."

Casement had other frustrations as well. His indignation at the wrongs of colonial rule had no room for expression in his work as a consul. He had a vague interest in Irish history but could not pursue this in the

---

concert that night in Brussels, for otherwise, exasperated with her husband's coldness and public philandering, she no longer lived with him. Severely dressed in black and sometimes wearing a man's top hat, she spent most of her time at the elegant Belgian resort of Spa, nursing her sorrows in the company of an odd menagerie of animals that included several parrots and a llama.

Clementine, the youngest of the three daughters, was the only one with whom Leopold was now on speaking terms. Prince Victor Napoleon, the balding Bonaparte heir to the vanished French imperial throne, was her true love, but he did not pass muster with Leopold. For his African adventures the king needed the good will of France's republican government, which had deposed the Bonapartes. Leopold refused his consent to the marriage. The timid Clementine acquiesced, serving the king as palace hostess; she would marry Victor Napoleon only after her father's death.

tropics. He had ambitions as a writer but no outlets except long-winded reports that left the Foreign Office staff in London amused; few other consuls routinely sent twenty-page dispatches from West African ports. He wrote large quantities of mediocre verse but managed to publish almost none.

Other white men in the Congo considered the new British consul an eccentric. When traveling for the first time as consul from Matadi to Leopoldville, for instance, Casement did not take the new railway; he walked more than two hundred miles — in protest against high railway fares. On later trips he did use the railway, one baffled Congo state official reported back to Brussels, but "he always traveled second class. In all his movements he is always accompanied by a big bulldog with large jaws."

At the back of his mind was something further, which Casement could not share even with close friends or relatives, although several had their suspicions. He was a homosexual. In a poem that could never be published in his lifetime he wrote:

> *I sought by love alone to go*
> *Where God had writ an awful no*
>
> *. . . .*
>
> *I only know I cannot die*
> *And leave this love God made, not I.*

Casement lived in a time when to be found out meant disgrace or worse. It was in 1895 that Oscar Wilde, a fellow Irishman, was sentenced to two years at hard labor for "committing acts of gross indecency with other male persons." In the spring of 1903, as Casement was returning to the Congo from home leave in Europe, another case captured the headlines, that of Major General Sir Hector Macdonald, among the most decorated British soldiers of his time. Exposed as a homosexual and scheduled for court-martial, he killed himself in a Paris hotel room.

"News of Sir Hector Macdonald's suicide in Paris!" Casement wrote in his diary on April 17, 1903. "The reasons given are pitiably sad. The most distressing case this surely of its kind." Two days later, he added, "Very sorry at Hector Macdonald's terrible end." Eleven days after that, in the Congo port of Banana, thoughts of Macdonald pursued Casement through a sleepless night: "A dreadful room at Hotel. Sandflies. Did not close my eyes. Hector Macdonald's death very sad."

Casement must have known that if he ever acquired powerful enemies, he would be open to blackmail. Yet with a touch of unconscious self-destructiveness, he kept a meticulous diary of his assignations, almost all of which were paid for. On that same voyage from England to the Congo, he taunted fate by recording all his sexual encounters along the way. Madeira: "Agostinho kissed many times. 4 dollars." Las Palmas: "No offers." Shipboard: "Down and oh! oh! quick, about 18." Boma: "Tall, 'How much money?'" If the diary were discovered by someone who wished him ill, he would be destroyed. Until then, it was a time bomb, with a fuse of unknown length.

In May 1903, the month following his diary entries about Macdonald's suicide, Casement found something to be happy about; moreover, it was something that promised a big advance in his career. For two years, he had been sending reports to the Foreign Office about the brutal conditions in Leopold's Congo. Now that the Congo protest resolution had been unanimously passed by the House of Commons, the British government had to make a high-profile move in response.

The previous year, Casement had cabled London proposing that he make an investigative trip to the rubber-producing areas of the interior. He was given permission, but home leave in England and Ireland delayed the trip. The parliamentary debate immediately put it back on the agenda, and soon after returning to the Congo, Casement was under way.

He knew the journey would be arduous; writing to a friend later, Casement quoted an African proverb: "A man doesn't go among thorns unless a snake's after him — or he's after a snake." He added, "I'm after a snake and please God I'll scotch it."

To carry out his investigation, Casement could have taken the new railway up to Stanley Pool and spent a few weeks touring areas within easy reach of the comfortable brick house where he stayed there. He didn't. Instead, he spent more than three and a half months in the interior. In order not to depend on the authorities for his transportation — a key hold they had over many visitors — he rented a narrow, iron, single-decker steamboat from some American missionaries and traveled far up the Congo River. He spent seventeen days at Lake Tumba, where the state ran its rubber slavery operations with no intermediaries; he visited concession-company territory; he directed his steamer up side rivers and walked when the rivers gave out; he counted the exact number of people held hostage in a village that had not delivered its rubber quota; he canoed across a river and walked several miles through a flooded forest to meet one victim and inspect his injuries in person.

Sometimes Casement stayed overnight at a mission station; sometimes he camped in a riverside clearing or on an island. ("Hippo downstream. Saw three pelicans feeding, close to us. Also saw a beautiful Egyptian ibis, black body, white wings; a lovely fellow in full flight over us.") He was traveling, as always, with his beloved bulldog, John, and he brought with him as cook and helper an otherwise unidentified man who appears in his diary only as Hairy Bill. "Poor old Hairy Bill. A queer life." Hairy Bill's repertoire as chef seems to have been limited to three dishes: chicken, custard, and something known as boiled or stewed sugar. "Chicken, chicken, custard, custard . . . every day. . . . Goddam," writes Casement. Sometimes he turns sarcastic: "We had boiled sugar again for change, also custard." Or: "Stewed sugar and custard again twice daily for a month and beats me hollow."

Casement sent a ceaseless flow of dispatches to the Foreign Office. "They'll curse me at F.O.," he noted with satisfaction. Surely others cursed him too. He penned a torrent of letters to Congo state officials condemning specific atrocities and, most undiplomatically, the entire way the colony was run. "That system, Monsieur le Gouverneur-Général, is wrong — hopelessly and entirely wrong. . . . Instead of lifting up the native populations submitted to and suffering from it, it can, if persisted in, lead only to their final extinction and the universal condemnation of civilized mankind." Small wonder that word filtered back to a worried Leopold that his regime would not be treated kindly in the British consul's report. Similar rumors also reached E. D. Morel, who eagerly waited for Casement's return. To the British foreign secretary, Casement exulted, in a most unconsular manner, that he had "broken into the thieves' kitchen."

He was a man possessed. His anger at what he saw had a dramatic effect on many of the other Europeans he encountered; it was as if his visible outrage gave them permission to act on stifled feelings of their own. Two missionaries Casement visited were so inspired by his example that they promptly set off on their own investigative trips; one began writing critical letters to the governor general. Casement, heading downriver, met the steamer of the veteran British missionary George Grenfell heading up, and the two men stopped and talked. After listening to Casement, Grenfell promptly resigned from Leopold's sham Commission for the Protection of the Natives. (A fruitless gesture, incidentally: the king had let the commission's mandate expire a few months earlier, without informing any of its members.) The Italian consul in the Congo, disturbed by what Casement told him, abandoned plans for a European holiday and made an investigative journey of his own that confirmed Casement's findings.

Casement's daily diary entries are far more moving to read than his carefully worded official report; his horror pulses through the cryptic pages.

June 5: The country a desert, no natives left.

July 25: I walked into villages and saw the nearest one — population dreadfully decreased — only 93 people left out of many hundreds.

July 26: Poor frail folk . . . — dust to dust ashes to ashes — where then are the kindly heart, the pitiful thought — together vanished.

August 6: Took copious notes from natives. . . . They are cruelly flogged for being late with their baskets [of rubber]. . . . Very tired.

August 13: A. came to say 5 people from Bikoro side with hands cut off had come as far as Myanga intending to show me.

August 22: Bolongo quite dead. I remember it well in 1887, Nov., full of people then; now 14 adults all told. I should say people wretched, complained bitterly of rubber tax. . . . 6:30 passed deserted side of Bokuta. . . . Mouzede says the people were all taken away by force to Mampoko. Poor unhappy souls.

August 29: Bongandanga . . . saw rubber "Market," nothing but guns — about 20 armed men. . . . The popln. 242 men with rubber all guarded like convicts. To call this "trade" is the height of lying.

August 30: 16 men women and children tied up from a village Mboye close to the town. Infamous. The men were put in the prison, the children let go at my intervention. Infamous. Infamous, shameful system.

August 31: In the evening a dance was organised in my honour; all the local chiefs and their wives, etc., came (at L.'s orders) to it. Poor souls. I was sorry for it, of all the forced enjoyment I ever saw this took the cake.

September 2: Saw 16 women seized by Peeters's sentries and taken
off to Prison.

September 9: 11.10 passed Bolongo again. The poor people put off
in canoe to implore my help.

Living long after the movement against slavery and well before the appearance of organizations like Amnesty International, Casement in his
diary wrote in the tones of the Abolitionists: "Infamous. Infamous,
shameful system." But the official report he composed subsequently is in
the language that Amnesty and similar groups would later make their
own: formal and sober, assessing the reliability of various witnesses, filled
with references to laws and statistics, and accompanied by appendices and
depositions.

In late 1903, Casement sailed back to Europe to prepare his report. He
spent some weeks in London dictating and correcting, and made his final
revisions on a train while returning from a visit to Joseph Conrad and his
family at their country house. The information in Casement's report was
largely familiar to people like E. D. Morel and his small group of supporters, but for the first time it was to be laid out with the authority of His
Britannic Majesty's Consul. The report was all the more authoritative
because Casement was a veteran of Africa who made frequent compari-
sons between the Congo he had once known and the same territory
under the rubber terror.

Again and again Casement describes hands being cut off corpses.
Sometimes it wasn't the hands. His report quotes one witness:

"The white men told their soldiers: 'You kill only women; you cannot
kill men.' So then the soldiers when they killed us (here P.P. who was
answering stopped and hesitated, and then pointing to the private parts of
my bulldog — it was lying asleep at my feet) then they cut off those
things and took them to the white men, who said: 'It is true, you have
killed men.'"

Despite the restrained tone and careful documentation, the report's
accounts of sliced-off hands and penises was far more graphic and forceful than the British government had expected. The Foreign Office, already uneasy, began getting urgent requests to delay publication from Sir
Constantine Phipps, the fervently pro-Leopold British minister to Brussels. Phipps, a conceited man of limited intelligence, couldn't believe

"that Belgians, members of a cultivated people amongst whom I had lived, could, under even a tropical sky, have perpetrated acts of refined cruelty." The only reason the companies used "sentries," he explained to the foreign secretary, was to *protect* the rubber harvesters during their work. "Please manage to prevent issue of report by Casement until after 10th instant, date on which I must unavoidably encounter King of the Belgians," Phipps telegraphed. "The publication will inevitably put me in an awkward position at court."

More pressure came from another quarter. Urged on by an apprehensive Leopold, Sir Alfred Jones of the Elder Dempster line twice visited the Foreign Office to try to soften the report, or to at least get an advance copy for the king.

Casement was so distressed by what he had seen in the Congo that the Foreign Office could not control him, and he gave several interviews to the London press. Their publication made it hard to censor or postpone his report, though Foreign Office officials did water it down by removing all names. When the report was finally published, in early 1904, readers found statements by witnesses that read: "I am N.N. These two beside me are O.O. and P.P." Or: "The white man who said this was the chief white man at F.F. . . . His name was A. B." This lent the report a strangely disembodied tone, as if horrible things had been done but not to or by real people. It also made it impossible for Casement to defend himself by reference to specific people and places when Leopold's staff issued a long reply. Belgian newspapers tied to Congo business interests joined in the attack; one, *La Tribune Congolaise,* said that the people Casement had seen with missing hands "were unfortunate individuals, suffering from cancer in the hands, whose hands thus had to be cut off as a simple surgical operation."

Casement was both angry and disappointed. Mercurial (he himself had at first wanted to protect his witnesses by omitting their names, then changed his mind) and easily offended, he sent off an eighteen-page letter of protest to the Foreign Office and threatened to resign. In his diary he wrote that his superiors were "a gang of stupidities"; one in particular was "an abject piffler." In a letter, he called them a "wretched set of incompetent noodles."

But then, at last, Casement found someone with whom he could share his feelings. He had avidly read Morel's writings while still in the Congo, and the men were eager to meet. "The man is honest as day," Casement wrote in his diary after the long-awaited meeting took place. "Dined at

Comedy [a restaurant] together late and then to chat till 2 A.M. M. sleeping in study." Casement was staying at a friend's house in Chester Square; Morel left after breakfast the next morning.

It is easy to imagine the two men talking that night: the tall, black-bearded Casement, simmering with fury at what he had seen; Morel, with his handlebar mustache, almost a decade younger, also big, but stocky, filled with his own earnest anger at the evidence he had uncovered in Europe. In a sense, each had seen half of what made up Leopold's "Free State." Together, they had as full a version of the story as was likely to be told. Morel remembered the meeting for the rest of his life:

> I saw before me a man, my own height, very lithe and sinewy, chest thrown out, head held high — suggestive of one who had lived in the vast open spaces. Black hair and beard covering cheeks hollowed by the tropical sun. Strongly marked features. A dark blue penetrating eye sunken in the socket. A long, lean, swarthy Vandyck type of face, graven with power and withal of great gentleness. An extraordinarily handsome and arresting face. From the moment our hands gripped and our eyes met, mutual trust and confidence were bred and the feeling of isolation slipped from me like a mantle. Here was a man, indeed. One who would convince those in high places of the foulness of the crime committed upon a helpless race. . . . I often see him now in imagination as I saw him at that memorable interview, crouching over the fire in the otherwise unlighted room . . . unfolding in a musical, soft, almost even voice, in language of peculiar dignity and pathos, the story of a vile conspiracy. . . . At intervals he would rise, and with swift silent steps, pace the room; then resume his crouching attitude by the fire, his splendid profile thrown into bold relief by the flames.
>
> I was mostly a silent listener, clutching hard upon the arms of my chair. As the monologue of horror proceeded . . . I verily believe I *saw* those hunted women clutching their children and flying panic stricken to the bush: the blood flowing from those quivering black bodies as the hippopotamus hide whip struck and struck again; the savage soldiery rushing hither and thither amid burning villages; the ghastly tally of severed hands. . . .
>
> Casement read me passages from his report, which he was then writing, whose purport was almost identical with oft-re-

peated sentences of my own. He told me that he had been amazed to find that I, five thousand miles away, had come to conclusions identical with his in every respect. . . . An immense weight passed from me.

It was long hours past midnight when we parted. The sheets of his voluminous report lay scattered upon the table, chairs and floor. And it was with the debris of that Report around me, that Report which was . . . to tear aside the veil from the most gigantic fraud and wickedness which our generation has known, that I slept in my clothes upon the sofa; while its author sought his bedroom above.

A few weeks later, Casement visited Morel's home at Hawarden, a small Welsh village near the border of England; he jotted in his diary, "Talked all night nearly, wife a good woman." He was trying to persuade Morel to found an organization devoted solely to campaigning for justice in the Congo, but Morel was at first reluctant. The Aborigines Protection Society was wary at the prospect of a new group encroaching on its turf and perhaps cutting into its fundraising. But Morel's wife, Mary, agreed with Casement, and it may have been at her urging that Morel went to Ireland to talk further with Casement. He wrote: "Casement's plan found fervid support in my wife, and if I crossed the Irish Channel . . . to meet him . . . it was very largely owing to [her] influence. . . . It was . . . on that Irish soil . . . fertilised by so many human tears, that Casement and I conspired further . . . [and] discussed ways and means and drew up a rough plan of campaign."

The men talked over dinner at the Slieve Donard Hotel in Newcastle, where Morel became convinced that "the Congo evil was a special and extraordinary evil calling for special means of attack. . . . If the British people could be really roused, the world might be roused. . . . Britain had played that part before [in the campaign against slavery]. . . . Could we raise a throbbing in that great heart of hers?"

Although he was between posts, Casement was still a member of the consular service, so Morel would have to run the new organization. "But how were the vulgar details to be overcome? I explained to Casement that I had no money. . . . Neither had he. . . . Without a moment's hesitation he wrote out a cheque for £100." For Casement this was more than a month's income.

Shortly afterward, Casement wrote to Morel, "We shall grow in numbers day by day until there go up from the length and breadth of England one overwhelming Nay!"

A few weeks after their dinner in Ireland, Morel formed the Congo Reform Association. Using some of Casement's donation, he bought the first supplies, including a typewriter. He rounded up the public endorsement of an impressive list of lords, earls, businessmen, churchmen, members of Parliament, and, to evoke the heritage of the battle against slavery, the great-grandson of the famous British Abolitionist William Wilberforce. The C.R.A. attracted more than a thousand people to its first meeting, in Liverpool's Philharmonic Hall, on March 23, 1904.

Although Casement and Morel each had his prickly side, the friendship between them was immediate and lasting. "I think Casement is about as near to being a saint as a man can be," Morel wrote to a friend. Each now had the perfect ally. The relationship deepened over the years; in their many letters back and forth, Casement became "Dear Tiger" and Morel "Dear Bulldog." Leopold was "the King of Beasts."

Although he could be only a silent partner in the reform campaign, Casement urged on Bulldog with enthusiastic advice about political strategy, about whom to lobby, even about what clothes to wear. Without the Foreign Office's knowledge, he helped to raise money for the campaign. Morel, for his part, encouraged Casement to return to the Congo to conduct a further investigation. The consul replied that officials might "hang me as they did Stokes — and one couldn't do better than be hanged in order to end that den of devils." This is not the last time that we will hear from Casement a hint of a desire for martyrdom.

That meeting between Bulldog and Tiger as they plotted their attack on the King of Beasts would later be compared by their admirers with the legendary conversation beneath a spreading tree between William Wilberforce and William Pitt the Younger, more than a hundred years earlier, which marked the beginning of the British antislavery movement. But like the British Abolitionists, Morel and Casement were for the moment safe in England; for all their good will, they were not themselves subject to the lash of the *chicotte* or the weight of shackles. They were white men trying to stop other white men from brutalizing Africans. Most of the Africans who fought this battle in the Congo perished, their very names unrecorded. In a sense, we honor Morel and Casement in their stead.

The two men, however, were far more than armchair do-gooders.

They were people of conviction — and both ended up paying a high price. At the time they met and shared their passion about the Congo in December 1903, Morel and Casement did not know that more than a dozen years later they would have something else in common. Each would be taken, in custody, through the gates of London's Pentonville Prison. One would never emerge.

14

TO FLOOD HIS DEEDS
WITH DAY

THE CRUSADE that E. D. Morel now orchestrated through the Congo
Reform Association exerted a relentless, growing pressure on the
Belgian, British, and American governments. Almost never has one man,
possessed of no wealth, title, or official post, caused so much trouble for
the governments of several major countries. Morel knew that officials
like Foreign Secretary Sir Edward Grey would act only "when kicked,
and if the process of kicking is stopped, he will do nothing." To this
kicking, Morel devoted more than a decade of his life.

In addition to running the Congo Reform Association, Morel continued to spend part of each workday, which sometimes stretched to sixteen or eighteen hours, editing his *West African Mail*. "People don't seem
altogether to realize that — apart from everything else — I turn out a
weekly paper," he wrote to a fellow activist, "plus a monthly organ for
the C.R.A. whose size sometimes has been very great and would have
kept an ordinary individual pretty well busy all the month. It is only
because I am an exceptionally *rapid worker* that I have been able to do
it all."

Another reason Morel could do it all was that he had a devoted wife to
run his household. Indeed, he is one of the few people in this entire story
who was happily married. Mary Richardson Morel raised their five children and encouraged her husband's cause in every way. She took a particular liking to Casement, agreeing with him that her husband ought to
form an organization that focused exclusively on the Congo. As with so
many couples of their day, we do not know how many of Morel's memo-

rable achievements should also be credited to her. "I always think of her as part of you," John Holt, his long-time staunch supporter and confidant, wrote him, "the two constituting the Morel of Congo reform."

Morel was not without flaws. He could be bullheaded; he rarely admitted any mistakes; and in his newspaper he ran an occasional picture of himself, enthusiastic reviews of his books, resolutions thanking him for his good work, interviews with himself reprinted from other papers, and an editorial "wish[ing] Mr. Morel 'God-speed' on his journey" when he went abroad to campaign for Congo reform. He sometimes clashed with colleagues who were, he felt, getting too much of the limelight — although seldom with Casement, whom he venerated. Like many enormously productive people, he had spells of depression and self-pity. "My home life is reduced to microscopic proportions. . . . Personally I am at the end of my tether," he wrote in 1906 to Mark Twain, declaring that he would go on with his Congo work nonetheless, because "those wretched people out there have no-one but us after all. And they have the right to live."

His politics also had limitations. Some of these he shared with most other Europeans of his time, from his faith in the magic of free trade to his belief that African men had a higher sexual drive than white men and could pose a danger to white women. Other quirks were more rooted in his single-minded passion for stopping the atrocities in King Leopold's Congo. The picture Morel gives in his writings of Africans in the Congo before whites arrived is that of Rousseau's idealized Noble Savage: in describing traditional African societies he focuses on what was peaceful and gentle and ignores any brutal aspects — which occasionally included, for example, long before the Force Publique made it the order of the day, cutting off the hands of one's dead enemies.

More important, Morel was so enraged by Leopold's villainy that he ignored his own country's use of forced labor — wide, though far less murderous — in its African colonies, particularly in the east and south. There was nothing inherently wrong with colonialism, he felt, if its administration was fair and just. He believed this to be the case in the British colonies in west Africa, where, to be sure, there was no rubber terror and no massive seizure of all so-called vacant land. In the later stages of his Congo campaign, he even found time to go to Nigeria and write a generally approving book about British rule there.

But whatever his faults, when it came to campaigning against injustice in the Congo, Morel had an unswerving, infectious sense of right and wrong. A superb speaker, he regularly addressed crowds of several thousand people with no notes. Between 1907 and 1909 alone, he spoke at some fifty mass meetings throughout Great Britain. "Sometimes . . ." he wrote, "I have had bursts of fury . . . when some story more abominable than the rest moved me in a special way, and when I should have stopped at very little if any of Leopold's crew had been about. . . . [I have experienced] exhilaration when I had driven home some good thrust, or when that something or other which it is difficult to name gripped me on the platform and I felt I had a great audience in the hollow of my hand."

Morel considered his movement to be in the grand tradition of such British humanitarian crusades as the righteous outrage provoked by the Turkish massacres of Bulgarians in 1876 and of Armenians in the 1890s. Above all, he saw himself as a moral heir to the antislavery movement. He began his blistering *Red Rubber: The Story of the Rubber Slave Trade Flourishing on the Congo in the Year of Grace 1906* with an epigraph from the great American Abolitionist William Lloyd Garrison:

> *The standard of emancipation is now unfurled . . .*
> *I will not equivocate,*
> *I will not excuse,*
> *I will not retreat a single inch:*
> *And I will be heard,*
> *Posterity will bear testimony that I was right.*

The tradition of British radicalism from which Morel came was rooted in the Nonconformist — that is, Protestant, but not Church of England — churches and in the Clapham Sect, the humanitarian evangelical group to which the antislavery leader William Wilberforce had belonged. In the early nineteenth century these humanitarians had focused their zeal on improving the condition of all sorts of oppressed groups: prisoners, factory workers, child laborers, the insane. Theirs, however, was not the from-the-bottom-up politics later adopted by Marxists and trade unionists; it was the top-down reformism of the relatively well-born. They aimed at ending the death penalty, corporal punishment, and cruelty to animals. When they turned their attention overseas, it was to push for the abolition of the slave trade and to send missionaries abroad to uplift the "natives" in the far reaches of the world. (Indeed, it was the Nonconformist churches, especially the Baptists, that sent the British missionaries to the Congo.)

Significantly, Morel's humanitarian political ancestors, unlike his socialist contemporaries, had firmly believed that improving the lot of downtrodden people everywhere was good for business. Better treatment of colonial subjects would "promote the civil and commercial interests of Great Britain. . . ." declared a parliamentary select committee in the 1830s. "Savages are dangerous neighbours and unprofitable customers, and if they remain as degraded denizens of our colonies, they become a burden upon the State."

Such humanitarians never saw themselves as being in conflict with the imperial project — as long as it was British imperialism. "Morally emancipation put the British on a special plane. . . ." as James Morris sums it up in his history of the British Empire. "If so much could be achieved by agitation at home, what might not be done if the moral authority of England were distributed across the earth — to tackle the evils of slavery, ignorance and paganism at source, to teach the simpler peoples the benefits of Steam, Free Trade and Revealed Religion, and to establish not a world empire in the bad Napoleonic sense, but a Moral Empire of loftier intent? So was evolved the chemistry of evangelical imperialism."

This was the tradition in which Morel felt at home, and it was a tradition that perfectly suited his organizational talent. Although without old-school ties to them, he had the knack of making the wealthy, the powerful, and the famous believe they did credit to themselves by supporting his Congo crusade. Month after month, the front page of the Congo Reform Association's periodical carried a full-page portrait photo of a prominent supporter — a lord, an earl, a member of Parliament, a mustachioed retired colonial governor. After the association's founding in Liverpool, Morel saw to it that the first meeting of the group's executive committee was held in a room secured by a sympathetic M.P. at the House of Commons. Almost every major C.R.A. public meeting after that had at least one bishop on the platform. Having the apparent blessing of both church and state, Morel found that few influential Britons could resist his entreaties to lend their names to the cause of Congo reform.

One of his political limitations was, in fact, a source of his immense success as an organizer. If he had believed, as we might conclude today, that Leopold's rape of the Congo was in part a logical consequence of the very idea of colonialism, of the belief that there was nothing wrong with a country being ruled other than by its own inhabitants, Morel would have been written off as being on the fringe. No one in England would have paid much attention to him. But he did not believe this; he believed with all his heart that Leopold's system of rule constituted a unique form of evil. People in England's ruling circles, therefore, could support his crusade without feeling their own interests threatened.

Yet despite some blind spots, Morel was at the far edge of the humanitarian tradition. His beliefs were implicitly more subversive than he allowed himself to recognize. He saw brutality in the Congo not as a specific imperfection to be wiped out in the way one could wipe out child labor or capital punishment, by passing a law against it, but as part of a complex, deeply embedded "System," as he called it — forced labor plus the massive European takeover of African land. This angle of vision is much closer to Marxism than to uplift-the-downtrodden humanitarianism, although Morel probably never read a word of Marx in his life. He never resolved the conflict between these two ways of seeing the world, and much of the drama of his later life lay in the constant tension between them.

⁂

"Morel has never had an equal as organizer and leader of a Dissenting movement," writes the historian A.J.P. Taylor. "He knew exactly where to look for rich sympathizers; and he took money from them without altering the democratic character of [his movement]. Millionaires and factory workers alike accepted his leadership." Among the millionaires were Quakers like the wealthy but plain-living chocolate manufacturer William Cadbury. Subsidies from these supporters kept the *West African Mail* alive, and it was the newspaper, not the Congo Reform Association, that paid Morel's salary. Paradoxically, Sir Alfred Jones of the Elder Dempster line also invested a little money in the paper, doubtless hoping to soften the attitude of his former employee. But his hopes were in vain; Morel repeatedly attacked Jones without mercy, exposing his doings as Leopold's major British ally. When Jones saw he would have no influence, he pulled his advertising from the paper.

Morel knew exactly how to fit his message to his audience. He reminded British businessmen that Leopold's monopolistic system, copied by France, had shut them out of much Congo trade. To members of the clergy he talked of Christian responsibility and quoted the grim reports from the missionaries. And for all Britons, and their representatives in Parliament, he evoked the widespread though unspoken belief that England had a particular responsibility to make decency prevail in the universe.

One of the more surprising things about the Congo crusade was that, except for forays to speak at meetings, Morel conducted it largely from his study. During the first half of the Congo Reform Association's nine-year lifetime, he didn't even live in London. Until December 1908, the C.R.A.'s head office was in Liverpool; from there and from his home in nearby Hawarden, Morel kept up a voluminous correspondence. In the first six months of 1906, for instance, he wrote 3700 letters. More important, his prodigious output of books, pamphlets, and newspaper articles about the Congo inspired people to write to him. He carefully cross-checked news items for accuracy, studied newspapers and documents from Belgium, and corresponded with government officials, journalists, and traders in Europe and Africa. By 1908, he estimated that he had amassed about twenty thousand letters concerning the Congo. They served as the basis for much of his published work.

Despite his disdain for organized religion, his tone was that of an evangelical preacher. To him, Leopold and his supporters, such as "the reptile Congophile Press of Brussels and Antwerp," personified the Devil; the Congo administration was "a bad and wicked system, inflicting terrible wrongs upon the native races." Morel spoke effectively to the mood of the day because he shared it: the optimism, the boundless confidence of a society that had not yet seen or imagined the world wars, the belief that humankind had the capacity to briskly eradicate all barriers that lay in the path of progress. "Our forefathers smashed the over-sea slave-trade," he declared in his book *King Leopold's Rule in Africa,* "and we shall root out the modern inland slave-trade on the Congo."

He was eager to raise the Congo reform movement above partisan politics and religious differences. On the speaker's platform for his major events were always M.P.s from the three major parties, clergy from both the Church of England and the Nonconformist churches, and an assortment of right honourables, lord mayors, lord provosts, and other notables. He had a superb sense of how to build up to an event: a large regional Congo protest rally was often preceded by an afternoon meeting with the local mayor and dignitaries at city hall. The mayor would then be on stage that evening. Before the end of 1905, more than sixty mass meetings had adopted a resolution condemning Leopold's rule as a revival of the African slave trade and calling "upon His Majesty's Government to convoke an assembly of the Christian Powers . . . in order to devise and put in force a scheme for the good government of the Congo territories." In Liverpool, an audience overflowed an auditorium that seated nearly three thousand and filled two adjoining halls. Cries of "Shame! Shame!" resounded at similar mass meetings throughout England and Scotland.

A master of all the media of his day, Morel made particularly effective use of photography. A central part of almost every Congo protest meeting was a slide show, comprising some sixty vivid photos of life under Leopold's rule; half a dozen of them showed mutilated Africans or their cut-off hands. The pictures, ultimately seen in meetings and the press by millions of people, provided evidence that no propaganda could refute.

Slides also showed charts and graphs estimating Leopold's Congo profits; they even displayed poems, which made up in passion what they lacked in art:

> No zeal, no Faith, inspired this Leopold,
> Nor any madness of half-splendid birth.
> Cool-eyed, he loosed the hounds that rend and slay,
> Just that his coffers might be gorged with gold.
> Embalm him, Time! Forget him not, O Earth,
> Trumpet his name, and flood his deeds with day.

To flood Leopold's deeds with day required that Morel mobilize his fellow journalists. He knew the editors of most of the major British magazines and newspapers, and wrote regularly for many of them, including the most prestigious, the *Times*. When an editor needed to send a reporter to Belgium or the Congo, Morel always had a candidate to suggest. He engineered "the downfall," he happily claimed, of a *Times* Brussels correspondent whom he thought too friendly to Leopold. He fed information to sympathetic newspapers in Belgium, and through his connections to the Press Association wire service was able to distribute material worldwide. When the famous American correspondent Richard Harding Davis was sent to Africa by *Collier's* magazine, he went supplied with Morel's latest findings, and echoed them in what he wrote.

With a powerful boost from Casement's report, the international campaign mounted by Morel reached newspapers all over the world. His carefully kept files contain, for the ten years starting in 1902, 4194 clippings relating to the drive for Congo reform. Nor did he focus on newspapers alone: The author of a 1906 boy's adventure novel, *Samba: A Story of the Rubber Slaves of the Congo,* thanks C.R.A. officials in his preface "for their kindness in reading the manuscript and revising the proofs of this book, and for many most helpful suggestions and criticisms."

Morel described himself as "Congo possessed." A letter to his Quaker backer William Cadbury in 1906 shows how:

> *Book.* Out this week . . . [this was *Red Rubber*]
> *Glasgow.* Lord Provost has summoned a Town's meeting. Shall probably have to go. Am arranging for formation of local CRA. . . . Any prominent Friends in Glasgow you could drop a note to?
> *France.* A French C.R.A. will be formed this month. . . .
> *Rising tide.* Demands for literature literally coming *in shoals.* . . . Twelve to 20 letters per day for literature, information, etc.

Like the Abolitionists before him, Morel understood that every national organization had to have local branches, so the C.R.A. had "auxiliaries" throughout England and Scotland. These groups organized their members to send funds, to write to their representatives in Parliament, and to produce an unending flow of letters to local newspapers. A Ladies' Branch had two representatives on the C.R.A. Executive Committee. Through such means, Morel applied steady pressure on the British government. He and his supporters never doubted that if only Britain were to act, it could force Leopold to mend his ways or could wrest the Congo entirely from his grasp.

The most effective spokespeople of all, Morel knew, were those with firsthand knowledge. Starting in 1906, the returned Baptist missionaries the Reverend John Harris and his wife, Alice Seeley Harris — she had taken almost all the photographs Morel used — began working full time for the association. The Harrises' zeal matched Morel's. In their first two years with the C.R.A., one or both of them spoke in public on six hundred occasions. A woman in a large audience in Wales was so moved that she handed Alice Harris her jewels to be sold for the benefit of the movement. The Harrises displayed *chicottes* and shackles, and throughout England they led church congregations in special hymns on "Congo Sundays." To shocked audiences, they described personal experiences like this one, which John Harris later put down on paper:

> Lined up . . . are 40 emaciated sons of an African village, each carrying his little basket of rubber. The toll of rubber is weighed

and accepted, but . . . four baskets are short of the demand. The order is brutally short and sharp — Quickly the first defaulter is seized by four lusty "executioners," thrown on the bare ground, pinioned hands and feet, whilst a fifth steps forward carrying a long whip of twisted hippo hide. Swiftly and without cessation the whip falls, and the sharp corrugated edges cut deep into the flesh — on back, shoulders and buttocks blood spurts from a dozen places. In vain the victim twists in the grip of the executioners, and then the whip cuts other parts of the quivering body — and in the case of one of the four, upon the most sensitive part of the human frame. The "hundred lashes each" left four inert bodies bloody and quivering on the shimmering sand of the rubber collecting post.

Following hard upon this decisive incident was another. Breakfast was just finished when an African father rushed up the veranda steps of our mud house and laid upon the ground the hand and foot of his little daughter, whose age could not have been more than 5 years.

As Morel's campaign surged forward in Europe, frantic messages flowed from Brussels to the Congo capital of Boma and from there to the most remote outposts. Near the British mission station where the Harrises had been working, the state posted a deputy public prosecutor. The governor general wrote to him:

> The main reason for your being placed at Baringa is to keep the government regularly informed of everything of interest in the Baringa region concerning the missionaries' agitation. . . . [It] will probably be necessary for you to have several blacks working for you who could gather useful information in the villages of the region, especially when the missionaries go traveling.
>
> I authorize you to hire five workers towards this end; I have given instructions to the commissioner-general of the Equator district to furnish you the necessary funds. You will use the funds as seems best to you, whether in hiring black workers . . . or in giving presents to certain natives living in the villages who can keep you up to date. . . .

It goes without saying that this must be done with the greatest
discretion.

In the following months, the public prosecutor at Boma wrote to his
deputy at Baringa asking him to find out what plans were to be hatched
at a forthcoming meeting of Protestant missionaries. Some weeks later,
this was followed by a collection of seven months' worth of Morel's *West
African Mail* and the news that further issues would be forwarded as soon
as they arrived at the capital:

> I particularly draw your attention to the importance for the
> Government in noting all the inaccuracies in the missionaries'
> accusations, in order to show the bad faith that inspires their
> attacks against the State. It is important that each of these issues
> . . . be the object of your most careful examination, and of a
> report that you send me of inaccuracies. . . .

As the attacks on Leopold mounted, the regime steadily increased its
scrutiny of Morel's allies in the Congo. None was at more risk than
Hezekiah Andrew Shanu.

Britain had established its colonies in Africa long before Leopold, and
in its early days the Congo state turned to these territories to recruit
experienced laborers, soldiers, and other personnel. Shanu was born and
educated in what is today Nigeria and became a schoolteacher. In 1884,
he began working for Leopold's regime; one task was to recruit soldiers
from his homeland for the Force Publique. When he became a clerk and
French-English translator on the governor general's staff at Boma, he
brought his wife, brother-in-law, and other members of his family from
Lagos to live in the Congo. In 1893, he left state service to go into
business for himself. The following year he went to Belgium, where he
ordered himself a piano and a steam launch, and put his son in school. In
all countries with colonies there is a ready audience for grateful subjects,
and Shanu was received with much enthusiasm when he lectured on the
Congo and thanked the Belgians for their good works. One newspaper
noted approvingly that Shanu "expresses himself in French with the
greatest correctness;" another patronizingly remembered him as "a striking example of the perfectibility of the negro race." An august-looking
man, Shanu wore a starched white collar on public occasions, with the
ribbon of a Congo state medal on his jacket lapel.

After visits to England, France, and Germany, Shanu returned to the Congo and, in a remarkable move in this state set up by Europeans for their own benefit, became a successful businessman. In Boma, he opened a well-stocked store selling canned food and other supplies from Europe; in addition he operated a tailor's shop and laundry, and ran small lodging houses both in Boma and the railhead town of Matadi. He enjoyed photography, and had some of his pictures published in the Brussels magazine *Le Congo Illustré*. When he leased a house he owned to an early British vice consul, he made so great an impression that the man recommended Shanu to the Foreign Office as his replacement during a home leave. Shanu was also respected by his former employers. During a Force Publique mutiny at Boma in 1900, state officials gratefully accepted his help in preventing the rebellion from spreading to West Africans working in the town. He even offered to take up arms against the mutineers. "Monsieur Shanu, in these troubled moments, has given proof of his sincere loyalty to the State," wrote a high Congo official.

Up to this point Shanu had thrown in his lot completely with the Congo's rulers. But something — we do not know what — caused a change of heart, and he moved into the camp of Leopold's enemies. For a black man living in the Congo capital, this was a dangerous step. One sign of his changed attitude came when he apparently supplied Roger Casement with information about the mistreatment of West African workers in the Congo. In turn, it appears that Casement told Shanu about the campaign Morel was mounting in Europe. While Casement was in the interior in 1903 making his investigation, Shanu sent a check to Morel, asking for copies of his writings. Delighted to have an African ally right in the enemy's capital, Morel immediately wrote back, sending Shanu a subscription to his newspaper, a book, and some pamphlets. "I do not know what your views on the Congo question are," he wrote, "but if they agree with mine, I shall be very glad if you can let me have information from time to time." Some weeks later Morel wrote again, suggesting that Shanu could avoid catching the eye of the Boma postal censor by addressing his mail to Morel's father-in-law in Devon. Before long Shanu found some useful information to send.

After the protests against Leopold's rule began in Europe, the Congo state had periodically made a big show of prosecuting low-ranking white officials for atrocities against Africans. Occasionally the convicted men were sentenced to prison terms, although most were released after serving only a fraction of their time. But trials can be risky for repressive governments; they can put damaging material on the public record. Like other small-fry scapegoats in tyrannies the world over, the defendants accused of brutal massacres in the Congo usually said they were only following orders — and often could produce witnesses or documents to prove the claim. The state therefore took care to keep the transcripts of these trials secret, and for some years virtually nothing leaked out. Morel, knowing the evidence from these trials would be a source of ammunition for the Congo reform campaign, asked Shanu to find out what he could.

One especially revealing case came to a climax in early 1904. The main defendant, a trigger-happy rubber-company agent named Charles Caudron, was accused of several crimes, including the murder of at least 122 Africans. In part, he was put on trial so that the state could claim it was upholding human rights, but the authorities had other motives as well. Caudron had offended the Force Publique commander in his area, who thought he was the one to run any military operations there. And he had spread his reign of terror so wildly that he had disrupted rubber production in a highly profitable district.

The trial revealed much about government orders condoning the holding of hostages. Furthermore, the appeals court lowered Caudron's sentence because of "extenuating circumstances." Invoking the familiar lazy-native theme, the court referred to the "great difficulties under which [Caudron] found himself, accomplishing his mission in the midst of a population absolutely resistant to any idea of work, and which respects no other law than force, and knows no other means of persuasion than terror."

Shanu got hold of some of the court documents and secretly sent them to Morel, who published them immediately, claiming that this was "the most damaging blow ever received by the Congo State." That was an overstatement, but the material was indeed damaging. And what was most embarrassing in it came from the mouths of Congo state officials themselves. It caught the eye of the British Foreign Office and was reprinted in an official report.

Shanu's next contribution to the anti-Congo campaign, however, ended tragically. He acted as liaison between Morel and a Congo state official, the police chief of Boma, who claimed to have information to give or sell to the reformers. But the man turned treacherous; he attacked Morel in the Belgian press and exposed Shanu as Morel's accomplice. Morel, who considered Shanu a man "of unblemished reputation and of great courage," feared for Shanu's life and urged the British consul in

Boma to do all he could to protect him. He sent offers of help to Shanu and anxiously asked for news. When it came, it was not good. Because Shanu was a British subject, the Congo authorities did not want to risk an international incident by arresting him. Instead, they harassed him unremittingly, even rescinding the medal he had been awarded for his work for the state. They then ordered all state employees not to patronize his businesses. That guaranteed that these would fail. In July 1905 Hezekiah Andrew Shanu committed suicide.

⁂

At the turn of the century, the Élysée-Palace Hotel, near the Arc de Triomphe, was among the most elegant in Paris. One day a guest happened to notice a young woman, also staying at the hotel, whose name, like other details of her past, remains in question: it was Caroline, or perhaps Blanche, Delacroix, or perhaps Lacroix. Although still a teenager, Caroline was the mistress of Antoine-Emmanuel Durrieux, a former officer in the French Army. He attempted to support them both by betting on horse races. When his betting luck ran low, it appears, Durrieux also acted as Caroline's pimp. Their lodgings at the Élysée-Palace were a useful base for these operations, but they frequently left bills unpaid. An unexpected solution to these troubles appeared when a woman approached Caroline at the hotel and said, "Madame, I am sent to you by a gentleman who has noticed you. He is a very high personage but his exalted position obliges me to withhold his name."

A meeting was arranged for the following day. According to Caroline's not entirely reliable memoirs, Durrieux, in a top hat and pearl-gray gloves, binoculars hanging around his neck, left for the racetrack unawares. (More likely, he was fully aware and had been paid off in advance.) Caroline went to a secluded room in a building on the nearby rue Lord Byron. The high personage arrived, accompanied by two aides, who took seats on either side of Caroline and began asking her questions. "It was not really a conversation; it was rather a series of trite questions asked in rotation first by one, then by the other. . . . These questions obliged me to turn my head first to the right, then to the left. I answered them without having to think, their only aim, as I learned later, being to show off my two profiles to the mute personage." After looking over his new prize, the high personage smiled behind his beard and pronounced himself pleased. He invited Caroline to travel to Austria with him, and the next day a large sum of money arrived, as well as some empty trunks for Caroline to fill with new dresses of her choice. Her admirer had found the way to her heart, for she liked nothing better in the world than to buy clothes. Caroline was sixteen; King Leopold II was sixty-five.

Then, as now, nothing royal stayed secret long. Courtiers gossiped, servants whispered, and news of the scandalous romance soon filled the press of Europe. Leopold had long had a well-known taste for extremely young women, but losing his head completely over a sixteen-year-old call girl was a different matter entirely. His new mistress was young enough to be his granddaughter. Leopold's chaotic family life and sexual tastes are far more than incidental to the Congo story. Ironically, they probably lost him more popularity in Belgium* than any of the cruelties he perpetrated in Africa. This, in turn, meant that few of his people were willing to rally behind him when he became the target of an international protest movement.

The king's personal foibles also turned him into an irresistible target for a world press stirred up by Morel. The large beard, now turned white, made him a cartoonist's dream. His bulky, cloaked figure stalked through the pages of Europe's newspapers: his beard dripping blood, his hands clutching shrunken heads from the Congo, his eyes hungrily devouring the dancers of a *corps de ballet*. He sits down to dine on a severed African head garnished with bayonets. Tsar Nicholas II complains that his knout is ineffective, so his cousin Leopold, dressed in a tiger skin, recommends the *chicotte*. Leopold's rejected daughters sadly beg their father for Caroline's cast-off clothing. Leopold and the Sultan of Turkey share a good laugh and a bottle of wine while comparing the massacre of the Congolese to that of the Armenians.

Several years into the king's liaison with his new love, his long-suffering wife, Marie-Henriette, lover of horses and music, died. From this point on, the king's infatuation with Caroline became flagrantly open. He installed her in a grand mansion, the Villa Vanderborght, across the way from the royal complex at Laeken, and built a pedestrian bridge over the street so that he could slip across at will for visits.

He was wildly jealous of Caroline, apparently with reason; he once caught her in the Brussels villa with Durrieux, the former officer from

---

* Nor did they win him friends elsewhere: after he made a state visit to Germany, Kaiser Wilhelm II's puritanical wife, Augusta, sent her personal chaplain to exorcise the palace rooms Leopold had been staying in.

whom he thought he had stolen her. Durrieux, whom Caroline tried to pass off as her brother, seems to have shown up on other occasions as well. One newspaper informed its readers that Caroline and Durrieux had secret electric bells installed in all her residences so that servants could warn them if Leopold was approaching.

After she moved to Brussels, Caroline continued to make frequent trips to Paris to visit her dressmaker and her hatmaker. (During this period, she once bragged, she bought three million francs' worth of dresses at a single store, Callot's.) When she complained to the king that the evening express train back to Brussels departed too early and left her too little shopping time, Leopold, rather than risk her staying in Paris and out of his sight overnight, spoke to the head of the railway. From then on the train left an hour later.

Caroline quickly learned to make use of Leopold's quirks, such as his hypochondria. "One day when I needed some free hours for myself I obtained them by sneezing. How many times have I kept intriguing women away from the sovereign simply by telling him that they had colds!"

Leopold took Caroline with him everywhere. Ostensibly, she traveled incognito, but with an expanding retinue of servants this became difficult. Shocking everyone, she accompanied the king to London in 1901 for the funeral of his cousin Queen Victoria. The king did not entirely lose his interest in other young women — in Brussels, Paris, and elsewhere, he periodically sent his valet or another intermediary to look for candidates who met his detailed physical specifications — but Caroline was in a different category. The two of them seemed to trumpet, rather than disguise, their difference in age: she called him Très Vieux and he called her Très Belle. To the extent that someone like Leopold was capable of love, this teenage prostitute proved to be the love of his life.

But it was not only Leopold's liaison with Caroline that lost him popularity with Belgians. It began to dawn on his people that their country was gaining little financial benefit from the Congo: the bulk of the profits were going straight into Caroline's dresses and villas and, on a far larger scale, into the king's construction projects. Since Leopold had little taste for good works, literature, or drama — and a well-known dislike for music — he spent his money mostly on building things, the bigger the better.

For years the king had pled poverty, but as his triumphal arches, museums, and monuments sprouted around the country, he could keep up the pretense no longer. Belgians were even more upset when it became clear that their king was spending much of his newfound wealth abroad. He was soon one of the largest landowners on the French Riviera, where he built a dock for his fifteen-hundred-ton yacht, the *Alberta,* and had architects from Nice design and build a series of splendid villas. His property included most of the land at the end of the scenic fingertip of Cap Ferrat, then, as now, among the most expensive seaside real estate in the world.

On his young mistress Leopold showered castles and mansions. When she became pregnant, he and the French government split the cost of building a new road near her villa at Cap Ferrat, in order to give her carriage a smoother ride. When her son was born, he was given the title of Duke of Tervuren, and she became the Baroness de Vaughan. The king took her around the Mediterranean on his yacht, but the Belgian public loathed her, and her carriage was once stoned in the streets of Brussels. In the minds of Europeans, the king's public and private lives by now were wholly entwined. When Caroline's second son was born, he had a deformed hand. A cartoon in *Punch* showed Leopold holding the newborn child, surrounded by Congolese corpses with their hands cut off. The caption read: VENGEANCE FROM ON HIGH.

How did Leopold feel about being the target of such wrath? Clearly, it exasperated him; he once wrote to an aide, "I will not let myself be soiled with blood or mud." But the tone he sounded was always of annoyance or self-pity, never of shame or guilt. Once, when he saw a cartoon of himself in a German newspaper slicing off hands with his sword, he snorted, according to a military aide, and said, "Cut off hands — that's idiotic! I'd cut off all the rest of them, but not the hands. That's the one thing I need in the Congo!" Small wonder that when the king jokingly introduced Prime Minister Auguste Beernaert to a gathering as "the greatest cynic in the kingdom," Beernaert replied, deadpan, that he would not dare take precedence over His Majesty.

15

A RECKONING

As E. D. Morel, Roger Casement, and their allies caught Europe's attention with reports of the holocaust in central Africa, newspapers and magazines ran pictures of burned villages and mutilated bodies, and missionary witnesses spoke of the depopulation of entire districts. Looking at this written and photographic record today immediately raises a crucial question: what was the death toll in Leopold's Congo? This is a good moment to pause in our story to find an answer.

The question is not simple. To begin with, history in this case cannot have distinct lines drawn around it as it can, say, when we ask how many Jews the Nazis put to death between 1933 and 1945. King Leopold II's personal État Indépendant du Congo officially existed for twenty-three years, beginning in 1885, but many Congolese were already dying unnatural deaths by the start of that period, and important elements of the king's system of exploitation endured for many years after its official end. The rubber boom, cause of the worst bloodletting in the Congo, began under Leopold's rule in the mid-1890s, but it continued several years after the end of his one-man regime.

Furthermore, although the killing in the Congo was of genocidal proportions, it was not, strictly speaking, a genocide. The Congo state was not deliberately trying to eliminate one particular ethnic group from the face of the Earth. Instead, like the slave dealers who raided Africa for centuries before them, Leopold's men were looking for labor. If, in the course of their finding and using that labor, millions of people died, that to them was incidental. Few officials kept statistics about something they considered so negligible as African lives. And so estimating the number of casualties today requires considerable historical detective work.

In population losses on this scale, the toll is usually a composite of figures from one or more of four closely connected sources: (1) murder; (2) starvation, exhaustion, and exposure; (3) disease; and (4) a plummeting birth rate. In the worst period in the Congo, the long rubber boom, it came in abundance from all four:

1. *Murder.* Although outright murder was not the major cause of death in Leopold's Congo, it was most clearly documented. When a village or a district failed to supply its quota of rubber or fought back against the regime, Force Publique soldiers or rubber company "sentries" often killed everyone they could find. Those times when an eyewitness happened upon a pile of skeletons or severed hands, and a report survives, represent, of course, only a small proportion of the massacres carried out, only a few sparks from a firestorm. But among those scattered sparks are some that burn distinctly:

- In 1896, a German newspaper, the *Kölnische Zeitung,* published, on the authority of "a highly esteemed Belgian," news that 1308 severed hands had been turned over to the notorious District Commissioner Léon Fiévez in a single day. The newspaper twice repeated the story without being challenged by the Congo state. Several additional reports of that day's events, including some from both Protestant and Catholic missionaries, cited even higher totals for the number of hands. On a later occasion, Fiévez admitted that the practice of cutting hands off corpses existed; he denied only, with great vehemence, that he had ever ordered hands cut off living people.
- In 1899, a state officer, Simon Roi, perhaps not realizing that one of the people he was chatting with was an American missionary, bragged about the killing squads under his command. The missionary, Ellsworth Faris, recorded the conversation in his diary: "Each time the corporal goes out to get rubber, cartridges are given to him. He must bring back all not used; and for every one used he must bring back a right hand! . . . As to the extent to which this is carried on, [Roi] informed me that in six months they, the State, on the Momboyo River had used 6000 cartridges, which means that 6000 people are killed or mutilated. It means more than 6000, for the people have told

me repeatedly that the soldiers kill children with the butt of their guns."

• The punitive expeditions against the Budja rebels [see pages 192–193] altogether killed more than thirteen hundred Budjas. Reports of this appeared in various Belgian newspapers in 1900, one of which was subsidized by the Congo state. Dozens of other rebellions against rubber-collecting broke out throughout the territory over the next decade. Estimating the death toll caused by suppressing them all is impossible, but sometimes a stray statistic carries appalling implications, when we remember that soldiers were severely punished for "wasting" bullets on nonhuman targets. Among a raft of revealing documents from the A.B.I.R. concession company that Morel got hold of is a register showing that in the year 1903, a *single* one of the thirty-five rubber-collecting posts in A.B.I.R. territory was sent a total of 159 firearms and 40,355 rounds of ammunition.

The list of specific massacres on record goes on and on. The territory was awash in corpses, sometimes literally. Where a river flows into Lake Tumba, wrote the Swedish missionary E. V. Sjöblom, "I saw . . . dead bodies floating on the lake with the right hand cut off, and the officer told me when I came back why they had been killed. It was for the rubber. . . . When I crossed the stream I saw some dead bodies hanging down from the branches in the water. As I turned away my face at the horrible sight one of the native corporals who was following us down said, 'Oh, that is nothing, a few days ago I returned from a fight, and I brought the white man 160 hands and they were thrown into the river.'"

It was not only missionaries and visitors who recorded the mass murders. Many Force Publique officers kept astonishingly frank diaries about the death and destruction they left behind them.

• At the village of Bikoro on Lake Tumba, a Swedish officer of the Force Publique, Lieutenant Knut Svensson, may have been the cause of some of the mangled bodies his countryman Sjöblom had seen. Svensson noted in his diary a death toll of 527 people in four and a half months' time, upon the imposition of the rubber regime in 1894–1895. (According to oral tradition in the area today, Svensson would assemble the people of a recalcitrant village, on the pretext of signing a treaty or recruiting porters, and then simply open fire.)

• The diary of another officer, Charles Lemaire, is chilling in its casualness: "28 March 1891: . . . The village of Bokanga was burned. . . . 4 April 1891: A stop at Bolébo. . . . Since they wanted to meet us only with spears and guns, the village was burned. One native killed. . . . 12 April 1891: Attack on the Ikengo villages. . . . The big chief Ekélé of Etchimanjindou was killed and thrown in the water. . . . 14 June 1891: Expedition against the Loliva who refuse to come to the station. Dreadful weather; attack made in driving rain. The group of villages was large; couldn't destroy them all. Around 15 blacks killed. . . . 14 June 1891: At 5 A.M. sent the Zanzibari Metchoudi with about 40 men . . . to burn Nkolé. . . . The operation was successful and everything was burned. . . . 4 September 1891: At 4 A.M. preparations for attacking Ipéko. . . . The whole village was burned and the banana trees cut down. . . . 13 July 1892: The Bompopo villages were attacked 7 July by Lieutenant Sarrazijn; 20 natives killed; 13 women and children taken prisoner."

• From the diary of Louis Leclercq, another Force Publique officer: "21 June 1895. . . . Arrived at Yambisi at 10:20 A.M. Village abandoned. . . . We sent several groups of soldiers to scour the area; they came back several hours later with 11 heads and 9 prisoners. A canoe sent out hunting in the evening also brought back several heads. 22 June 1895: They brought us three prisoners in the morning, three others towards evening, and three heads. A man from Baumaneh running through the forest shouting for his lost wife and child came too close to our camp and received a bullet from one of our sentries. They brought us his head. Never have I seen such an expression of despair, of fear. . . . We burned the village."

The diaries of Lemaire and Leclercq — and others — go on in this vein for day after day, week after week.

Resistance of any kind, or even cutting corners, was fatal. E. D. Morel reprinted a message that a district commissioner, Jules Jacques,* sent to one of his underlings after finding that some villagers had severed vines, killing them, to extract the rubber, instead of merely tapping the vines as they were supposed to: "M. le Chef de Poste. Decidedly these people of [Inongo] are a bad lot. They have just been and cut some rubber

---

* Jacques later won glory in World War I, and today there is a statue of him in the main square of Diksmuide, Belgium.

vines. . . . We must fight them until their absolute submission has been obtained, or their complete extermination. . . . Inform the natives that if they cut another single vine, I will exterminate them to the last man."

Conrad was not making much up when he had Mr. Kurtz scrawl the infamous line "Exterminate all the brutes!"

2. *Starvation, exhaustion, and exposure.* As news of the terror spread, hundreds of thousands of people fled their villages. In retaliation, soldiers often took their animals and burned their huts and crops, leaving them no food. This pattern of action was established even before the rubber boom, when Leopold's soldiers were looking primarily for ivory and for porters and food for themselves. A Swedish lieutenant describes such a raid in 1885 in the lower Congo rapids district: "When we were approaching there was a terrible tumult in the village. The natives . . . were completely taken with surprise. We could see them gather what they could of their belongings and escape into the deep thick woods. . . . Before I left the place I had the village plundered of the large number of goats, hens and ducks that were there. . . . Then we abandoned the village and retired to a better place for our noon rest."

As they fled these expeditions, villagers sometimes abandoned small children for fear that their cries would give away their hiding places. As a result, many children starved. A small proportion of the population, lucky enough to live near the Congo's borders, escaped from the country. Some thirty thousand refugees, the French colonial governor estimated, had crossed into French territory by 1900. Others fled to British territory, although a number of them drowned in the Luapula River, which formed part of the border with British-owned Northern Rhodesia. But for most people there was nowhere to flee except deep into the rain forest or the swamps, where there was no shelter and little food. The American soldier of fortune Edgar Canisius saw refugees from his scorched-earth raids "living like wild beasts in the forest, subsisting on roots, and ants and other insects." A fellow Presbyterian missionary of William Sheppard's wrote, in 1899, "All the people of the villages run away to the forest when they hear the State officers are coming. To-night, in the midst of the rainy season, within a radius of 75 miles of Luebo, I am sure it would be a low estimate to say that 40,000 people, men, women, children, with the sick, are sleeping in the forests without shelter."

Around the same time, a young English explorer named Ewart S. Grogan walked the length of Africa and was shocked at what he saw in crossing a "depopulated and devastated" 3000-square-mile tract in the far northeastern part of the Congo: "Every village has been burnt to the ground, and as I fled from the country I saw skeletons, skeletons everywhere; and such postures — what tales of horror they told!"

Hunger also struck villagers who did not flee into the forest, because if they were near a rubber post they had to give up much of their bananas, manioc, fish, and meat to feed the soldiers. The village of Bumba in the A.B.I.R. concession, for example, had only a hundred families, but it was expected each month to deliver fifteen kilos of yams or similar vegetables, in addition to five pigs or fifty chickens. Furthermore, villages like this one usually had to come up with all the food while their able-bodied men were in the forest, desperately searching for rubber. Without the manpower to clear new garden plots, so essential in farming the fragile soil of the rain forest, the women often replanted worn-out fields. Harvests declined, and in the old A.B.I.R. region the period is remembered today as *lonkali,* the time of famine.

Untold thousands of people, women, children, and the elderly, died as hostages. Soldiers kept them in dirt compounds, often in chains, feeding them little or nothing until the men of a village brought in the demanded amount of rubber — something that might take weeks. In one stockade in 1899, prisoners were found to be dying at the rate of three to ten a day.

3. *Disease.* As with the decimation of the American Indians, disease killed many more Congolese than did bullets. Europeans and the Afro-Arab slave-traders brought to the interior of the Congo many diseases previously not known there. The local people had no time to build up immunities — as they largely had to malaria, for instance. Both new illnesses and old ones spread rapidly, because huge numbers of Congolese were now forced to travel long distances: as men conscripted to be long-haul porters or to work as steamboat crews (a large boat required from twenty to sixty woodcutters) or as soldiers impressed into the Force Publique. The most notorious killers were smallpox and sleeping sickness, although less dramatic lung and intestinal infections also took a high toll.

Smallpox had been endemic in parts of coastal Africa for centuries, but the great population movements of the imperial age spread the illness throughout the interior, leaving village after village full of dead bodies. A Kuba king — the successor to the one who had welcomed William Sheppard to the kingdom — died from the disease. Smallpox inspired a particular terror. The Africans called it "the sickness from above" or "the sickness of heaven," because the terrifying disease seemed to come from no familiar source. One traveler to the Congo came on a deserted town where a fifteen-foot boa constrictor was dining on smallpox victims' flesh, and on another where the vultures were so gorged that they were too heavy to fly.

Sleeping sickness also spread lethally up the rivers. Half a million Congolese were estimated to have died of it in 1901 alone. The disease is caused by a parasite first spread by the bite of the pink-striped tsetse fly, about the size of a horsefly, with a distinctive high-pitched buzz. Once contracted by humans, sleeping sickness becomes highly contagious. It can cause fever, swelling of the lymph glands, a strange craving for meat, and a sensitivity to cold. At last comes the immense lethargy that gives the illness its name.

Faced with undeniable evidence of massive population loss, Leopold's apologists, then and now, blame sleeping sickness. And it is true that sleeping sickness and the other diseases would doubtless have taken many lives even if the Congo had come into the twentieth century under a regime other than Leopold's. But the story is more complicated, for disease rarely acts by itself alone. Epidemics almost always take a drastically higher and more rapid toll among the malnourished and the traumatized: the Nazis and Soviets needed no poison gas or firing squads to finish off many of those who died in their camps. Today, thanks in part to our century of famines and barbed wire, epidemiologists understand all too well the exact mechanisms by which this happens. Even in the Congo, one did not have to be a physician to see that those who were dying of disease were not dying of disease alone. Charles Gréban de Saint-Germain, a magistrate at Stanley Falls, wrote in 1905: "Disease powerfully ravages an exhausted population, and it's to this cause, in my opinion, that we must attribute the unceasing growth of sleeping sickness in this region; along with porterage and the absence of food supplies, it will quickly decimate this country. I've seen nowhere in the Congo as sad a spectacle as that along the road from Kasongo to Kabambare. The villages for the most part have few people in them; many huts are in ruins; men, like women and children, are thin, weak, without life, very sick, stretched out inert, and above all there's no food."

4. *Plummeting birth rate.* Not surprisingly, when men were sent into the forest in search of rubber for weeks at a time, year after year, and women were held hostage and half-starved, fewer children were born. A Catholic

missionary who worked for many years in the Lake Mai Ndombe district, a major rubber area, noticed this pattern. When he arrived, in 1910, he was surprised by the almost total absence of children between the ages of seven and fourteen, although there were many of other ages. This pinpoints the period from 1896 to 1903 — just when the rubber campaign was at its height in the district. A witness in a nearby area at that very time was Roger Casement, on his investigative trip. He estimated that the population had dropped by 60 percent and wrote that "the remnant of the inhabitants are only now, in many cases, returning to their destroyed or abandoned villages. . . . A lower percentage of births lessen[s] the population. . . . Women refuse to bear children, and take means to save themselves from motherhood. They give as the reason that if 'war' should come to a woman 'big with child' or with a baby to carry, 'she' cannot well run away and hide from the soldiers." Part of the population loss in the Congo resulted, then, when families, terrorized and torn apart by the rubber campaign, simply stopped having children.

No territory-wide census was taken in the Congo until long after the rubber terror was over. But Daniel Vangroenweghe, a Belgian anthropologist who worked in a former rubber area in the 1970s, found persuasive demographic evidence that large numbers of men had been worked to death as rubber slaves or killed in punitive raids — and he discovered the evidence in the regime's own statistics. No other explanation accounts for the curious pattern that threads through the village-by-village headcounts taken in the colony long before the first territorial census. These local headcounts consistently show far more women than men.

At Inongo in 1907, for example, there were 309 children, 402 adult women, but only 275 adult men. (This was the very town for which, some ten years earlier, the district commissioner had ordered "absolute submission . . . or . . . complete extermination.") At nearby Iboko in 1908 there were 322 children, 543 adult women, but only 262 adult men. Statistics from numerous other villages show the same pattern. Sifting such figures today is like sifting the ruins of an Auschwitz crematorium. They do not tell you precise death tolls, but they reek of mass murder.

During Leopold's rule, by how much, from all four causes, did the Congo population shrink? Just as when historians chart population loss from the Black Death in fourteenth-century Europe, they can be more confident of the percentage than they are of absolute numbers. They have, after all, no census data. Interestingly, some estimates of population loss in the Congo made by those who saw it firsthand agree with some of those made by more scientific methods today.

An official Belgian government commission in 1919 estimated that from the time Stanley began laying the foundation of Leopold's state, the population of the territory had "been reduced by half." Major Charles C. Liebrechts, a top executive of the Congo state administration for most of its existence, arrived at the same estimate in 1920. The most authoritative judgment today comes from Jan Vansina, professor emeritus of history and anthropology at the University of Wisconsin and perhaps the greatest living ethnographer of Congo basin peoples. He bases his calculations on "innumerable local sources from different areas: priests noticing their flocks were shrinking, oral traditions, genealogies, and much more." His estimate is the same: between 1880 and 1920, the population of the Congo was cut "by at least a half."

Half of what? Only in the 1920s were the first attempts made at a territory-wide census. In 1924 the population was reckoned at ten million, a figure confirmed by later counts. This would mean, according to the estimates, that during the Leopold period and its immediate aftermath the population of the territory dropped by approximately ten million people.

※※※

Burned villages, starved hostages, terrified refugees dying in swamps, orders for "extermination" — even in crass, purely monetary terms, aren't these inefficient means of doing business? Massacring huge numbers of people may frighten the survivors into gathering rubber, but doesn't it destroy the labor force? Indeed it does. Belgian administrators ordered the census taken in 1924 because they were deeply concerned about a shortage of available workers. "We run the risk of someday seeing our native population collapse and disappear," fretfully declared the permanent committee of the National Colonial Congress of Belgium that year. "So that we will find ourselves confronted with a kind of desert."

Why, then, did the killings go on for so long? The same irrationality lies at the heart of many other mass murders. In the Soviet Union, for example, shooting or jailing political opponents at first helped the Communist Party and then Josef Stalin gain absolute power. But after there were no visible opponents left, seven million more people were executed, and many millions more died in the far-flung camps of the gulag. So many engineers were seized that factories came to a halt; so many railway men died that some trains did not run; so many colonels and generals were shot that the almost leaderless Red Army was nearly crushed by the German invasion of 1941.

In the Congo, as in Russia, mass murder had a momentum of its own. Power is tempting, and in a sense no power is greater than the ability to take someone's life. Once under way, mass killing is hard to stop; it becomes a kind of sport, like hunting. Congo annals abound in cases like that of René de Permentier, an officer in the Equator district in the late 1890s. The Africans nicknamed him Bajunu (for *bas genoux,* on your knees), because he always made people kneel before him. He had all the bushes and trees cut down around his house at Bokatola so that from his porch he could use passersby for target practice. If he found a leaf in a courtyard that women prisoners had swept, he ordered a dozen of them beheaded. If he found a path in the forest not well-maintained, he ordered a child killed in the nearest village.

Two Force Publique officers, Clément Brasseur and Léon Cerckel, once ordered a man hung from a palm tree by his feet while a fire was lit beneath him and he was cooked to death. Two missionaries found one post where prisoners were killed by having resin poured over their heads, then set on fire. The list is much longer.

Michael Herr, the most brilliant reporter of the Vietnam War, captures the same frenzy in the voice of one American soldier he met: "We'd rip out the hedges and burn the hooches and blow all the wells and kill every chicken, pig and cow in the whole fucking ville. I mean, if we can't shoot these people, what the fuck are we doing here?" When another American, Francis Ford Coppola, tried to put the blood lust of that war on film, where did he turn for the plot of his *Apocalypse Now?* To Joseph Conrad, who had seen it all, a century earlier, in the Congo.

16

"JOURNALISTS WON'T GIVE YOU RECEIPTS"

As the Congo reform crusade reached its height, the man in England whose name was most indelibly linked to the territory passed from the scene. After having been elected to Parliament, Sir Henry Morton Stanley found serving there a bore. The rousing adventure stories he liked to tell on the lecture circuit were no substitute for a polished House of Commons debating style. Stanley lacked something else useful in Parliament: a sense of humor. He soon resigned.

The years of battling malaria, dysentery, and other tropical diseases had taken their toll. Only in his early sixties, this surprisingly small man with close-cropped white hair and mustache and a ruddy, weathered face moved ever more slowly. He avidly followed the news of the Boer War, fulminating against the rebels who dared to challenge British rule. Filled with self-pity and calling himself "a man who had given up his life for his country and for Africa," he worked fitfully on his autobiography. Although he had been a fast, prolific writer all his life, he left this book unfinished, perhaps fearful of being caught in the web of contradictory stories he had spun about his childhood and youth. He, his wife, Dorothy, and an adopted son divided their time between a London home and an elegant mock-Tudor country mansion in Surrey. They named a pond, a stream, and a pine grove on their estate after the scenes of his fame: Stanley Pool, the Congo River, and the Ituri forest.

Stanley was rumored to be unhappy with the chamber of horrors the Congo had become, but the few public statements he made were all in Leopold's defense. His health grew worse, probably exacerbated by the myriad of hovering doctors eager to give their famous patient all the latest treatments: strychnine injections, ammonia, ether, and electric pulses. On May 10, 1904, Stanley heard Big Ben strike in the night, and murmured, "How strange! So that is time! Strange!" Those were his last words.

Stanley was one of the most lionized Englishmen of his time, and while he lived, his display of loyalty to Leopold was worth far more than any publicity the king could have bought. But with Stanley gone, Casement's report released, and Morel's attacks on the increase, Leopold needed new defenses. Signs of these showed up in an unexpected place.

Luxury train travel had reached a high point during the first decade of the twentieth century. Cities across Europe were linked together by the comfortable sleeping cars of the Compagnie Internationale de Wagons-Lits. For the well-to-do, boarding an overnight express train meant clouds of hissing steam on the platform, a porter carrying suitcases, and a sleeping car attendant folding down the bed. By the middle of the decade, these elite travelers could count on a small addition to the ritual. On the table in the sleeping compartment would be found a monthly magazine, with three parallel columns of type in English, French, and German, called *The Truth about the Congo*. Its free distribution to this select captive audience of wealthy Europeans was a publicist's dream. A major stockholder of the Compagnie Internationale de Wagons-Lits was King Leopold II. The king had begun his counteroffensive.

Stimulated by Morel, attacks on Leopold were now coming from all quarters. During the decade, branches or affiliates of the Congo Reform Association would spring up in Germany, France, Norway, Switzerland, and other countries. Eight members of the Swedish Parliament signed a statement supporting the C.R.A. Among his supporters Morel could count Prince Boris Czetwertynski, of a distinguished Polish noble family, the famous novelist Anatole France, and the Nobel Prize–winning Norwegian writer Björnstjerne Björnson. In Switzerland, wrote one witness, men grew pale and tears collected in women's eyes when Alice Harris's pictures of maimed children were shown at a Congo protest meeting. A speaker attacked the Congo administration at a big public meeting in Australia; a series of talks was given in New Zealand. In Italy, one of Leopold's critics was so vociferous that the Congo state consul in Genoa, Giovanni Elia, challenged him to a duel. (Both men were lightly wounded, the consul on the nose, his opponent on the arm.) Morel and his supporters seemed to the king an international conspiracy. So he fought back internationally.

Belgium's lack of great-power status meant that Leopold was dependent on cunning, above all on his skill at manipulating the press. As he waged his countercampaign, the king showed himself to be as much a master of the mass media as his archenemy Morel. He dispatched an aide on a secret mission to British Africa to search out abuses to match those Casement had found in the Congo. He made sure there were frequent articles in *The Truth about the Congo* along the lines of "Opium in British India" and derogatory news items from all over the British Empire: floggings in South Africa, human sacrifices in Nigeria, abuses in Sierra Leone and Australia. Then, calling in his chits, Leopold threatened to take away his friend Sir Alfred Jones's lucrative Congo shipping contract if Jones did not manage to dampen British criticism.

Jones promptly went to work. He paid £3000 for long trips to the Congo by two travelers. One was his friend Viscount William Mountmorres, a young man who indirectly owed Jones his job. Mountmorres obligingly published a favorable book about the Congo in 1906: "It is astounding to witness the whole-hearted zeal with which the officials . . . devote themselves to their work." While Mountmorres acknowledged some excesses, he found most of the Congo "to be well and humanely-governed." Mountmorres's volume reminds one of Beatrice and Sidney Webb's famously cheerful account of their visit to the young Soviet Union. Like the Webbs, Mountmorres assumed that any laws and regulations on the books were carefully followed. The *chicotte,* he stressed, could be used only after a formal inquiry in which the accused had the right to call witnesses, and could be applied only to the buttocks. Also, "not more than twenty strokes may be inflicted in any case except for habitual thieving, when a maximum of fifty may be ordered, but in this case the punishment must be spread over a series of days, and not more than twenty strokes given on any one day." (In practice, this was followed about as rigorously as the early Soviet decree outlawing the death penalty.)

The other voyager Jones sponsored was Mary French Sheldon, a London publisher and travel writer. Once in the Congo, she depended for her travel on the steamboats of the state and its company allies (something Casement had been careful not to do), and officials spared no effort in showing her the territory's delights. Everywhere she went, hostages were released so that she would see no one in custody. According to one missionary, at Bangala on the Congo River the state agent even "pulled down an old prison, and levelled the ground, and made it all nice, because she was coming." Things went seriously awry only once, when a local station chief got his instructions garbled. Confusing Mrs. Sheldon with another VIP he had been told to prepare for, from the Liverpool School of Tropical Medicine, he assembled for her inspection in a clearing the most severely crippled people and the worst cases of disease he could find. But no matter; Mrs. Sheldon fell in love with a steamboat captain and had a good time. Leopold granted her an audience when she was on her way home, and Jones helped place her enthusiastic articles in newspapers. "I have witnessed more atrocities in London streets than I have ever seen in the Congo," she wrote in the *Times* in 1905. On her return, she gave a speech and slide show for five hundred people at London's Savoy Hotel, for which Leopold paid the bill. The king then put her on his payroll at fifteen hundred francs a month (about $7500 today) to lobby members of Parliament.

While launching these counterattacks on his British critics in public, Leopold simultaneously tried to co-opt them, always using go-betweens to cover his tracks. A Paris attorney approached a board member of the Congo Reform Association: if the C.R.A. would draft a reform plan and a proposed budget for the Congo, he could guarantee, he said, that His Majesty would read it with great interest. Morel rejected this as "extraordinarily impudent." Leopold's British Baptist friend Sir Hugh Gilzean Reid made a similar overture to the Aborigines Protection Society; it too was rebuffed.

The king did get some artful revenge on one opponent, the influential French journalist Pierre Mille, an ally of Morel's who had fiercely and repeatedly attacked the king in print. One day a courtier brought word that Mille was quietly visiting Brussels with a woman not his wife. Leopold found out where they were staying and sent them an invitation to visit the great greenhouses at the château of Laeken. Mille and his lady friend accepted, and they appeared so delighted that Leopold thought he had won over a major critic. But soon after, Mille resumed his attacks. The king then asked the Belgian embassy in Paris to find Mille's home address. To it he sent a huge bouquet of flowers, with a card bearing the royal coat of arms and the message, "To Monsieur and Madame Pierre Mille, in memory of their visit to Laeken."

Leopold's public relations campaign was mounted by an elaborate staff.

In September 1904, he had called together a group of his top advisers and laid plans for a Press Bureau. It would be headquartered well away from public scrutiny behind several innocuous front organizations: the German-based Committee for the Protection of Interests in Africa, the Bureau of Comparative Legislation in Brussels, and the Federation for the Defense of Belgian Interests Abroad, which operated in many countries.

Within a year or two, new pro-Leopold books began coming off the presses. The Press Bureau secretly subsidized several Belgian newspapers and a magazine, published in Edinburgh, called *New Africa — The Truth on the Congo Free State.* Taking a cue from Morel, Leopold ordered up more than two dozen pamphlets. His British publicist, Demetrius C. Boulger (who was on a 1250-franc monthly retainer, plus bonuses), wrote one called, perhaps too defensively, *The Congo State is* NOT *a Slave State.** Another, *A Complete Congo Controversy, illustrating the controversial methods of Mr. Morel, Hon. Sec. Congo Reform Association,* appeared over the signature of one Lieutenant Colonel James Harrison, billed as "a country gentleman of absolutely independent mind, a sportsman and a traveller, and a familiar figure in London Social and Political Circles." Harrison's main qualification as a Congo expert was his having made a big-game hunting expedition there, during which, he found, "the natives were cheerful and satisfied."

The main work of the Press Bureau, however, was done under cover. Its agents surreptitiously passed cash to editors and reporters all over Europe; by 1907, the Brussels correspondents of both the *Times of London* and Germany's *Kölnische Zeitung* were on the take. Two editors of a major newspaper in Vienna received the equivalent of more than $70,000 in today's money. In Italy, Elia, the dueling consul, made payments to two newspapers, planted favorable articles elsewhere, arranged for people to write a pro-Leopold pamphlet and book, and paid off at least one legislator. The newspaper *Corriere della Sera* refused a large bribe and launched an investigation instead.

The bureau focused much of its attention on Germany, now a major power in Africa. The country was a particular problem because Kaiser

---

* It used, among other things, the lazy-native theme in justifying Leopold's methods: "To draw up a scheme by which the black race can be made to work without pressure or compulsion in some form or other is beyond the powers of human ingenuity."

Wilhelm II personally loathed Leopold; at one point he called him "Satan and Mammon in one person." The Press Bureau organized the usual array of pro-Leopold lectures and pamphlets in German, but that was only the beginning. Ludwig von Steub, a banker who served as honorary Belgian consul in Munich, operated as a German bagman for Leopold. In Berlin, the *National-Zeitung* was writing fiercely in 1903 of "the unscrupulous businessman who lives in the palace in Brussels," but von Steub, knowing that the newspaper was in financial difficulties, acted accordingly. By 1905, the paper moved onto the fence: "It is certainly not easy for a German to arrive at a clear opinion in questions where so many interests are at stake, notably those of the British rubber merchants." Later that year it devoted an entire page to a glowing portrait of a prosperous Congo state, shamefully calumnized by a clique of foreign merchants and missionaries who spread "old wives' tales" and "hateful peddlar's stories." By 1906 it was publishing Leopold's decrees. In 1907 its editor was decorated by the king.

Readers observed similar mysterious transformations in other German newspapers. The *Münchener Allgemeine Zeitung,* for example, once adamantly opposed to Leopold's rule, suddenly began publishing pro-Leopold Congo news items from "a most reliable source" or "a Congolese source" or "a well-informed source." The newspaper's Brussels correspondent, not in on the take, sent home more critical reports, including a long piece that apparently got into the paper without first being read by the editor in chief. In the very next issue, an editor's note began, "Contrary to the opinions we published in an earlier issue, another source, no doubt better informed on the situation in the Congo, has sent us the following commentary. . . ."

Bribes are usually hard to trace, but we know something about Leopold's in Germany because of an amusing chain of events. Exposés damaged the Press Bureau's effectiveness, and in 1908 its German payoff operations were ordered shut down. But poor von Steub in Munich didn't understand the message or couldn't bring himself to stop doing this interesting work. He kept on paying out his bribes — and then became upset when he wasn't reimbursed. He soon was bombarding officials in Brussels with obsequious, complaining letters, which somehow escaped destruction and were discovered in the archives more than fifty years later. In them von Steub described his work in ever greater detail, to ever higher officials. "According to the opinion of all the colonial experts, the good will of the German government [toward the

Congo] is due mainly to my activity," he wrote to the Belgian foreign minister. "To abandon the flag at such an important moment and to leave the field free for the enemy seemed a crime to me. . . . On January 1 and April 1 I made all the usual payments, and I dare hope to at least have my expenses covered." Later, more desperate than ever, he describes his "payments to organs of the press" and explains why he isn't submitting paperwork to back up his claims: "In giving me my assignment, M. Liebrechts [the Congo state's secretary general of the interior] told me, 'Journalists and writers won't give you receipts, so don't ask for any.'"

Despite the king's efforts to stem it, the outpouring of criticism spread rapidly. As soon as the Congo Reform movement was well under way in England, E. D. Morel set his sights on the United States. That nation had, Morel told every American who would listen, a special responsibility to bring Leopold's bloody rule to an end, because it was the first country to have recognized the Congo.

In September 1904, at the invitation of a group of American Congo missionaries who were already denouncing the king's rule, Morel crossed the Atlantic. Shortly after he disembarked in New York, he was received by President Theodore Roosevelt at the White House. He next spoke at a human rights conference in Boston and spurred his allies to found the American Congo Reform Association. Its first head was Dr. G. Stanley Hall, president of Clark University, remembered today mainly for later inviting Sigmund Freud to the United States. The association's vice presidents soon included several churchmen, President David Starr Jordan of Stanford University, Booker T. Washington, and Mark Twain. Washington took a delegation of black Baptists to the White House to urge President Roosevelt to put pressure on Leopold, lobbied members of the Senate Foreign Relations Committee, and, encouraged by Morel, joined Twain in speaking about the Congo at public meetings in several cities. "Dr. Washington is no small enemy to overcome," one of Leopold's agents in the United States wrote the king. Leopold unsuccessfully tried to get Washington off the case by offering him an all-expenses-paid trip to the Congo, and, when that didn't work, a trip to Belgium.

Deeply impressed after meeting Morel in New York, Twain three times went to the nation's capital to lobby. "I think I have never known him to be so stirred up on any one question as he was on that of the cruel treatment of the natives in the Congo Free State. . . ." Washington wrote of Twain. "I saw him several times in connection with his efforts to bring about reforms in the Congo Free State, and he never seemed to tire of talking on the subject." Twain had lunch with Roosevelt — news Morel eagerly passed on to the British Foreign Office — met with the secretary of state, and wrote to Morel that the cause of Congo reform in the United States was a "giant enterprise . . . [that] needs an organization like U.S. Steel." In 1905 he wrote a pamphlet, *King Leopold's Soliloquy,* an imaginary monologue by Leopold. It went through many printings and garnered royalties that the author donated to the Congo Reform Association. Much of the monologue is about Leopold's media campaign. "In these twenty years I have spent millions to keep the Press of the two hemispheres quiet, and still these leaks keep occurring," says Twain's exasperated king, who rages against "the incorruptible *kodak.* . . . The only witness I have encountered in my long experience that I couldn't bribe." In Twain's pamphlet, Leopold attacks William Sheppard by name and denounces the black man's "meddlesome missionary spying." Although it is painted with too broad a brush and is far from Twain's best work, *King Leopold's Soliloquy* provoked the royal propaganda machine to rush out an anonymous forty-seven-page pamphlet, *An Answer to Mark Twain.*

Just as he had done in England, Morel smoothly shaped his message for different American constituencies. Most of his allies were progressive intellectuals like Mark Twain, but he was willing to sup with the devil to help his cause. He made shrewd use of Senator John Tyler Morgan, the former Confederate general who had helped to engineer U.S. recognition of Leopold's Congo twenty years earlier. Morgan, still thundering away about sending blacks back to Africa so as to make an all-white South, wanted the abuses in the Congo cleaned up with no delay. Otherwise, how could black Americans be persuaded to move there? He hoped to see ten million of them "planted" in the Congo, he told Morel. With prodding from Morel, Morgan kept the issue of Congo atrocities alive in the Senate.

The veteran British Baptist missionaries John and Alice Harris, who followed Morel to America, addressed more than two hundred public meetings in forty-nine cities. At one meeting in Chicago an old woman who had been born a slave tried to donate her life savings to the cause of Congo reform; the reformers would accept only one dollar. Speaking tours by other activists followed. John Harris enthusiastically reported to Morel from Washington, "Telegrams, petitions, private letters are rolling in here by the thousands. . . . The President . . . with a little more pressure will take some action."

Secretary of State Elihu Root, who found himself on the receiving end of all the pressure, recalled later in some exasperation, "The very people who are most ardent against entangling alliances insist most fanatically upon our doing one hundred things a year on humanitarian grounds. . . . The Protestant Church and many good women were wild to have us stop the atrocities in the Congo. . . . People kept piling down on the [State] Department demanding action." Petition-signers included the governor of Massachusetts and every member of the Commonwealth's senate, a group of Yale professors and officials, university presidents, divinity school deans, bishops, and newspaper editors. A Congo resolution was passed by the convention of the National Women's Christian Temperance Union.

Although Morel had vocal individual supporters throughout Europe, only in the United States did the cause of Congo reform become the full-scale crusade it was in England. Horrified to see the movement against him spreading to a new continent, Leopold leaped into action. When Morel spoke in Boston in 1904, no fewer than six of the king's spokesmen showed up to demand equal time. When the influential Senator Henry Cabot Lodge of Massachusetts arrived in Paris for a visit the following year, the king immediately sent an emissary to invite him to dinner in Brussels. "He named six different days, so there was no escape," Lodge wrote to President Roosevelt. Lodge was impressed by Leopold; he described him as "a shrewd, active able man of business — a cross between [railroad barons] Jim Hill & Harriman, between the great organizer & promoter & the speculator. He knows everybody & about everybody."

Using his knowledge "about everybody," Leopold targeted an even more powerful senator, Nelson W. Aldrich of Rhode Island. Aldrich, a multimillionaire, a card-playing partner of J. Pierpont Morgan, the father-in-law of John D. Rockefeller, Jr., and chairman of the Senate Finance Committee, was the ultimate Washington power broker. "I'm just a president," Roosevelt once told the journalist Lincoln Steffens, "and he has seen lots of presidents."

Leopold courted Aldrich and other influential Americans by promising them a share of the loot. He gave major Congo concession rights to Aldrich, the Guggenheim interests, Bernard Baruch, John D. Rockefeller, Jr., and the financier Thomas Ryan, a close friend and former legal client of Secretary of State Root. A letter of advice to the king from one of his

American agents made clear the strategy Leopold was following: "Open up a strip of territory clear across the Congo State from east to west for benefit of American capital. Take the present concessionaires by the throat if necessary, and compel them to share their privileges with the Americans. In this manner, you will create an American vested interest in the Congo which will render the yelping of the English agitators and the Belgian Socialists futile." Leopold also gave more than three thousand Congo artifacts to the American Museum of Natural History, knowing that J. P. Morgan was on its board.

With Senator Aldrich, Leopold's largesse worked. The State Department was under constant pressure from the reformers to appoint an American consul general to the Congo who could follow up Roger Casement's investigation with one of his own. To get the reformers off his back, Secretary of State Root nominated the consul general they had suggested, but when Aldrich let it be known he would block that choice in the Senate, Root withdrew the nomination.

His eye on key American ethnic voting blocs, Leopold also played the role of the victimized Catholic. His representatives in Rome successfully convinced the Vatican that this Catholic king was being set upon by unscrupulous Protestant missionaries. A stream of messages in Latin* flowed from the Holy See across the Atlantic to the designated Catholic point-man for Leopold in the United States, James Cardinal Gibbons of Baltimore — who, as it happened, was another card-playing companion of Senator Aldrich. Cardinal Gibbons believed that the Congo reform crusade was the work of "only a handful of discontented men . . . depending largely upon the untrustworthy hearsay evidence of natives." He spoke out loudly for Leopold, who awarded him the Grand Cross of the Order of the Crown.

Leopold had a full squadron of lobbyists in the United States. Professor Alfred Nerincx, of George Washington University, helped put out a new English-language magazine on the Congo, gave speeches, and saw to it that favorable articles appeared in highbrow magazines. Frederick Starr, an oddball University of Chicago anthropologist who was a big believer in the inferiority of "primitive" peoples, received one of Leopold's innumerable medals and a full-year, all-expenses-paid tour of the Congo. In

---

* "*Probe novit summus Pontifex ea omnia, quae exagitata fuerunt contra Gubernium Status Congi Independentis seu Belgici, per aliquos missionarios protestantes anglicos. . . .*"

return he produced a series of fifteen enthusiastic articles in the *Chicago Daily Tribune* under the heading "Truth about the Congo Free State," later reprinted as a book.* Henry Wellington Wack, an attorney for a patent-medicine firm, published a thick book that soon appeared in thousands of American libraries. Instructions from Brussels were that Wack was "to act as if he were not in the State's employ, but merely an impartial publicist."

Another American agent, however, proved less reliable. In setting up his U.S. lobbying effort, the king had made a rare and disastrous misstep.

For any well-heeled Californian who found himself on trial in 1904, a likely defense lawyer might have been Colonel Henry I. Kowalsky of San Francisco. Kowalsky was a classic American type: the flamboyant trial lawyer who himself skirts the edge of the law and whose showman's dazzle attracts a roster of famous friends and acquaintances. A bon vivant, raconteur, and big spender who ran up legendary hotel bills, the gregarious Kowalsky's larger-than-life persona and courtroom skills won him a broad range of clients. Some were boxers and underworld figures; some were previously unknown relatives or common-law wives, whom he had a great knack for finding when there was a will that could be contested. Like many a colonel of his day, Kowalsky had never been in the army, although he let Europeans believe he had been.

It was not just Kowalsky's personality that was larger than life. A renowned amateur chef, he consumed a vast amount of his own and others' cooking. "Compared with him," a reporter later observed when the portly William Howard Taft was in the White House, "President Taft is a top worker in a team of acrobats." Kowalsky's enormous neck cascaded over his collar; his voice had a husky wheeze; and when a San Francisco newspaper asked local luminaries for their favorite recipes one Christmas, Kowalsky slyly submitted one for roast jowls.

He also suffered from narcolepsy, the disease that causes uncontrollable short spells of sleep. "There is scarcely a man familiar with the life of San Francisco who has not seen Kowalsky fall asleep on the street, sitting in

---

* Here, for example, is Starr on the *chicotte:* "Many a time . . . I have seen a man immediately after being flogged, laughing and playing with his companions as if naught had happened."

the lobby of a hotel, trying a case in court or occupying a box at a theater," observed a reporter. He may, in fact, have had more control over this problem than he admitted; a journalist covering one trial noticed that "he awakes just in time to interpose the most pertinent legal objections to questions.

"And it is these sudden awakenings," the story went on, "that have occasioned such havoc among the furniture of Judge Graham's court. When a man of some 300 pounds — to put it conservatively — awakes with a start, it is apt to jar the strongest chair made. . . . A few times more and there is an ominous creak, and then a crack and a smash. 'There goes another,' murmurs Bailiff McGenity as the colonel abandons his ruined chair and draws up a firm one." At the end of this particular trial, Kowalsky grandly presented the court with a special chair he had ordered built — of solid oak, held together by iron bolts, its legs reinforced with iron bracing.

When Kowalsky was on the other side of a bitter legal battle with the famous gunfighter Wyatt Earp, the short-fused Earp threatened to shoot Kowalsky on sight. The two men ran into each other in a San Francisco saloon. Earp forced Kowalsky into a back room, pulled out a revolver, and told the lawyer to get ready to meet his maker. Kowalsky's jowly face dropped onto his chest and he dozed off. Earp stormed from the room, saying, "What can you do with a man who goes to sleep just when you're going to kill him!"

Kowalsky had an unerring eye for the pathway to a lucrative client, and he spotted one when Prince Albert, heir apparent to the Belgian throne, came to California. Albert was traveling incognito, but Kowalsky recognized and befriended him, and was rewarded in 1904 with an invitation to Belgium. There, he was received on board the royal yacht at Ostend and introduced to Leopold.

Looking at Kowalsky, the king saw an American who was active in the Republican Party, then in power, and a man who portrayed himself as a lobbyist extraordinaire, able to thwart the troublesome do-gooders intent on causing trouble for His Majesty. With Morel starting to stir up the American public, there seemed no time to waste. The king hired Kowalsky, gave him detailed instructions, and provided enough money for a luxurious office on Wall Street. As Kowalsky prepared to move to New York, his friends in San Francisco — judges, businessmen, an admiral, and some rival lawyers who may have been happy to see him leave town — gave him a farewell banquet that doubtless added a few more pounds to his already awesome frame. "I shall not closely follow the text of the toast which has been assigned me," said the mayor of San Francisco. "Like our guest, it is too large a subject." Another speaker commented that it was fortunate Leopold had not sent Kowalsky directly to the Congo, where "the cannibals of Africa would have taken pleasure in so choice a morsel."

Kowalsky replied to the toasts, "When I leave you, it is only because I have heard the clarion call of duty in the interest of humanity and civilization." The clarion call included an annual retainer of 100,000 francs, about $500,000 in today's money. In his new role, Kowalsky was received by President Roosevelt, to whom he gave a photograph of Leopold in a silver frame, an album of photos of the Congo, and a memorandum asking him not to be deceived by jealous missionaries and Liverpool merchants.

Someone taken by surprise by all this was Baron Ludovic Moncheur, the Belgian minister to the United States, who had just penned a rapturous article, "Conditions in the Congo Free State," for the influential *North American Review* and who thought *he* was leading Leopold's American propaganda effort. He was horrified by the sudden appearance of Kowalsky, who had the unmistakable look of a shyster. On the very day of Kowalsky's farewell banquet in San Francisco, Moncheur learned with dismay, the lawyer had had a fistfight in court with a creditor. Moncheur and his aides sent off a frantic stream of messages to Brussels.

At the Royal Palace, no underling dared openly oppose a new favorite of the king's, but Moncheur did at last receive a coded telegram from a top executive for Congo affairs: "I have your information on Kowalsky. Do you think the situation is such that we should cancel his mission? — which would be difficult for us, however. Wouldn't it be better to try to give him another mission in Africa or China?"

"It would be worse than useless to send him to the Congo," one of Moncheur's aides replied, "unless one could hope that he wouldn't come back." Moncheur followed this up with a prescient warning about Kowalsky: "If he took me to be the cause of his disgrace, he could make scenes that would produce a scandal in the press."

Cautiously, Congo state officials asked Kowalsky to come to Brussels, where they requested that he undertake an urgent mission to Nigeria. Kowalsky was interested enough to buy himself a sun helmet and an elephant gun, but he then turned down the assignment, probably having guessed that he was being put out of circulation. Because he knew too much, Leopold's worried Congo aides did not dare fire him, so they sent him back to the United States with more lobbying instructions, which barely disguised their mounting anxiety: "Colonel Kowalsky's mission is to enlighten senators and congressmen as to the justice of our cause, and to ward off the passing of unfavorable resolutions by them." However: "He will be careful not to call at the White House except in case of absolute necessity. . . . He will make no public speeches except after taking the Belgian Minister's advice."

Kowalsky was now out of the loop, and a year after Leopold had hired him, the king let his contract expire. In vain, the lawyer bombarded Leopold with letters (all beginning "My dear Majesty . . .") touting his work for the Congo cause, denouncing his rivals among Leopold's other American lobbyists (he called one "a characterless, unworthy, and unprincipled ingrate" with a "rascally hand"), and making extravagant claims for himself. "It was a mighty task, and I worked night and day. . . . I have travelled thousands of miles in this cause." He tried to flatter the king into putting him back on the payroll: "I confess having conceived an affection for your Majesty such as I felt for my much beloved and lamented father." To Kowalsky's annual retainer, Leopold added a hefty 125,000 francs on condition that he leave quietly, all the while soothing him with hints that at some future date the king might need his services again.

At last, however, the spurned Kowalsky did what Moncheur and his colleagues at the Belgian embassy had been dreading. On December 10, 1906, readers of William Randolph Hearst's *New York American* picked up their newspapers to find a front-page exposé on the workings of the American Congo lobby. KING LEOPOLD'S AMAZING ATTEMPT TO INFLUENCE OUR CONGRESS EXPOSED. . . . FULL TEXT OF THE AGREE- MENT BETWEEN KING LEOPOLD OF BELGIUM AND HIS PAID AGENTS IN WASHINGTON. Although Kowalsky indignantly maintained that someone had robbed his office, he had, it appears, sold Hearst his complete Congo correspondence.

Every day for a week, Hearst played the story for all it was worth, splashing tens of thousands of words and dozens of photographs across the pages of the *American* and the many other newspapers he owned. There could not have been a worse catastrophe for Leopold, for, in order to highlight its scoop, the *American* dramatized the king's villainy by reprinting Morel's severed-hands photos and trumpeting all the Congo reformers' atrocity charges: INFAMOUS CRUELTIES. . . . TORTURE OF WOMEN AND CHILDREN. . . . U.S. AMAZED AT CRIMES OF CONGO.

The documents revealed that, in addition to Kowalsky's salary and keep-quiet payment, Leopold had promised Kowalsky an additional 100,000 francs in the king's Congo state bonds "if the American Government does not make any declaration harmful to the Congo State, and if Congress passes no unfavourable resolutions before the end of the next session." A letter from Kowalsky to the king boasted of a $1000 bribe he had paid to an unnamed prominent journalist, who was, he claimed, "the President's personal friend," from whose services "we got hundreds of thousands in advertising our cause." Kowalsky also boasted that he had quashed an exposé in *Munsey's Magazine* by going to "the editor, my personal friend, who destroyed the article and published one very complimentary to Your Majesty's interest instead."

The most enticing revelation of all was that Kowalsky had used Leopold's money to bribe Thomas G. Garrett, a staff member of the Senate Foreign Relations Committee, to help derail Congo protest resolutions. Garrett, Kowalsky extravagantly told the king, had "stood at the door of the committee room and held back the demanding, howling missionaries, ministers, and religious cranks, as well as some agents of the Liverpool outfit. All this time I was at my post, and only when Congress closed did I breathe safely." On the *American*'s front page appeared a photograph of a handwritten letter on U.S. Senate stationery from Garrett to Kowalsky, asking for part of the promised payment.

Garrett was promptly fired. Hours after the story broke, Senator Lodge of Massachusetts, where the American Congo Reform Association had its headquarters, introduced a resolution calling for an international investigation of the Congo scandal. Skillful lobbying by Moncheur and backroom maneuvering by Senator Aldrich got the resolution watered down before it was passed, but the entire episode dramatically changed the climate in Washington. Secretary of State Root reversed the government's previous hands-off policy and decided to cooperate with the British in putting pressure on Leopold to end his rule over the territory. The Kowalsky revelations — swiftly and jubilantly reprinted by Morel, both in England and in a pamphlet in French for Belgium — created a major setback for Leopold. The tide was turning against the king.

Around the time that he hired Kowalsky, Leopold had begun maneuvers on a completely different front. Remembering how effectively his sham Commission for the Protection of the Natives had silenced his critics in the 1890s, he decided it was time for another commission. This one would go to the Congo, investigate the situation, and clear his name.

To his new Commission of Inquiry, he appointed three judges: one Belgian, one Swiss, and one Italian. The commission, however, was not as neutral as it appeared. The Italian, Baron Giacomo Nisco, worked not in Italy, but in the Congo state as chief judge. It was he, in fact, who in the notorious Caudron case [see page 220] had reduced the prisoner's sentence on grounds that a certain amount of "force" and "terror" was unavoidable. Furthermore, none of the three judges knew any African language or even enough English to talk directly to the highly critical British and American missionaries. The commission was told to hold hearings, hear witnesses, and issue a report. On the long voyage to the Congo, the king surely hoped, the old Africa hand Baron Nisco would enlighten his two fellow judges about the natives' need for firm discipline.

The commission spent several months taking 370 depositions. It held its sessions everywhere, from the verandas of rubber-collecting posts to the deck of its steamboat, the *Archiduchesse Stéphanie,* named after one of the daughters Leopold was not speaking to. There was much ceremony: scarlet judicial robes and black ones, interpreters, scribes, guards with rifles and fixed bayonets. A parade of witnesses offered horrifying testimony. One of the most impressive was Chief Lontulu of Bolima, who had been flogged with the *chicotte,* held hostage, and sent to work in chains. When his turn came to testify, Lontulu laid 110 twigs on the commission's table, each representing one of his people killed in the quest for rubber. He divided the twigs into four piles: tribal nobles, men, women, children. Twig by twig, he named the dead.

Word about the testimony quickly got back to Brussels, but Leopold did not realize what effect it was having on the commissioners. Then, in March 1905, from the Congo's capital at Boma came a curious warning signal that all might not turn out well for the king. Paul Costermans, the territory's acting governor general and, to the extent possible for a person high up in such a system, a man of personal integrity, was briefed on the commission's findings. He then alarmed his aides by plunging into a deep depression. Some two weeks later, after writing a series of farewell letters, he slit his throat with a razor.

Another bad omen for Leopold was the news that one of the judges, while listening to a succession of witnesses with atrocity stories, had broken down and wept. It was now obvious to the king that the process had backfired: to his horror what was intended to be a sham investigation had slipped out of his control and become a real one. Although Morel lacked the official verbatim transcripts, he quickly published as a pamphlet the information his missionary friends and their African parishioners had given the commission, and he sent a copy to every member of the Belgian Parliament.

On their return to Europe, the commissioners deliberated and produced a 150-page report. Even though it was couched in bland and bureaucratic language, Leopold saw that it repeated almost every major criticism made by Casement and Morel. He was furious. By the fall of 1905, he could no longer delay publication of the report that all Europe was waiting for. Politicians and journalists were already speculating about its contents. But Leopold had one more trick up his sleeve, perhaps the most dazzling stroke of showmanship in his long career.

With his modern sense of public relations, the king understood brilliantly that what matters, often, is less the substance of a political event than how the public perceives it. If you control the perception, you control the event. He also knew that journalists dread having to digest a long official report when writing against a tight deadline — all the more so when the material is in a foreign language. On November 3, 1905, the day before the Commission of Inquiry report was scheduled for release, every major paper in England received a document with a cover letter explaining that it was a "complete and authentic résumé of the report." This timely and helpful summary came from the West African Missionary Association, which surely sounded reliable. Missionaries, after all, had been among the Congo state's most consistent critics. Most conveniently of all, the summary was in English.

Delighted, nearly all the British newspapers published the summary, thinking they were getting a one-day jump on the big news of the week. The Associated Press transmitted the summary to the United States, where it was also picked up by major newspapers. Only during the next few days, as reporters and editors had time to read the full text of the report in French, did they realize that the so-called summary had little to do with the report. Again and again it took major points in the report and "summarized" them beyond recognition. For example, where the report said, "We have ourselves described the disastrous effects of porterage, and

shown that the excessive labor imposed on the natives in the neighborhood of certain important posts had the effect of depopulating the country," the summary said. "In order to avoid the regrettable consequences of
[porterage] while awaiting the building of the railways, the Commission
suggests that the waterways should be utilized."

And what, the journalists began to wonder, was the West African
Missionary Association? They were able to trace it to the office of a
London lawyer, but he refused to reveal the address of his client. A day or
two later, relenting, he directed questioners to a one-room office across
the street, with a freshly painted sign on the door. It was occupied only by
a watchman. The lawyer then produced a list of the association's board
members, but none of those whom reporters were able to reach had
ever attended a meeting. Further investigation revealed that the "summary" had been brought to England by a Belgian priest to whose church
Leopold had recently made a large donation. The West African Missionary Association, never heard from before publishing its influential summary, would never be heard from again.

17

NO MAN IS A STRANGER

I T IS IN THE RAW, unedited testimony given to the Commission of Inquiry that King Leopold II's rule is at last caught naked. There could be no excuse that this was information gathered by the king's enemies, for the three commissioners had been sent by Leopold himself. There could be no excuse that people were fabricating stories, for sometimes many witnesses described the same atrocity. And there could be no excuse that witnesses were lazy malcontents, for many risked their lives by even speaking to the commissioners. When Raoul Van Calcken, an A.B.I.R. official, found two Africans, Lilongo and Ifomi, traveling to meet the commission, he ordered them seized. "He then told his sentries to tie us to two trees with our backs against the trees and our feet off the ground," Lilongo told a British missionary. "Our arms were stretched over our heads. . . . Look at the scars all over my body. We were hanging in this way several days and nights. . . . All the time we had nothing to eat or drink, and sometimes it was raining and at other times the sun was out. . . . We cried and cried until no more tears would come — it was the pain of death itself. Whilst we hung there three sentries and the white man beat us in the private parts, on the neck and other parts of the body with big hard sticks, till we fainted." Ifomi died, and Van Calcken ordered his body thrown in a river. Lilongo survived, testified before the commission, and was carried home by his younger brother.

The testimony given before the commission by Lilongo and other witnesses appears on forms, each headed with the full title of the commission ("The Commission of Inquiry instituted by the decree of the

King-Sovereign dated July 23, 1904") and the names and titles of the three commissioners, followed by blanks for the names of the secretary, the witness, who swears to tell the whole truth and nothing but the truth, and the interpreter. Then comes the story.

Witness Ilange Kunda of M'Bongo: "I knew Malu Malu [Quickly Quickly, the African name for Force Publique Lieutenant Charles Massard]. He was very cruel; he forced us to bring rubber. One day, I saw him with my own eyes kill a native named Bongiyangwa, solely because among the fifty baskets of rubber which had been brought, he found one not full enough. Malu Malu ordered the soldier Tshumpa to seize [Bongiyangwa] and tie him to a palm tree. There were three sets of bonds: one at knee height, a second at stomach height, and a third crushing his arms. Malu Malu had his cartridge-pouch on his belt; he took his rifle, fired from a distance of about 20 meters, and with one bullet he killed Bongiyangwa. . . . I saw the wound. The unhappy man gave one cry and was dead."

Witness M'Putila of Bokote: "As you see, my right hand is cut off. . . . When I was very small, the soldiers came to make war in my village because of the rubber. . . . As I was fleeing, a bullet grazed my neck and gave me the wound whose scars you can still see. I fell, and pretended to be dead. A soldier used a knife to cut off my right hand and took it away. I saw that he was carrying other cut-off hands. . . . The same day, my father and mother were killed, and I know that they had their hands cut off."

Witness Ekuku, paramount chief of Boiéka: "I knew Jungi well. He died about two months ago from the whipping he received. I saw him hit and I saw him die. It was about three or four meters from the white man's veranda, at the spot I showed you, between the two cactuses. They stretched him out on the ground. The white man Ekotolongo [Molle] held his head, while Nkoi [Ablay], standing at his feet, hit him with a cane. Three canes were broken during the execution. Finally Nkoi kicked Jungi several times and told him to get up. When he didn't move, Ekate said to the white man, 'This man is dead. You've killed him. . . .' The white man replied, 'I don't give a damn. The judges are white men like me.' . . . Jungi was buried the next day. . . . Jungi was an old man but he had been healthy."

Witness Mingo of Mampoko: "While I was working at brick-making at Mampoko, twice the sentries Nkusu Lomboto and Itokwa, to punish me, pulled up my skirt and put clay in my vagina, which made me suffer greatly. The white man Likwama [a company agent named Henri Spelier] saw me with clay in my vagina. He said nothing more than, 'If you die working for me, they'll throw you in the river.'"

And so the statements continue, story after story, by the hundreds. Here at last was something the rest of the world had seldom heard from the Congo: the voices of the Congolese themselves. On few other occasions in the entire European Scramble for Africa did anyone gather such a searing collection of firsthand African testimony. The effect on anyone who read these stories could be only that of overwhelming horror.

However, no one read them.

Despite the report's critical conclusions, the statements by African witnesses were never directly quoted. The commission's report was expressed in generalities. The stories were not published separately, nor was anyone allowed to see them. They ended up in the closed section of a state archive in Brussels. Not until the 1980s were people at last permitted to read and copy them freely.

※※※※※

At the time he applied his artful spin control to the release of the Commission of Inquiry report, Leopold was seventy. As he grew older he seemed always in motion. He avoided Brussels as much as he could, and even while there showed his distaste for things Belgian by having all the meat for his table sent from Paris. He preferred to be abroad. He bought Caroline a French château and often stayed there with her. He liked to visit Paris, where he once took the entire French Cabinet out to dinner. Each winter he traveled south to the Riviera in his private railway car, its green leather chairs embossed with gold. While snowbound Belgians fumed and couriers shuttled to and from Brussels, he lived and worked for months on his yacht, the long, sleek *Alberta*, which could travel under steam or sail.

During these Riviera winters, Leopold installed Caroline in a luxurious home on shore, the Villa des Cèdres. "Every evening," she writes, "a steam launch took the king . . . to a pier leading to my villa through a subterranean passage. Speaking about this, I can't help remarking on the extraordinary taste of the king for everything which . . . had a secret and mysterious character. Anyone could sell him any house so long as it was built on the side of an abandoned quarry or if it had secret staircases."

Even when he could bring himself to remain in his own frustratingly small country, Leopold moved back and forth between the château at

Laeken, the Chalet Royal on the beach at Ostend, and two other châteaux. Squadrons of craftsmen continually renovated these buildings, adding new rooms, outbuildings, and façades. At Laeken workmen installed an elevator done in Italian Renaissance style, and, open to the public, a million-franc "Chinese pavilion" (equipped, strangely, with a French restaurant). It was intended to be the first of a series of buildings representing different regions of the world. Leopold's ceaseless architectural fiddling extended to buildings he could see as well as those he lived in. He wanted, for instance, "to adorn the heart of Ostend with attractive *uniform* façades." He offered a neighbor twenty-five thousand francs to put a façade on his house designed by Leopold's favorite architect, the Frenchman Charles Girault. When the landowner declined, the house was expropriated.

The king often went to see Girault in Paris, seating himself at a table in the architect's studio and poring through stacks of blueprints. He liked visiting building sites. "Ask the Minister of Public Works to be at the Brussels Palace at 9 Wednesday," he instructed his private secretary one day in 1908. "I want to go with him to St. Gilles Park and be there at 9:30. Then to the Cinquantenaire arch at 11. Then lunch at the Palace around 12:30, then go to Laeken at 2. A stop at the bridge over the canal opposite Green Avenue. At 3, Van Praet Avenue and the Japanese Tower. At 4 the Meysse road and the Heysel road." When he ordered some building done in the neighborhood of the Royal Palace in Brussels, Leopold had a special tower of wooden scaffolding erected, from which he could watch the progress of the work.

With his visitors, the monarch was always subtly bargaining for ways to extend his power. Théophile Delcassé, the French foreign minister, observed that Leopold's "only failing is that he cannot hide his intelligence: one gets suspicious, and afraid of being led up the garden path." The South African diamond king Cecil Rhodes, the one other white man whose boundless reach in Africa matched Leopold's, once joked that he had declined an invitation to a meal at the palace because "each dinner accepted cost a province."

At Laeken, servants were used to seeing the king's large, bearded, bald-headed figure with its severe brown eyes and big nose, dressed in a lieutenant general's uniform and walking for hours, leaning on his oak cane, among the palm trees and other tropical plants in the greenhouses and on the paths of the château's large park. His eccentricities multiplied. Sometimes he rode to rendezvous with Caroline on a large tricycle, which he referred to as *"mon animal."* He still feared germs and became convinced that it was good for his health to drink huge quantities of hot water each day; servants kept a decanter always at the ready. Court protocol remained as formal as ever, the tone set by Leopold, who spoke slowly and majestically, "as if," Joseph Conrad and Ford Madox Ford wrote in their thinly disguised portrait of him in their novel, *The Inheritors,* "he were forever replying to toasts to his health." Leopold had also begun speaking of himself in the third person. "Bring Him some hot water!" "Call Him his doctor!" "Give Him his cane!"

The command he really wanted to give was: "Don't take away His Congo!" For thanks to Morel's campaign and his own Commission of Inquiry report, from all sides pressure was mounting on him to divest himself of the country he considered his private property. Only one alternative to Leopold's control of the Congo was ever really considered: its becoming a colony of Belgium. Even Morel, frustrated by the lack of other politically viable choices, reluctantly advocated what was known as "the Belgian solution." If such a move were accompanied by the proper reforms — and Morel constantly insisted on these — he believed the rights of the Congolese might be better protected in a Belgian colony open to scrutiny and under the rule of law than in a secretive royal fief. That few reformers considered anything but the "Belgian solution" seems surprising to us today, but we forget that in the first decade of the century, the idea of independence and self-government in Africa was voiced by almost no one, except for a few beleaguered rebels deep in the Congo rain forest. In 1890, George Washington Williams had called for the Congo to be under rule that would be "local, not European; international, not national." But it would be more than three decades later before even the most ardently anticolonialist intellectuals, in Europe, Africa, or the Americas, said much like this again.

To Leopold, the international explosion of bad publicity triggered by the Kowalsky disaster was a turning point: instead of grandly bequeathing the Congo to Belgium at his death as he had planned, he understood that he would have to make the change before then. With his extraordinary knack for making the best of an apparently difficult situation, he began to maneuver. If these do-gooders were forcing him to give up his beloved colony, he decided, he was not going to give it away. He would *sell* it. And Belgium, the buyer, would have to pay dearly.

Oddly enough, Leopold had the Belgian government cornered. The Congo reform movement had reached such a pitch of fervor that Belgium's international reputation was at stake. And the British public's capacity for moral outrage had a power independent of government: at about this time, for example, some British humanitarians were organizing a boycott of Portuguese products because of Portugal's use of forced labor in Africa. Furthermore, if Belgium didn't take over the colony soon, some powerful country might: France and Germany, long jealous of the king's lucrative rubber profits, had their eye on pieces of Congo territory. President Roosevelt hinted that he was willing to join Britain in convening an international conference to discuss the Congo's fate. Three times the British and American ministers in Brussels went, together, to see the Belgian minister of foreign affairs and press for Belgian annexation. But sharply limited as Leopold's powers were in Belgium itself, the worried Belgian government had no legal authority over him in his role as ruler of the Congo. In the end, the king held the key cards, and he knew it.

How much, then, could he get the government to pay him for his colony? Negotiations began at the end of 1906 but soon bogged down, because the government could not get an accounting of the secretive Congo state's finances. If you are buying a business enterprise, after all, you want to see the balance sheet. Leopold was wintering in the sun at Cap Ferrat, and the government dispatched the secretary general of the Foreign Ministry, Baron Léon van der Elst, to see him. The king received the baron on his yacht, showered him with hospitality for several days, and showed him through the gardens of his expanding array of properties on shore. But when the baron asked for financial data, Leopold replied that the Congo state "is not beholden to anyone except to its founder. . . . No one has the right to ask for its accounts." One reason for his obstinacy, it became clear when auditors finally got to see some numbers, was that the twenty-five million francs the Belgian government had loaned him in 1890, plus nearly seven million more he had borrowed a few years later, were missing. An Antwerp newspaper suggested that the money had gone to Caroline. The king huffed and puffed and deflected further questioning.

Negotiations dragged on through 1907 and into early 1908. Leopold grumped and raged at the officials who tried to talk with him. At one point he slammed the door in his secretary's face, accusing him of being in league with the forces trying to take away his Congo. But like his charm, the king's tantrums were calculated. With the time that they bought him, he secretly did everything possible to hide his bewildering web of Congo-related riches, all the while claiming that he had no such wealth at all: "I am the ruler of the Congo, but the prosperity of the country no more affects me financially than the prosperity of America increases the means of President Roosevelt," he told an American correspondent. "I have not one cent invested in Congo industries, and I have not received any salary as Congo executive."

Finally the king hinted that he was ready to give in. He named his price. He yielded a little, but not much, and in March 1908 the deal was done. In return for receiving the Congo, the Belgian government first of all agreed to assume its 110 million francs' worth of debts, much of them in the form of bonds Leopold had freely dispensed over the years to favorites like Caroline. Some of the debt the outmaneuvered Belgian government assumed was in effect to itself — the nearly 32 million francs worth of loans Leopold had never paid back.

As part of the deal, Belgium also agreed to pay 45.5 million francs toward completing certain of the king's pet building projects. Fully a third of the amount was targeted for the extensive renovations under way at Laeken, already one of Europe's most luxurious royal homes, where, at the height of reconstruction, 700 stone masons, 150 horses, and seven steam cranes had been at work following a grand Leopoldian blueprint to build a center for world conferences.

Finally, on top of all this, Leopold was to receive, in installments, another fifty million francs "as a mark of gratitude for his great sacrifices made for the Congo." Those funds were not expected to come from the Belgian taxpayer. They were to be extracted from the Congo itself.

In November 1908, as solemn ceremonies at Boma marked the Congo's formal change of ownership, an unusual drama was unfolding far inland. The mere fact that it had begun under Leopold's state and continued uninterrupted in the new Belgian colony suggests that the difference between the two regimes was not what the reformers had hoped for. At center stage was the black American missionary William Sheppard.

Sheppard's article from a decade earlier, about his discovering eighty-one severed hands being smoked over a fire, had been one of the most widely quoted pieces of testimony about the Congo. "His eyewitness account," writes one scholar, "was cited by almost every American reformer, black or white." For some years now Sheppard had had a strong ally in his boss, William Morrison, a white minister who had headed the Southern Presbyterian Congo mission since 1897. Morrison was a fearless opponent of the regime, a friend of Morel's, and a leader in inspiring his fellow missionaries, American, British, and Scandinavian, to speak out. He had bombarded officials in Boma with letters of protest, published an open letter to Leopold, and delivered an influential speech when passing through London. In the United States, he had led a group of Presbyterians to see President Theodore Roosevelt about the Congo. The regime, in turn, hated Morrison as much as it did Sheppard.

Sheppard and Morrison were the most outspoken of any of the American Congo missionaries, whose protests had long nettled Leopold. He had ordered missionary magazines searched for their hostile articles; some copies still survive, heavily marked in blue pencil by palace aides. Leopold could not get at his real target, Morel, safe in England, but he had tried persistently to intimidate Morel's sources: in 1906 he had issued a decree mandating a fine or a five-year jail term for any calumny against a Congo state official. A British Baptist missionary who fed information to Morel was soon put on trial. He was convicted, fined a thousand francs plus court costs, and, less of a crusader than Sheppard or Morrison, he left the country. The little band of American Presbyterians saw it was now riskier to speak out; the authorities were watching them closely, both in Africa and abroad. Unknown to them, Moncheur, the Belgian minister to Washington, had attended in Virginia one of the many head-line-making speeches denouncing Congo atrocities that was given by Sheppard, whose reputation for stirring oratory packed many a church or hall during his home leaves.

As the end of Leopold's rule approached, the Compagnie du Kasai, a concession company of a new generation that was the de facto government of the area where the Presbyterians were working, was trying to extract all the rubber it could while the boom lasted. The Kasai River basin, where exploitation had begun a little later than elsewhere, had become the Congo's most lucrative source of rubber. And who now suddenly reappears on the scene, visiting the area for some months as inspector general of the Compagnie du Kasai, having risen in the world since we met him last? Léon Rom, the one-time collector of severed heads. His transformation into a Congo company official was a common one for retired Force Publique officers.

In the Kasai region, the normally unwarlike Kuba people had risen in revolt against the rubber terror, spurred on, as in similar doomed uprisings elsewhere in southern Africa, by elders with a fetish said to change the white man's bullets into water. The rebels burned trading posts and a mission station; when bullets did not turn to water, some 180 of them were killed. Writing in the annual newsletter the American Presbyterians published for their supporters back home, the *Kassai Herald,* William Sheppard described the toll taken on the Kuba. Significantly, he first celebrated the Kubas' history, writing in a way that no white missionary would have done:

> These great stalwart men and women, who have from time im-memorial been free, cultivating large farms of Indian corn, peas, tobacco, potatoes, trapping elephants for their ivory tusks and leopards for their skins, who have always had their own king and a government not to be despised, officers of the law established in every town of the kingdom, these magnificent people, perhaps about 400,000 in number, have entered a new chapter in the history of their tribe. Only a few years ago, travelers through this country found them living in large homes, having from one to four rooms in each house, loving and living happily with their wives and children, one of the most prosperous and intelligent of all the African tribes. . . .
>
> But within these last three years how changed they are! Their farms are growing up in weeds and jungle, their king is practically a slave, their houses now are mostly only half-built single rooms and are much neglected. The streets of their towns are not clean and well-swept as they once were. Even their children cry for bread.
>
> Why this change? You have it in a few words. There are armed sentries of chartered trading companies who force the men and women to spend most of their days and nights in the forests making rubber, and the price they receive is so meager that they cannot live upon it. In the majority of villages these people have not time to listen to the Gospel story, or give an answer concern-ing their soul's salvation.

Sheppard's story appeared in January 1908, the month Léon Rom returned to Belgium from a six-month business trip to the Kasai. Soon after, Rom's colleagues at the Compagnie du Kasai began to threaten, bluster, and demand a retraction, which Morrison and Sheppard refused to make. Morrison sent company officials forceful letters listing more specific charges, which upset them still further. The two missionaries were legally vulnerable, since technically they had published the article in the Congo itself. In England, Morel reprinted Sheppard's article, and also a photograph the missionaries had sent him, of forced laborers, tied to one another by ropes around their necks.

While the company was still complaining about the offending article, the British vice consul to the Congo, Wilfred Thesiger, paid a three-month visit to the Kasai basin to prepare a report on conditions there. Nervous officials monitored his travels, remembering all too well the international furor caused by Roger Casement's report four years earlier. To the authorities' dismay, Thesiger stayed with the American Presbyterians at their mission and traveled on their steamboat, the *Lapsley*. As someone who understood the local languages and who knew the district well, Sheppard acted as guide to Thesiger, taking him to thirty-one Kuba villages. After they departed, a suspicious station chief grilled villagers the two men had spoken to, and worriedly reported to his superiors that "Sheppard pointed to the Consul and said, 'You see this white man, when he returns to Europe he will tell the State officials whatever you tell him, because he is very powerful.' In the Bakuba villages [Thesiger] . . . asked any questions Sheppard suggested." Thesiger soon submitted an excoriating report on starvation and brutality in the Kasai to the British Parliament. One passage, describing Kuba homes falling into ruin while people were put to work as rubber slaves, closely echoed Sheppard's article. The Compagnie du Kasai's stock price plummeted. Company and Congo state officials, furious, blamed Sheppard.

The company could not legally punish the Presbyterians for helping Thesiger, but it could do so for their publishing Sheppard's 1908 article. In February 1909 it filed suit for libel against Sheppard, as writer of the article, and Morrison, as its publisher, demanding eighty thousand francs in damages. The two men, firm in their convictions, decided that if the judge ruled against them, they would, as Morrison wrote home, "prefer to go to prison rather than pay the fine." Abroad, their supporters rallied to their defense. "Morrison in the dock," wrote Sir Arthur Conan Doyle (ignoring the black defendant, Sheppard), "makes a finer Statue of Liberty than Bartholdi's in New York harbour." In Washington, the affair was discussed at a Cabinet meeting. The American legation in Brussels informed the Belgian government that the United States viewed the trial with "acute interest and no little concern," and suggested that U.S. recognition of the new Belgian claim to the Congo might hinge on the result.

The trial took place in Leopoldville, some six hundred miles down the

Kasai and Congo rivers from the Presbyterian mission. A photo shows Morrison and Sheppard before the trial, standing under some palm trees on each side of a dozen Kubas who were prepared to testify in their defense. The Kubas are naked above the waist. Morrison, the white man, looks resigned behind his heavy beard, as if preparing for one more ordeal in a saintly life that will be rewarded in Heaven, but certainly not before then. He wears a black hat, black suit, and scuffed shoes. Sheppard, the black man, wears a white suit and white hat. His shoes gleam; his chest is arched out; he stands a head taller than everyone else and seems to be enjoying the moment immensely. There is something proud and inclusive in his stance toward the Kubas, as if they are junior kinsmen.

The trial's opening date was set — deliberately, the missionaries thought — during the dry season on the Kasai River. After the steamboat carrying the two defendants and their Kuba witnesses encountered low water, the captain refused to go farther. A new date was fixed.

Morel telegraphed his friend and ally Émile Vandervelde, leader of the Belgian socialists, asking him to recommend an "honest young Belgian lawyer" for the two missionaries. Vandervelde, a leading figure in European democratic socialism, was also an attorney. To everyone's surprise, he declared that he would take on the case himself, *pro bono*. The trial was postponed yet again so that Vandervelde could travel out to the Congo. As he was preparing to leave Belgium, someone criticized him for traveling all the way to Africa to defend a couple of "strangers." Unspoken, perhaps, was the fact that one of those strangers was black.

Vandervelde replied, "No man is a stranger in a court of justice."

Newly arrived in the Congo, the anticlerical Vandervelde, president of the Second International and friend or acquaintance of all the great left-wing figures of his day, found himself living in a mission station and cruising Stanley Pool in the mission steamboat, which flew the American flag. He watched with great amusement as missionaries carried out baptisms by total immersion and prayed for a favorable verdict.

At last the trial began, in a Leopoldville courtroom of wood and brick, its windows open to the breeze. On a technicality, the court had dropped the charge against Morrison, leaving Sheppard the only defendant. In this frontier outpost, dotted with mango, palm, and baobab trees, and with its forced labor gangs, military barracks, and a firing range where Europeans practiced shooting on Sundays, the trial was definitely the biggest show in town. Over thirty foreign Protestant missionaries packed the courtroom in a show of support. They and other supporters of Sheppard sat on one side of the courtroom; on the other side were Catholic missionaries, Congo state officials, and other backers of the Compagnie du Kasai. Onlookers who couldn't fit in the room watched through the open door and windows. The Compagnie du Kasai officials wore white suits and white sun helmets; Sheppard looked natty in a dark coat with a handkerchief in his breast pocket.

After the judge rang a small bell to begin the proceedings and the lawyer for the Compagnie du Kasai spoke, Vandervelde rose to make the most of his unusual forum. Sheppard, he told the judge, was "no longer of England or America, but of the Kasai. . . . His only motive in revealing the condition of the natives amongst whom he lives is humanitarian." Vandervelde "made a magnificent defense," Morrison reported. "His speech was a marvel of eloquence, invincible logic, burning sarcasm, and pathetic appeal for justice to be done not only for us Missionaries but especially for the native peoples. He held the audience in the Courtroom spell-bound for over two hours." Sheppard, the accused, was also moved. "The trial is the talk of the whole country," he wrote, and the spectators "were so affected that their handkerchiefs were freely used." According to Sheppard, even the Catholic priests — usually staunch allies of the state — were weeping, and one of them came up and congratulated Vandervelde after his speech. "It is said there has never been such a speech as that made in Congo."

The trial won Sheppard some attention back home. Under the headlines AMERICAN NEGRO HERO OF CONGO and FIRST TO INFORM WORLD OF CONGO ABUSES, the *Boston Herald* wrote, "Dr. Sheppard has not only stood before kings, but he has also stood against them. In pursuit of his mission of serving his race in its native land, this son of a slave . . . has dared to withstand all the power of Leopold."

After the closing arguments, the judge announced that he would give his decision in two weeks. In the end, it was politics, not Vandervelde's eloquence or the missionaries' prayers, that dictated the results. The presence of the American consul general and vice consul in the courtroom was a reminder of the problems Belgium might face if Sheppard were found in the wrong. Similarly, the judge knew he would not have a promising career in the Congo if he found that Sheppard's accusations against the company were true. Steering a cautious middle course, he made adroit use of the fact that (even though there were no other such companies in the area) Sheppard's article had not specifically named the Compagnie du Kasai, but had only attacked "armed sentries of chartered trading companies." Thus, the judge declared, most improbably, "the defendant Sheppard did not intend to make an attack on the said company. . . . The article did not and could not refer to the Compagnie du Kasai." In effect, Sheppard was found innocent, without the Compagnie du Kasai's being found guilty. The company, however, had to pay court costs.

Far up the Kasai River, the missionaries' wives knew that their husbands had vowed to go to jail rather than pay the damages if the judgment went against them. The sign that this had happened would be if the men were not on board the Presbyterian steamboat when it returned from Leopoldville. As people anxiously waited at the mission station, there seems to have been a warmth and camaraderie among these black and white Americans that would have been inconceivable back home. "Mrs. Morrison and I waited almost breathlessly for the return of our loved ones," wrote Lucy Gantt Sheppard. "As the *Lapsley* came steaming in, hundreds of Christians began singing hymns and waving their hands and shouting for joy. It was a glorious time — a time for thanksgiving."

Back in Europe, there was no thanksgiving for Leopold. In December 1909, less than two months after the Sheppard trial, the seventy-four-year-old king fell gravely ill with an "intestinal blockage," possibly a euphemism for cancer. Crowded out of the château of Laeken by his endless renovations, surrounded as always by sheaves of architectural drawings, the king was living in an outbuilding, the Palm Pavilion, amid the great greenhouses. Caroline and their two sons rushed to Leopold's side, and Leopold's private chaplain performed a hasty wedding. With things now straightened out with the church, the king could receive last rites. Nonetheless, Caroline, who stayed by his side, had to disappear from sight every time a visitor arrived.

Leopold's rejected daughters, Louise and Stephanie, came to Brussels, hoping for a reconciliation and for changes in their favor in the royal will. Obstinate to the last, their father turned them away. The royal physician, Dr. Jules Thiriar, who had also served as a dummy stockholder for the king in several Congo corporations, ordered an operation, but it was unsuccessful. Parliament had just passed a pet bill of Leopold's, instituting compulsory military service. When he came out of the anesthetic after his surgery, the king signed the bill with a trembling hand. The next day he seemed to rally, demanding newspapers and giving orders to prepare for a departure for the Riviera. A few hours later he was dead. One of the myriad of hovering officials led the weeping Caroline from his bedside.

If we are to believe Caroline's account, Leopold, just after the secret wedding, had turned to Baron Auguste Goffinet, one of the plump, bearded, slightly cross-eyed twins who had been among his closest aides for more than thirty years, and declared, "I present you my widow. I place her under your protection during the few days she'll spend in Belgium after my death." It is likely that the king did say something like this, for he knew that his three daughters and the Belgian public hated Caroline — and that they would do so all the more when they discovered that in his last days he had transferred to her a fortune in Congo securities, on top of some six million francs he had already given her.

Princess Louise's lawyers came after the securities, so when Caroline went to her Brussels villa, she found it padlocked and guarded, the windows boarded up. It was the same story at the French castle she had been given by Leopold. But with the help of the king's loyalists, who were seen removing papers from his desk in his final hours, Caroline got herself and much of her money away to Paris.

Less than a year later, she remarried — her husband none other than the former French officer, Durrieux, her original boyfriend and pimp. If she shared some of her fortune with him, his was surely one of the most successful feats of pimpery of all time. Of Caroline and Leopold's two sons, one died a few years after his father. The other lived a long, quiet life on the income from capital once wrested from the labor of Congo rubber slaves; he died in 1984. Perhaps the most interesting of Leopold's descendants was his granddaughter Elizabeth, the only child of Stephanie and Crown Prince Rudolf of Austria-Hungary. She married a socialist politician and became known as the Red Archduchess.

At his death, Leopold was little mourned by his people. They much preferred his nephew and successor, Albert I, modest, likable, and — extremely rare for a European monarch — visibly in love with his wife. As for the world outside Belgium, thanks to Morel and his allies, it now thought of Leopold not in terms of the monuments and buildings he was so proud of, but of the severed hands. The American poet Vachel Lindsay declaimed:

> *Listen to the yell of Leopold's ghost*
> *Burning in Hell for his hand-maimed host.*

Hear how the demons chuckle and yell
Cutting his hands off, down in Hell.

But the battle over how Leopold and his works would be remembered
had only begun.

The life of a major figure in the early stages of that battle, Roger Casement, had now taken some new turnings. When Casement's report was
published, he had been interviewed by newspapers, wined and dined by
the London literary world, awarded a medal by the British king, attacked
by the Belgian king, defended by Morel and the reform movement, and
then vindicated triumphantly by Leopold's own Commission of Inquiry.

But Casement had to earn a living. By 1906, he was once again serving
as British consul in a remote spot, this time Santos, Brazil, where the
consulate was an empty, whitewashed room in a coffee warehouse. He
wore a dress uniform for ceremonial occasions (white gloves, gold braid
on collar and cuffs, a sword, and a hat with a cockade), but his daily work
was anything but glamorous. Exasperatedly summing up his entire consular career, Casement later wrote, "My predecessor in Santos had a wire
netting up to the ceiling to prevent . . . distressed British subjects throwing things at him. . . . At Delagoa Bay [in Mozambique] I could not
afford a secretary or clerk. I had to sit in my office for two years and open
the door to everyone who came in. I was bottle washer and everything
else. . . . I have known ladies to come in and ask me for their cab fare. I
have been asked to pronounce a divorce and been upbraided for not
doing it. Once a woman came into my office in Delagoa Bay and fainted
on the sofa, and that woman remained in the house for a week."

When he was not bailing drunken sailors out of jail or performing
other consular duties, Casement was becoming ever more involved with
his native Ireland. On home leave he met members of the movement to
revive what he called the "lovely, glorious language" of Gaelic and, with
it, the roots of Irish culture. He visited the movement's language school at
Cloghaneely, where he was photographed, arms crossed tightly on his
stomach, as if holding in some anxiety, his tall frame seated awkwardly
amid solemn Gaelic League members in long Victorian cutaways and vests.

"In those lonely Congo forests where I found Leopold," he wrote to a
friend, "I found also myself, the incorrigible Irishman." To another, he

said that "it was only because I was an Irishman that I could understand *fully*, I think, the whole scheme of wrongdoing at work on the Congo." He had come to feel that Ireland, like the Congo, was a colony, and that there, too, the core injustice was the way the colonial conquerors had taken the land. "I realised that I was looking at this tragedy [in the Congo] with the eyes of another race of people once hunted themselves."

True enough, but was the "race of people once hunted themselves" only the Irish? Being a gay man in an unforgiving age, Casement surely felt hunted every day of his adult life. That was a cause too dangerous to openly take on, but embracing Irish nationalism was possible, and Casement did so with characteristic passion. Although he never fully mastered the language, he sometimes used the Gaelic form of his name, Ruari MacAsmund, and tried Gaelic in his letters. On his way to take up his post in Brazil, his baggage stuffed with books on Ireland, he wrote to a friend, "Remember my address is Consulate of Great Britain and *Ireland,* Santos — not British Consulate!!" He had special stationery printed to emphasize this. From Brazil, he wrote home, "Send me news of Congo and Ireland — nothing else counts."

On one trip home, his ship anchored at Rio de Janeiro. "Casement came ashore and we talked for a time before going back to his liner for lunch," the British vice consul later recalled. "Half-way out to the ship, the villainous Brazilian boatmen who were rowing us out suddenly rested on their oars and, as was often their wont, tried to hold us up for more money than the price already agreed on. But by then Casement was launched on a tremendous monologue about Irish Home Rule and nothing could stem the flood. For a while the boatmen tried to shout him down, but it was impossible. Finally they gave up in disgust and we continued on our way, with Casement still going strong on Ireland."

Generous as always (he helped support a ne'er-do-well brother for some years) and frequently in debt, Casement somehow managed to contribute more than £85 in "Payments to Irish Causes in 1907" out of his salary. More and more, he came to see the world in terms of colonizers and colonized. His letters are filled with discomfort at working for the biggest colonizer of them all, and he gently chided his friend E. D. Morel for believing England to be morally superior to the other colonial powers: "I have no use for your British government. . . . You are one of the few, my dear Bulldog, who do not realise the national characteristics — and it is for that I love you. When I think what J.B. [John Bull] has done to Ireland I literally weep to think I must still serve — instead of fight. . . . I do not agree with you that England and America are the two great humanitarian powers. . . . [They are] materialistic first and humanitarian only a century after."

Morel advised Casement not to sacrifice his pension rights by prematurely leaving the consular service. He understood Casement's frustrations, but was wise enough to know that some of them came from the man, not the job. "You are a difficult man to help," he once wrote to Casement. "You are very proud, for which I admire you, in the first place. Also, forgive me for saying so, it is a little difficult sometimes to know exactly anything [that] could be done that would fall in with your exact wishes."

Casement worried about Morel's welfare as much as Morel did about his. He knew that Morel, having poured all his energy into Congo reform, had not been able to put aside any money for his old age. In London on leave, Casement began collecting funds for this purpose, contributing £50 himself. "My hope now," he wrote to William A. Cadbury, the Quaker chocolate manufacturer, "is that we may raise from £10,000 to £15,000 possibly & with this sum . . . invested for the wife and children the besetting fear and dread that weighs on his mind may be removed forever, & his whole personality released for greater good and more work for Africa, or elsewhere where such a fearless soul as his is needed." Casement followed this with a blizzard of letters and personal visits to other Congo reform supporters. He fell short of his target, but he succeeded in gathering several thousand pounds. He, and Morel even more so, were skilled at something essential to political crusades: fundraising.

Suddenly an opportunity arose for Casement to repeat his famous Congo investigative journey, this time in another part of the world. Reports filtering back to England described atrocities committed against Indians in the remote Putumayo region of the Amazon River basin by officials of the Peruvian Amazon Rubber Company. British humanitarians, labor unions, and church groups were demanding action. The firm was incorporated in London, and some of the mistreated workers were British subjects, contract laborers from Barbados. The Foreign Office sent Casement to investigate.

For Casement, the Putumayo was the Congo all over again, from the long, dreary journeys on crowded steamboats to the swarms of rain forest mosquitoes to the shootings, shackles, beheadings, mutilations, and kidnappings of a slave-labor system driven by Europe's insatiable demand for wild rubber. Casement weighed and tried to carry the Indians' rubber loads. He measured the stocks into which people were locked to be flogged with a tapir-hide whip, which resembled the *chicotte*.

In reporting to the Foreign Office, Casement knew everything had to be precise and well documented. But his other writings from this time show a romantic idealization of the oppressed. The Irish, he felt, were "white Indians"; poverty-stricken Galway was the "Irish Putumayo." In a magazine article, he argued that the Putumayo Indians were morally superior to their white overlords; the Indian was "a Socialist by temperament, habit, and possibly, an age-long memory of Inca and pre-Inca precept." (Some of the smaller peoples crushed by their armies might not have seen the Incas so benignly.)

Despite succumbing to his own version of the Noble Savage myth, Casement got the job done. As with the Congo, he was not content just to carry out his Foreign Office assignment; he wrote voluminous letters to influential people, raised money, and fed pages of suggested questions to sympathetic members of Parliament. In the middle of this work, he received a startling piece of news: on recommendation of the foreign secretary, he was to be knighted. He agonized for days over whether to refuse the knighthood, feeling, as he explained to a friend, that "until Ireland is safe and her outlook happy no Irishman has any right to be accepting honours." Finally he said yes, but when it came to the day of the actual ceremony — which would have required him to kneel before the British king — he pled ill.

While in the Putumayo, Casement's life had been all work, as in the Congo, with scarcely a thought for anything else. But on the long voyages to and from South America he filled his diary again with a record of assignations. On shipboard: "Captain's steward, an Indian boy of 19, broad face." In Pará, Brazil: "Shall I see Joao, dear old soul! I'll get up early. . . . To Cemetery and lo! Joao coming along, blushed to roots of hair with joy." He seemed to become more heedless in his meetings. Passing through Pará again: "Dinner at 8 P.M. and out to cemetery and met Friend. . . . Police passing behind paling — but he laughed. . . . $10." Still undiscovered, the time bomb's fuse burned on.

One evening in 1910, a year after King Leopold died, London theatergoers attending a new play, based on the Sherlock Holmes story *The Speck-*

led Band, noticed a trio of men in the audience: the famous journalist E. D. Morel, with his trademark mustache; the black-bearded Sir Roger Casement, deeply tanned from his time in the Putumayo; and the creator of Sherlock Holmes, Sir Arthur Conan Doyle, host of the other two.

Conan Doyle was Morel's most important new recruit to the cause of Congo reform. His help was eagerly welcomed by Morel, whose job had been made more difficult by the Belgian takeover of the Congo and Leopold's death the following year. Morel had suffered the worst setback that can happen to a crusader: he had lost his villain. It is always tempting to believe that a bad system is the fault of one bad man. Morel never gave in to that temptation, but he feared that his supporters would. For the Congo reformers, being able to demonize Leopold had been a double-edged sword. With the king now gone, the movement could easily falter, so Conan Doyle's influential support had come at just the right time.

In 1909 the novelist had spoken side by side with Morel to huge crowds: 2800 in Edinburgh, 3000 in Plymouth, 5000 in Liverpool. He wrote an introduction to Morel's newest book and also published a book of his own based on Morel's vast store of material, *The Crime of the Congo,* which sold twenty-five thousand copies a week when it first appeared and was immediately translated into several languages. With all the fervor of a late convert, he was one of the few people in Europe whose denunciations were even more impassioned than Morel's. He called the exploitation of the Congo "the greatest crime which has ever been committed in the history of the world."

Morel considered the Belgian takeover of the Congo only "a partial victory." He knew that the system Leopold had set up would not be quickly dismantled; it was too profitable. The same men who had been district commissioners and station chiefs for Leopold would now simply get their paychecks from a different source. The Force Publique didn't even bother to change its name. The new Belgian minister of colonies was a former official of a company that had used thousands of forced laborers to build railways in the eastern Congo. The head of the Belgian Senate committee that approved the new colonial budget — which *increased* "taxes in kind" on Africans, Morel pointed out — was a shareholder in the notorious rubber concession company, A.B.I.R. As long as there was big money to be made from rubber, white men, with the help of the gun and the *chicotte,* would force black men to gather it. Coached by Morel, Conan Doyle wrote, in one of many letters to the editor he sent to various British newspapers, "So long as in any report of Congo reforms, such a sentence occurs as 'Adult natives will be compelled to work,' there can be no true reform whatever."

Morel now concentrated on trying to make the Foreign Office demand that the Belgian government eliminate the hated Leopoldian "System" of forced labor and confiscation of the products of the land. The final picture in the Congo Reform Association slide show was of a British warship — which Morel urged be sent to Boma to block the Congo River. Earl Grey, the foreign secretary, refused, limiting his pressure on Belgium to withholding British recognition of the Belgian Congo. Morel threw himself into his organizing with more intensity than ever, turning out another book and an undiminished stream of pamphlets, articles, and issues of the Congo Reform Association's magazine. He packed the Royal Albert Hall to the highest balconies with a huge Congo protest meeting, endorsed by 20 bishops and 140 members of Parliament.

Change seemed to be on its way in the Congo. The new Belgian king, Albert I, who had actually visited the territory just before taking the throne and seen people without hands, let it be known that he thought forced labor a scandal and lobbied for major reforms. (He would lose his youthful idealism later in life, unfortunately.) Morel was delighted, but such news made it hard to keep his followers fired up. By 1910, the American Congo Reform Association had faded away. "Americans . . ." Morel wrote to one of his hundreds of correspondents, "have not got very much staying-power."

Morel tried valiantly to keep his followers focused on the issue of land ownership, so much more important but so much less dramatic than Leopold's personal villainy had been. He had long believed that "the root of the evil [will remain] untouched . . . till the native of the Congo becomes once more owner of his land and of the produce which it yields."

Although Morel never intended it to be, his vocal insistence on African land rights was taken by many people, particularly in the Foreign Office, as implicitly threatening not just to Belgian but to British practice in Africa. "The Native question is not so simple as he thinks," the foreign secretary wrote to Lord Cromer, a Morel supporter. "We do not, in our own Colonies, say that all the land and produce of the soil belongs to the Natives." In believing that Congo land *did* belong to the Africans, Morel was inherently more radical than almost all of those he worked with. Once again, Morel the crusader for justice was in unspoken tension with

Morel the British patriot, whose newest celebrity ally, Conan Doyle, had once been president of the Boys' Empire League. In Morel's writing of this period, we can begin to see signs of how his involvement with the Congo had changed and deepened him. In 1909, decades ahead of his time and in stark contrast to the self-congratulatory mood around him, he wrote a trenchant warning of the "far-reaching consequences over the wider destiny, not only of South Africa, but of all Negro Africa" that would flow from the fact that Britain had set up the new, independent Union of South Africa with an all-white legislature.

All did not look bleak to Morel, however. In the fall of 1909, the Belgian colonial minister announced major reforms, to be phased in over three years. Morel strongly protested that the transition period was too long. But over this time letters from his missionary correspondents turned hopeful. Similarly encouraging news came from inspection tours by British consuls. Reports of atrocities against rubber workers slowed to a trickle. In 1912, Alice and John Harris — now running the newly merged Anti-Slavery and Aborigines Protection Society — returned from a trip to the Congo and reported "immense improvement."

Morel was locked in a double race against time: against the inevitable British recognition of the Congo as a Belgian colony, which finally came in 1913, and against the waning fervor of his supporters. Even Casement felt that "the break-up of the pirate's stronghold [was] nearly accomplished" and urged Morel to declare the campaign over. Despite some doubts voiced in his private correspondence, Morel decided to publicly claim victory. "I do not wish to paint the present in roseate hues. The wounds of the Congo will take generations to heal. But . . . the atrocities have disappeared. . . . The revenues are no longer supplied by forced or slave labour. The rubber tax has gone. The native is free to gather the produce of his soil. . . . A responsible Government has replaced an irresponsible despotism." The one major goal not achieved, he acknowledged, was African ownership of land.

On June 16, 1913, the Congo Reform Association held its final meeting, at the Westminster Palace Hotel in London. Many of the principal British supporters of the cause were together for the last time: John and Alice Harris, the Archbishop of Canterbury, explorers, missionaries, editors, M.P.s. Sir Roger Casement, William Cadbury, John Holt, Émile Vandervelde, Pierre Mille, and the writer John Galsworthy sent letters or telegrams of support that were read aloud. As the organization he founded, which had roiled the political waters of several countries for nearly a decade, officially went out of business, E. D. Morel was only thirty-nine years old.

A series of distinguished speakers praised him. Morel seldom liked sharing too much of the limelight, but when he replied on this occasion, he gave the greatest credit to someone else: "While I was listening to all that was being said, I had a vision. The vision of a small steamer ploughing its way up the Congo just ten years ago this month, and on its decks a man that some of you know; a man of great heart . . . Roger Casement." The meeting marked the end of the first major international human rights movement of the twentieth century. "We have struck a blow for human justice," Morel told the assembled dignitaries, "that cannot and will not pass away." It would take another generation to judge whether this was true.

18

VICTORY?

Both in Africa and Europe, Leopold's death had promised to mark the end of an era. Many Belgians felt relieved; at last they would be rid of the multiple embarrassments of his youthful mistress, his unseemly quarrels with his daughters, and the sheer nakedness of his greed. But it was soon clear that Leopold's ghost would not vanish so easily. The king who had died while in possession of one of Europe's largest fortunes had tried to take it with him. After a fashion, he had succeeded.

Not long before his death, it turned out, Leopold had surreptitiously ordered the establishment of a foundation, based in Germany, to which he transferred some twenty-five million francs' worth of paintings, silver-ware, crystal, jewelry, furniture and the like, plus another twenty million francs in securities. Some of the foundation's income was to be reinvested, its charter said, and the remainder was to be spent — "according to the directions left by the Founder" — on the grand, showy projects he loved: palaces, monuments, and public buildings. He was afraid that future small-minded Belgian governments would not spend money in such ways, and he was also trying, as always, to keep his wealth from going to Louise, Stephanie, and Clementine. "The king has but two dreams," a former Cabinet minister reportedly said during Leopold's last years; "to die a billionaire, and to disinherit his daughters."

The German foundation was not the only place Leopold had tried to hide his fortune. Fifty-eight pieces of real estate in Brussels, purchased for the king by his faithful aide Baron Auguste Goffinet, turned out to belong to another secret company. A third shadowy entity, the Residential

275

and Garden Real Estate Corporation of the Côte d'Azur, held possession of Leopold's panoply of Riviera properties. Some of these villas were earmarked as permanent vacation homes for future Belgian kings; others were to be part of a huge health resort, with parks, gardens, sports facilities, and cottages, providing free holidays for white officials returning from their labors in the Congo. Furthermore, these several corporate hiding places held more than twenty-five million francs' worth of Leopold's Congo bonds.

The Belgian government's effort to clear up the dead king's financial morass dragged on for years. Since the entities involved had been variously incorporated in Belgium, France, and Germany, the process of straightening everything out was wholly disrupted by World War I. The health resort was never built. The grand World School of Colonialism, which Leopold had enthusiastically planned, was left unfinished, its lavish foundations already laid outside Brussels. Somerset Maugham eventually bought one of the king's many Riviera villas. The grounds of another were turned into a zoo, known today for its troupe of performing chimpanzees.

Only in 1923, fourteen years after his death, was the last of Leopold's financial thicket untangled. Investigators trying to figure out his finances discovered, among other things, that some of the riches he had disposed of had in fact belonged to his crazed sister Carlota, still very much alive. Leopold, her legal guardian, had helped himself to certain properties of hers that he wanted, illegally substituting for them some of his Congo state bonds.

The one-time Empress of Mexico long outlived her brother. When she received a visitor, it was in a room with twenty or more chairs lined up. Carlota would enter the room and solemnly greet an imaginary guest in each chair before talking with her caller. As the years passed, she spent endless hours changing her clothes and doing her hair. Then one day she reportedly caught sight of herself in a mirror, realized that she was no longer a youthful beauty, and ordered all the mirrors in her château smashed. At a party forty-five years after her husband's execution, she exclaimed, puzzled, "And Maximilian isn't here!" She was probably one of the few people in Belgium who barely noticed the four-year German occupation during World War I. She died in 1927, at the age of eighty-six, muttering madly about imaginary kingdoms and dynasties to the very end.

Even today, researchers are not completely sure which of Leopold's baubles were paid for out of which hidden pockets. Nor is it possible to answer fully a larger question: how much profit altogether did the king draw from the Congo in his lifetime? In answer to this question, the Belgian scholar Jules Marchal, the leading historian of this period, makes a "conservative" estimate, not including some smaller or hard-to-trace sources of money, of 220 million francs of the time, or $1.1 billion in today's dollars.

One of the lawsuits provoked by Leopold's financial tangles was filed by Princesses Stephanie and Louise. They claimed that since the wealth in the secret foundation and companies had been their father's, it was now in part theirs. The Belgian government, however, eventually got most of the funds.

There was no lawyer to argue that the money should have been returned to the Congolese.

The final meeting of the Congo Reform Association, in 1913, marked the end of the most important and sustained crusade of its sort between the Abolitionism of the early and middle nineteenth century and the world-wide boycott and embargo against apartheid-era South Africa in the 1970s and 1980s. But the Congo reform movement, heroic though it was, leaves some troubling questions in its wake. The most important is, did it do any lasting good?

For many years, the conventional answer was yes. The glare of publicity surrounding the Casement and Commission of Inquiry investigations had sparked a new outbreak of rebellions in some areas that caused a noticeable, although temporary, reduction of rubber gathering. Later, E. D. Morel and his allies could point to the marked drop-off in reports of atrocities after the transfer to Belgium. Oblique testimony to the importance of wresting the Congo away from Leopold came even from Alexandre Delcommune, a long-time Congo businessman and adminis-trator, a ruthless robber baron. (It was a steamboat from Delcommune's company that Joseph Conrad was hired to command.) Delcommune once wrote that if Leopold's rule had lasted another ten years, "one would no longer have found a single rubber vine, or perhaps a single native." Did the Congo reformers, then, save millions of lives?

It would be a fitting climax to our story if this were so, for a splendid movement deserves splendid results. The organizing by E. D. Morel, the acts of witness of George Washington Williams, William Sheppard, and

Roger Casement, and the deaths of Andrew Shanu and of rebel leaders like Nzansu, Mulume Niama, and Kandolo should not have been in vain. But the truth is more somber.

Reports of abuses against gatherers of wild rubber in the Congo did drop off markedly after the Belgian takeover of 1908. In the following years there was far less news of villages burned or of women and children held hostage. There was no more officially sanctioned severing of hands. What lay behind the change, however, was not a kinder and gentler regime brought about by the reformers, but several other developments. One was the gradual shift from wild rubber to cultivated rubber. Another was the introduction of a new method of forcing people to work that drew much less protest from missionaries and humanitarians: taxes.

The Belgian administrators who took over from Leopold saw that they needed plantations of cultivated rubber, because if all the rubber harvested came from wild vines, Africans desperate to meet their quotas would cut them all down; vines were already becoming scarce in parts of the country. Look again at the statement from Alexandre Delcommune on the previous page. He sounds just as concerned about the possible disappearance of wild rubber as of Congolese.

The imposition of a heavy head tax forced people to go to work on the plantations or in harvesting cotton, palm oil, and other products — and proved an effective means of continuing to collect some wild rubber as well. Until the 1920s white traders bought wild rubber from villagers pressed to pay their taxes.

The central part of what Morel had called the "System," forced labor, remained in place, applied to all kinds of work. Forced labor became particularly brutal during the First World War. In 1916, an expanded Force Publique invaded German East Africa, today's Tanzania. Like the other Allied powers, Belgium had its eye on getting part of Germany's slice of the African cake in the postwar division of the spoils. Enormous numbers of Congolese were conscripted as soldiers or porters. In 1916, by colonial officials' count, one area in the eastern Congo, with a population of 83,518 adult men, supplied more than three million man-days of porterage during the year; 1359 of these porters were worked to death or died of disease. Famines raged. A Catholic missionary reported, "The father of the family is at the front, the mother is grinding flour for the soldiers, and the children are carrying the foodstuffs!"

The years after the war saw the growth of copper, gold, and tin mining. As always, the profits flowed out of the territory. It was legal for mine management to use the *chicotte,* and at the gold mines of Moto, on the upper Uele River, records show that 26,579 lashes were administered in the first half of 1920 alone. This figure was equal to eight lashes per full-time African worker. Techniques for gathering forced labor for the mines were little different from those employed in Leopold's time. According to the historian David Northrup, "a recruiter from the mines went around to each village chief accompanied by soldiers or the mines' own policemen, presented him with presents, and assigned him a quota of men (usually double the number needed, since half normally deserted as soon as they could). The chief then rounded up those he liked the least or feared or who were least able to resist and sent them to the administrative post tied together by the neck. From there they were sent on to the district headquarters in chains. . . . Chiefs were paid ten francs for each recruit." If a worker fled, a member of his family could be imprisoned — not so different from the old hostage system.

As elsewhere in Africa, safety conditions in the mines were abysmal: in the copper mines and smelters of Katanga, five thousand workers died between 1911 and 1918. When the vaunted Matadi-Leopoldville railroad was rebuilt with a wider gauge and partly new route by forced labor between 1921 and 1931, more workmen on the project perished than had died when the line was laid in the 1890s. To the Africans throughout the Congo conscripted to work on these and other new enterprises, the Great Depression, paradoxically, brought lifesaving relief.

With the start of the Second World War, the legal maximum for forced labor in the Congo was increased to 120 days per man per year. More than 80 percent of the uranium in the Hiroshima and Nagasaki bombs came from the heavily guarded Congo mine of Shinkolobwe. The Allies also wanted ever more rubber for the tires of hundreds of thousands of military trucks, Jeeps, and warplanes. Some of the rubber came from the Congo's new plantations of cultivated rubber trees. But in the villages Africans were forced to go into the rain forest, sometimes for weeks at a time, to search for wild vines once again.

Although they failed to end forced labor, the Congo reformers for roughly a decade were spectacularly successful in keeping the territory in the spotlight. Seldom has so much outrage poured down for so long upon such a distant target. This raises another major question about the movement: Why the Congo?

An ancient English law made it a crime to witness a murder or discover a corpse and not raise a "hue and cry." But we live in a world of corpses, and only about some of them is there a hue and cry. True, with a population loss estimated at ten million people, what happened in the Congo could reasonably be called the most murderous part of the European Scramble for Africa. But that is so only if you look at sub-Saharan Africa as the arbitrary checkerboard formed by colonial boundaries. If you draw boundaries differently — to surround, say, all African equatorial rain forest land rich in wild rubber — then what happened in the Congo is, unfortunately, no worse than what happened in neighboring colonies: Leopold simply had far more of the rubber territory than anyone else. Within a decade of his head start, similar forced labor systems for extracting rubber were in place in the French territories west and north of the Congo River, in Portuguese-ruled Angola, and in the nearby Cameroons under the Germans. For the concession companies in the Cameroons, "the 'model' from which they professed to derive their inspiration," writes one historian, "was . . . that of King Leopold II's ventures in the Congo Free State, the dividends of which evoked admiration in stock-broking circles."

In France's equatorial African territories, where the region's history is best documented, the amount of rubber-bearing land was far less than what Leopold controlled, but the rape was just as brutal. Almost all exploitable land was divided among concession companies. Forced labor, hostages, slave chains, starving porters, burned villages, paramilitary company "sentries," and the *chicotte* were the order of the day. Thousands of refugees who had fled across the Congo River to escape Leopold's regime eventually fled back to escape the French. The population loss in the rubber-rich equatorial rain forest owned by France is estimated, just as in Leopold's Congo, at roughly 50 percent. And, as in Leopold's colony, both the French territories and the German Cameroons were wracked by long, fierce rebellions against the rubber regime. The French scholar Catherine Coquéry-Vidrovitch has published a chilling graph showing how, at one French Congo post, Salanga, between 1904 and 1907, the month-by-month rise and fall in rubber production correlated almost exactly to the rise and fall in the number of bullets used up by company "sentries" — nearly four hundred in a busy month.

During this period a scandal erupted in France when two white men were put on trial for a particularly gruesome set of murders in the French Congo; to celebrate Bastille Day, one had exploded a stick of dynamite in a black prisoner's rectum. Copying Leopold, the government tried to calm things down in 1905 by sending to Africa a commission of inquiry. To lead it, the famous explorer de Brazza was brought out of retirement. It was hoped that he would not say anything embarrassing about the territory he himself had won for France, whose capital city was named Brazzaville.

Plans, however, went awry. Orders for cosmetic changes to be made during de Brazza's visit, such as unchaining the forced laborers, did not reach all the way into the interior before de Brazza got there. Horrified by what he saw, he began compiling a report that promised to be searingly critical, but, to the government's relief, he died on the way home. He was given an impressive state funeral, and the minister of colonies himself pronounced a flowery eulogy over his grave in Paris's Père Lachaise cemetery: "Brazza is not dead . . . his passion lives. . . . He is the example . . . of the eternal traditions of justice and humanity which are the glory of France." The eternal traditions of justice and humanity did not allow for the release of de Brazza's draft report. It was promptly suppressed by the same minister, with the endorsement of Parliament, and was never published. The lucrative concession-company system continued, with few changes. In the 1920s, construction of a new railway through French territory bypassing the big Congo River rapids cost the lives of an estimated twenty thousand forced laborers, far more than had died building, and later rebuilding, Leopold's railway nearby.

(There is a curious footnote to the story of the French Congo. Who, by way of strawmen and dummy corporations, was discovered to be a major shareholder in five of the concession companies there, and the majority shareholder in three of these? King Leopold II. Belgian government investigators discovered this in the course of trying to untangle Leopold's finances after his death. Fearing that the French would be upset to find their Congo partly owned by the king next door, they successfully kept the news quiet for some years, and did not sell the shares until the 1920s. Leopold also held big blocks of shares in several concession companies in Germany's Cameroons.)

The exclusive focus of the reform movement on Leopold's Congo seems even more illogical if you reckon mass murder by the percentage of the population killed. By these standards, the toll was even worse among the Hereros in German South West Africa, today's Namibia. The killing there was masked by no smokescreen of talk about philanthropy. It was genocide, pure and simple, starkly announced in advance.

After losing much of their land to the Germans, the Hereros rebelled in 1904. In response, Germany sent in a heavily armed force under Lieutenant General Lothar von Trotha, who issued an extermination order (*Vernichtungsbefehl*):

"Within the German boundaries every Herero, whether found with or without a rifle, with or without cattle, shall be shot. . . .

"Signed: The Great General of the Mighty Kaiser, von Trotha."

In case everything was not clear, an addendum specified: "No male prisoners will be taken."

Of an estimated eighty thousand Hereros who lived in the territory in 1903, fewer than twenty thousand landless refugees remained in 1906. The others had been driven into the desert to die of thirst (the Germans poisoned the waterholes), were shot, or — to economize on bullets — bayoneted or clubbed to death with rifle stocks.

Von Trotha's extermination order stirred some protests in Germany itself, but internationally it was greeted with silence, even though the Congo reform campaign was then flying high. Morel and other Congo reformers paid so little attention that five years later John Holt, the businessman who was one of Morel's two main financial backers, could ask him, "Is it true that the Germans butchered the Hereros — men, women, and children? . . . I have never heard of this before."

Around the time the Germans were slaughtering Hereros, the world also was largely ignoring America's brutal counterguerrilla war in the Philippines, in which U.S. troops tortured prisoners, burned villages, killed 20,000 rebels, and saw 200,000 more Filipinos die of war-related hunger or disease. Britain came in for no international criticism for its killings of aborigines in Australia, in accordance with extermination orders as ruthless as von Trotha's. And, of course, in neither Europe nor the United States was there major protest against the decimation of the American Indians.

When these other mass murders went largely unnoticed except by their victims, why, in England and the United States, was there such a storm of righteous protest about the Congo? The politics of empathy are fickle. Certainly one reason Britons and Americans focused on the Congo was that it was a safe target. Outrage over the Congo did not involve British or American misdeeds, nor did it entail the diplomatic, trade, or military consequences of taking on a major power like France or Germany. Morel had something of a blind spot about Germany, but, although he had his hands more than full with Leopold, to his great credit he repeatedly and forcefully attacked France for adopting the Leopoldian system wholesale in its equatorial African colonies and reaping a lethal rubber harvest second only to the king's. His words drew little response among his fellow Britons, who saw World War I on the horizon and knew that France would be their chief ally.

What happened in the Congo was indeed mass murder on a vast scale, but the sad truth is that the men who carried it out for Leopold were no more murderous than many Europeans then at work or at war elsewhere in Africa. Conrad said it best: "All Europe contributed to the making of Kurtz."

In the years following Leopold's death, the other actors in the Congo drama passed from the scene. In 1910, William Sheppard returned to the United States for good. Just after being vindicated in the Compagnie du Kasai libel trial, he was forced to resign his post as a missionary because he had been caught having extramarital affairs with African women. He was briefly placed on probation by the church and then allowed to resume work as a minister in the United States, where word of the scandal was never made public. His health was weakened after dozens of bouts of fever during his twenty years in Africa, and he lived out most of his remaining years as pastor of Grace Presbyterian Church in Louisville, Kentucky, where his wife, Lucy, taught Sunday school and led the choir.

Sheppard continued to write and speak widely about Africa, even though, in his Southern Presbyterian church, this meant having to talk before segregated congregations. At different times, each of the two great archrivals, Booker T. Washington and W.E.B. Du Bois, invited Sheppard to join him on the speaker's platform, and Sheppard obliged. But this man, who was so honored in the black community, who had been the first foreign visitor to meet the Kuba king, who had been received in the White House, had returned to an American South where he was still a second-class citizen. Years later, a white woman in Sheppard's home town of Waynesboro, Virginia, said of him: "He was such a good darky. When he returned from Africa he remembered his place and always came to the back door." When Sheppard died in Louisville at the age of sixty-two, in 1927, more than a thousand people came to his funeral.

On the other side of the country, the lawyer Henry Kowalsky's great bulk hastened his end. He was found dead at the age of fifty-six, in 1914, on the floor of his apartment in San Francisco's Palace Hotel. In Belgium,

Léon Rom, his head-collecting days long past, collapsed in his office at the Compagnie du Kasai in 1924. Joseph Conrad, who had so acutely captured the essence of Rom and of fortune-hunters like him in *Heart of Darkness,* died in England the same year. The only public figure from the Congo controversy to survive into our time was the missionary, reformer, and photographer Alice Harris, who died in 1970 at the age of one hundred.

Another major figure in the Congo story did not meet his end so peacefully.

In 1913, Sir Roger Casement retired from the British consular service and was free at last to throw himself into the cause that now consumed him: freedom for his homeland. Returning to Ireland, he helped to found the Irish Volunteers, an armed militia, and traveled the country to speak at mass meetings. A comrade left this description of him in Dublin in 1914: "Looking outward before the window curtains, stood Roger Casement . . . [with] the apparent dejection which he always wore so proudly, as though he had assumed the sorrows of the world. His face was in profile to me, his handsome head and noble outline cut out against the lattice-work of the curtain and the grey sky. His height seemed more than usually commanding, his black hair and beard longer than usual. His left leg was thrown forward and the boot was torn in a great hole — for he gave his substance away always, and left himself thus in need."

"It is quite clear to every Irishman," Casement wrote, "that the only rule John Bull respects is that of the rifle." He set off across the Atlantic to raise funds from Irish-Americans for buying black-market guns, but shortly after he arrived in the United States, World War I began. Any talk of Home Rule for Ireland, the British said, would have to wait. Casement responded with an open letter declaring that the Irish people should never "contribute their blood, their honour and their manhood in a war that in no wise concerns them. . . . Ireland has no blood to give to any land, to any cause but that of Ireland. . . . Let our graves be in that patriot grass whence alone the corpse of Irish nationality can spring to life."

He shaved off his beard and, using a false passport, headed from New York to Germany. The militant Irish nationalists wanted the Germans to declare that if they won the war, Ireland would receive independence. In return, they hoped to arm and train an Irish Brigade of freedom fighters from among Irish prisoners of war now held in Germany. And if the Irish Brigade could not fight in Ireland itself, Casement thought, it would fight beside the Egyptians, another colonial people yearning for freedom from

Britain. His plan, he wrote in his diary, was to "link the green flag of Ireland with the green flag of the Prophet & . . . drive the allies into the sea."

Casement's dreams won little sympathy from the Irish prisoners of war. They were professional soldiers, many with ancestors who had served in the same British regiment. Of some 2200 Irish Catholic POW's, fewer than sixty joined the Irish Brigade, where they were given German uniforms with a harp and shamrock on the collar. Casement occasionally marched with the brigade in training, but, scarcely larger than an Irish platoon, it never went to war.

The Germans were highly uneasy with Casement's anticolonialism and wanted to get this restless romantic off their hands; he was eager to return to Ireland to join his comrades underground. On April 21, 1916, off the west coast of Ireland, a German submarine captain released Casement, two companions, and their supplies in a small boat. When he asked Casement whether there was any more clothing he needed, Casement replied, "Only my shroud."

In a way, Casement had been waiting for this moment of homecoming and martyrdom all his life. "When I landed in Ireland that morning (about 3 A.M.), swamped and swimming ashore on an unknown strand. . . . I was for one brief spell happy and smiling once more . . . and all around were primroses and wild violets and the singing of the skylarks in the air, and I was back in Ireland again."

He was captured a few hours later. His mind was filled with thoughts of primroses and skylarks, but his pockets held a railway ticket stub for the trip from Berlin to Wilhelmshaven, a German submarine port, and a diary with the entry, supposedly in code, "April 12: left Wicklow in Willie's yacht." Among the items police found buried on the beach where he had landed were three Mauser pistols, ammunition, binoculars, maps, and a copy of *The Rubaiyat of Omar Khayyám*.

Two days later, Casement was charged with high treason, the first knight of the realm to be so accused in several hundred years. He was held incommunicado in the Tower of London, and the British wasted little time in putting him on trial. Guards led him to and from court in handcuffs. Like almost all of his Congo reform movement friends, Sir Arthur Conan Doyle strongly disapproved of his action, but he contributed £700 toward Casement's defense. He and many other famous writers signed petitions asking that Casement's life be spared. However, Joseph Conrad, Casement's 1890 roommate from Matadi, refused to sign; he was as staunch a patriot of his adopted country, England, as Casement was an opponent.

Money and messages of support arrived from around the world. From the United States, the Negro Fellowship League sent King George V an appeal for clemency: "We feel so deeply grateful to this man for the revelations he made while British Consul in Africa, touching the treatment of the natives of the Congo. But for him, the world might not know of the barbarous cruelties." George Bernard Shaw drafted a speech for Casement to give at his trial, but Casement rejected it and gave his own.

"Self-government is our right," he declared. "A thing born in us at birth; a thing no more to be doled out to us or withheld from us by another people than the right to life itself — than the right to feel the sun or smell the flowers, or to love our kind. . . . Where men must beg with bated breath for leave to subsist in their own land, to think their own thoughts, to sing their own songs, to garner the fruits of their own labours . . . then surely it is braver, a saner and a truer thing, to be a rebel . . . than tamely to accept it as the natural lot of men." Like far too few nationalists, Casement's passion for freedom applied to all peoples, not just his own. For his time he was rare, perhaps unique, in proclaiming something in common between the struggle for freedom of Europeans like the Irish and of Africans like the Egyptians and the Congolese. His speech quickly entered the annals of anticolonialism, where it made a deep impression on a young man who would later help lead his own country to independence, Jawaharlal Nehru. "It seemed to point out," he said, "exactly how a subject nation should feel."

Found guilty, Casement was moved to London's Pentonville Prison, a massive, forbidding structure built in 1842 to hold convicts in solitary confinement under a strict rule of silence. At his former lodgings in London, Scotland Yard had already found some of his diaries. The authorities immediately made photographic copies of the entries about his homosexual experiences and showed them around widely: to the king, to influential citizens in their London clubs, to members of Parliament. Journalists were invited in for a look, and one set of copies went to Washington. The government wanted to discredit Casement and to discourage any more notables from speaking up for clemency. The diaries helped to seal his doom.

An imprisoned pacifist caught a glimpse of Casement watching the sunset sky through his Pentonville cell window. He looked "wonderfully calm . . . he seemed already to be living in another world; there was not a trace of anxiety or fear in his features." On the morning of August 3, 1916, guards tied his hands behind his back. "He marched to the scaffold," said a priest who accompanied him, "with the dignity of a prince and towered straight over all of us." The hangman called him "the bravest man it fell to my unhappy lot to execute." In one of the last letters he wrote from his cell, less than a week before he was hanged, Casement looked back over his life: "I made awful mistakes, and did heaps of things wrong and failed at much — but . . . the best thing was the Congo."

Like his friend Casement, E. D. Morel had also been transformed by the long struggle over the Congo. In the final decade of his life he fought his bravest, loneliest battle of all. And this time there were no lords and bishops cheering him on.

In the closing years of the Congo reform movement, Morel saw how much his cause was being hindered by the Entente Cordiale between Paris and London, studded with secret clauses, in which the two countries subordinated everything to preparations for a coming European war. At the beginning of August 1914, he was on a rare seaside vacation with his daughter in Dieppe, France. Newly mobilized reservists filled the streets as the two caught a packed boat across the Channel to England, their holiday cut short by the looming conflict. In London, Morel and his friend Charles Trevelyan, M.P., filled with foreboding, walked through an empty House of Commons as crowds in the street outside roared their support for war.

Morel was among the handful of people on either side in Europe who said openly that the war was madness. Through a series of treaties kept secret from the public and Parliament, he argued, England had become caught up in a needless cataclysm. He was not a pacifist; he said he would fight if England were attacked, but it had not been. He was asked to resign his position as a Parliamentary candidate for the Liberal Party. With a small, beleaguered group of like-minded men and women, Morel formed the Union of Democratic Control, which quickly became the main voice of antiwar dissent in England. UDC activists found that their mail was being opened by Scotland Yard and their telephone calls tapped. Mobs broke up their meetings, tearing down banners, throwing stink bombs, and beating up speakers and members of the audience. Before long, no one in London would rent the UDC a meeting hall. On all sides, former admirers deserted Morel. When one old journalist friend, now in uniform, deigned to greet him in the street, Morel was so moved that he wept, saying, "I did not think anyone would speak to me now."

In the UDC, as in the Congo reform movement, Morel became the dominant figure. "I felt something volcanic in the man," wrote a colleague. There were "fires smouldering always at his heart." As before, his wife, Mary, supported him wholeheartedly, joining the organization's council. He set up branches of the UDC all over England, edited the group's monthly newspaper, and wrote his usual stream of articles and pamphlets, plus two books. But the work was far harder now, for England was in the grip of war fever, the wartime censor banned some of his writing, and his mailbox was filled with hate mail. Police raided both the UDC office and the Morel family's home, where they took papers and correspondence from his study. Of one of the works Morel managed to get published while enduring all this, *Ten Years of Secret Diplomacy,* the historian A.J.P. Taylor writes, "All the later studies of 'war-origins' stem from [it] . . . the interwar historians were . . . cut from his cloak. . . . Morel caused more than a change of method; he caused a change of outlook."

Today we see so clearly that the 8.5 million dead and 21 million wounded of World War I were a needless, avoidable tragedy that we forget how few people had the courage to call it that at the time. As the war went on, Morel came under heightened attack. A fierce blast against the British antiwar movement in the *Daily Sketch* noted, "If you meet pacifists in debate and question their facts you always find yourself referred to one authority — Morel. . . . To kill this conspiracy we must get hold of the arch-conspirator." His office was under constant police surveillance. WHO IS MR. E. D. MOREL? read a headline in the *Daily Express,* AND WHO PAYS FOR HIS PRO-GERMAN UNION? The *Evening Standard* called him "Germany's agent in this country."

It was while undergoing attacks like these that Morel got the news of Casement's arrest. Morel's fellow UDC members warned him that they were in enough trouble as it was and urged him not to support his friend who, unlike them, actually had been collaborating with the Germans. So Morel, although he must have agonized about it, did not visit Casement in prison during the few months he had left to live. Casement, generous-spirited as ever, sent word that he fully understood. A friend who had seen him wrote to Morel: "He told me that he thought you were *quite right* to have accepted the decision of your colleagues, that there was no question about it."

Throughout the war, Morel stuck to his beliefs, as passionate and unyielding now, when all were against him, as he had been in the days of Congo reform, when much of the British establishment had been on his side. He called for a negotiated peace and an end to secret treaties. And he argued, with great prescience, against the harsh peace terms he was certain would be imposed on Germany. With tsarist Russia on the Allied side, he wrote, it was ridiculous to claim that the war was one between democracy and autocracy. He demanded disarmament, an agreement that no land would be transferred without a plebiscite of its inhabitants, and an International Council of all nations.

"The War of 1914–1918 changed everything for me. . . ." writes Bertrand Russell, another man who boldly challenged the chauvinist fever. "I lost old friends and made new ones. I came to know some few people whom I could deeply admire, first among whom I should place E. D. Morel. . . . With untiring energy and immense ability in the face of all the obstacles of propaganda and censorship, he did what he could to enlighten the British nation as to the true purposes for which the Government was driving the young men to the shambles. More than any other opponent of the War he was attacked by politicians and the press. . . . In spite of all this his courage never failed." Russell declared of Morel, "No other man known to me has had the same heroic simplicity in pursuing and proclaiming political truth."

British government records show that high officials in many departments long conferred about how best to get Morel "safely lodged in gaol," as one man in the Foreign Office put it, without giving him the public forum of a trial, at which he could deploy his persuasiveness as a speaker and his awesome command of information. In 1917, they found an appropriate technicality, and arrested him for violating an obscure law against sending antiwar literature to neutral countries. He was denied bail and promptly sentenced to six months at hard labor.

Morel describes a curious event at his sentencing in 1917: "A picturesque feature in this otherwise squalid legal landscape was provided by an individual crossing the body of the Court from somewhere behind me while my counsel was pleading, and handing up a note to the prosecuting counsel, who opened it, read it, and nodded, whereupon the individual regained his seat, but not before I had recognised in him the same individual who . . . acting as an accredited representative of King Leopold II, had publicly opposed me in America in the course of my mission to the United States." Leopold had died eight years earlier, and Morel's trip to the United States had been five years before that. Some half-dozen of the king's paid lobbyists had taken to the field against him then; he does not tell us which of them made this mysterious appearance in the courtroom, as if Leopold were still sending orders from the grave.

Guards took Morel through the gates of Pentonville Prison a year after Roger Casement had been executed there. The man in the cell on one side of Morel had stolen three bottles of whiskey; on the other side was someone who had raped a child. In one of the monthly letters, which were all he was permitted to write to his wife, he referred to "this, the 1st time in the last twenty years we have not written to each other daily when absent."

He spent his prison days in a dust-filled room sewing canvas mail-bags and weaving rope into hammocks and mats for the navy, all in silence: no conversation between prisoners was allowed at work. He was locked in his cell each night from four P.M. until eight the next morning. Supper, eaten alone in the cell, was "a piece of bread, half-a-pint of coldish porridge at the bottom of a tin which earlier in the day may have contained red-herrings and still bears traces of them, and a pint of hot, greasy cocoa which one learns to regard as a veritable nectar of the gods, especially in cold weather." Once or twice during the night there would be clicking sounds as a warder opened the peephole in each cell door to check on the prisoners. At night there was "the cold of a cold cell — like nothing on earth. Nothing seems proof against it."

In the prison chapel prisoners sat, again in silence, watched by warders on raised platforms while officials made announcements of battlefield victories in the war Morel opposed. Sometimes at work he was made to carry big slabs of jute, whose weight he estimated at close to a hundred pounds each, to the prison workshop. This made him think wryly of the African porters who had carried his baggage through the Nigerian countryside half a dozen years before. "But memory remains, experience is a great teacher, there is much to be learned here too, and, after all, one has lived to play both parts." A man imprisoned for burglary, sensing that Morel was someone important, called him "sir."

Two months after his release, in early 1918, Bertrand Russell, soon to go to jail himself, wrote worriedly to Gilbert Murray: "I saw E. D. Morel yesterday for the first time since he came out, & was impressed by the seriousness of a six months' sentence. His hair was completely white (there was hardly a tinge of white before) — when he first came out, he collapsed completely, physically & mentally, largely as the result of insufficient food."

Morel resumed his speaking and writing, but his once sturdy figure was now painfully thin. Not long after his release, he had the first of several heart attacks. But in the next few years he also had the satisfaction of being publicly vindicated. There *were* secret treaties among the Allied powers, it turned out. And many of the Fourteen Points President Woodrow Wilson proposed for the peace settlement sounded as if they had been copied from one of Morel's pamphlets. The UDC's wartime support had come partly from trade unionists and — to Morel's surprise, for this former shipping company official had never previously thought himself a socialist — he found himself treated as a hero by the Labour Party. In 1922, standing for a House of Commons seat on the Labour ticket, he had the great pleasure of defeating a former minister of the Cabinet that had sent him to jail during the war — a member of Parliament named Winston Churchill.

Morel proved enormously popular with his constituents in Dundee, Scotland. They reelected him in 1923 and again the following year, when twenty thousand saw him off at the railway station as he left for London. In Parliament, he rapidly became Labour's most prominent and respected voice on foreign policy. When, in early 1924, the party leader Ramsay MacDonald became Britain's first Labour prime minister, many expected him to name Morel foreign secretary. But this was not to be. For the leader of a shaky coalition government, Morel was too fiercely independent a moralist and a crusader — and perhaps a potential rival for the leadership. MacDonald kept the foreign secretary's position for himself. As a consolation, he nominated Morel as Britain's candidate for the Nobel Peace Prize.

Although Morel was only fifty-one years old, prison, wartime persecution, his disappointment at not receiving a Cabinet post, and the grueling pace of his work over several decades all began to take their toll. He had to lie down periodically, stretched out on the terrace of the House of Commons, and he and his wife often drove for rests to her family's home in Devonshire. On November 12, 1924, out for a walk in the woods with his sister-in-law, Morel said he felt tired, sat down, and leaned against a tree to rest. He never got up.

He was remembered at large memorial services in Dundee, in London, and in New York. "Morel," said the French writer Romain Rolland, "will tower above the age as the years pass."

19

THE GREAT FORGETTING

O NE OF THE MORE eerie experiences for a visitor to the old Soviet Union was strolling through the spacious galleries of the Museum of the Revolution on Moscow's Gorky Street. You could look at hundreds of photographs and paintings of fur-hatted revolutionaries behind snowy barricades, innumerable rifles, machine guns, flags and banners, a large collection of other relics and documents, and find no clue that some twenty million Soviet citizens had died in execution cellars, in manmade famines, and in the gulag.

Today that museum in Moscow has changed in ways its creators could never have imagined. But on the other side of Europe is one that has not changed in the slightest. To see it, take the short walk from the European Union headquarters complex in Brussels to the beginning of the Number 44 tram line. The tram carries you through the shady, pleasant Forêt de Soignes on the outskirts of the city to the ancient ducal borough of Tervuren. In the eighth century, Saint Hubert, the patron saint of hunters, lived here and pursued game in these woods. Today, grandly overlooking a park, in an enormous Louis XV–style palace built by King Leopold II, is the Royal Museum of Central Africa. On a typical day it will be swarming with hundreds of visitors, from schoolchildren filling in blank spots in workbooks to elderly tourists arriving in air-conditioned buses.

The museum houses one of the world's largest collections of Africana. It takes a full day to see all the exhibits, from Stanley's cap to Leopold's cane, from slave manacles to a dugout canoe big enough for a hundred men. One gallery full of weapons and uniforms celebrates the "antislavery campaigns" of the 1890s — against the "Arab" slavers, of course. A plaque lists the names of several dozen Force Publique officers who "rest in African earth." Other plaques in this "memorial hall" have the names of hundreds more white pioneers who died in the Congo. Another gallery holds stuffed wild animals: elephants, chimpanzees, gorillas. An old black-and-white film plays continually on a TV monitor, showing Pende masked dances, the Kuba king at court, Ntomba funeral rites — an Africa composed entirely of exotic costumes and pounding drums. Everywhere, preserved in glass cases, are objects from the Congo's manifold cultures: spears, arrows, pipes, masks, bowls, baskets, paddles, scepters, fish traps, musical instruments.

One temporary exhibit shows a remarkable type of sculpture from the lower part of the Congo River: three-foot-high wooden statues, the chest and neck of each one studded with hundreds of nails, spikes, and tiny razorlike blades. The statues look like bristling, tortured dwarfs. A sign explains that each is an *nkondi,* a fetish to combat witches and other evildoers. Every nail and blade stands for an oath or an appeal for retaliation against an injustice. But of any larger injustice in the Congo, there is no sign whatever. For in none of the museum's twenty large exhibition galleries is there the slightest hint that millions of Congolese met unnatural deaths.

There is no hint of these deaths anywhere in Brussels. The rue Bréderode, where part of the Congo administration and the most important Congo companies once had headquarters, still runs past the back of the Royal Palace. But today the spot where Joseph Conrad had his job interview is occupied by a government tax-collection office. On another side of the palace, a larger-than-life statue of Leopold on horseback stares metallically out at a freeway underpass. And yet the blood spilled in the Congo, the stolen land, the severed hands, the shattered families and orphaned children, underlie much that meets the eye. The ornate, columned Royal Palace itself was renovated to its present splendor with Congo profits, as was the more grandly situated, domed château of Laeken, where the royal family lives, with its stunning array of greenhouses containing more than six acres of glass. Each spring the greenhouses are briefly opened to the public, and thousands of visitors walk past a bust of Leopold, decorated with camelias and azaleas. At Laeken also stands the five-story Japanese Tower, an architectural oddity that Leopold saw at a Paris world's fair, took a fancy to, and bought with his Congo money. Dominating part of the city's skyline is the grandest Congo-financed extravagance of all, the huge Cinquantenaire arch, studded with heroic statuary; it looks like a swollen combination of the Arc de Triomphe and the Brandenburg Gate, with curving wings added. The arch's massive stone and concrete bulk brings to mind Conrad's description of the unnamed European capital in *Heart of Darkness* as "the sepulchral city." But of the millions of Africans whose labors paid for all this and sent them to sepulchers of unmarked earth, there is no sign.

Brussels is not unique. In Berlin, there are no museums or monuments to the slaughtered Hereros, and in Paris and Lisbon no visible reminders of the rubber terror that slashed in half the populations of parts of French and Portuguese Africa. In the American South, there are hundreds of Civil War battle monuments and preserved plantation manor houses for every exhibit that in any way marks the existence of slavery. And yet the world we live in — its divisions and conflicts, its widening gap between rich and poor, its seemingly inexplicable outbursts of violence — is shaped far less by what we celebrate and mythologize than by the painful events we try to forget. Leopold's Congo is but one of those silences of history.

The Congo offers a striking example of the politics of forgetting. Leopold and the Belgian colonial officials who followed him went to extraordinary lengths to try to erase potentially incriminating evidence from the historical record. One day in August 1908, shortly before the colony was officially turned over to Belgium, the king's young military aide Gustave Stinglhamber walked from the Royal Palace to see a friend in the Congo state offices next door. The midsummer day seemed particularly warm, and the two men went to an open window to talk. Stinglhamber sat down on a radiator, then jumped to his feet: it was burning hot. When the men summoned the janitor for an explanation, he replied, "Sorry, but they're burning the State archives." The furnaces burned for eight days, turning most of the Congo state records to ash and smoke in the sky over Brussels. "I will give them my Congo," Leopold told Stinglhamber, "but they have no right to know what I did there."

At the same time the furnaces roared in Brussels, orders went from the palace to the Congo commanding the destruction of records there. Colonel Maximilien Strauch, the king's long-time *consigliere* on Congo matters, later said, "The voices which, in default of the destroyed archives, might speak in their stead have systematically been condemned to silence for considerations of a higher order." Seldom has a totalitarian regime gone to such lengths to destroy so thoroughly the records of its work. In their later quests for a higher order, Hitler and Stalin in some ways left a far larger paper trail behind them.

The same kind of deliberate forgetting took place in the minds of the men who staffed the regime. Forgetting one's participation in mass murder is not something passive; it is an active deed. In looking at the memories recorded by the early white conquistadors in Africa, we can sometimes catch the act of forgetting at the very moment it happens. It is not a moment of erasure, but of turning things upside down, the strange reversal of the victimizer mentally converting himself to victim. Take, for example, a moment in the memoirs of Raoul de Premorel, who ran rubber-collecting posts in the Kasai region of the Congo from 1896 to 1901. Here is his description of how he dealt with the alleged ringleader of a mutiny:

> I had two sentries drag him to the front of the store, where his wrists were tied together. Then standing him up against a post with his arms raised high above his head they tied him securely to a cross beam. I now had them raise him by tightening the rope until just his toes touched the floor. . . . So I left the poor wretch. All night long he hung there, sometimes begging for mercy, sometimes in a kind of swoon. All night long his faithful wife did what she could to alleviate his suffering. She brought him drink and food, she rubbed his aching legs. . . . At last when the morning came and my men cut him down, he dropped unconscious in a heap on the ground. "Take him away," I ordered. . . . Whether he lived or not, I do not know. . . . Now sometimes in my sleep I think I am the poor devil and half a hundred black fiends are dancing . . . about me. I wake up with a great start and I find myself covered with a cold sweat. Sometimes, I think it is I who have suffered most in the years that have passed since that night.

Sometimes, I think it is I who have suffered most. . . . Throughout history, people with blood on their hands have used such rationalizations. But the process of forgetting the killings of Leopold's Congo received an unexpected boost when Belgium itself was seen as victim instead of conqueror. The world was shocked by Germany's unprovoked invasion of neutral Belgium in August 1914, as well as by German killings of many Belgian civilians in the opening weeks of the war.

During the next four years, first the British and then the American governments used the sufferings of "brave little Belgium" to whip up war fever in countries that had not themselves been attacked. Newspaper stories, cartoons, posters, and patriotic speeches luridly denounced mass rapes of Belgian women by German soldiers. The Germans, it was said, crucified Belgian babies on the doors of houses. And, in a striking but unconscious echo of the imagery of the Congo reform movement, the press in the Allied countries reported that German soldiers were cutting off the hands and feet of Belgian children. An exiled Belgian writer even wrote a poem on the subject.*

These shocking reports of severed hands and feet were so widespread that a rich American tried to adopt maimed Belgian children; but, even with offers of a reward, none could be found. In the end, the mass rape, mutilation, and crucifixion charges also turned out to be false. During and after the war, though, no one in the Allied countries wanted to be reminded that, only a decade or two earlier, it was the King of the Belgians whose men in Africa had cut off hands. And so the full history of Leopold's rule in the Congo and of the movement that opposed it dropped out of Europe's memory, perhaps even more swiftly and completely than did the other mass killings that took place in the colonization of Africa.

In the quiet village of Hoepertingen, an hour east of Brussels by train, Jules Marchal and his wife live in a modest, rambling house with a small cherry orchard. Once a year they spend a few weeks on ladders, with baskets, harvesting cherries to sell through the local farmers' co-operative. Marchal was born here, and at seventy-three he fits the part of a town

---

* It ends:

> Et quand ils rencontraient quelque Teuton frappé
> Par une balle adroite, au bord d'un chemin proche,
> Souvent ils découvraient, dans le creux de ses poches,
> Avec des colliers d'or et des satins fripés,
> Deux petits pieds d'enfant atrocement coupés.

And when they [Belgians] find some Hun struck down
By a well-aimed bullet, at a nearby roadside,
Often they find, in the folds of his pockets,
With gold rings and crumpled satin,
Two children's feet, cruelly cut off.

elder: a gold tooth, suspenders, a ruddy, kindly face, white hair. His white mustache gives him a slight resemblance to pictures of Stanley in the explorer's last years. But there the similarity ends.

Marchal is a retired diplomat. In the early 1970s, he was Belgian ambassador to a group of three countries in West Africa: Ghana, Liberia, and Sierra Leone. One day he noticed a story in a Liberian newspaper that referred, in passing, to ten million deaths in King Leopold's Congo.

"I was startled," says Marchal. "I wrote to the foreign minister in Brussels. I said, 'I have to write a letter to the editor correcting this story, this strange slander on our country. But I don't know the history of that period. Could you please have someone send me some information?'

"I waited. But I never got an answer. And that's when my curiosity began."

Marchal is a careful, methodical man, the sort of person who likes to read a book in its original language, to trace a piece of information to its source, to get his history not from someone else's summary, but from the original documents. His interest ignited, he now read enough about early Congo history to discover that finding official documents might not be so easy, given Leopold's week-long bonfire. However, certain crucial papers had escaped the furnace in 1908, and among them were the transcripts — never published — of the testimony given by African witnesses before the 1904–1905 Commission of Inquiry. Conveniently for him, Marchal discovered, this important collection of records had eventually ended up filed in the archives of the Belgian Foreign Ministry, his own employer. He looked forward to examining them.

Marchal next served in another post in Africa, "but the Congo always stayed in my head. There was an air of something rotten about it. I learned that there had been this huge campaign, in the international press, from 1900 to 1910; millions of people had died, but we Belgians knew absolutely nothing about it. And so when I arrived in 1975 for a post at the Foreign Ministry in Brussels, the first thing I did was to go to the ministry archives and ask to see the Commission of Inquiry testimony."

Impossible, he was told. The testimony papers were stamped *Ne pas à communiquer aux chercheurs* — no access for researchers. Marchal protested that it was seventy years after the commission had delivered its report, and that he was of ambassadorial rank. It made no difference. He was not allowed to see the files.

"There was a rule in the Foreign Ministry archives. They were not permitted to show researchers material that was bad for the reputation of

Belgium. But *everything* about this period was bad for the reputation of Belgium! So they showed nothing." Marchal, now obsessed with the subject, had another decade and a half to serve before retirement. He remained in the foreign service, returning to Africa as an ambassador and also working in several desk jobs in Brussels. He devoted all of his spare time to research and writing about Leopold's Congo. After he retired, in 1989, he worked at his project full time. Four decades as a civil servant had given him unusual skill in locating revealing information in government records, and he traveled to every archive in Europe and the United States that had material about this period. He found collections of private papers in Belgium that had been beyond reach of Leopold's fire. He found that often the most revealing material lay in the letters and reports of low-ranking, idealistic young colonial officers, newly arrived in the Congo and shocked that African realities did not match the noble rhetoric they had heard in Europe. He studied the files of missionary societies and of companies that had done business in Africa. He went to Ireland to look at Casement's papers and to visit the beach where Casement had landed on his last, fatal mission.

While Marchal was still a Belgian diplomat, he wrote under a pseudonym — Delathuy, the maiden name of his great-grandmother. "A remarkable woman. But she had been written out of the family history because she had had a child out of wedlock. Her name was never mentioned. It was taboo. Like the history of the millions killed." Marchal wrote his history of Leopold's Congo in his native Dutch, then revised and translated it for a four-volume edition in French. Although virtually ignored in Belgium, his books are the definitive scholarly study of the subject, a magisterial, scrupulously documented account unsurpassed in any language. It might never have been written had he not seen that Liberian newspaper article.

As Marchal describes his work, he seems a man possessed. His voice rises, he gesticulates. He pulls books and papers off his shelves and burrows into drawers to find photographs. The photos are of every house in England where E. D. Morel lived. "Morel has been treated in Belgium as a traitor and a bad man. I want to put him in his rightful place."

It upset Marchal that he had been representing his country for many years while knowing nothing of this piece of its past, and it rankled him even more to be denied access to the archives of his own ministry. At one point, a senior official told him, "You can see the files, but only if you promise not to write anything based on them." Marchal refused the bargain. Only after badgering ministry officials for eight years was he allowed to look at the Commission of Inquiry testimony. He has published an annotated collection of it as a book.

There was a further reason that Marchal was distressed by what he learned. Before joining the Belgian diplomatic service when he was in his early forties, he had worked in the Congo for nearly twenty years, in its last years as a Belgian colony and its first as an independent country, starting as a young assistant district administrator for the colonial regime. Years later, on first learning about the turn-of-the-century history, Marchal and his wife, Paula, carefully sifted their memories to see whether there were any clues, anything people had said, that could be understood in a new light. He remembered one such episode:

"When I arrived in the Congo in 1948, my very first job was to go around and distribute medals to the village chiefs who had gathered rubber for the government during the Second World War. You know they made everyone go back into the forest then, and tap wild rubber. I had to give decorations to about a hundred chiefs. I had a corporal and six or seven soldiers who went to all the villages with me. The corporal, he said to me, 'The rubber *this* time, that was nothing. But the first time, *that* was terrible.' Only thirty years later did I understand what he was talking about."

༺༝༛༝༺

In all of Africa, the colonizers wrote the school textbooks; together with widespread book-banning and press censorship, this accomplished the act of forgetting for the written record. In the Congo, throughout the half-century of Belgian rule that followed Leopold's death, textbooks for Africans praised Leopold and his works as lavishly as Soviet schoolbooks praised Lenin. For example, a 1959 text for young Congolese soldiers studying to become NCOs in the Force Publique explained that history "reveals how the Belgians, by acts of heroism, managed to create this immense territory." Fighting the "Arab" slavers, "in three years of sacrifice, perseverance and steadfast endurance, they brilliantly completed the most humanitarian campaign of the century, liberating the decimated and exploited peoples of this part of Africa." As for critics, who go unnamed: "The criticisms emitted in the course of defamatory campaigns undertaken by jealous foreigners . . . were shown to amount to nothing."

This officially decreed forgetting could not, of course, reach all the way to the villages, where there remains some lore about the rubber terror. But even that collective memory today is more scanty than one would expect. A handful of dedicated anthropologists have helped find and preserve these memories — often a fragmentary local legend about an extraordinarily cruel person from the period remembered as *la guerre du Blanc* [the white man's war], or, in the Mongo language, *lokeli,* "the overwhelming." Sometimes, in conjunction with information gathered by witnesses like Casement or the missionaries, the villain of legend can be identified as a district commissioner or rubber-company agent or a chief who collaborated with the conquerors. Sometimes the period of terror is stamped into the language itself. In the Mongo tongue, "to send someone to harvest rubber" is an idiom meaning "to tyrannize."

Relatively little collective memory of the rubber era has survived in rural Africa, because oral tradition is usually a matter of remembering kings, dynasties, victories in battle. And those dynasties which have survived almost always did so by collaborating with the colonial rulers. As Jan Vansina observes in his history of the Kuba people: "No account of those events [the Leopold-era rubber slavery] appeared in the dynastic traditions. The rulers who had benefited from the system were not about to commit this to official memory." In the cities, where many Congolese now live, the process of rapid urbanization itself has brought drastic upheaval. For example, what was, just over a hundred years ago, the small village of Kinshasa is today a sprawling, chaotic metropolis of some five million people, many of them recently arrived from rural areas in a desperate search for work. Such changes have strained and loosened the connecting links by which lore is passed from one generation to another. Traditional cultures have been much weakened, and disappearing with them is the very memory of the forces that first shattered them.

Decades after Leopold's death a curious legend developed in the Congo. The king, it was believed, had not died at all but had come to live in his former colony. He had been transformed into a Catholic bishop, Jean-Félix de Hemptinne, an autocratic nobleman who long weilded great political influence in the Congo. (The legend was clearly sparked by de Hemptinne's large white beard and figure, which were of Leopoldian dimensions.) De Hemptinne was Leopold reincarnated, it was said, or maybe he was the king's illegitimate son, and in this role he was a shadowy figure behind the scenes at pivotal moments, ordering the police to fire on striking mineworkers in one notorious episode, ordering a judge to be tough on an accused prisoner in another.

It needed no reincarnation, however, for Leopold to leave his mark. History lies heavy on Africa: the long decades of colonialism, several hundred years of the Atlantic and Arab world slave trade, and — all too often ignored — countless centuries of indigenous slavery before that. From the colonial era, the major legacy Europe left to Africa was not democracy as it is practiced today in countries like England, France, and Belgium; it was authoritarian rule and plunder. On the whole continent, perhaps no nation has had a harder time than the Congo in emerging from the shadow of its past.

When independence finally came to the Congo, the country fared badly. Like most other colonial powers in Africa, Belgium was taken by surprise by the demand for self-rule that swept across the continent in the 1950s, igniting mass demonstrations in Leopoldville in 1959 that were bloodily suppressed by the Force Publique. Until then, Leopold's heirs had thought independence might come, but decades hence. Some Africans were being trained for that distant day; but when pressure grew and independence came in 1960, in the entire territory there were fewer than thirty African university graduates. There were no Congolese army officers, engineers, agronomists, or physicians. The colony's administration had made few other steps toward a Congo run by its own people: of some five thousand management-level positions in the civil service, only three were filled by Africans.

King Baudouin of Belgium arrived in Leopoldville to grant, officially and patronizingly, the Congo its freedom. He said, "It is now up to you, gentlemen, to show that you are worthy of our confidence." An angry, impromptu speech in reply by Patrice Lumumba caught the world's attention. Barely a month earlier, an election had made Lumumba a coalition-government prime minister. It was the first democratic national election the territory had ever had. In substance if not form, it would be, for more than thirty-five years, the last. Lumumba believed that political independence was not enough to free Africa from its colonial past; the continent must also cease to be an economic colony of Europe. His speeches set off immediate alarm signals in Western capitals. Belgian, British, and American corporations by now had vast investments in the Congo, which was rich in copper, cobalt, diamonds, gold, tin, manganese, and zinc. An inspired orator whose voice was rapidly carrying beyond his country's borders, Lumumba was a mercurial and charismatic figure.

His message, Western governments feared, was contagious. Moreover, he could not be bought. Finding no sympathy in the West, he asked for help from the Soviet Union. Anathema to American and European capital, he became a leader whose days were numbered. Less than two months after being named the Congo's first democratically chosen prime minister, a U.S. National Security Council subcommittee on covert operations, which included CIA chief Allen Dulles, authorized his assassination. Richard Bissell, CIA operations chief at the time, later said, "The President [Dwight D. Eisenhower] would have vastly preferred to have him taken care of some way other than by assassination, but he regarded Lumumba as I did and a lot of other people did: as a mad dog . . . and he wanted the problem dealt with."

Alternatives for dealing with "the problem" were considered, among them poison (a supply of which was sent to the CIA station chief in Leopoldville), a high-powered rifle, and free-lance hit men. But it proved hard to get close enough to Lumumba to use these, so, instead, the CIA supported anti-Lumumba elements within the factionalized Congo government, confident that before long they would do the job. They did. After being arrested and suffering a series of beatings, the prime minister was secretly shot in Elizabethville in January 1961. A CIA agent ended up driving around the city with Lumumba's body in his car's trunk, trying to find a place to dispose of it. We cannot know whether, had he survived, Lumumba would have stayed true to his rhetoric and to the hopes he embodied for so many people in Africa and elsewhere. But the United States saw to it that he never had a chance. Like millions of Congolese before him, he ended up dumped in an unmarked grave.

The key figure in the Congolese forces that arranged Lumumba's murder was a young man named Joseph Désiré Mobutu, then chief of staff of the army and a former NCO in the old colonial Force Publique. Early on, the Western powers had spotted Mobutu as someone who would look out for their interests. He had received cash payments from the local CIA man and Western military attachés while Lumumba's murder was being planned. Wearing dark glasses and his general's uniform with gold braid and a sword, he later met President Kennedy at the White House in 1963. Kennedy gave him an airplane for his personal use — and a U.S. Air Force crew to fly it for him. With United States encouragement, Mobutu staged a coup in 1965 that made him the country's dictator. And in that position he remained for more than thirty years.

Further U.S. military aid helped Mobutu repel several attempts to overthrow him. Some of his political enemies he ordered tortured and killed; some he co-opted into his ruling circles; others he forced into exile. The United States gave him well over a billion dollars in civilian and military aid during the three decades of his rule; European powers — especially France — contributed more. For its heavy investment, the United States and its allies got a regime that was reliably anti-Communist and a secure staging area for CIA and French military operations, but Mobutu brought his country little except a change of name, in 1971, to Zaire.

Government-owned media began referring to Mobutu variously as the Guide, the Father of the Nation, the Helmsman, and the Messiah. With American and European approval, the country's wealth flowed mainly into the pockets of the Messiah and foreign mining companies. Mobutu's loyalty to his Western backers made him a popular visitor to Washington, where he shrewdly abandoned his military uniform for civilian dress, a carved ebony cane, and a trademark African-looking leopard-skin hat that had actually been made by an elegant Paris milliner. Ronald Reagan received him at the White House several times, praising him as "a voice of good sense and good will." George Bush greeted him as "one of our most valued friends." He added, "I was honored to invite President Mobutu to be the first African head of state to come to the United States for an official visit during my presidency."

Mobutu and his entourage helped themselves to state revenue so freely that the Congolese government ceased to function. When he ran out of money to pay the army and other state workers in 1993, he printed up a new kind of currency. Because shopkeepers would not accept it, soldiers rioted, looting shops, government buildings, and private homes. Hundreds of people were killed. For years, garbage piled up in heaps, uncollected. A few foreign airlines continued to stop in the country, but they avoided leaving their planes overnight; insurance would not cover it. Government support of schools and hospitals dwindled to almost nothing. The U.S. embassy advised its staff in the capital not to unlock car doors or roll down windows when stopped by police at roadblocks: they should show their papers through the window only, lest their wallets be taken.

Before Mobutu was overthrown, in 1997, his thirty-two years in power had made him one of the world's richest men; his personal wealth at its peak was estimated at $4 billion. He spent much of his time on his yacht, on the river at Kinshasa, formerly Leopoldville. One of the big lakes he renamed Lake Mobutu Sese Seko. He acquired palatial homes in France, Belgium, Portugal, Spain, Switzerland, and elsewhere. He made no distinction between state assets and his own; in a single year, he dispatched a state-owned jet airliner thirty-two times to Venezuela to ferry five thousand long-haired sheep to his ranch at Gbadolite; while his yacht was being renovated in 1987, he simply took over the most comfortable of the few remaining passenger boats still operating on the river system. And he demanded, and got, a piece of the action in almost every major corporation operating in the country.

It is an oversimplification to blame Africa's troubles today entirely on European imperialism; history is far more complicated. And yet, consider Mobutu again. Aside from the color of his skin, there were few ways in which he did not resemble the monarch who governed the same territory a hundred years earlier. His one-man rule. His great wealth taken from the land. His naming a lake after himself. His yacht. His appropriation of state possessions as his own. His huge shareholdings in private corporations doing business in his territory. Just as Leopold, using his privately controlled state, shared most of his rubber profits with no one, so Mobutu acquired his personal group of gold mines — and a rubber plantation. Mobutu's habit of printing more money when he needed it resembled nothing so much as Leopold's printing of Congo bonds.

"Those who are conquered," wrote the philosopher Ibn Khaldūn in the fourteenth century, "always want to imitate the conqueror in his main characteristics — in his clothing, his crafts, and in all his distinctive traits and customs." Mobutu's luxurious Villa del Mare, a pink-and-white marble colonnaded château at Roquebrune-Cap-Martin on the French Riviera, complete with indoor and outdoor swimming pools, gold-fitted bathrooms, and heliport, lay a mere dozen miles down the coast from the estates Leopold once owned at Cap Ferrat. From one cape you can see the other.

✦✦✦✦

What epitaph can we write for the movement that worked so hard for justice in the Congo a hundred years ago?

The Congo reform movement had two achievements that lasted far beyond its own time. First, through the efforts of E. D. Morel, Roger Casement, and equally brave but lesser-known figures like George Washington Williams, William Sheppard, and Hezekiah Andrew Shanu, it put a remarkable amount of information on the historical record. And there it remains, despite the strenuous efforts of Leopold and his admirers, then and now, to burn it, to ignore it, to distort it with mythologizing. That record of truth matters, especially for a continent whose history is otherwise so filled with silences.

The movement's other great achievement is this. Among its supporters, it kept alive a tradition, a way of seeing the world, a human capacity for outrage at pain inflicted on another human being, no matter whether that pain is inflicted on someone of another color, in another country, at another end of the earth.

When the Congo reformers spoke at hundreds of mass meetings throughout Britain and the United States, they showed slides: photographs of adults and children with their hands cut off, forced laborers at work as porters, a devastated village. LANTERN LECTURE ON THE CONGO ATROCITIES, read an advertisement. "60 excellent Photographic Lantern Slides from Photographs taken by Mrs. Harris, late of Baringa, Congo Free State. Descriptive lecture, revised by the Rev. J. H. Harris & Mr. E. D. Morel." These slides were black and white, approximately three inches square, made for "magic lantern" projectors. Someone who goes in search of those slides today can find them. They rest in two dusty wooden boxes on a storage shelf on the ground floor of a small, low-rent building in south London. The building is the office of Anti-Slavery International, formerly the Anti-Slavery Society, formerly the Anti-Slavery and Aborigines Protection Society, formerly the British and Foreign Anti-Slavery Society. John and Alice Harris ran the society for many years after their work with Morel. In continuous existence since 1839, it is the oldest human rights organization on earth. Today, in that room with the boxes of slides, men and women in their twenties briskly come and go, carrying posters, video cassettes, and bundles of pamphlets — about child labor in Bangladesh and Nepal and Malaysia, women in household slavery in the Middle East, debt bondage in Brazil, child prostitution in Thailand, genital mutilation of women in Africa, the exploitation of immigrant domestic servants in England.

The tradition that is alive in that London office has grown and broadened in the last two hundred years. Today we are less likely to speak of humanitarianism, with its overtones of paternalistic generosity, and more likely to speak of human rights. The basic freedoms in life are not seen as gifts to be doled out by benevolent well-wishers, but, as Casement said at his trial, as those rights to which all human beings are entitled from birth. It is this spirit which underlies organizations like Amnesty International, with its belief that putting someone in prison solely for his or her opinions is a crime, whether it happens in China or Turkey or Argentina, and Médecins Sans Frontières, with its belief that a sick child is entitled to medical care, whether in Rwanda or Honduras or the South Bronx.

The Congo reform movement at its best not only helped to shape and strengthen this set of beliefs; it went beyond them. Human rights groups today usually deal with results — a man in jail, a woman in servitude, a child without medicine. E. D. Morel talked, as well, about causes: above all, the theft of African land and labor that made possible Leopold's whole system of exploitation. It was this radicalism, in the best and deepest sense of the word, that underlay the passion of the leading Congo reformers and that led Morel and Casement, after their battle for justice in the Congo, to Pentonville Prison.

The larger tradition of which they are a part goes back to the French Revolution and beyond; it draws on the example of men and women who fought against enormous odds for their freedom, from the slave revolts of the Americas to the half-century of resistance that brought Nelson Mandela to power in South Africa. During its decade on the world stage, the Congo reform movement was a vital link in that chain, and there is no tradition more honorable. At the time of the Congo controversy a hundred years ago, the idea of full human rights, political, social, and economic, was a profound threat to the established order of most countries on earth. It still is today.

NOTES

BIBLIOGRAPHY

ACKNOWLEDGMENTS

INDEX

NOTES

Sources are given for direct quotations, which are identified by their closing words, for most numbers and statistics, and for many other points of information. I have not identified sources when the facts involved are not in dispute and can easily be found in one — or usually several — of the key books acknowledged at the beginning of the Bibliography.

Some works cited only once or twice are referred to in the source notes but are not listed in the Bibliography.

For abbreviated references to one of several books by the same author — as in Morel 5, Stengers 2, Marchal 3 — consult the Bibliography.

INTRODUCTION

page
1 *Morel in Antwerp:* Morel 5, chapters 4 and 5.
2 *nearly three hundred a year:* in 1907, for example. *Official Organ* . . . April 1908, p. 24.
2 *letter of protest to the* Times: 23 Dec. 1908, Morel 5, p. 208.
2 *"so strongly and so vehemently":* Morel 5, p. xiv.
4 *"history of human conscience":* "Geography and Some Explorers," *Last Essays,* ed. Richard Curle (London: J. M. Dent & Sons, 1926), p. 17, excerpted in Conrad, p. 187.

PROLOGUE: "THE TRADERS ARE KIDNAPPING OUR PEOPLE"

6 *early European maps and images of Africa:* See Klemp.
7 *"edge of the world":* Forbath, p. 41.
8 *"without resistance":* Forbath, p. 73.
8 *"in his household":* Forbath, p. 73.
8 *Mbanza Kongo:* Balandier, p. 30 ff.
8 *ManiKongo:* Vansina 1, pp. 41–45.

9 *sophisticated and well-developed state:* see Balandier; Cuvelier; Hilton, chapters 1–3; and
   Vansina 1, chapter 2.

10 *"of their faith":* *Relations sur le Congo du père Laurent de Lucques (1700–1717),* ed. Jean
   Cuvelier (Brussels: Institut Royal Colonial Belge, 1953), p. 338, quoted in Balandier, p. 81.

11 *fifteen thousand slaves a year:* Vansina 1, p. 149.

11 *"she is dying":* Miller, p. xiii. This list of slaves is from 1736.

11 *Atlantic slave trade and the Kongo kingdom:* Miller is the best source, although he
   concentrates on a later period.

12 *"that of Affonso":* quoted in Davidson 1, p. 138.

12 *"speaking of our Savior":* Rui de Aguiar to King Manuel I, 25 May 1516, quoted in
   Affonso, p. 117.

12 selective *modernizer:* Vansina 1, pp. 45–58.

12 *first known documents:* Albert S. Gérard, *African Language Literature: An Introduction to
   the Literary History of Sub-Saharan Africa* (Harlow, Essex: Longman, 1981), p. 287.

13 *"transport of slaves":* Affonso to João III, 6 July 1526, Affonso, p. 156.

13 *"red-hot iron":* Affonso I to João III, 18 Oct. 1526, Affonso, p. 167.

13 *"selling them as captives":* Affonso I to João III, 25 Aug. 1526, Affonso, p. 159.

14 *"obedient to us and content":* Affonso I to João III, 6 July 1526, Affonso, pp. 155–156.

14 *"no slave has ever left":* João III to Affonso, 1529 (n. d.), Affonso, p. 175.

14 *"He is again crucified":* Affonso to Manuel I, 31 May 1515, Affonso, p. 103.

14 *"their fathers and mothers":* Affonso I to João III, 25 Mar. 1539, Affonso, p. 210.

15 *ancestral ghosts:* see, for instance, Harms 2, p. 210.

16 *"wars and miseries":* Haveaux, p. 47.

16 *deadly transformations began:* Miller, pp. 4–5.

16 *"sold them to the white men":* Weeks, pp. 294–295.

17 *"of this animal":* Instructions to Mr. Tudor, 7 Feb. 1816, quoted in Anstey 1, p. 5.

18 *"masses of quartz":* Forbath, p. 177.

18 *"of the Thames":* *Narrative of the Expedition to explore the River Zaire, usually called the
   Congo . . .* (London: 1818), p. 342, quoted in Anstey 1, p. 9.

1. "I SHALL NOT GIVE UP THE CHASE"

21 *John Rowlands/Henry Morton Stanley:* The best sources on Stanley's life are the careful,
   thorough biographies, Bierman and McLynn 1 and 2. Hall was a pioneer biographical debunker but does not give specific sources. Stanley 5, Stanley's own
   autobiography, the only source for much of his youth, omits and embellishes a
   great deal, often revealingly so.

21 *"sound whipping":* Stanley 5, p. 8.

22 *"utter desolateness":* Stanley 5, p. 10.

22 *"things they should not":* Bierman, p. 8.

22 *"as with a snap":* Stanley 5, p. 29.

23 *"to sail in this ship?":* Stanley 5, p. 67.

23 *"want a boy, sir?":* Stanley 5, p. 87.

23 *"big talk and telling stories":* New Orleans *Daily States,* 16 Apr. 1891, quoted in
   Bierman, p. 29.

24 *"almost broke my spine":* Stanley 5, p. 33.

24 *"God bless you!"*: Stanley 5, p. 113.

24 "you are to bear my name": Stanley 5, p. 121.

24 *"esteemed him as he deserved?"*: Draft for Stanley's unfinished autobiography, quoted in McLynn 1, pp. 37–38.

25 *"through excess of sentiment, into folly"*: Stanley 5, pp. 107–111.

26 *"debauchery . . . whirlpool of sin"*: Bierman, p. 48.

26 *"on the warpath"*: Newspaper dispatch of 25 May 1867, quoted in Bierman, p. 47.

27 *"we were here all the time"*: reportedly said by Dr. Hastings Banda of Malawi, quoted in McLynn 3, p. ix.

27 *too vile to be spoken of:* West, pp. 22–23.

28 *"in the emancipation of slaves"*: Honour, p. 264.

29 "BUT FIND LIVINGSTONE!": Stanley 1, pp. xvi–xvii.

29 *"all the subsequent professional travel writers"*: George Martelli, *Leopold to Lumumba: A History of the Belgian Congo 1877–1960* (London: Chapman & Hall, 1962), p. 10.

30 *"bring his bones to you"*: *Stanley's Despatches to the New York Herald 1871–72, 1874–77,* ed. Norman R. Bennett (Boston: Boston University Press, 1970), p. 23, quoted in Bierman, p. 101.

30 *"the Arab . . . the Banyan . . . the half-castes"*: Stanley 1, p. 6.

31 *"too ungrateful to suit my fancy"*: Slade 2, p. 23.

31 *"sometimes to an extravagant — activity"*: Bierman, p. 97.

31 *"well flogged and chained"*: Stanley 1, p. 318.

31 *"thorn clumps and gum trees!"*: *Stanley's Despatches to the New York Herald,* p. 76, quoted in Bierman, p. 109.

31 *"their next resting place?"*: Stanley 1, pp. 112–113.

31 *march to the sea:* McLynn 1, p. 204.

32 *"fellow Missourian"*: Hall, p. 99.

2. THE FOX CROSSES THE STREAM

33 *Leopold II:* Emerson is the standard scholarly biography of Leopold. Ascherson does a better job of capturing the spirit of the man but is scantily footnoted.

34 *"by this last report"*: Queen Marie-Louise to Leopold, 28 June 1849, reprinted in Freddy, p. 27.

34 *"That is Leopold's way!"*: Emerson, p. 23.

35 *"saying disagreeable things to people"*: Aronson, p. 35.

35 *"by nun I mean the Duke of Brabant"*: Madame de Metternich, quoted in Ascherson, p. 34.

35 *"I shall not go on living much longer"*: Joanna Richardson, *My Dearest Uncle. Leopold I of the Belgians* (London: Jonathan Cape, 1961), p. 188, quoted in Ascherson, p. 36.

36 *"has now borne fruit"*: Leopold to Albert, 19 Nov. 1857, quoted in Emerson, p. 56.

36 *"richest countries in the world"*: Emerson, p. 19.

37 *"makes now out of her colonies"*: Leopold to Brialmont, quoted in Ascherson, p. 46.

37 *"corrupt peoples of the Far East"*: L. Le Febve de Vivy, *Documents d'histoire précoloniale belge* (Brussels: Académie Royale des Sciences Coloniales, 1955), p. 20, quoted in Stengers 7, p. 19. On Money, also see Money, Stengers 1, p. 145 fn., and Marchal 1, pp. 40–41.

38 *"times as big as Belgium"*: Leopold to Lambermont, 11 June 1861, quoted in Roeykens, pp. 413–414 fn.

38 *"let such a fine prey escape"*: Leopold to Brialmont, 16 May 1861, quoted in Stengers 7, p. 21.

38 *"got to make her learn"*: L. le Febve de Vivy, *Documents d'histoire précoloniale belge* (Brussels: Académie Royale des Sciences Coloniales, 1955), p. 23, quoted in Ascherson, p. 58.

39 *"'a great veterinarian'?"*: Daye, pp. 438–439.

39 *"without knowing how to wear it"*: Marshal Canrobert, quoted in Daye, p. 92.

39 *"banned by a malignant fairy"*: Aronson, pp. 34–35.

39 *"his admirable wife"*: Louise, p. 34.

39 *"to me or my sisters"*: Louise, p. 29.

40 *Laeken and its greenhouses*: Goedleven, pp. 69–75.

40 *"Little?"*: Stinglhamber and Dresse, p. 256.

41 *"Muchachos, aim well"*: Hyde, p. 291.

41 *"I am starving, literally starving!"*: Hyde, p. 226. See also O'Connor, pp. 271–273.

42 *"anything to be done in Africa"*: Leopold to Lambermont, 22 Aug. 1875, quoted in Roeykens, pp. 95–96.

42 *100,000 francs*: Roeykens, p. 73.

43 *"letters must be written after the names"*: Vandewoude, p. 434.

44 *"even the Ink and the Ammunition"*: Rawlinson to Lady Rawlinson, 11 Sept. 1876, quoted in Pakenham, p. 21.

44 *Leopold's speech to the Geographical Conference*: reprinted in P. A. Roeykens, *Léopold II et la Conférence géographique de Bruxelles (1876)* (Brussels: Académie Royale des Sciences Coloniales, 1956), pp. 197–199. See Bederman for a short treatment of the conference.

46 *"greatest humanitarian work of this time"*: Pakenham, p. 22.

3. THE MAGNIFICENT CAKE

47 *wielding the whip and the gun*: And much worse; see Marchal 1, pp. 28–32.

47 *"Exploration of Africa"*: Stanley 2, vol. 2, pp. 346–347.

48 *"we shall call Stanley Pool!'"*: Stanley 5, p. 329.

49 *"three or four score villages"*: Stanley 7, p. 199.

49 *"quiet the mocking"*: Stanley 7, p. 125.

50 *"as if they were monkeys"*: Bierman, p. 182.

50 *"safe in London"*: McLynn 2, p. 11.

50 *"species of human vermin"*: *New York Herald*, 17 Sept. 1877, quoted in McLynn, vol. 2, p. 11.

50 *"for they are the envoys of God"*: McLynn 1, p. 257.

50 *"in chains for 6 months"*: Stanley 7, p. 87.

50 *"such miserable slaves"*: Stanley 7, p. 195.

50 *"until death relieves them"*: Stanley to Alice Pike, 25 Dec. 1874, quoted in Bierman, p. 163.

51 *"angry with Central Africa"*: Alice Pike to Stanley, 13 Oct. 1874, quoted in McLynn 1, p. 248.

52 *"attend you in your sleep!"*: Stanley 2, vol. 2, pp. 148–152.

53 *"the poor young man was dead":* Stanley 2, vol. 1, p. 190.

53 *"take his last gasp":* Stanley 2, vol. 1, p. 91.

53 *"and not disturb him":* Stanley 7, p. 130.

54 *"the strong Basoko with jeers":* Ward, p. 110.

54 *part of white anatomy:* Hulstaert, p. 52.

55 *"commerce to West Central Africa":* Daily Telegraph, 12 Nov. 1877, quoted in Stanley 3, vol. 1, p. vi.

55 *"through a rock tunnel":* Stanley 2, vol. 2, p. 261–262.

56 *"until I meet you":* Stanley to Alice Pike, 14 Aug. 1876, quoted in Bierman, p. 189.

57 *footnote:* quoted in Bierman, p. 214.

57 *"indecency of their nakedness":* Stanley 2, vol. 2, p. 59.

57 *"western half of the Dark Continent":* Stanley 2, vol. 2, p. 99.

57 *"commerce with Central Africa":* Stanley 7, p. 40.

57 *"reached the Lualaba":* Leopold to Greindl, 30 May 1877, quoted in Roeykens, p. 235.

58 *"this magnificent African cake":* Leopold to Solvyns, 17 Nov. 1877, quoted in part in Pakenham, p. 38, and in part in Ascherson, p. 104.

59 *Sanford's business troubles:* Fry 1, esp. pp. 78–89.

59 *"loves and appreciates you":* Greindl to Sanford, 28 Nov. 1877, quoted in Fry 1, p. 133.

60 *"called a pirate":* Hall, p. 245.

4. "THE TREATIES MUST GRANT US EVERYTHING"

61 *time spent in Africa:* Marchal 1, p. 49.

64 *"has been a nose-bleed?":* Stanley 5, p. 351.

65 *the real purpose of their work:* Marchal 1, p. 49.

65 *"explorations are intended":* "The Whitehall Review and the King of the Belgians," in *The Whitehall Review,* 2 Aug. 1879, p. 269. Quoted in Stengers 3, p. 122.

65 *"doesn't grasp that":* Leopold to Strauch, 8 Jan. 1884, quoted in Stanley 6, pp. 20–21.

66 *the elephants:* Anstey 1, p. 75.

66 *"traffic in slaves":* speech of 6 Mar. 1879, reprinted in Bontinck, p. 74.

66 *"to the cause of progress":* Stengers 3, p. 144.

67 *"believe in Kings forever":* William T. Hornaday, *Free Rum on the Congo* (Chicago: Women's Temperance Publication Association, 1887), pp. 44–45, quoted in Stengers 4, p. 260.

67 *"free negro republics":* Col. Maximilien Strauch, quoted in Bierman, p. 225.

67 *"Some in the Congo?":* Eugène Beyens to Léon Lambert, 3 Nov. 1882, quoted in Stengers 3, p. 142.

67 *"retain all the powers":* Strauch to Stanley, undated, Stanley 6, pp. 22–23.

67 *"shame and discomfort":* Stanley to Strauch, 12 June 1881, Stanley 6, p. 49.

68 *"able to use it as before":* Stanley 6, p. 44.

68 *"the ranks of soldier-laborers":* Stanley 3, vol. 2, pp. 93–94.

68 *"Breaker of Rocks":* Stanley 3, vol. 1, pp. 147–148, p. 237. See also Marchal 1, p. 52, for a corrective.

68 *"weak-minded . . . so many idle hands":* Stanley 3, vol. 2, pp. 376–377.

68 *"clothesless . . . unabashed nudity":* Stanley 3, vol. 2, p. 100.

69 *"chieftainship to wear them":* Stanley 3, vol. 1, pp. 130–131.

69 *"entrusted to me":* Pakenham, p. 150.

69 *"underbred . . . white children":* Stanley 3, vol. 1, p. 459.

70 *"when I most need you?":* Frank Hird, *H. M. Stanley: The Authorized Life* (London: S. Paul & Co., 1935), p. 186, quoted in Bierman, p. 235.

70 *"perhaps Chinese coolies":* Leopold to Stanley, 31 Dec. 1881, quoted in Emerson, p. 96.

70 *"carry on trade":* FO 84/1802, 15 Nov. 1882, quoted in Stengers 3, p. 133.

70 *"custom of every country":* Leopold to Stanley, 31 Dec. 1881, quoted in Emerson, p. 96.

71 *"claim to manhood":* Stanley 3, vol. 1, p. 466.

71 *"must grant us everything":* Leopold to Strauch, 16 Oct. 1882, reprinted in Stanley 6, p. 161.

71 *"bottles of gin":* Stanley 3, vol. 1, p. 185.

72 *"property of the said Association":* Stanley 3, vol. 2, pp. 196–197.

72 *as diverse as the land:* There is a vast anthropological literature on the Congo basin. See especially Vansina 1 and 3, and, for a highly readable treatment of the Pygmies, Turnbull.

73 *harsh as warfare elsewhere:* Vellut, p. 701; Vansina 2, p. 144, p. 343.

74 *spot in the rain forest:* Vansina 1, p. 100.

74 *"take in a herring":* Stanley to Sanford, 4 Mar. 1885, reprinted in Bontinck, p. 300.

5. FROM FLORIDA TO BERLIN

75 *"a gentleman . . . evidently a good feeder":* New York Times, 6 Apr. 1883, 13 Apr. 1883.

75 *President Arthur's trip to Florida:* New York Times, 5–15 Apr. 1883. On Arthur generally, see Reeves.

76 *Sanford's Florida business troubles:* Fry 1, pp. 100–106.

77 *a special code:* Bontinck, pp. 139–140.

77 *"population of several millions":* Leopold to Arthur, 3(?) Nov. 1883, quoted in Bontinck, pp. 135–136.

78 *The copy, however, had been altered:* Stengers 3, p. 128 fn. and p. 130 fn.

78 *"discovered by an American":* Sanford to Frelinghuysen, 30 Dec. 1882, quoted in Carroll, p. 115.

78 *"the neutrality of the valley":* President Arthur's message to Congress, 4 Dec. 1883, quoted in Bontinck, p. 144.

79 "ENCHANTED WITH ÉMILE": Strauch to Sanford, 6 Dec. 1883, quoted in Bontinck, p. 146.

79 *"gastronomic campaign":* Anonymous letter-writer in the *Times* of Philadelphia, 31 Jan. 1885, quoted in Bontinck, p. 160.

79 *"queenly presence too":* Latrobe to Sanford, 18 Mar. 1884, quoted in Bontinck, p. 189.

79 *"enforced negro rule . . . innocent woman":* Fry 2, pp. 56–57.

79 *"general exodus":* Fry 2, p. 56.

79 *"home of the negro":* Fry 2, p. 185.

80 *"field for his efforts":* Congressional Record, 7 Jan. 1890, quoted in Carroll, pp. 332–333.

80 *footnote:* Carroll, p. 337.

80 *"more congenial fields than politics":* Sanford to Evarts, 21 Jan. 1878, quoted in Bontinck, p. 29.

80 *"modern Israelites":* "American Interests in Africa," *The Forum* 9 (1890), p. 428, quoted in Roark 1, p. 169.

80 *"over the Southern states":* ibid., p. 428, quoted in Meyer, p. 28 fn.

80 *"adjacent rivers"*: Bontinck, p. 171.

80 *"secure their welfare"*: U.S. Senate, *Occupation of Congo in Africa,* S. Rept. 393, 48th Congress, 1st sess., 1884, p. 9, quoted in Normandy, p. 171.

81 *"both the King and Queen"*: Gertrude Sanford to Henry Sanford, April 1884, quoted in Fry 1, p. 148.

81 *"flag of a friendly Government"*: Bontinck, p. 201.

81 *statement was reprinted:* Stanley 3, vol. 2, p. 420.

82 *"new life of the Association"*: Stanley 3, vol. 2, p. 383.

82 *large monthly stipend:* of 1000 francs. Stengers 7, p. 48.

82 *"be established in the Congo"*: Leopold to Strauch, 26 Sept. 1883, quoted in Pakenham, p. 245.

82 *"its work was completed"*: Emerson, p. 108.

83 *"and eradicate it"*: Emerson, p. 108.

83 *"get away with anything"*: Emerson, p. 109.

83 *the role of Bleichröder:* Stern, p. 403–409.

84 *"slaughtered game during our travels"*: Hall, p. 265.

84 *"end be their improvement"*: J. S. Mill, *"On Liberty" In Focus,* eds. John Gray and G. W. Smith (London: Routledge, 1991), p. 31.

85 *owed a large sum of money:* Anstey 1, p. 68; Pakenham, p. 247.

85 *"of that continent very well"*: Stanley's journal, 24 Nov. 1884, quoted in McLynn 2, pp. 86–87.

86 *"the utmost freedom of communication"*: John A. Kasson, an American delegate, in U.S. Senate, *Report of the Secretary of State Relative to Affairs of the Independent State of the Congo,* p. 42., quoted in Clarence Clendenen, Robert Collins, and Peter Duignan, *Americans in Africa 1865–1900* (Stanford: The Hoover Institution on War, Revolution, and Peace, 1966), p. 57.

86 *"its illustrious creator"*: H. L. Wesseling, *Divide and Rule: The Partition of Africa, 1880–1914* (Westport, CT: Praeger, 1996).

87 *"as the Congo's 'proprietor'"*: Stengers 2, p. 262. See also Jean Stengers in *La Nouvelle Clio* IX (1950), p. 515.

6. UNDER THE YACHT CLUB FLAG

88 *the king was named: Pall Mall Gazette,* 10 Apr. 1885, p. 9; and 11 Apr. 1885, p. 3.

89 *umbrellas and parasols: New York Times,* 5 June 1917 and 15 June 1917.

89 *"topic of conversation around me"*: Louise, p. 32.

90 *"and they have not"*: Hilaire Belloc, *The Modern Traveller* (1898).

90 *430 whites working in the Congo:* census taken 31 Dec. 1889, reported in *Le Mouvement Géographique,* 23 Mar. 1890.

91 *"offer my services"*: Henry Sanford to Gertrude Sanford, 30 Aug. 1884, quoted in Fry 1, p. 150.

91 *the Sanford Exploring Expedition:* Fry, pp. 157–163; White.

91 *this was not true:* Van der Smissen, vol. 1, p. 127.

92 *"with your Congo!"*: Stinglhamber and Dresse, p. 142.

92 *honorary president:* Lagergren, p. 198 fn.

93 *"receptions and balls"*: Kirk to Wylde, 24 Apr. 1890, quoted in Miers, p. 102.

93 *"a new pretty woman"*: Liebrechts, pp. 29–30.

93 *the king had betrayed him:* Meyer, p. 37; Fry 1, p. 168.

94 *"greatest sovereign is your own"*: Emerson, p. 149.

95 *"over l'État Indépendant du Congo"*: Mutamba-Makombo, p. 32.

95 *"throws away the peel"*: August Beernaert in Jean Stengers, *Belgique et Congo: L'élaboration de la charte coloniale* (Brussels: La Renaissance du Livre, 1963), p. 98, quoted in Emerson, p. 64.

95 *"in ample time to prepare"*: Stanley to Mackinnon, 23 Sept. 1886, quoted in Bierman, p. 256.

95 *"I can't talk to women"*: Hall, p. 274.

96 *"her sweet scented notes"*: Stanley to Mackinnon, 23 Sept. 1886, quoted in Bierman, p. 256.

96 *"I will never give it up!"*: Stengers 2, p. 287.

96 *"resources of civilisation"*: the *Times*, 14 Jan. 1887, quoted in Emerson, p. 157.

97 *"to overcome barbarism"*: *Globe*, 19 Jan. 1887, quoted in McLynn 2, p. 146.

98 *"frenzy of rage"*: *The Diary of A. J. Mounteney Jephson*, ed. Dorothy Middleton (Cambridge: Cambridge University Press, 1969), p. 228 (26 Feb. 1888), quoted in Bierman, p. 289.

99 *"catch some more of their women"*: James S. Jameson, *The Story of the Rear Column of the Emin Pasha Relief Expedition*, ed. Mrs. J. A. Jameson (London: R. H. Porter, 1890), p. 92 (21 July 1887), quoted in Bierman, p. 297.

99 *"burn all the villages round"*: *The Diary of A. J. Mounteney Jephson*, ed. Dorothy Middleton (Cambridge: Cambridge University Press, 1969), p. 203 (10 Dec. 1887), quoted in Bierman, p. 286.

99 *"poured into the village"*: Stairs's journal, 28 Sept. 1887, quoted in Bierman, p. 281.

99 *by his Piccadilly taxidermist*: Bierman, p. 298.

99 *"peace of mind"*: Stanley 4, vol. 1, p. 396.

100 *"leave without me!"*: *Die Tagebüchen von Dr Emin Pascha*, ed. Franz Stuhlmann (Hamburg: G. Westerman, 1916–1927), vol. 4, p. 202, 14 Jan. 1889, quoted in McLynn 2, pp. 262–263.

100 *"well-selected and iced"*: Stanley 4, vol. 2, p. 458.

100 *"was most exhilarating!"*: *Funny Folks*, quoted in Bierman, p. 340.

7. THE FIRST HERETIC

102 *several different lives*: unless otherwise noted, biographical facts about Williams are taken from Franklin.

103 *he had never earned*: Marchal 1, p. 176.

103 *"That day will come!"*: Franklin, pp. 10–11.

104 *"so much native ability"*: *New York Times*, 22 Jan. 1883, quoted in Franklin, p. 116.

104 *"greatest historian of the race"*: W.E.B. Du Bois, "The Negro in Literature and Art," *Annals of the American Academy of Political and Social Science* 49 (Sept. 1913), p. 235, quoted in Franklin, p. 133.

105 *Williams, Arthur, and Sanford*: Bontinck, pp. 221, 442.

105 *when he visited London*: Marchal 1, p. 178.

106 *"with complete success"*: *L'Indépendance Belge*, 1 Nov. 1889, quoted in Marchal 1, p. 180.

106 *"a pleasant and entertaining . . . mercy, and justice . . . good listener"*: *Boston Herald*, 17 Nov. 1889, quoted in Franklin, pp. 181–182.

107 *"within a few days"*: Williams 3, p. 265.

108 *"loaded on to the steamer"*: J. Rose Troup, *With Stanley's Rear Column* (London: Chapman & Hall, 1890), p. 124, quoted in Sherry, p. 59. See De Premorel pp. 42–44 for another description of steamer travel.

108 *"Siberia of the African Continent"*: Williams to Huntington, 14 Apr. 1890, quoted in Franklin, p. 191.

108 Open Letter quotations: Williams 1, pp. 243–254.

111 *"introduced this . . . just, not cruel"*: Williams 3, pp. 277–279.

112 *"crimes against humanity"*: Williams to Blaine, 15 Sept. 1890, quoted in Bontinck, p. 449.

112 *"attempt at blackmail"*: *New York Herald,* 14 Apr. 1891.

112 *"natives of that country"*: Huntington to Mackinnon, 20 Sept. 1890, quoted in Franklin, p. 208.

112 *"truth in his pamphlets"*: Vivian to Salisbury, 4 Apr. 1891, quoted in Franklin, p. 210.

112 *"un vrai scandale"*: Émile Banning, *Mémoires politiques et diplomatiques: comment fut fondé le Congo belge* (Paris: La Renaissance du Livre, 1927), p. 295, quoted in Bontinck, p. 448.

112 *"First of all . . . not a colonel"*: *Journal de Bruxelles* 12, 13, 14 June 1891, quoted in Franklin, pp. 211–212.

113 *"the American traveler"*: *La Réforme,* 15 June 1891, quoted in Marchal 1, p 195.

113 *"in its own defense"*: Franklin, p. 213.

113 *"Colonel Williams and others"*: Gosselin to Salisbury, 19 July 1891, quoted in Franklin, p. 215.

113 *"an embarrassingly formidable opponent"*: Cookey, p. 36.

114 *"action of the State"*: Grenfell to Baynes, 23 June 1890; quoted in Franklin, p. 194.

8. WHERE THERE AREN'T NO TEN COMMANDMENTS

115 *Boma in the 1890s:* see numerous articles in *La Belgique Coloniale,* esp. 18 Dec. 1897, p. 607, and 28 Aug. 1898, p. 411.

116 *"learn to stoop"*: Aronson pp. 141–142.

116 *Fischer's of Strasbourg:* Gann and Duignan 2, p. 106.

116 *brides from Europe:* Leclercq, pp. 284–285.

118 *"ivory had disappeared"*: Obdeijn, p. 202.

118 *"lessen its deficit"*: Leopold to Beernaert, 19 June 1891, reprinted in Van der Smissen, vol. 2, p. 212.

118 *"the sanctity of work"*: Interview by Publishers' Press, in the *New York American,* 11 Dec. 1906.

118 *four francs per kilo:* Marchal 1, p. 212.

119 *twenty-two pounds:* Constant De Deken, *Deux Ans au Congo* (Antwerp: Clément Thibaut, 1902), p. 72 fn., cited in Samarin, p. 118.

119 *"A file of poor devils . . . up to the job"*: Courouble, pp. 77, 83.

119 *three thousand porter loads:* Samarin, p. 120.

120 *"overwork in their villages"*: Picard, pp. 96–97.

120 *not one returned:* Marchal 1, p. 202.

120 *"each of the children"*: Marchal 4, p. 317.

121 *"give the military salute"*: Marchal 4, pp. 325–326. Lefranc's account, which he wrote for the Belgian newspaper *L'Express de Liège* on 1 June 1908, was also reprinted as a pamphlet by the Congo Reform Association.

121   "A mediocre agent": Marchal 4, p. 318.

121   "without asking questions": quoted as epigraph in Katz.

122   "become used to it": Sereny, p. 200.

122   "never made any lethal injections": KL Auschwitz Seen by the SS: Hoess, Broad, Kremer, ed. Jadwiga Bezwinska and Danuta Czech (Oswiecimiu, Poland: Panstwowe Museum, 1978), quoted in Katz, pp. 54–55.

122   "punishment for his own gang": De Premorel, p. 63.

123   footnote: Jules Marchal unearthed this remarkable photo, which was first used by Morel before he became editor of the West African Mail. Marchal 2, p. 116; Marchal 3, p. 39.

123   "walk into fire as if to a wedding": Bricusse, p. 85.

123   more than nineteen thousand officers and men: Gann and Duignan 2, p. 79.

123   more than half the state's budget: Marchal 1, p. 354.

124   different ethnic groups staged major rebellions: Isaacman and Vansina is the best short summary.

124   Mulume Niama: Marchal 4, pp. 27–28; Flamant, pp. 182–183.

125   fifty thousand men a year by the mid-1890s: Marchal 1, p. 323.

125   "cannot feel surprised": Karl Teodor Andersson, 28 Dec. 1893, Missionsförbundet 1894, p. 83.

125   "the rebels have not fled . . . leaders in those times": C. N. Börrisson, 2 Feb. 1894, Missionsförbundet 1894, pp. 132–134.

126   Rommel and Nzansu: Axelson, pp. 259–260; Marchal 1, pp. 320–321.

127   "rather than with the hunted": Casement 3, p. 166.

127   ordered her killed: Marchal 1, p. 373.

127   Kandolo: One thing that can mislead the unwary researcher is that three different men named Kandolo figure in Congo history of this period, one of whom was a leader of another mutiny, that of 1897 in the northeast.

127   snatched the whip out of his hands: Van Zandijcke, p. 182.

128   thirteen years after the uprising began: De Boeck, pp. 104, 125. See the other extensive treatments of the uprising in Flament and Van Zandijcke, and a summary in Marchal 1, pp. 372–376.

128   "worthy of a better cause": Flament, p. 417. The best treatment of this uprising is in De Boeck.

128   quotations from Father Achte: De Boeck, pp. 224–228. De Boeck has rescued this valuable piece of testimony, earlier accessible only in truncated versions.

129   starting in the 1960s: De Boeck's entire book is premised on this point.

130   Bongata in 1892: Vangroenweghe, p. 43.

130   instead of paying chiefs for them: Marchal 1, p. 216.

130   "drowned trying to escape": Marchal 1, p. 224.

130   instead of heavy iron ones: Marchal 1, p. 227.

130   "pulls the whole file off and it disappears": Marchal 1, p. 231.

131   the campaign against the "Arabs": See Marchal 1, chapter 14.

133   "to the white men's town at Nyangwe": Canisius, pp. 250–256.

133   the rigors of Leopold's regime: see Marchal 2, part V, for the best treatment of the role of Catholic missionaries.

134   "1500 children and administrative personnel": Leopold to Van Eetvelde, 27 Apr. 1890, quoted in Marchal 2, p. 209.

134 *"the most male children possible":* Governor general's circular, 4 June 1890, quoted in Marchal 2, p. 177.

134 *"was sounded by bugles": Het H. Misoffer. Tijdschrift van de Norbertijner Missiën* 1899, p. 226, quoted in Marchal 2, p. 298.

135 *often over 50 percent:* Marchal 2, pp. 181–182.

135 *within the following few weeks:* Marchal 2, p. 179.

135 *"praying for our great king":* Marchal 2, p. 221.

135 *"Once more, I thank you":* Bauer, p. 216.

135 *"that shepherd":* Daye, p. 399.

136 *"That is forbidden!":* O'Connor, p. 346.

136 *"in the face of the enemy":* Gann and Duignan 2, pp. 62–63.

137 *only fined five hundred francs:* Lagergren, p. 195.

137 *"trader!! Why not!":* Slade 2, p. 116.

137 *Léon Rom's career:* The principal sources (all more or less hagiographic) are *Biographie coloniale belge,* vol. 2, cols. 822–826; Janssens and Cateaux, vol. 1, pp. 125–132 and vol. 2, pp. 197–200; Lejeune-Choquet, pp. 114–126; *Bulletin de l'Association des Vétérans coloniaux,* June 1946, pp. 3–5; Sidney Langford Hinde, *The Fall of the Congo Arabs* (New York: Negro Universities Press, 1969; reprint of 1897 edition), pp. 232, 235, 244–245; and Rom's own unpublished *Notes. Mes Services au Congo de 1886 à 1908.* The first three, as well as Arnold, are useful guides for career details, sanitized, of many other Congo state European personnel of this time.

137 *"as proof of surrender":* Janssens and Cateaux, vol. 2, pp. 199–200.

138 *"Master, they're going to kill you!":* Lejeune-Choquet, pp. 123–124.

138 *many butterfly specimens:* Albert Chapaux, *Le Congo* (Brussels: Charles Rozez, 1894), p. 470.

138 *"can raise a thirst":* from "Mandalay" in *Barrack Room Ballads* (London: Methuen, 1892).

138 *a third of white Congo state agents died there:* Marchal 1, p. 210. See Gann and Duignan 2, p. 68, for a similar figure, almost as high, for military men only, prior to 1906.

139 *"plein de tristesse/Pour le Congo":* Picard, pp. 145–146.

139 *"the river will kill the white man":* L. Dieu, *Dans la brousse congolaise* (Liège: Maréchal, 1946), pp. 59–60, quoted in Slade 2, p. 72.

9. MEETING MR. KURTZ

140 *"I shall go there":* Joseph Conrad, *A Personal Record* (London: J. M. Dent & Sons, 1912), p. 13, excerpted in Conrad, p. 148.

141 *Conrad in the Congo:* Unless otherwise noted, biographical facts about Conrad in the Congo are taken from Nadjer, the most careful biographer when it comes to this period of the novelist's life.

141 *"realities of a boy's daydreams!":* Joseph Conrad, "Geography and Some Explorers," in *Last Essays,* ed. Richard Curle (London: J. M. Dent & Sons, 1926), p. 17, excerpted in Conrad, pp. 186–187.

142 *missionary doctor:* Lapsley, p. 83. Conrad's various biographers have not noticed this.

142 *"not a thought in his head":* Edward Garnett's introduction to *Letters from Conrad 1895–1924,* p. xii. (London: Nonesuch Press, 1928), excerpted in Conrad, p. 195.

142 *"Soundings in fathoms: 2, 2, 2, 1, 1, 2, 2, 2"*: Joseph Conrad, *Congo Diary and Other Uncollected Pieces,* ed. Zdzislaw Najder (New York: Doubleday, 1978), reprinted in Conrad, p. 182.

142 *"everything you had known"*: Conrad, p. 35.

142 *"lost in the depths of the land"*: Conrad, p. 12.

143 *"narrow white line of the teeth"*: Conrad, p. 57.

143 *"beyond the actual facts of the case"*: Joseph Conrad, "Author's Note" to *Youth: A Narrative; and Two Other Stories* (London: William Heinemann, 1921), reprinted in Conrad, p. 4.

143 *"bights swung between them, rhythmically clinking"*: Conrad, p. 19.

144 *"now and then . . . bullet-hole in the forehead"*: Conrad, p. 23.

144 *"met an off[ic]er . . . Saw another dead body . . . tied up to a post"*: Joseph Conrad, *Congo Diary and Other Uncollected Pieces,* ed. Zdzislaw Najder (New York: Doubleday, 1978), reprinted in Conrad, pp. 160, 161, 165.

144 *"several abandoned villages"*: Conrad, p. 23.

144 *"precious trickle of ivory"*: Conrad, p. 21.

144 *"The word 'ivory' . . . could earn percentages"*: Conrad, pp. 26–27.

145 *famed for his harem:* Marchal 1, p. 284.

145 *captured and beheaded him:* Times of London, 8 Dec. 1892, quoted in Sherry, pp. 110–111.

145 *Rom:* see biographical references in preceding chapter.

145 *"a flower-bed in front of his house!"*: E. J. Glave in *The Century Magazine,* Sept. 1897, p. 706.

145 *Rom:* see biographical references on p. 319.

146 *a young officer he had met:* Any meeting between Conrad and Rom would have taken place at the beginning of August, when Conrad passed through Leopoldville, or in the next day or two, before his boat left neighboring Kinshasa. Conrad was again at Leopoldville/Kinshasa from late September to late October and would have had ample opportunity to hear stories of Rom then. Rom himself had already left for his next post on September 2, 1890, while Conrad was upriver. I am indebted to Jules Marchal for finding this date in the state personnel archives. The *Biographie Coloniale belge* wrongly implies a later departure date. For other white collectors of Congolese heads whose boasts may also have helped inspire Conrad's creation of Mr. Kurtz, see pp. 99, 166, and 196–197.

146 *"The horror! The horror!"*: Conrad, p. 68.

146 *"when you look into it too much"*: Conrad, p. 10.

146 *"real work is done in there"*: Conrad, p. 13.

146 *"spark from the sacred fire"*: Conrad, p. 8.

146 *"under the English flag all over the world"*: Frances B. Singh, "The Colonialistic Bias of *Heart of Darkness,*" in *Conradiana* 10 (1978), reprinted in Conrad, p. 278.

146 *"less savage than the other savages"*: Mark Twain, *More Tramps Abroad* (London: Chatto & Windus, 1897) pp. 137–138, quoted in C. P. Sarvan, "Racism and the *Heart of Darkness,*" *International Fiction Review* 7 (1980), reprinted in Conrad, p. 284.

146 *"weird incantations"*: Conrad, p. 65.

146 *"passionate uproar"*: Conrad, p. 38.

146 *"some satanic litany"*: Conrad, p. 66.

147 *"lo! the darkness found him out"*: Chinua Achebe, "An Image of Africa: Racism in Conrad's *Heart of Darkness*," reprinted in Conrad, p. 261.

147 *"the Company was run for profit"*: Conrad, p. 16.

147 *footnote*: Conrad and Hueffer, p. 165.

147 *"the noble cause"*: Conrad, p. 12.

147 *"science and progress"*: Conrad, p. 28.

147 *"sketch in oils"*: Conrad, p. 27.

147 *"vibrating with eloquence . . . Exterminate all the brutes!"*: Conrad, pp. 50–51.

148 *in a Belgian museum*: the Musée Royal de l'Afrique Centrale at Tervuren.

148 *"he generally responds with something stupid"*: Rom, *Le Nègre du Congo*, pp. 5–6.

148 *"they will have at the next stop"*: Rom, *Le Nègre du Congo*, p. 84.

149 *"getting himself adored"*: Conrad, p. 56.

149 *"He makes his agents . . . the role of a second Rom"*: Leclercq, p. 264.

149 *"in front of the station!"*: Wahis to Van Eetvelde, 2 Nov. 1896, quoted in Marchal 1, p. 298.

10. THE WOOD THAT WEEPS

150 *"burns like the altar flame"*: Tennant to Stanley, 6 May 1890 and 9 May 1890, quoted in McLynn 2, pp. 328–329.

151 *"like a monkey in a cage"*: Stanley's journal, 9 Sept. 1890, quoted in McLynn 2, p. 334.

151 *"he considered sex for the beasts"*: McLynn 2, p. 334.

152 *"general mediocrity"*: McLynn 2, p. 376.

152 *"untrained, undisciplined, loutish and ill-bred"*: Stanley to Mackinnon, 25 Dec. 1890, quoted in McLynn 2, p. 337.

152 *William Sheppard*: The most thorough study of Sheppard is Phipps. See also Schall, Shaloff, Roth, Walter Williams, Sheppard, and numerous articles by and about Sheppard in the *Southern Workman*.

152 *"to the homes of their ancestors"*: Shaloff, p. 15.

153 *in the process*: *The Missionary*, vol. xxvi, no. 6, pp. 219–220.

153 *as much as he did other visitors*: Lapsley, p. 44.

154 *"furnishes a handle I hope to use on him"*: Lapsley to his "Aunt Elsie," in Lapsley, p. 83. A misprint in Lapsley erroneously dates this letter 1891.

154 *"black white man, as they call Sheppard"*: Lapsley to "Aunt Elsie," Lapsley, p. 83.

154 *"thankful to God for Sheppard"*: Lapsley to his mother, 22 Dec. 1890, Lapsley, p. 94.

154 *"I let him do most of the buying"*: Lapsley, p. 108.

154 *"the dense darkness . . . filled with superstition and sin"*: William Sheppard in the *Southern Workman* 44 (1915), pp. 166, 169, quoted in Schall, pp. 114–115.

154 *"I would be happy, and so I am"*: Sheppard to Dr. S. H. Henkel, 5 Jan. 1892, quoted in Shaloff, p. 29.

154 *"the names they gave us"*: Sheppard, "Yesterday, To-day and To-morrow in Africa," in *Southern Workman*, Aug. 1910, p. 445.

155 *"my people"*: Walter Williams, p. 138.

155 *"the country of my forefathers"*: letter from Sheppard to *The Missionary*, Sept. 1890, quoted in Walter Williams, p. 138.

155 *"and on the 26th of March died"*: S. C. Gordon to Sheppard, quoted in Shaloff, p. 30.

155　*"he alone speaks of all the Europeans"*: Ernest Stache to the Board of World Missions of the Presbyterian Church, 7 Aug. 1892, quoted in Shaloff, p. 32.

155　*strayed from his marriage*: Phipps, p. 118; Benedetto, pp. 30, 423–425.

156　*"got theirs from the Bakuba!"*: Sheppard in the *Southern Workman,* Dec. 1893, pp. 184–187, quoted in Walter Williams, p. 143.

156　*"came from a far-away land"*: Sheppard, "African Handicrafts and Superstitions," *Southern Workman,* Sept. 1921, pp. 403–404.

156　*the first foreigner*: Vansina 2, p. 3.

157　*a former king*: This is the way Sheppard usually told the story, as, for example, when he spoke at Hampton on 14 Nov. 1893 (reprinted in the *Southern Workman,* April 1895, "Into the Heart of Africa," p. 65): "You are Bo-pe Mekabé, who reigned before my father and who died." Although on several occasions (*Southern Workman,* April 1905, p. 218, and Sept. 1921, p. 403), he said he was taken for a dead son of the present king.

157　*footnote*: Shaloff, p. 45.

157　*information for later scholars*: Vansina 2 is the definitive scholarly treatment of the Kuba. To avoid confusion, however, in quotations from Sheppard and elsewhere, I have generally used Sheppard's spelling of African names.

157　*"the highest in equatorial Africa"*: Sheppard, p. 137.

157　Presbyterian Pioneers in Congo: A later edition is called *Pioneers in Congo.*

157　*"and the rope was drawn up"*: Sheppard, p. 119.

159　*to aides for action*: Liebrechts, pp. 37–38.

160　*eight times his annual salary*: Harms 3, p. 132.

160　*nearly thirty times what it had been six years earlier*: Harms 3, pp. 130–131.

160　*increased ninety-six times over*: Nelson, p. 82.

161　*"tapping some vines"*: *Official Organ,* Sept. 1907, p. 10.

161　*"must be compelled to do it"*: Louis Chaltin, journal, 16 July 1892, quoted in Northrup, p. 51.

161　*"the requisite amount of rubber had been collected"*: Pulteney to FO, 15 Sept. 1899, FO 10/731, no. 5, quoted in Cookey, pp. 50–51 fn.

162　*"unchain the prettiest ones and rape them"*: Bricusse, p. 81.

162　*"will usually decide to send representatives"*: Donny, vol. 1, pp. 139–140.

163　*three to four kilos of dried rubber per adult male per fortnight*: Harms 3, p. 132.

163　*against leopards*: Daniel Vangroenweghe "Le *Red Rubber* de l'Anversoise, 1899–1900, Documents inédits" in *Annales Aequatoria* 6 (1985), p. 57.

163　*and squeeze the rubber out*: Harms 1, p. 81.

163　*forty-seven thousand rubber gatherers*: Harms 1, p. 79.

163　*four hundred men with baskets*: Harms 3, p. 134.

164　*"use them as slaves — as I liked"*: Canisius, p. 267.

164　*some of the strongest resistance to Leopold's rule*: Marchal 4, pp. 106–107.

164　*"I counted them, 81 in all"*: Sheppard diary, 14 Sept. 1899, Sheppard Papers.

164　*"to show the State how many we have killed"*: Sheppard in *The Missionary,* Feb. 1900, p. 61.

165　*"cut off hands, noses and ears"*: Charles Lemaire, *Belgique et Congo* (Gand: A. Vandeweghe, 1908), p. 64, quoted in Vangroenweghe, p. 46.

165　*"cut off a hand from a living man"*: Ellsworth E. Faris, journal, 23 Aug. 1899, quoted in Morel 5, p. 248.

165 *"keeper of the hands"*: Vangroenweghe, p. 234.

165 *"Arches of the Severed Hands"*: Parliamentary debate of 28 Feb. 1905, quoted in Vangroenweghe, p. 288.

166 *"rape their own mothers and sisters"*: Boelaert, pp. 58–59.

166 *"allowed five hundred others to live"*: Bricusse, p. 56. (11 June 1894).

166 *shoot holes in Africans' ear lobes*: Guy Burrows, *The Curse of Central Africa* (London: R. A. Everett & Co., 1903), pp. xviii–xix.

166 *large doses of castor oil*: de Premorel, p. 64.

166 *he made them eat it*: Marchal 4, p. 85.

166 *rubbed with excrement*: Marchal 1, p. 391.

166 *contained chopped-up hands*: Bremen 1, pp. 119–120.

11. A SECRET SOCIETY OF MURDERERS

167 *"except money!"* Bauer, p. 169.

167 *"one day or another come on to the market"*: conversation of 30 Aug. 1892 in Auguste Roeykens, *Le baron Léon de Béthune au service de Léopold II* (Brussels: Académie Royale des Sciences d'Outre-Mer, 1964), p. 56, quoted in Stengers 2, p. 286.

168 *"moving Europe so deeply"*: Emerson, pp. 193–194.

168 *understated the state's real profits*: Marchal 1, p. 353.

168 *more than a hundred million francs*: Vangroenweghe, p. 87.

169 *Leopold's daily routine*: For eyewitness accounts, see Stinglhamber and Dresse, especially pp. 38–50, and Carton de Wiart, especially pp. 44 and 123–130.

169 *"I'll also take some cutlets"*: Stinglhamber and Dresse, p. 88.

170 *"thinking that Africans are black?"*: Emerson, p. 221.

170 *"by the hands of giants"*: C. Vauthier, "Le chemin de fer du Congo de Matadi à Léopoldville. Les environs de Matadi et le massif de Palabala," in *Bulletin de la Société Géographique d'Anvers* 13 [1887?], pp. 377–378, quoted in Kivilu, p. 324.

170 *twelve miles in length*: Cornet, p. 376.

170 *"what would it cost?"*: Leopold to Thys, 31 May 1888, quoted in Cornet, p. 236.

170 *east coast and then home*: Cornet, p. 236.

171 *each telegraph pole one European life*: Axelson, p. 204.

171 *close to 1800 a year*: Marchal 3, p. 143, p. 153.

171 *forced them back*: Cornet, p. 209.

172 *eleven million pounds*: Gann and Duignan 2, p. 123.

172 *footnote*: Emile Wangermée, journal, 31 Jan. 1899, quoted in Lagergren, p. 294 fn.

172 *"to save us from the rubber trouble?"*: Regions Beyond, April 1897, quoted in Slade 1, p. 251.

173 *"We want to die"*: Axelson, pp. 259–260.

173 *"(toujours désagréable)"*: J. De Witte, *Monseigneur Augouard* (Paris: Émile-Paul Frères, 1924), p. 71, quoted in Slade 1, p. 255.

173 *"time of service will soon be finished"*: Morel 3, pp. 43–44.

173 *reportedly paid a visit*: Fox Bourne to Morel, 21 Nov. 1903, quoted in Louis 1, p. 99 fn.

174 *"dared to kill an Englishman"*: Lionel Decle in the *Pall Mall Gazette*, 11 June 1896, quoted in Louis 3, p. 575.

174 *"faced the facts of the situation":* 21 Sept. 1896, quoted in Lagergren, p. 197 fn.

175 "En domptant l'Arabe inhumain": Louis Graide, "Les Belges au Congo," in F. Alexis-M. *Soldats et Missionnaires au Congo de 1891 à 1894* (Lille: Desclée, de Brouwer & Cie., 1896).

175 *the Congolese at Tervuren:* See Marchal 2, pp. 78–80, Gerard, p. 181, Debrunner, pp. 340–342, *Le Mouvement Géographique,* 27 June 1897 and 18 July 1897, and *La Belgique Coloniale,* 4 July 1897 and 5 Sept. 1897.

176 *footnote:* The poem by M.E.Buhler appeared in the *New York Times* of Sept. 19, 1906. This and other press clippings are reprinted in *Ota Benga: The Pygmy in the Zoo,* by Phillips Verner Bradford and Harvey Blume (New York: St. Martin's Press, 1992).

176 *"first sign of civilization":* La Belgique Coloniale, 4 July 1897, p. 314.

177 *"the great warrior":* La Belgique Coloniale, 4 July 1897.

177 *"an example of humanity!":* Bruxelles-Exposition, n.d., quoted in *La Belgique Coloniale,* 5 Sept. 1897, p. 423.

178 *"a magnificent field for [Belgian] enterprise":* "The Belgians in Africa," 22 Feb. 1894. (Name of periodical is missing in the Morel Papers microfilm.)

178 *"involuntary shudder of repulsion":* Morel 5, p. 27.

179 *"greatly troubled at the 'indiscretion'":* Morel 5, pp. 28–29.

180 *"to what usage was this armament put?":* Morel 5, p. 36.

180 *"into whose pocket did the unavowed surplus go?"* Morel 5, pp. 39–40.

180 *"to pay for what was coming out."* Morel 5, p. 36.

180 *were destined for Africans:* Gann and Duignan, p. 149.

181 *"with a King for a croniman":* Morel 5, pp. 41–42.

12. DAVID AND GOLIATH

186 *"set their African house in order":* Morel 5, pp. 47–48.

186 *"presence was unwelcome":* Morel 5, p. 48.

186 *"a vast destruction of human life":* Morel 5, p. 5.

186 *"no turning back":* Morel 5, p. 49.

187 *"temperamentally impossible":* Morel 5, p. 30.

188 *"these deeds must* of necessity *take place":* Morel 3, p. 8 fn.

189 *"'Ending date . . . Observations'":* West African Mail, 13 Jan. 1905, p. 996.

189 *"feeding of hostages":* Special Congo Supplement to the West African Mail, Jan. 1905.

189 *from a post in Brussels:* A. and J. Stengers, "Rapport sur une mission dans les archives anglaises," in *Bulletin de la Commission Royale d'Histoire,* vol. CXXIV (1959), pp. ciii–civ.

189 *the company's agents in the Congo:* Morel 1, p. 31.

190 *in the original French: Official Organ,* Sept.–Nov. 1908.

190 *"of the various districts":* Morel 3, p. 24.

190 *"in connection with this circular,* verbally": Morel 3, p. 25.

190 *"What can I do?":* Morel 3, p. 56.

191 *"at a distance of fully four feet":* Morel 3, p. 47.

191 *"tongues were hanging out":* Morel 3, p. 57.

191 *list of the dead: Official Organ,* Jan. 1906, p. 15.

192 *"the peoples of the Congo may ever have . . . the advantages of your enlightened rule":* Morel 5, p. 115.

192   *"choice and copious"*: Morel 5, p. 128.

192   *"I enjoyed myself most thoroughly"*: Morel 5, p. 129.

193   *"other service than rubber-gathering"*: Canisius, pp. 75–80.

193   *"that civilization was dawning"*: Canisius, p. 99.

193   *"literally shrieked with pain"*: Canisius, pp. 92–93.

193   *"to starvation and smallpox"*: Canisius, p. 113.

193   *"men, women and children"*: Canisius, p. 142.

193   *"to the monthly crop"*: Ibid.

194   *"governed with humanity"*: Resolution of 20 May 1903, quoted in Cline, p. 37.

194   *"the Armenians or the Bulgarians"*: Georges Lorand, in *La Réforme,* 14 Sept. 1896, quoted in Lagergren, p. 199 fn.

13. BREAKING INTO THE THIEVES' KITCHEN

195   *"to send reports soon"*: PRO HO 161, quoted in Reid, p. 42. See also PRO FO 629/10,11,12.

195   *Roger Casement:* Reid and Inglis are the best of the many biographers of Casement. Inglis gives much more space to his African experiences, but lacks source notes.

195   *"Knight errant he was"*: Stephen Gwynn, *Experiences of a Literary Man* (London: T. Butterworth, 1926), p. 258, quoted in Reid, p. 63.

196   *"would never make money"*: W. Holman Bentley, quoted in Vangroenweghe, p. 276.

196   *"specimen of the capable Englishman"*: Stanley's journal, 15 Apr. 1887, quoted in McLynn 2, p. 171.

196   *to the dog to eat:* McLynn 2, pp. 174–175.

196   *"nothing but devastation behind it"*: Camille Janssen, in *Bulletin de la Société Belge d'Études Coloniales* (1912), p. 717.

196   *"stimulate their prowess in the face of the enemy"*: Casement to Foreign Office, 14 Jan. 1904, PRO FO 10/807, quoted in Casement 5, p. i.

196   *"most intelligent and very sympathetic"*: Joseph Conrad, *Congo Diary and Other Uncollected Pieces,* ed. Zdzislaw Najder (New York: Doubleday, 1978), reprinted in Conrad, p. 159.

197   *"His greatest charm . . . He purrs at you"*: Ernest Hambloch, *British Consul: Memories of Thirty Years' Service in Europe and Brazil* (London: G. G. Harrap, 1938), p. 71, quoted in Reid, p. 5 fn.

197   *saw Casement once more:* the clear implication of Conrad's letter to Cunninghame Graham of 26 Dec. 1903 ("I have seen him start off into an unspeakable wilderness . . . A few months afterwards it so happened that I saw him come out again"), quoted in Reid, p. 14.

197   *"talked there till 3 in the morning"*: Conrad to John Quinn, 24 May 1916, quoted in Frederick Karl, *Joseph Conrad: The Three Lives* (New York: Farrar, Straus & Giroux, 1979), p. 286. Sometimes foggy about dates, Conrad, echoed by one or two of his more careless biographers, placed this meeting in 1896. But that could not have been; Casement was in Africa that year. Jane Ford (in "An African Encounter, A British Traitor and *Heart of Darkness,*" *Conradiana,* vol. 27, no. 2, 1995, p. 125) believes the encounter probably occurred in 1898 — which would have made it just before Conrad started writing *Heart of Darkness.*

197 *"things I never did know"*: Conrad to Cunninghame Graham, 26 Dec. 1903, quoted in Reid, p. 14.

197 *"in any shape or form"*: Casement to Fox-Bourne, 2 July 1894, quoted in Reid, p. 20.

198 *"in the character"*: Singleton-Gates, p. 91.

198 *"advise him of"*: Louis 1, p. 103.

198 *"listen to a drunken sailor's complaint"*: Inglis, p. 41.

199 *"big bulldog with large jaws"*: Marchal 3, p. 187.

199 *"And leave this love God made, not I"*: Inglis, pp. 382–383.

199 *diary entries on Macdonald*: Casement 2, pp. 121, 123, 125 (17, 19 and 30 Apr. 1903).

200 *"Agostinho . . . How much money?"*: Casement 2, pp. 111, 115, 119, 129 (13, 20 Mar.; 6 Apr.; 12 May 1903).

200 *brutal conditions in Leopold's Congo*: Marchal 3, pp. 189–190.

200 *Casement was under way*: Marchal 3, p. 192; Inglis, p. 69.

200 *"please God I'll scotch it"*: Casement to Poultney Bigelow, 13 Dec. 1903, quoted in Reid, p. 53.

201 *"in full flight over us"*: Casement 2, p. 145 (2 July 1903).

201 *"poor old Hairy Bill. . . . beats me hollow"*: Casement 2, pp. 147, 149 (8, 9, 10, 13 July 1903).

201 *"curse me at F.O."*: Casement 2, p. 137 (11 June 1903).

201 *"condemnation of civilized mankind"*: Casement to Fuchs, 15 Sept. 1903, quoted in Casement 5, p. v.

201 *"into the thieves' kitchen"*: Casement to Lansdowne, no. 34 Africa, 15–16 Sept. 1903, FO 10/805, quoted in Louis 1, p. 107.

201 *letters to the governor general*: Lagergren, pp. 323–329.

202 *diary entries, 5 June–9 Sept.*: Casement 2, pp. 135, 153, 155, 157, 159, 163, 165.

203 *"'you have killed men'"*: Casement 3, p. 114.

204 *"acts of refined cruelty"*: Phipps to Lansdowne, 27 Feb. 1904, quoted in Louis 1, pp. 112–113.

204 *"awkward position at court"*: Phipps to Barrington, 5 Feb. 1904, quoted in Louis 1, p. 111 fn.

204 *"I am N.N. . . . his name was A.B."*: Casement 3, p. 112.

204 *"as a simple surgical operation"*: Special Congo Supplement to the West African Mail, June 1904.

204 *"gang of stupidities"*: Casement 2, p. 183 (1 Dec. 1903).

204 *"an abject piffler"*: Casement 2, p. 185 (16 Dec. 1903).

204 *"incompetent noodles"*: Casement to Nightingale, 8 Sept. 1904, quoted in Reid, p. 65.

205 *"M. sleeping in study"*: Casement 2, p. 183 (10 Dec. 1903).

206 *"sought his bedroom above"*: Morel 5, pp. 160–162.

206 *"wife a good woman"*: Casement 2, p. 189 (5 Jan. 1904).

206 *"drew up a rough plan of campaign"*: Morel 5, pp. 163–164.

206 *"in that great heart of hers?"*: Morel 5, pp. 164–165.

206 *"he wrote out a cheque for £100"*: Morel 5, p. 165.

207 *"one overwhelming Nay!"*: Inglis, p. 92.

207 *"as near to being a saint as a man can be"*: Morel to Holt, 12 July 1910, quoted in Porter, p. 267.

207 *"to end that den of devils"*: Casement to Morel, 4 July 1906, quoted in Louis 1, p. 119.

14. TO FLOOD HIS DEEDS WITH DAY

209 *"he will do nothing"*: Morel to Guthrie, 25 Feb. 1910, quoted in Morel 5, p. 195 fn.

209 *"that I have been able to do it all"*: Morel to Brabner, 14 Sept. 1908, quoted in Morel 5, p. 211.

210 *"the Morel of Congo reform"*: Holt to Morel, quoted in Adams, p. 179.

210 *"'God-speed' on his journey"*: *West African Mail*, 23 Sept. 1904, p. 601.

210 *"And they have the right to live"*: Morel to Mark Twain, quoted in Hawkins 1, p. 167.

210 *the hands of one's dead enemies:* Vansina 2, pp. 144, 343; Vellut, p. 701.

211 *"in the hollow of my hand"*: Morel to Holt, 1910, quoted in Morel 5, p. 217.

212 *"a burden upon the State"*: Furley, pp. 141–142.

212 *"chemistry of evangelical imperialism"*: James Morris, *Heaven's Command: An Imperial Progress* (New York: Harcourt Brace Jovanovich, 1973), p. 39.

213 *"accepted his leadership"*: Taylor, p. 133.

214 *"the reptile Congophile Press of Brussels and Antwerp"*: Morel 1, p. 261.

214 *"terrible wrongs upon the native races"*: Morel 1, p. x.

214 *"inland slave-trade on the Congo"*: Morel 1, p. xvii.

214 *"good government of the Congo territories"*: Cookey, p. 149.

215 *"and flood his deeds with day"*: William Watson, "Leopold of Belgium," in the Congo Reform Association's slide show. The poem also appeared in the *West African Mail,* 21 Sept. 1906, p. 608, and, in a slightly different version identified as being from Watson's *New Poems* (Lane), in the *African Mail,* 26 Nov. 1909, p. 80.

215 *"the downfall"*: note to himself, 14 June 1907, quoted by Cline, p. 58.

215 *4,194 clippings:* The sum of various subtotals given in *Inventaire des microfilms des Papiers Morel, series A, B, E, F, G, H, I, se rapportant à l'histoire du Congo et conservés à la British Library of Political and Economic Science, London School of Economics* (Brussels: Fonds National de la Recherche Scientifique, 1961).

215 *Samba: A Story of the Rubber Slaves of the Congo,* by Herbert Strang (London: Hodder and Stoughton, 1906), p. vi.

216 *"literature, information, etc"*: Morel to Cadbury, Oct. 1906, quoted in Cline, p. 54.

216 *for the benefit of the movement: West African Mail,* 24 Aug. 1906, p. 520.

217 *"more than 5 years"*: John Harris, unpublished autobiographical ms., quoted in Louis 6, p. 833.

218 *"with the greatest discretion"*: Wahis to Charles Smets, 26 Jan. 1906, De Ryck Collection.

218 *"send me of inaccuracies"*: Weber to Naur, 16 Aug. 1906, De Ryck Collection.

218 *Hezekiah Andrew Shanu:* Unless otherwise noted, all information on Shanu comes from Marchal 3, pp. 142, 167–168, 191, 231, 296–302, 330–332, plus a few details from Lemaire 1, pp. 42–44, and *Biographie Coloniale Belge,* vol. 4, cols. 838–839.

218 *"with the greatest correctness"*: *Le Mouvement Géographique,* 30 Sept. 1894, p. 85.

218 *"of the negro race"*: *La Chronique Coloniale et Financière,* 11 Dec. 1904, p. 1.

219 *"loyalty to the State"*: Memorandum by Albrecht Gohr, director of justice, 27 July 1900, quoted in Marchal 3, p. 297.

219 *"from time to time"*: Morel to Shanu, 4 Sept. 1903, quoted in Morel 5, p. 157.

220 *"means of persuasion than terror"*: Marchal 3, p. 231.

220 *"ever received by the Congo State"*: Morel 1, p. 135.

220 *the Caudron case*: Morel 1, pp. 135–153.

220 *"unblemished reputation and of great courage"*: Morel 5, p. 156.

221 *"to withhold his name"*: De Vaughan, p. 48.

221 *"to the mute personage"*: De Vaughan, p. 51.

222 *footnote*: Stinglhamber and Dresse, p. 306.

223 *left an hour later*: De Vaughan, p. 123.

223 *"telling him that they had colds!"*: De Vaughan, p. 67.

224 *"be soiled with blood or mud"*: Leopold to Liebrechts, 31 Jan. 1899, quoted in Marchal 2, p. 96.

224 *"the one thing I need in the Congo!"*: Stinglhamber and Dresse, p. 136.

224 *not dare take precedence over His Majesty*: Ascherson, p. 142.

15. A RECKONING

226 *without being challenged by the Congo state*: Marchal 1, p. 339.

226 *even higher totals for the number of hands*: Marchal 1, p. 339.

226 *hands cut off living people*: Lagergren, p. 297.

227 *"with the butt of their guns"*: this statement was quoted in Casement's report, repeated by Morel, and is quoted in Lagergren, p. 288, and Marchal 3, pp. 197–198.

227 *40,355 rounds of ammunition*: West African Mail, 17 Feb. 1905, p. 111.

227 *"'they were thrown into the river'"*: Speech by Sjöblom in London, 12 May 1897, quoted in Morel 3, p. 43.

227 *rubber regime in 1894–1895*: Lagergren, p. 121.

227 *simply open fire*: Vangroenweghe, p. 59.

228 *"13 women and children taken prisoner"*: Lemaire 2, pp. 18, 20, 23, 30, 36, 48.

228 *"We burned the village"*: Leclercq, pp. 244–445.

228 *footnote*: Marchal 1, p. 362.

229 *"exterminate them to the last man"*: West African Mail, 16 Mar. 1906, p. 1219.

229 *"Exterminate all the brutes!"*: Conrad, p. 51.

229 *"better place for our noon rest"*: P. Möller, Tre Ar i Kongo (Stockholm: P. A. Norstedt, 1887), pp. 234–235, quoted in Kivilu, p. 338.

229 *French territory by 1900*: Morel 3, p. 63.

229 *"roots, and ants and other insects"*: Canisius, p. 170.

229 *"sleeping in the forests without shelter"*: William Morrison, letter from Luebo, 15 Oct. 1899, in The Missionary, Feb. 1900, p. 67.

230 *"depopulated and devastated. . . . what tales of horror they told!"*: From Cape to Cairo: the First Traverse of Africa from South to North (London: Hurst and Blackett, 1900), quoted in Morel 3, p. 58.

230 *five pigs or fifty chickens*: Nelson, p. 100.

230 *three to ten a day*: Harms 3, p. 134.

231 *too heavy to fly*: McLynn 3, p. 245.

231 *in 1901 alone*: McLynn 3, p. 238.

231 *blame sleeping sickness*: For a modern example of this, see Jean Stengers in Morel 5, p. 255.

231 *"above all there's no food"*: Marchal 4, p. 49.

232 *noticed this pattern*: Vangroenweghe, p. 233.

232 *"hide from the soldiers":* Casement 3, p. 140.
232 *show the same pattern:* Vangroenweghe, pp. 233, 237.
233 *"been reduced by half":* L. Guebels, *Relation complète des travaux de la Commission Permanente pour la Protection des Indigènes* (Elisabethville: 1954), pp. 196–197.
233 *"and much more":* interview, Sept. 1995.
233 *"by at least a half":* Jan Vansina, introduction to Vangroenweghe, p. 10.
233 *reckoned at ten million: La Question sociale au Congo: Rapport au comité du congrès colonial national* (Brussels: Goemaere, 1924), p. 7.
233 *"confronted with a kind of desert": La Question sociale au Congo: Rapport au comité du congrès colonial national* (Brussels: Goemaere, 1924), p. 101.
234 *killed in the nearest village:* Vangroenweghe, p. 60.
234 *cooked to death:* Marchal 4, p. 26.
234 *then set on fire:* Vangroenweghe, p. 115.
234 *"are we doing here?":* Michael Herr, *Dispatches* (New York: Alfred A. Knopf, 1977), p. 29.

16. "JOURNALISTS WON'T GIVE YOU RECEIPTS"

235 *"for his country and for Africa":* McLynn 2, p. 405.
236 *"So that is time! Strange!":* Stanley 5, p. 515.
236 *wrote one witness:* Daniel Bersot in the foreword to *Sous la Chicotte* (Geneva: A. Jullien, 1909).
236 *on the arm:* Liane Ranieri, *Les Relations entre l'État Indépendant du Congo et l'Italie* (Brussels: Académie Royale des Sciences d'Outre-Mer, 1959), p. 195.
237 *those Casement had found in the Congo:* Marchal 4, p. 12.
237 *"Opium in British India":* in *La Vérité sur le Congo,* Jan. 1905, p. 8.
237 *"It is astounding . . . humanely-governed":* Mountmorres, pp. 99–100, 159.
237 *"on any one day":* Mountmorres, pp. 105–106.
238 *"because she was coming":* John Weeks to Morel, 7 Nov. 1904, in the *West African Mail,* 10 Mar. 1905, p. 1186.
238 *worst cases of disease he could find:* Marchal 3, p. 304.
238 *"than I have ever seen in the Congo": Times,* 3 Feb. 1905, quoted in Bontinck, p. 456.
238 *for which Leopold paid the bill:* Marchal 3, p. 316.
238 *"extraordinarily impudent":* Morel to Fox, 18 Oct. 1905, quoted in Cookey, p. 143.
238 *"in memory of their visit to Laeken":* Stinglhamber and Dresse, pp. 334–335.
239 *operated in many countries:* Willequet, pp. 109–113.
239 *footnote:* Demetrius C. Boulger, *The Congo State is* NOT *a Slave State: A Reply to Mr. E. D. Morel's Pamphlet Entitled "The Congo Slave State"* (London: Sampson Low, Marston, 1903), p. 3.
239 *"cheerful and satisfied":* interview with Harrison in the *Journal of Commerce,* 23 June 1904.
239 *at least one legislator:* Marchal 4, pp. 12–21.
239 *launched an investigation instead: Official Organ,* #1, 1909, p. 64.
240 *"Satan and Mammon in one person":* Willequet, letter reproduced following p. 36.
240 *"the unscrupulous businessman who lives in the palace in Brussels": National-Zeitung,* 22 May 1903, quoted in Wllequet, p. 150.
240 *"the British rubber merchants": National-Zeitung,* 4 Mar. 1905, quoted in Willequet, pp. 150–151.

240 *"old wives' tales . . . hateful peddlar's stories"*: National-Zeitung, 30 May 1905, quoted in Willequet, p. 152.

240 *"the following commentary"*: Münchener Allgemeine Zeitung, 1 Mar. 1906, quoted in Willequet, pp. 159 160.

241 *"due mainly to my activity"*: Von Steub to Davignon, 21 May 1909, quoted in Willequet, p. 114 fn.

241 *"have my expenses covered"*: Von Steub to Davignon, 21 May 1909, quoted in Willequet, p. 128.

241 *"to organs of the press"*: Von Steub to Davignon, 14 Sept. 1909, quoted in Willequet, p. 130.

241 *"'don't ask for any'"*: Von Steub to Denyn, 8 Oct. 1909, quoted in Willequet, p. 130.

241 *Mark Twain and Congo reform:* see Hawkins 1.

241 *"no small enemy to overcome"*: Kowalsky to Leopold, undated, in New York American, 11 Dec. 1906.

241 *Booker T. Washington and Congo reform:* Harlan 1, pp. 270–271; Harlan 2, pp. 75–77.

242 *"talking on the subject"*: Booker T. Washington in "Tributes to Mark Twain," *North American Review* 191, no. 655 (June 1910), p. 829, quoted in Shelley Fisher Fishkin, *Was Huck Black?: Mark Twain and African-American Voices* (New York: Oxford University Press, 1993), p. 106.

242 *"needs an organization like U.S. Steel"*: Twain to Morel, c. 12 Jan. 1906, reprinted in Wuliger, p. 236.

242 *royalties that the author donated:* Maxwell Geismar, *Mark Twain: An American Prophet* (Boston: Houghton Mifflin, 1970), p. 222.

242 *"these leaks keep occurring"*: Twain, p. 1.

242 *"that I couldn't bribe"*: Twain, p. 66.

242 *"meddlesome missionary spying"*: Twain, p. 36.

242 *he told Morel:* Morgan to Morel, 6 Oct. 1904, quoted in Baylen, p. 129.

242 *in forty-nine cities: Congo News Letter,* April 1906 and April 1907.

242 *would accept only one dollar: Official Organ,* April 1906, p. 10.

243 *"will take some action"*: Harris to Morel, 14 Feb. 1906, quoted in Cookey, p. 174.

243 *"demanding action"*: Philip C. Jessup, *Elihu Root, 1905–1937,* vol. 2 (New York: Dodd, Mead, 1938), pp. 61–62, quoted in Shaloff, p. 90.

243 *"everybody & about everybody"*: Lodge to Roosevelt, 6 July 1905, quoted in Sternstein, p. 192.

243 *"seen lots of presidents"*: *The Autobiography of Lincoln Steffens* (New York: Harcourt Brace Jovanovich), 1931, p. 506, quoted in Sternstein, p. 193.

244 *"the English agitators and the Belgian Socialists futile"*: Wack to Leopold, n.d., quoted in the *New York American,* 13 Dec. 1906.

244 *footnote:* Cardinal Gotti to Gibbons, 24 Nov. 1904, quoted in Slade 1, p. 310n.

244 *"hearsay evidence of natives"*: Gibbons to Morel, 21 Oct. 1904, quoted in Morel 5, p. 183.

245 *footnote:* Starr, p. 91.

245 *"an impartial publicist"*: New York American, 12 Dec. 1906.

245 *"in a team of acrobats"*: San Francisco Call, 15 Jan. 1911.

246 *"a box at a theater"*: San Francisco Examiner, 29 Nov. 1914.

246 *"draws up a firm one"*: San Francisco Call, 15 Jan. 1911.

246 *"just when you're going to kill him!"*: San Francisco Bulletin, 18 Nov. 1914.

247 *"too large a subject"*: Mayor E. E. Schmits, *Speeches Made,* p. 10.

247 *"so choice a morsel"*: A. Reuf, *Speeches Made*, p. 26.

247 *"humanity and civilization"*: *Speeches Made*, p. 40.

247 *"mission in Africa or China?"*: de Cuvelier to Moncheur, 4 Feb. 1905, quoted in Marchal 4, p. 270.

247 *"wouldn't come back"*: Nerincx to de Cuvelier, 11 Feb. 1905, quoted in Marchal 4, p. 270.

247 *"a scandal in the press"*: Moncheur to de Cuvelier, 19 Feb. 1905, quoted in Marchal 4, p. 271.

248 *"taking the Belgian Minister's advice"*: *New York American*, 10 Dec. 1906.

248 *"a characterless . . . lamented father"*: Kowalsky to Leopold, n.d., reprinted in *New York American*, 11 Dec. 1906.

248 *a hefty 125,000 francs*: Marchal 4, p. 272.

249 INFAMOUS CRUELTIES . . . WOMEN AND CHILDREN: *New York American*, 10 Dec. 1906.

249 *"crimes of Congo"*: *New York American*, 11 Dec. 1906.

249 *"the end of the next session"*: *New York American*, 10 Dec. 1906.

249 *"the President's personal friend . . . Your Majesty's interest instead"*: Kowalsky to Leopold, n.d., in *New York American*, 11 Dec. 1906.

249 *"did I breathe safely"*: Kowalsky to Leopold, n.d., in *New York American*, 11 Dec. 1906.

250 *Commission of Inquiry*: see Congo Reform Association; Vangroenweghe; Marchal 4, pp. 111–122; Cookey, pp. 132–151.

251 *broken down and wept*: Conan Doyle, p. 75; Morel in *Penny Pictorial*, Oct. 1907, article 4 in series.

251 *"complete and authentic résumé of the report"*: *Daily Chronicle*, 7 Nov. 1905.

252 *"We have ourselves . . . should be utilized"*: *Daily Chronicle*, 7 Nov. 1905.

252 *West African Missionary Association*: *Daily Chronicle*, 7, 11, 14, and 15 Nov. 1905; *Daily News*, 15 Nov. 1905.

17. NO MAN IS A STRANGER

253 *"till we fainted"*: *Regions Beyond*, Jan.–Feb. 1906, p. 46; also *Official Organ*, Jan. 1906, p. 5.

254 *"gave one cry and was dead"*: *Procès-Verbaux*, 2 Nov. 1904.

254 *"had their hands cut off"*: *Procès-Verbaux*, 21 Nov. 1904.

254 *"but he had been healthy"*: *Procès-Verbaux*, 5 Jan. 1905.

255 *"throw you in the river"*: *Procès-Verbaux*, 2 Jan. 1905.

255 *"if it had secret staircases"*: De Vaughan, pp. 99–100.

256 *"with attractive uniform façades"*: Leopold to Goffinet, 23 Jan. 1906, quoted in Ranieri, p. 247.

256 *"and the Heysel road"*: Carton de Wiart, p. 177.

256 *"led up the garden path"*: Ascherson, p. 219.

256 *"cost a province"*: Stinglhamber and Dresse, p. 59.

257 *"toasts to his health"*: Conrad and Hueffer, p. 120.

257 *"Give Him his cane!"*: Bauer, p. 163, de Lichtervelde, p. 323.

257 *"international, not national"*: Williams 3, p. 279.

257 *said much like this again*: Even as late as 1919, when the Second Pan-African Congress of black American, Caribbean, and African leaders met in Paris under the leadership of W.E.B. Du Bois, it did not advocate full independence for African colo-

nies. *Pan-Africanism,* eds. Robert Chrisman and Nathan Hare (New York: Bobbs-Merrill, 1974), p. 302.

257 *turning point:* Stengers 7, p. 176.

258 *press for Belgian annexation:* Cookey, p. 210.

258 *"to ask for its accounts":* Baron Léon Van der Elst, "Souvenirs sur Léopold II," in *Revue Générale,* 1923, quoted in Emerson, p. 259.

258 *to take away his Congo:* Carton de Wiart, p. 188.

259 *"any salary as Congo executive":* interview with Publishers' Press, in the *New York American,* 11 Dec. 1906.

259 *"made for the Congo":* Marchal 4, p. 349.

259 *"almost every American reformer, black or white":* Normandy, p. 300.

259 *William Morrison:* see Marchal 3, pp. 75–91; Shaloff, pp. 84–94; and Vinson. Dozens of Morrison's letters are reprinted in Benedetto.

260 *left the country:* Slade 1, p. 317.

260 *home leaves:* Phipps, pp. 95–96.

261 *some 180 of them were killed:* Marchal 4, p. 225.

261 *"concerning their soul's salvation":* from "From the Bakuba Country," by W. H. Sheppard, *The Kassai Herald,* 1 Jan. 1908, pp. 12–13. Sheppard Papers.

262 *"asked any questions Sheppard suggested":* Kocher to the State Prosecutor, 31 July 1908, quoted in Martens, p. 398.

262 *eighty thousand francs in damages:* American Consul General Handley to the Assistant Secretary of State, 21 Sept. 1909. Sheppard Papers.

262 *"pay the fine":* Morrison to Chester, 9 Aug. 1909, reprinted in Benedetto, p. 383.

262 *"in New York harbour":* Conan Doyle, p. iv.

262 *"no little concern":* State Dept. to H. L. Wilson, 2 July 1909, quoted in Shaloff, p. 119.

263 *"young Belgian lawyer":* Morel to Vandervelde, July 1909, quoted in Slade 1, p. 371 fn.

263 *"in a court of justice":* Vinson, p. 99.

263 *prayed for a favorable verdict:* Vandervelde, pp. 90–91.

264 *"amongst whom he lives is humanitarian":* *Official Organ,* No. 5, Jan. 1910, p. 465.

264 *"for over two hours":* Morrison to Conan Doyle, n.d., reprinted in *Official Organ,* no. 5, Jan. 1910.

264 *"were so affected . . . made in Congo":* William Sheppard, "The Days Preceding the Trial," in the *Christian Observer,* 10 Nov. 1909.

264 *"all the power of Leopold":* Phipps, p. 106.

265 *"could not refer to the Compagnie du Kasai":* Shaloff, p. 125.

265 *"a time for thanksgiving":* Phipps, p. 106.

266 *"in Belgium after my death":* De Vaughan, p. 201.

267 *"Cutting his hands off, down in Hell":* Vachel Lindsay, "The Congo," in *The Congo and Other Poems* (New York: Macmillan, 1916).

267 *"remained in the house for a week":* Casement in 1913 [?], Singleton-Gates and Girodias, p. 317.

267 *"lovely, glorious language":* Casement to Gertrude Bannister, March 1904, quoted in Inglis, p. 113.

267 *"the incorrigible Irishman":* Casement to Alice Green, Spring 1907, quoted in Inglis, p. 152.

268 *"wrongdoing at work on the Congo":* Casement to Cadbury, 7 July 1905, quoted in Porter, p. 267.

268 *"people once hunted themselves"*: Casement to Alice Green, quoted in Inglis, p. 125.

268 *"not British Consulate!!"*: Casement to Alice Green, 21 Sept. 1906, quoted in Reid, p. 78.

268 *"nothing else counts"*: Casement to Parry, 9 Oct. 1906, quoted in Reid, pp. 80–81.

268 *"still going strong on Ireland"*: interview with Sir Gerald Campbell in MacColl, p. 73 fn.

269 *"humanitarian only a century after"*: quoted in Adams, p. 203.

269 *"with your exact wishes"*: Morel to Casement, 12 June 1913, quoted in Reid, p. 173.

269 *"a fearless soul as his is needed"*: Casement to Cadbury, 4 July 1910, quoted in Reid, p. 97.

270 *"white Indians . . . Irish Putumayo"*: from a comment by Casement written on a letter from Charles Roberts, 6 June 1913, quoted in Reid, p. 172.

270 *"pre-Inca precept"*: Casement, "The Putumayo Indians" in the *Contemporary Review*, September 1912, quoted in Inglis, p. 206.

270 *"any right to be accepting honours"*: Casement to Alice Green, 21 June 1911, quoted in Reid, p. 137.

270 *"boy of 19, broad face"*: Casement 4, p. 289 (20 Nov. 1910).

270 *"blushed to roots of hair with joy"*: Casement 4, p. 221 (9 Aug. 1910).

270 *"laughed . . . $10."*: Casement's diary for 16 Aug. 1911, quoted in Inglis, p. 194.

271 *"in the history of the world"*: Conan Doyle to the *Times*, 18 Aug. 1909, reprinted in Conan Doyle 2, p. 138.

271 *"partial victory"*: Morel to Weeks, 9 Nov. 1908, quoted in Cline, p. 64.

272 *"no true reform whatever"*: Conan Doyle to the *Daily Express*, 13 Apr. 1910, reprinted in Conan Doyle 2, p. 152.

272 *"not got very much staying-power"*: Morel to Claparède, 23 Mar. 1910, quoted in Morel 5, p. 202.

272 *"the produce which it yields"*: Morel in the *Morning Post*, 4 June 1907, quoted in Louis 4, p. 280.

272 *"produce of the soil belongs to the Natives"*: Grey to Cromer, 13 Mar. 1908, quoted in Morel 5, p. 199 fn.

273 *"but of all Negro Africa"*: *African Mail*, 27 Aug. 1909, p. 463.

273 *"immense improvement"*: *Official Organ*, no. 10, August 1912, p. 799.

273 *"nearly accomplished"*: Casement to Morel, 13 June 1912, quoted in Louis 1, p. 119.

273 *"replaced an irresponsible despotism"*: Morel's speech to the executive committee of the C.R.A., 25 Apr. 1913, in *Official Organ*, July 1913, pp. 986–987.

274 *"A man of great heart . . . Roger Casement"*: Supplement to the *African Mail*, 27 June 1913, p. 12.

274 *"will not pass away"*: Supplement to the *African Mail*, 27 June 1913, p. 6.

18. VICTORY?

275 *"to disinherit his daughters"*: Robert E. Park, "A King in Business: Leopold II of Belgium, Autocrat of the Congo and International Broker," reprinted in Stanford M. Lyman, *Militarism, Imperialism, and Racial Accomodation: An Analysis and Interpretation of the Early Writings of Robert E. Park* (Fayetteville: University of Arkansas Press, 1992), p. 214.

276 *huge health resort*: Stinglhamber and Dresse, p. 131.

276 *twenty-five million francs' worth of Leopold's Congo bonds:* Marchal 4, p. 432.

276 *some of his Congo state bonds:* Stengers 1, pp. 172, 275.

276 *to the very end:* Hyde, pp. 321–324; Ridley, p. 290; Gene Smith, p. 290; Foussemagne, p. 378. However, most reports of the last six decades of Carlota's life are second or third hand, because the Belgian royal family kept her secluded from public view.

277 *out of which hidden pockets:* Stengers 1 is the most exhaustive study of Leopold's finances, but even it finds some questions unanswerable.

277 *$1.1 billion in today's dollars:* A condensed version of Marchal's calculations (in a letter to the author, answering a question on this point, 30 July 1997) are as follows:

- Loans to the Congo state not invested in the Congo but spent by Leopold in Europe: 110 million francs (Jean Stengers "La dette publique de l'État Indépendant du Congo (1879–1908)," in *La dette publique aux XVIIIe et XIXe siècles: son développement sur le plan local, régional et national* (Brussels: Crédit Communal de Belgique, 1980), p. 309).

- Estimated off-the-books rubber profits for the peak boom years, 1898–1908, mainly from rubber gathered on state land, and also including profits from the state's share of the major concession companies (A.B.I.R., the Compagnie du Kasai, and the Société Anversoise du Commerce au Congo): 110 million francs.

  Not included in the calculations are profits from earlier rubber harvests or from the state share in more than half a dozen smaller companies.

277 *"or perhaps a single native":* Alexandre Delcommune, *L'Avenir du Congo Belge Menacé* (1919), quoted in Michel Massoz, *Le Congo de Léopold II (1878–1908),* (Liège: Soledi, 1989), p. 576.

278 *died of disease:* Northrup, p. 109.

278 *"carrying the foodstuffs!":* quoted in Northrup, p. 107.

279 *in the first half of 1920 alone:* Northrup, p. 161.

279 *"paid ten francs for each recruit":* Northrup, p. 99.

279 *Katanga mines, Matadi-Leopoldville railroad:* Jules Marchal, work in progress.

279 *80 percent of the uranium:* Cornevin 2, pp. 286–288.

279 *search for wild vines once again:* Anstey 2, pp. 144–152.

280 *"admiration in stockbroking circles":* Suret-Canale, p. 21.

280 *just as brutal:* Suret-Canale, pp. 20–28; West, pp. 165–181; Coquéry-Vidrovitch 1, pp. 171–197.

280 *at roughly 50 percent:* Vansina 3, p. 239.

280 *fierce rebellions against the rubber regime:* Vansina 3, p. 242.

280 *nearly four hundred in a busy month:* Coquéry-Vidrovitch 1, p. 181.

281 *"which are the glory of France":* Étienne Clémentel, quoted in Pakenham, p. 639.

281 *the lives of an estimated twenty thousand forced laborers:* Coquéry-Vidrovitch 1, p. 195.

281 *discovered to be a major shareholder:* Stengers 1, pp. 278–279, Marchal 3, p. 45.

282 *extermination order* (Vernichtungsbefehl): Swan, p. 51; Pakenham, p. 611.

282 *"never heard of this before":* Holt to Morel, 5 Oct. 1909, quoted in Louis 5, p. 34.

283 *"contributed to the making of Kurtz":* Conrad, p. 50.

283 *never made public:* Benedetto, pp. 30, 423–425.

283 *and Sheppard obliged:* Roth, p. 283.

283 *"and always came to the back door"*: Phipps, preface.

284 *"and left himself thus in need"*: Darrell Figgis, *Recollections of the Irish War* (New York: Doubleday, Doran & Co., 1927) p. 11, quoted in Reid, p. 190.

284 *"is that of the rifle"*: Casement to Morten, 1 May 1914, quoted in Sawyer, p. 114.

284 *"Irish nationality can spring to life"*: Roger Casement in the *Irish Independent*, 5 Oct. 1914, quoted in Singleton-Gates and Girodias, pp. 357–358.

285 *"drive the allies into the sea"*: Casement on 28 Sept. 1915, quoted in Reid, p. 309.

285 *"Only my shroud"*: Basil Thompson [Casement's Scotland Yard interrogator], *Queer People* (London: Hodder and Stoughton, 1922), p. 87.

285 *"I was back in Ireland again"*: Casement to his sister Nina, 15 July 1916, quoted in Reid, p. 351.

285 *"left Wicklow in Willie's yacht"*: Inglis, p. 313.

286 *"know of the barbarous cruelties"*: Inglis, p. 364.

286 *"the natural lot of men"*: reprinted in Singleton-Gates and Girodias, p. 498.

286 *"how a subject nation should feel"*: Inglis, p. 346.

287 *"not a trace of anxiety or fear in his features"*: A. Fenner Brockway, quoted in Inglis, p. 368.

287 *"towered straight over all of us"*: Father Thomas Carey, writing on 5 Aug. 1916, quoted in Reid, p. 448.

287 *"lot to execute"*: Ellis [the executioner] in *The Catholic Bulletin*, Aug. 1928, quoted in Reid, p. 448.

287 *"the best thing was the Congo"*: Casement to Morten, 28 July 1916, quoted in Reid, pp. 436.

288 *"anyone would speak to me now"*: Adams, p. 212.

288 *"at his heart"*: Swanwick, p. 187.

288 *and the Morel family's home*: Swartz, p. 105; Swanwick p. 98.

288 *"a change of outlook"*: Taylor, p. 120.

288 *"get hold of the arch-conspirator"*: *Daily Sketch*, 1 Dec. 1915, quoted in Cline, p. 103, and Swartz, p. 111.

288 HIS PRO-GERMAN UNION?: *Daily Express*, 4 Apr. 1915, quoted in Cline, p. 110.

288 *"Germany's agent in this country"*: *Evening Standard*, 7 July 1917, quoted in Adams, p. 210.

288 *"there was no question about it"*: Alice Green to Morel, quoted in McColl, pp. 273–274.

289 *"his courage never failed"*: *The Autobiography of Bertrand Russell*, vol. 2 (Boston: Little, Brown, 1968), pp. 36–37.

289 *"proclaiming political truth"*: Bertrand Russell, *Freedom versus Organization, 1814–1914* (New York, 1962), p. 402, quoted in Swartz, p. 50.

289 *"safely lodged in gaol"*: Minute by M. N. Kearney, 10 Oct. 1916, FO 371/2828/202398, PRO, quoted by Cline, p. 111.

289 *"my mission to the United States"*: *The Persecution of E. D. Morel: The Story of his Trial and Imprisonment*. With an introduction by Sir D. M. Stevenson and a prefatory note by Thomas Johnston (Glasgow: Reformers' Bookstall, 1918), p. 11.

290 *"to each other daily when absent"*: Adams, p. 180.

290 *"especially in cold weather"*: Morel 4, p. 60.

290 *"proof against it"*: Morel 4, p. 62.

290 *"lived to play both parts"*: Morel 4, p. 66.

291 *"the result of insufficient food":* Russell to Murray, 27 Mar. 1918, in *The Autobiography of Bertrand Russell,* vol. 2 (Boston: Little, Brown, 1968), p. 108.

291 *as he left for London:* "E. D. Morel" by F. Seymour Cocks, in *Foreign Affairs: A Journal of International Understanding,* vol. VI no. 6, Dec. 1924, p. 118.

291 *"as the years pass":* Morel Papers F 1, 7, quoted in Marchal 3, p. 10.

19. THE GREAT FORGETTING

294 *"the sepulchral city":* Conrad, p. 27.

294 *"no right to know what I did there":* Stinglhamber and Dresse, pp. 52–53.

294 *"for considerations of a higher order":* Strauch to Wauters, 1911, quoted in Stanley 6, p. xi.

295 *"in the years that have passed since that night":* De Premorel, p. 97.

296 *footnote:* Émile Verhaeren. "La Belgique sanglante," quoted in Read, p. 35.

296 *to be false:* Read, pp. 78–96.

296 *Jules Marchal:* interviewed September 1995.

298 *idealistic young colonial officers:* such as Lefranc (pp. 120–121) or Gréban de Saint-Germain (p. 231).

299 *"exploited peoples of this part of Africa":* État Major de la Force Publique, *L'Afrique et le Congo jusqu'à la création de l'État Indépendant du Congo* (Leopoldville: 1 June 1959), pp. 10–11, quoted in Stengers 5, p. 165.

299 *"to amount to nothing":* État Major de la Force Publique, *L'Etat Indépendant du Congo (1885–1908)* (Leopoldville: 1 Oct. 1959), p. 145, quoted in Stengers 5, p. 165.

300 *dedicated anthropologists:* The pioneering work of two Belgian priests, Fathers Edmond Boelaert and Gustave Hulstaert, deserves special mention. See also Vangroenweghe and Anstey 3.

300 *"the overwhelming":* Nelson, p. 104.

300 *an idiom meaning "to tyrannize":* Vangroenweghe, p. 234.

300 *"to commit this to official memory":* Vansina 2, p. 230.

300 *a curious legend:* Fabian, pp. 27–28, 55, 60, 261.

301 *only three were filled by Africans:* Stengers 7, p. 271.

301 *"worthy of our confidence":* Bremen 2, p. 145.

302 *authorized his assassination:* Kelly, pp. 57–60. Kelly's careful account is based on both interviews and documents, particularly the landmark report of November 20, 1975, from the U.S. Senate investigation headed by Senator Frank Church: *Alleged Assassination Plots Involving Foreign Leaders: An Interim Report of the Select Committee to Study Governmental Operations With Respect to Intelligence Activities.*

302 *"the problem dealt with":* John Ranelagh, *The Agency: The Rise and Decline of the CIA* (New York: Simon & Schuster, 1986), p. 342, quoted in Kelly, p. 59.

302 *find a place to dispose of it:* John Stockwell, *In Search of Enemies* (New York: W. W. Norton, 1978), p. 105, cited by Kelly, p. 71.

302 *was being planned:* Young, p. 325; Kelly, pp. 52, 170.

303 *several attempts to overthrow him:* Kelly, p. 178.

303 *"voice of good sense and good will":* Winternitz, p. 270.

303 *"during my presidency":* George Bush, on 29 June 1989, quoted in Kelly, p. 1.

303 *estimated at $4 billion: The Guardian,* 13 May 1997.

304 *sheep to his ranch at Gbadolite: Africa: Dispatches from a Fragile Continent* (New York: Norton, 1990), by Blaine Harden, p. 38.

304 *"his distinctive traits and customs":* Pascal Bruckner, *The Tears of the White Man: Compassion as Contempt* (New York: The Free Press, 1986), p. 84.

BIBLIOGRAPHY

The researcher who wants the most comprehensive bibliography of modern scholarship on the colonial Congo should turn to *Bibliographie historique du Zaïre à l'époque coloniale (1880–1960): travaux publiés en 1960–1996* (Louvain, Belgium: Enquêtes et Documents d'Histoire Africaine, 1996), edited by Jean-Luc Vellut. What follows is a list of the works I used.

The tyranny of alphabetical order cannot do justice to the help that other people's books gave me in writing this one. So let me first make a particularly low bow to those volumes on which I drew the most.

Primary sources penned by some of the central characters in this story include the works listed here by King Affonso I, Roger Casement, Joseph Conrad, William Sheppard, Henry Morton Stanley, George Washington Williams, and E. D. Morel. There is no comprehensive edition of King Leopold II's voluminous, revealing output of letters and memoranda, but hundreds of them do appear in Édouard Van der Smissen's *Léopold II et Beernaert: d'après leur correspondance inédite de 1884 à 1894.* Some are also reprinted in François Bontinck's *Aux Origines de l'État Indépendant du Congo,* an important collection of letters and documents on the early days. Robert Benedetto's new anthology has made a large collection of source material on the Presbyterian missionaries' work for human rights easily available for the first time.

Most of the major European and American figures — but none of the African ones — have had biographies written of them. I have drawn particularly on those of Stanley by John Bierman and Frank McLynn, of Casement by Brian Inglis and B. L. Reid, and of the studies (although none of them is the full-scale biography the man deserves) of E. D. Morel by Catherine Cline, A.J.P. Taylor, F. Seymour Cocks, and W. S. Adams. John Hope Franklin's biography of George Washington Williams rescued Williams from obscurity and provided most of my source material for Chapter 8. Of the various biographies of Leopold, those by Barbara Emerson and Neal Ascherson were essential; most of the material about life in the king's household comes from the memoirs of his aides, Gustave Stinglhamber and Baron Carton de Wiart.

Thomas Pakenham's *The Scramble for Africa* is a comprehensive diplomatic overview of that period whose novelist's-eye array of detail I have gratefully stolen from. In the Prologue, I was also inspired by *The River Congo* by Peter Forbath, one of the few writers to recognize the drama and tragedy of the life of King Affonso I. A number of scholarly books written in recent decades form a mine of information. Among them, I have found especially helpful the studies by Ruth Slade, Robert Harms, Stanley Shaloff, S.J.S. Cookey, David Lagergren, and the many works by Jean Stengers. Jacques Willequet's *Le Congo Belge et la Weltpolitik (1894–1914)* has all the delicious material about Leopold's press bribery operation.

Finally, several Belgians have recently provided a refreshing change to the decades of sugar-coated Congo history that has usually been their country's norm. *Du Sang sur les Lianes,* by Daniel Vangroenweghe, is passionate and highly useful. Guy De Boeck's study of the Force Publique mutinies points out how these are the precursors of anticolonial guerrilla wars of more than half a century later. And the French-language edition of Jules Marchal's four-volume history of the Congo, from 1876 to 1910, is, for this crucial period, the best scholarly overview by far, encyclopedic in scope. In countless places in this volume, I am in his debt, as will be anyone who writes about this era for years to come.

PUBLISHED SOURCES

Adams, W. S. *Edwardian Portraits.* London: Secker & Warburg, 1957.

Affonso I. *Correspondance de Dom Afonso, roi du Congo 1506–1543.* Eds. Louis Jadin and Mireille Decorato. Brussels: Académie Royale des Sciences d'Outre-Mer, 1974.

Annexe aux Annales du Musée du Congo, Ethnographie et Anthropologie, Série IV — Fascicule I. *L'État Indépendant du Congo — Documents sur le pays et ses habitants.* Brussels: 1903.

Anstey, Roger.

   1. *Britain and the Congo in the Nineteenth Century.* Oxford: Clarendon Press, 1962.

   2. *King Leopold's Legacy: The Congo Under Belgian Rule 1908–1960.* London: Oxford University Press, 1966.

   3. "The Congo Rubber Atrocities — A Case Study." *African Historical Studies* IV, no. 1 (1971): pp. 59–76.

Arnold, Nicolas, et al. *À nos héros coloniaux morts pour la civilisation 1876–1908.* Brussels: La Ligue du Souvenir Congolais, 1931.

Aronson, Theo. *Defiant Dynasty: The Coburgs of Belgium.* New York: Bobbs-Merrill, 1968.

Ascherson, Neal. *The King Incorporated: Leopold II in the Age of Trusts.* London: George Allen & Unwin, 1963.

Axelson, Sigbert. *Culture Confrontation in the Lower Congo: From the Old Congo Kingdom to the Congo Independent State with Special Reference to the Swedish Missionaries in the 1880s and 1890s.* Falköping, Sweden: Gummessons, 1970.

Balandier, Georges. *Daily Life in the Kingdom of the Kongo from the Sixteenth to the Eighteenth Century.* Trans. Helen Weaver. London: George Allen & Unwin, 1968.

Bauer, Ludwig. *Leopold the Unloved: King of the Belgians and of Wealth.* Boston: Little, Brown, and Company, 1935.

Bawele, Mumbanza Mwa. "Afro-European Relations in the Western Congo Basin c. 1884–1885." In Förster, Mommsen, and Robinson, below.

Baylen, Joseph O. "Senator John Tyler Morgan, E. D. Morel, and the Congo Reform Association." *The Alabama Review* (April 1962): pp. 117–132.

Bederman, Sanford H. "The 1876 Brussels Geographical Conference and the Charade of European Cooperation in African Exploration." *Terrae Incognitae* 21 (1989): pp. 63–73.

Benedetto, Robert, ed. *Presbyterian Reformers in Central Africa: A Documentary Account of the American Presbyterian Congo Mission and the Human Rights Struggle in the Congo, 1890–1918.* Leiden: E. J. Brill, 1996.

Bierman, John. *Dark Safari: The Life behind the Legend of Henry Morton Stanley.* New York: Alfred A. Knopf, 1990.

Biographie Coloniale Belge, vols. I–VI (volume VI: *Biographie Belge d'Outre-Mer*). Brussels: Académie Royale des Sciences Coloniales/Académie Royale des Sciences d'Outre-Mer, 1948–1968.

Birmingham, David, and Phyllis M. Martin, eds. *History of Central Africa,* vol. 2. New York: Longman, 1983.

Boahen, A. Adu, ed. *General History of Africa,* vol. VII. Paris: UNESCO, 1985.

Bobb, F. Scott. *Historical Dictionary of Zaire.* Metuchen, NJ: Scarecrow Press, 1988.

Boelaert, E. "Ntange." *Aequatoria* XV, no. 2: pp. 58–62; and no. 3: pp. 96–100. Coquilhatville, Belgian Congo: 1952.

Bontinck, François. *Aux Origines de l'État Indépendant du Congo. Documents tirés d'Archives Américaines.* Publications de l'Université Lovanium de Léopoldville. Louvain, Belgium: Éditions Nauwelaerts, 1966.

Breman, Jan.
1. "Primitive Racism in a Colonial Setting." In *Imperial Monkey Business: Racial Supremacy in Social Darwinist Theory and Colonial Practice.* Ed. Jan Breman. Amsterdam: VU University Press, 1990.
2. "The Civilization of Racism: Colonial and Postcolonial Development Policies." In above volume.

Bricusse, Georges. *Les carnets de campagne de Georges Bricusse (6 février 1894–18 juillet 1896).* Ed. Pierre Salmon. Brussels: Édition CEMUBAC, 1966.

Buell, Raymond Leslie. *The Native Problem in Africa.* New York: Macmillan, 1928.

Canisius, Edgar. *A Campaign Amongst Cannibals.* London: R. A. Everett & Co., 1903. (Published in one volume with Captain Guy Burrows, *The Curse of Central Africa,* under the latter title).

Carton de Wiart, Baron E. *Léopold II: Souvenirs des dernières années 1901–1909.* Brussels: Les Ouvres Goemaere, 1944.

Casement, Roger.
1. *The Crime Against Europe: The Writings and Poetry of Roger Casement.* Ed. Herbert O. Mackey. Dublin: C. J. Fallon, 1958.
2. "The 1903 Diary." In Singleton-Gates and Girodias, below.
3. "The Congo Report." In Singleton-Gates and Girodias, below.
4. "The 1910 Diary." In Singleton-Gates and Girodias, below.
5. *Le Rapport Casement* (annotated edition). Eds. Daniel Vangroenweghe and Jean-Luc Vellut. Louvain, Belgium: Université Catholique de Louvain, 1985.

Chanaiwa, D. "African Initiatives and Resistance in Southern Africa." In Boahen, above.

Cline, Catherine Ann. *E. D. Morel 1873–1924: The Strategies of Protest.* Belfast: Blackstaff Press, 1980.

Cocks, F. Seymour. *E. D. Morel: the Man and His Work.* London: George Allen & Unwin, 1920.

Conan Doyle, Sir Arthur.
1. *The Crime of the Congo.* New York: Doubleday, Page & Company, 1909.
2. *Letters to the Press.* Eds. John Michael Gibson and Richard Lancelyn Green. London: Secker & Warburg, 1986.

Le Congo Belge en Images. Brussels: J. Lebègue & Cie., 1914.

Congo Reform Association. *Evidence Laid Before the Congo Commission of Inquiry at Bwembu, Bolobo, Lulanga, Baringa, Bongandanga, Ikau, Bonginda, and Monsembe.* Liverpool: 1905.

Conrad, Joseph. *Heart of Darkness: An Authoritative Text; Backgrounds and Sources; Criticism.* Ed. Robert Kimbrough. Norton Critical Edition, 3d ed. New York: W. W. Norton & Co, 1988.

Conrad, Joseph, and Ford M. Hueffer [Ford Madox Ford]. *The Inheritors.* Garden City, NY: Doubleday, Page & Company, 1914.

Cookey, S.J.S. *Britain and the Congo Question: 1885–1913.* London: Longmans, Green & Co., 1968.

Coquéry-Vidrovitch, Catherine.
1. *Le Congo au temps des grandes compagnies concessionnaires 1898–1930.* Paris: Mouton, 1972.
2. "The Colonial Economy of the Former French, Belgian and Portuguese Zones 1914–35." In Boahen, above.

Cornet, René J. *La Bataille du Rail.* Brussels: Éditions L. Cuypers, 1958.

Cornevin, Robert.
1. "The Germans in Africa before 1918." In Gann and Duignan 1, below, vol. 1.
2. *Histoire du Zaïre: des Origines à nos Jours.* 4th edition. Paris: Académie des Sciences d'Outre-Mer, 1989.

Courouble, Léopold. *En Plein Soleil: Les Maisons du Juge — Le Voyage à Bankana.* Brussels: La Renaissance du Livre, 1930.

Cuvelier, Jean. *L'Ancien royaume de Congo: Fondation, découverte, première évangélisation de l'ancien Royaume de Congo. Règne du Grand Roi Affonso Mvemba Nzinga († 1541).* Bruges, Belgium: Desclée de Brouwer, 1946.

Davidson, Basil.
1. *The African Awakening.* London: Jonathan Cape, 1955.
2. *The African Slave Trade.* Revised and expanded edition. Boston: Little, Brown and Co., 1980.
3. *African Civilization Revisited: From Antiquity to Modern Times.* Trenton, NJ: Africa World Press, 1991.
4. *Africa in History: Themes and Outlines.* Revised and expanded edition. New York: Collier Books, 1991.

Daye, Pierre. *Léopold II.* Paris: Arthème Fayard et Cie., 1934.

De Boeck, Guy. *Baoni: Les Révoltes de la Force Publique sous Léopold II, Congo 1895–1908.* Brussels: Les Éditions EPO, 1987.

Debrunner, Hans Werner. *Presence and Prestige: Africans in Europe. A History of Africans in Europe before 1918.* Basel: Basler Afrika Bibliographien, 1979.

De Lichtervelde, Comte Louis. *Léopold of the Belgians.* New York: Century Co., 1929.

Depelchin, Jacques. *From the Congo Free State to Zaire: How Belgium Privatized the Economy. A History of Belgian Stock Companies in Congo-Zaire from 1885 to 1974.* Trans. Ayi Kwei Armah. Dakar, Senegal: Codesria, 1992.

De Premorel, Raoul. *Kassai: The Story of Raoul de Premorel, African Trader.* Ed. Reginald Ray Stuart. Stockton, CA: Pacific Center for Western Historical Studies, 1975.

De Vaughan, Baroness, with Paul Faure. *A Commoner Married a King.* New York: Ives Washburn, 1937.

Donny, Albert, et al. *Manuel du voyageur et du résident au Congo.* 5 vols. (Brussels: Hayez, 1897–1901).

Duignan, Peter. "The USA, the Berlin Conference, and its Aftermath 1884–1885." In Förster, Mommsen, and Robinson, below.

Dumont, Georges-Henri. *Léopold II.* Paris: Fayard, 1990.

Emerson, Barbara. *Leopold II of the Belgians: King of Colonialism.* London: Weidenfeld and Nicolson, 1979.

Fabian, Johannes. *Remembering the Present: Painting and Popular History in Zaire.* Berkeley: University of California Press, 1996.

Fetter, Bruce.
   1. *Colonial Rule and Regional Imbalance in Central Africa.* Boulder, CO: Westview Press, 1983.
   2. (ed.) *Demography from Scanty Evidence: Central Africa in the Colonial Era.* Boulder, CO: Lynne Rienner Publishers, 1990.

Flament, F., et al. *La Force Publique de sa naissance à 1914: Participation des militaires à l'histoire des premières années du Congo.* Brussels: Institut Royal Colonial Belge, 1952.

Forbath, Peter. *The River Congo: The Discovery, Exploration and Exploitation of the World's Most Dramatic River.* New York: Harper & Row, 1977.

Förster, Stig, Wolfgang J. Mommsen, and Ronald Robinson. *Bismarck, Europe, and Africa: The Berlin Africa Conference 1884–1885 and the Onset of Partition.* London: Oxford University Press, 1988.

Foussemagne, H. de Reinach. *Charlotte de Belgique: Impératrice du Mexique.* Paris: Plon-Nourrit et Cie., 1925.

Franklin, John Hope. *George Washington Williams: A Biography.* Chicago: University of Chicago Press, 1985.

Freddy, G. *Léopold II intime.* Paris: Félix Juven, 1905.

Fry, Joseph A.
   1. *Henry S. Sanford: Diplomacy and Business in Nineteenth-Century America.* Reno: University of Nevada Press, 1982.
   2. *John Tyler Morgan and the Search for Southern Autonomy.* Knoxville: University of Tennessee Press, 1992.

Furley, Oliver. "The Humanitarian Impact." In *Britain Pre-eminent: Studies of British World Influence in the Nineteenth Century,* ed. C. J. Bartlett. London: Macmillan, 1969.

Gann, L. H., and Peter Duignan.
   1. (eds.) *Colonialism in Africa 1870–1960.* 5 vols. Cambridge: Cambridge University Press, 1969.
   2. *The Rulers of Belgian Africa 1884–1914.* Princeton: Princeton University Press, 1979.

Gérard, Jo. *Le Pharaon des Belges: Léopold II.* Brussels: Éditions J. M. Collet, 1984.

Gifford, Prosser, and William Roger Louis, eds.
   1. *Britain and Germany in Africa: Imperial Rivalry and Colonial Rule.* New Haven: Yale University Press, 1967.
   2. *France and Britain in Africa: Imperial Rivalry and Colonial Rule.* New Haven: Yale University Press, 1971.

Glave, E. J. "Cruelty in the Congo Free State." *The Century Magazine* (Sept. 1897): pp. 699–715.

Goedleven, Edgard. *The Royal Greenhouses of Laeken.* Brussels: Lannoo/Duculot/Inbel, 1989.

Grand-Carteret, John. *Popold II, Roi des Belges et des Belles: Devant l'Objectif Caricatural.* Paris: Louis-Michaud, 1908.

Gründer, Horst. "Christian Missionary Activities in Africa in the Age of Imperialism and the Berlin Conference of 1884–1885." In Förster, Mommsen, and Robinson, above.

Halen, Pierre, and János Riesz, eds. *Images de l'Afrique et du Congo/Zaïre dans les lettres françaises de Belgique et alentour: Actes du colloque international de Louvain-la-Neuve (4–6 février 1993).* Brussels: Éditions du Trottoir, 1993.

Hall, Richard. *Stanley: An Adventurer Explored.* London: Collins, 1974.

Harlan, Louis R.
1. *Booker T. Washington: The Wizard of Tuskegee 1901–1915.* New York: Oxford University Press, 1983.
2. *Booker T. Washington in Perspective: Essays of Louis R. Harlan,* ed. Raymond W. Smock. Jackson: University Press of Mississippi, 1988.

Harms, Robert.
1. "The End of Red Rubber: A Reassessment." *Journal of African History* XVI, no. 1 (1975): pp. 73–88.
2. *River of Wealth, River of Sorrow: The Central Zaire Basin in the Era of the Slave and Ivory Trade, 1500–1891.* New Haven, Yale University Press, 1981.
3. "The World ABIR Made: The Maringa-Lopori Basin, 1885–1903." *African Economic History* 22 (1983): pp. 125–39.

Haveaux, G. L. *La Tradition Historique des Bapende Orientaux.* Brussels: Institut Royal Colonial Belge, 1954.

Hawkins, Hunt.
1. "Mark Twain's Involvement with the Congo Reform Movement: 'A Fury of Generous Indignation'." *The New England Quarterly* (June 1978): pp. 147–175.
2. "Joseph Conrad, Roger Casement and the Congo Reform Movement." *Journal of Modern Literature* 9, no. 1 (1981–82): pp. 65–80.

Headrick, Daniel R. *The Tools of Empire: Technology and European Imperialism in the Nineteenth Century.* New York: Oxford University Press, 1981.

Hilton, Anne. *The Kingdom of Kongo.* Oxford: Clarendon Press, 1985.

Honour, Hugh. *The Image of the Black in Western Art,* vol. IV, part 1. Cambridge: Menil Foundation/Harvard University Press, 1989.

Hulstaert, G. "Documents africains sur la pénétration européenne dans l'Equateur." *Enquêtes et Documents d'Histoire africaine* 2 (1977). [Louvain, Belgium.]

Hyde, H. Montgomery. *Mexican Empire: The History of Maximilian and Carlota of Mexico.* London: Macmillan, 1946.

Hyland, Paul. *The Black Heart: A Voyage into Central Africa.* New York: Henry Holt and Company, 1989.

Inglis, Brian. *Roger Casement.* London: Hodder and Stoughton, 1973.

Isaacman, A., and J. Vansina, "African Initiatives and Resistance in Central Africa, 1880–1914." In Baohen, above.

Janssens, Édouard, and Albert Cateaux. *Les Belges au Congo.* 3 vols. Antwerp: J. van Hille-De Backer, 1907–1912.

Katz, Fred E. *Ordinary People and Extraordinary Evil: A Report on the Beguilings of Evil.* Albany: State University of New York Press, 1993.

Kelly, Sean. *America's Tyrant: The CIA and Mobutu of Zaire.* Washington, D.C.: American University Press, 1993.

Kivilu, Sabakinu. "La région de Matadi dans les années 1880." In *Le Centenaire de l'État Indépendant du Congo: Recueil d'études.* Brussels: Académie Royale des Sciences d'Outre-Mer, 1988.

Kiwanuka, M. Semakula. "Colonial Policies and Administrations in Africa: The Myths of the Contrasts." In *The Colonial Epoch in Africa.* Ed. Gregory Maddox. New York: Garland Publishing, 1993.

Klemp, Egon, ed. *Africa on Maps Dating from the Twelfth to the Eighteenth Century.* New York: McGraw-Hill, 1970.

Lagergren, David. *Mission and State in the Congo: A Study of the Relations Between Protestant Missions and the Congo Independent State Authorities with Special Reference to the Equator District, 1885–1903.* Uppsala, Sweden: Gleerup, 1970.

Lapsley, Samuel. *Life and Letters of Samuel Norvell Lapsley: Missionary to the Congo Valley, West Africa 1866–1892.* Richmond, VA: Whittet & Shepperson, 1893. (Citations are to the full edition of 242 pages, not the abridged edition.)

Lederer, A. "L'Impact de l'arrivée des Européens sur les transports en Afrique Centrale." In *Le Centenaire de l'État Indépendant du Congo: Recueil d'études.* Brussels: Académie Royale des Sciences d'Outre-Mer, 1988.

Leclercq, Louis. "Les carnets de campagne de Louis Leclercq. Étude de mentalité d'un colonial belge." Ed. Pierre Salmon. In *Revue de l'Université de Bruxelles* Nouvelle Série 3 (February–April 1970): pp. 233–302.

Lejeune-Choquet, Adolphe. *Histoire militaire du Congo: explorations, expéditions, opérations de guerre, combats et faits militaires.* Brussels: Maison d'Édition Alfred Castaigne, 1906.

Lemaire, Charles.

1. *Au Congo: Comment les noirs travaillent.* Brussels: Imprimerie Scientifique Ch. Bulens, 1895.

2. "Charles Lemaire à l'Equateur: Son journal inédit. 1891–1895." Ed. Daniel Vangroenweghe. In *Annales Aequatoria* 7 (1986): pp. 7–73.

Liebrechts, Charles. *Congo: Suite à mes souvenirs d'Afrique.* Brussels: Office de Publicité, 1920.

Lindqvist, Sven. *"Exterminate All the Brutes": One Man's Odyssey into the Heart of Darkness and the Origins of European Genocide.* New York: New Press, 1996.

Louis, William Roger.

1. "Roger Casement and the Congo." *Journal of African History* V, no. 1 (1964): pp. 99–120.

2. "The Philosophical Diplomatist: Sir Arthur Hardinge and King Leopold's Congo, 1906–1911." *Bulletin des Séances de l'Académie Royale des Sciences d'Outre-Mer* (1965): pp. 1402–1430.

3. "The Stokes Affair and the Origins of the Anti-Congo Campaign, 1895–1896." *Revue Belge de Philologie et d'Histoire* 43 (1965): pp. 572–584.

4. "The Triumph of the Congo Reform Movement, 1905–1908." In *Boston University Papers on Africa,* vol. II. Ed. Jeffrey Butler. Boston: Boston University Press, 1966.

5. *Great Britain and Germany's Lost Colonies 1914–1919.* Oxford: Clarendon Press, 1967.

6. "Sir John Harris and 'Colonial Trusteeship.'" *Bulletin des Séances de l'Académie Royale des Sciences d'Outre Mer* 3 (1968): pp. 832–856.

Louise of Belgium, Princess. *My Own Affairs.* London: Cassell and Co., 1921.

Luwel, Marcel. "Roger Casement à Henry Morton Stanley: Un rapport sur la situation au Congo en 1890." *Africa-Tervuren* XIV, no. 4 (1968): pp. 85–92.

Lyons, Maryinez. *The Colonial Disease: A Social History of Sleeping Sickness in Northern Zaire, 1900–1940.* Cambridge: Cambridge University Press, 1992.

MacColl, René. *Roger Casement: A New Judgement.* New York: W. W. Norton & Co., 1957.

Marchal, Jules.

1. *L'État Libre du Congo: Paradis Perdu. L'Histoire du Congo 1876–1900,* vol. 1. Borgloon, Belgium: Éditions Paula Bellings, 1996.

2. *L'État Libre du Congo: Paradis Perdu. L'Histoire du Congo 1876–1900,* vol. 2. Borgloon, Belgium: Éditions Paula Bellings, 1996.

3. *E. D. Morel contre Léopold II: L'Histoire du Congo 1900–1910,* vol. 1. Paris: Éditions L'Harmattan, 1996.

4. *E. D. Morel contre Léopold II: L'Histoire du Congo 1900–1910,* vol. 2. Paris: Éditions L'Harmattan, 1996.

Martin, Phyllis M. "The Violence of Empire." In Birmingham and Martin, above.

McLynn, Frank.

1. *Stanley: The Making of an African Explorer.* London: Constable, 1989.

2. *Stanley: Sorcerer's Apprentice.* London: Constable, 1991.

3. *Hearts of Darkness: The European Exploration of Africa.* New York: Carroll & Graf, 1992.

Meyer, Lysle E. "Henry S. Sanford and the Congo: a Reassessment." *African Historical Studies* IV, no. 1 (1971): pp. 19–39.

Miers, Suzanne. "The Brussels Conference of 1889–1890: The Place of the Slave Trade in the Policies of Great Britain and Germany." In Gifford and Louis 1, above.

Miller, Joseph C. *Way of Death: Merchant Capitalism and the Angolan Slave Trade 1730–1830.* Madison: University of Wisconsin Press, 1988.

Money, J. W. B. *Java; or, How to Manage a Colony. Showing a Practical Solution of the Questions Now Affecting British India.* London: Hurst and Blackett, 1861.

Morel, E. D.

1. *King Leopold's Rule in Africa.* London: William Heinemann, 1904.

2. *Great Britain and the Congo: The Pillage of the Congo Basin.* London: Smith, Elder & Co., 1909.

3. *Red Rubber: The Story of the Rubber Slave Trade Which Flourished on the Congo for Twenty Years, 1890–1910.* New and revised edition. Manchester: National Labour Press, 1919.

4. "At Pentonville: September, 1917–January, 1918." In *Thoughts on the War: The Peace — and Prison,* ed. Robert Smillie. London: 1920.

5. *E. D. Morel's History of the Congo Reform Movement.* Eds. William Roger Louis and Jean Stengers. Oxford: Clarendon Press, 1968.

Mountmorres, Viscount William Geoffrey Bouchard de Montmorency. *The Congo Independent State: A Report on a Voyage of Enquiry.* London: Williams and Norgate, 1906.

Mutamba-Makombo. *L'histoire du Zaire par les Textes: Tome 2 — 1885–1955.* Kinshasa: EDIDEPS, 1987.

Mwembu, Dibwe Dia. "La Peine du Fouet au Congo Belge (1885–1960)." *Les Cahiers de Tunisie,* nos. 135–136 (1986): pp. 127–153.

Najder, Zdzislaw. *Joseph Conrad: A Chronicle.* New Brunswick, N.J.: Rutgers University Press, 1983.

Nelson, Samuel H. *Colonialism in the Congo Basin 1880–1940.* Athens, Ohio: Ohio University Center for International Studies, 1994.

Northrup, David. *Beyond the Bend in the River: African Labor in Eastern Zaire, 1865–1940.* Athens, Ohio: Ohio University Center for International Studies, 1988.

Obdeijn, Herman. "The New Africa Trading Company and the Struggle for Import Duties in the Congo Free State 1886–1894." *African Economic History* 12 (1983): pp. 193–212.

O'Connor, Richard. *The Cactus Throne: The Tragedy of Maximilian and Carlotta.* New York: G. P. Putnam's Sons, 1971.

Oliver, Roland, and Caroline Oliver, eds. *Africa in the Days of Exploration.* Englewood Cliffs, NJ: Prentice-Hall, 1965.

Pakenham, Thomas. *The Scramble for Africa: The White Man's Conquest of the Dark Continent from 1876 to 1912.* New York: Random House, 1991.

Phipps, William E. *The Sheppards and Lapsley: Pioneer Presbyterians in the Congo.* Louisville, KY: Presbyterian Church (USA), 1991.

Picard, Edmond. *En Congolie.* Brussels: Paul Lacomblez, 1896.

Porter, Bernard. *Critics of Empire: British Radical Attitudes to Colonialism in Africa 1895–1914.* New York: St. Martin's Press, 1968.

Ranieri, Liane. *Léopold II Urbaniste.* Brussels: Hayez, 1973.

Read, James Morgan. *Atrocity Propaganda 1914–1919.* New Haven: Yale University Press, 1941.

Reeves, Thomas C. *Gentleman Boss: The Life of Chester Alan Arthur.* New York: Alfred A. Knopf, 1975.

Reid, B. L. *The Lives of Roger Casement.* New Haven: Yale University Press, 1976.

Renoy, Georges. *Nous, Léopold II.* Zaltbommel, Holland: Bibliothèque Européenne, 1989.

Ridley, Jasper. *Maximilian and Juárez.* New York: Ticknor & Fields, 1992.

Roark, James L.
  1. *Masters Without Slaves: Southern Planters in the Civil War and Reconstruction.* New York: W. W. Norton & Co., 1977.
  2. "American Expansionism vs. European Imperialism: Henry S. Sanford and the Congo Episode, 1883–1885." *Mid-America: An Historical Review* LX (1978): pp. 21–33.

Roeykens, P. A. *Les Débuts de l'oeuvre africaine de Léopold II (1875–1879).* Brussels: Académie Royale des Sciences Coloniales, 1955.

Rom, Léon. *Le Nègre du Congo.* Brussels: Imprimerie Louis Vogels, 1899.

Rothstein, Andrew. *British Foreign Policy and Its Critics 1830–1950.* London: Lawrence and Wishart, 1969.

Rubin, William, ed. *"Primitivism" in 20th Century Art: Affinity of the Tribal and the Modern,* vol. 1. New York: Museum of Modern Art, 1984.

Samarin, William J. *The Black Man's Burden: African Colonial Labor on the Congo and Ubangi Rivers, 1880–1900.* Boulder, CO: Westview Press, 1989.

Sawyer, Roger. *Casement: The Flawed Hero.* London: Routledge & Kegan Paul, 1984.

Schall, Larryetta M. "William H. Sheppard: Fighter for African Rights." In *Stony the Road: Chapters in the History of Hampton Institute,* ed. Keith L. Schall. Charlottesville: University of Virginia Press, 1977.

Sereny, Gitta. *Into That Darkness: From Mercy Killing to Mass Murder.* New York: McGraw Hill, 1974.

Severin, Timothy. *The African Adventure.* London: Hamish Hamilton, 1973.

Shannon, R. T. *Gladstone and the Bulgarian Agitation 1876.* London: Thomas Nelson and Sons, 1963.

Shaloff, Stanley. *Reform in Leopold's Congo.* Richmond, VA: John Knox Press, 1970.

Sheppard, William H. *Presbyterian Pioneers in Congo.* Richmond, VA: Presbyterian Committee of Publication, 1916.

Shepperson, George. "Aspects of American Interest in the Berlin Conference." In Förster, Mommsen, and Robinson, above.

Sherry, Norman. *Conrad's Western World.* London: Cambridge University Press, 1971.

Singleton-Gates, Peter, and Maurice Girodias. *The Black Diaries: An Account of Roger Casement's Life and Times with a Collection of his Diaries and Public Writings.* New York: Grove Press, 1959.

Slade, Ruth.
1. *English-Speaking Missions in the Congo Independent State (1878–1908).* Brussels: Académie Royale des Sciences Coloniales, 1959.
2. *King Leopold's Congo: Aspects of the Development of Race Relations in the Congo Independent State.* London: Oxford University Press, 1962.

Smith, Gene. *Maximilian and Carlota: A Tale of Romance and Tragedy.* New York: William Morrow & Company, 1973.

Smith, Iain R. *The Emin Pasha Relief Expedition.* Oxford: Clarendon Press, 1972.

Speeches Made at Banquet Tendered to Col. Henry I. Kowalsky by his Friends. January five, Nineteen-five. San Francisco: 1905.

Stanley, Henry M.
1. *How I Found Livingstone: Travels, Adventures and Discoveries in Central Africa, Including Four Months' Residence with Dr. Livingstone.* London: Sampson Low, Marston, Low, and Searle, 1872.
2. *Through the Dark Continent; or, The Sources of the Nile Around the Great Lakes of Equatorial Africa and Down the Livingstone River to the Atlantic Ocean.* 2 vols. (First published 1878). 1899 edition reprinted by Dover Publications, New York, 1988.
3. *The Congo and the Founding of Its Free State: A Story of Work and Exploration.* 2 vols. New York: Harper & Brothers, 1885.
4. *In Darkest Africa; or, The Quest, Rescue and Retreat of Emin, Governor of Equatoria.* 2 vols. New York: Charles Scribner's Sons, 1890.
5. *The Autobiography of Sir Henry Morton Stanley.* Ed. Dorothy Stanley. Boston: Houghton Mifflin Company, 1909.
6. *Unpublished Letters.* Ed. Albert Maurice. London: W. & R. Chambers, 1955.
7. *The Exploration Diaries of H. M. Stanley.* Eds. Richard Stanley and Alan Neame. New York: Vanguard Press, 1961.

Starr, Frederick. *The Truth About the Congo: The Chicago Tribune Articles.* Chicago: Forbes & Co., 1907.

Stengers, Jean.
1. *Combien le Congo a-t-il coûté à la Belgique?* Brussels: Académie Royale des Sciences Coloniales, 1957.
2. "The Congo Free State and the Belgian Congo before 1914." In Gann and Duignan 1, above, vol. 1.
3. "King Leopold and Anglo-French Rivalry, 1882–1884." In Gifford and Louis 2, above.
4. "King Leopold's Imperialism." In *Studies in the Theory of Imperialism,* eds. Roger Owen and Bob Sutcliffe. London: Longman, 1972.
5. "Belgian Historiography since 1945." In *Reappraisals in Overseas History,* ed. P. C. Emmer and H. L. Wesseling. The Hague: Leiden University Press, 1979.

6. "Leopold II and the *Association du Congo.*" In Förster, Mommsen, and Robinson, above.

7. *Congo Mythes et Réalités: 100 Ans d'Histoire.* Paris: Éditions Duculot, 1989.

Stengers, Jean, and Vansina, Jan. "King Leopold's Congo, 1886–1908." In *The Cambridge History of Africa,* Vol. 6: *From 1870 to 1905,* ed. Roland Oliver and G. N. Sanderson. Cambridge: Cambridge University Press, 1985.

Stephanie of Belgium, H. R. H. Princess. *I Was to Be Empress.* London: Ivor Nicholson & Watson, 1937.

Stern, Fritz. *Gold and Iron: Bismarck, Bleichröder, and the Building of the German Empire.* New York: Alfred A. Knopf, 1977.

Sternstein, Jerome L. "King Leopold II, Senator Nelson W. Aldrich, and the Strange Beginnings of American Economic Penetration of the Congo." *African Historical Studies* II, no. 2 (1969): pp. 189–204.

Stinglhamber, Gustave, and Paul Dresse. *Léopold II au Travail.* Brussels: Éditions du Sablon, 1945.

Suret-Canale, Jean. *French Colonialism in Tropical Africa 1900–1945.* New York: Pica Press, 1971.

Swan, Jon. "The Final Solution in South West Africa." *MHQ: The Quarterly Journal of Military History* 3, no. 4 (1991): pp. 36–55.

Swanwick, H. M. *Builders of Peace: Being Ten Years' History of the Union of Democratic Control.* London: Swarthmore Press, 1924.

Swartz, Marvin. *The Union of Democratic Control in British Politics During the First World War.* Oxford: Clarendon Press, 1971.

Taylor, A. J. P. *The Trouble Makers: Dissent over Foreign Policy 1792–1939.* London: Hamish Hamilton, 1957.

Thompson, Robert S. "Léopold II et Henry S. Sanford: Papiers inédits concernant le Rôle joué par un Diplomate Americain dans la Création de l'E. I. du Congo." *Congo — Revue Générale de la Colonie Belge* II (1930): pp. 295–329.

Turnbull, Colin M. *The Forest People.* New York: Simon & Schuster, 1962.

Twain, Mark. *King Leopold's Soliloquy: A Defence of His Congo Rule.* Ed. E. D. Morel. London: T. Fisher Unwin, 1907.

Usoigwe, G. N. "European Partition and Conquest of Africa: An Overview." In Boahen, above.

Van der Smissen, Édouard, ed. *Léopold II et Beernaert: d'après leur correspondance inédite de 1884 à 1894.* Brussels: Goemaere, 1920.

Vandervelde, Émile. *Souvenirs d'un Militant Socialiste.* Paris: Les Éditions Denoël, 1939.

Vandewoude, Emile. "De Aardrijkskundige Conferentie (1976) vanuit het koninklijk Paleis genzien." In *La Conférence de Géographie de 1876: Recueil d'études.* Brussels: Académie Royale des Sciences d'Outre-Mer, 1976.

Vangroenweghe, Daniel. *Du Sang sur les Lianes.* Brussels: Didier Hatier, 1986.

Vansina, Jan.

1. *Kingdoms of the Savanna.* Madison: University of Wisconsin Press, 1966.

2. *The Children of Woot: A History of the Kuba Peoples.* Madison: University of Wisconsin Press, 1978.

3. *Paths in the Rainforest.* Madison: University of Wisconsin Press, 1990.

Van Zandijcke, A. *Pages d'Histoire du Kasayi.* Namur, Belgium: Collection Lavigerie, 1953.

Vellut, Jean-Luc. "La Violence Armée dans l'État Indépendant du Congo. *Cultures et Développement* 16, nos. 3–4 (1984): pp. 671–707.

Vinson, Rev. T. C. *William McCutchan Morrison: Twenty Years in Central Africa*. Richmond, VA: Presbyterian Committee of Publication, 1921.

Ward, Herbert. *A Voice from the Congo: Comprising Stories, Anecdotes, and Descriptive Notes*. London: William Heinemann, 1910.

Weeks, John H. *Among the Primitive Bakongo*. London: Seeley, Service & Co., 1914.

West, Richard. *Congo*. New York: Holt, Rinehart and Winston, 1972.

White, James P. "The Sanford Exploring Expedition." *Journal of African History* VIII, no. 2 (1967): pp. 291–302.

Willequet, Jacques. *Le Congo Belge et la Weltpolitik (1894–1914)*. Brussels: Presses Universitaires de Bruxelles, 1962.

Williams, George Washington.
1. *An Open Letter to His Serene Majesty Leopold II, King of the Belgians and Sovereign of the Independent State of Congo*. Reprinted in Franklin, above.
2. *A Report on the Proposed Congo Railway*. Reprinted in Franklin, above.
3. *A Report on the Congo-State and Country to the President of the Republic of the United States of America*. Reprinted in Franklin, above.

Williams, Walter L. "William Henry Sheppard, Afro-American Missionary in the Congo, 1890–1910." In *Black Americans and the Missionary Movement in Africa*, ed. Sylvia M. Jacobs. Westport, CT: Greenwood Press, 1982.

Winternitz, Helen. *East along the Equator: A Journey up the Congo and into Zaire*. New York: Atlantic Monthly Press, 1987.

Wuliger, Robert. "Mark Twain on *King Leopold's Soliloquy*." *American Literature* (May 1953): pp. 234–237.

Young, Crawford. "The Northern Republics 1960–1980." In Birmingham and Martin, above.

NEWSPAPERS AND PERIODICALS

La Belgique Coloniale (Brussels)
Le Congo Illustré (Brussels)
The Congo News Letter (Boston)
Missionförbundet (Stockholm)
Le Mouvement Géographique (Brussels)
Official Organ of the Congo Reform Association (Liverpool, London)
Regions Beyond (London)
Southern Workman (Hampton, VA)
West African Mail, later *African Mail* (Liverpool)

UNPUBLISHED AND ARCHIVAL SOURCES

Carroll, Murray Lee. *Open Door Imperialism in Africa: The United States and the Congo, 1876 to 1892*. Ph.D. thesis. University of Connecticut. 1971.

De Ryck, Maurice Martin. Zaire Colonial Documents Collection. University of Wisconsin.

Martens, Daisy S. *A History of European Penetration and African Reaction in the Kasai Region of Zaire, 1880–1908*. Ph.D. thesis. Simon Fraser University. 1980.

McStallworth, Paul. *The United States and the Congo Question, 1884–1914*. Ph.D. thesis. Ohio State University. 1954.

Normandy, Elizabeth L. *Black Americans and U.S. Policy Toward Africa: Two Case Studies from the pre–World War II Period.* Ph.D. thesis. University of South Carolina. 1987.

Procès-Verbaux de la Commission d'Enquête instituée par décret du 23 juillet 1904. Archives Africaines, Ministère des Affaires Etrangères, Brussels. (IRCB 717–718).

Rom, Léon. *Notes. Mes services au Congo de 1886 à 1908.* Musée Royal de l'Afrique Centrale. (Document MRAC-Hist-56.28).

Roth, Donald Franklin. *"Grace Not Race": Southern Negro Church Leaders, Black Identity, and Missions to West Africa, 1865–1919.* Ph.D. thesis. University of Texas at Austin. 1975.

Sheppard, William H. Papers. Hampton University, Hampton, Virginia.

ACKNOWLEDGMENTS

MY THANKS go to staff members at the Royal Geographical Society in London, Anti-Slavery International in London, the Musée Royal de l'Afrique Centrale in Tervuren, Belgium, the Musée Royal de l'Armée et d'Histoire Militaire in Brussels, Svenska Missionsförbundet in Stockholm, the American Baptist Historical Society in Rochester, New York, the Sanford Museum in Sanford, Florida, and the Department of History of the Presbyterian Church (USA) in Montreat, North Carolina, all of whom kindly responded to my requests for information, photographs, or other materials. Thanks also to Enid Schildkrout at the American Museum of Natural History in New York, to the archivists at Hampton University, Hampton, Virginia, who allowed me to look at William Sheppard's papers, to Ebba Segerberg for translations from the Swedish, and to David Raymond and Fritz Stern for some good bibliographic suggestions.

Writing this book helped me understand the essential role of libraries in preserving the records of history that powerful interests want forgotten or that people have chosen to ignore. I felt grateful to be able to borrow a book, even though — as I found in one case — I was the first person who had checked it out since 1937. Or — and this happened to me twice — to check out a library book from decades ago and find the pages still uncut. My thanks to the many helpful staff members at the various places I did research: the libraries at Northwestern University, Yale University, and Bates College; the New York Public Library; the library of Union Theological Seminary in New York; the Hoover and Green libraries at Stanford University, and, above all, the Doe, Moffitt, and Bancroft libraries of the University of California at Berkeley, where I did most of my work. Berkeley's rich range of materials from a century ago is eloquent testimony to what existed before small-minded politicians and tax-cutting fanatics began slashing the budgets of American public and state university libraries.

Although she was in the midst of finishing a remarkable book of her own, my wife, Arlie, talked, lived, and breathed this project with me every step of the way. By the time the manuscript was ready for her insightful reading, she knew the characters in the Congo story almost as if they were close friends of ours. I was lucky to have many real-life friends who also read the manuscript and gave me helpful comments, often drawing on their experience as writers, journalists, or historians: Ayi Kwei Armah, Harriet Barlow, Mary Felstiner, Laurie Flynn, David Hochschild, Patricia Labalme, Paul Solman, Allen Wheelis, Francis Wilson, and Blaikie, Monty, and Robert F. Worth. For critical readings and other support, I am also grateful to my agents, Denise Shannon and Georges Borchardt, and to my former editor at Houghton Mifflin, Dawn Seferian.

Almost every page of this book benefited immeasurably from intensive editorial consulting from Tom Engelhardt. Among American writers who care about their craft, Tom's name is a well-kept secret. There are few people alive for whom the act of critically reading, untangling and polishing a sentence, a paragraph, an entire book, is so much an act of the highest craftsmanship. If there were Oscars for editing, Tom would have won his long ago.

As a newcomer to this tragic patch of history, I was helped in my explorations by several people who know far more about it than I. Daniel Vangroenweghe read the manuscript and shared some documents with me. And I owe a special debt of gratitude to the two greatest scholars of this period, the anthropologist Jan Vansina and the historian Jules Marchal. Both generously responded to numerous calls and letters asking for information, and both read the manuscript with painstaking care, Marchal in two successive drafts, saving me from innumerable errors. They are not responsible for any mistakes that crept in by accident in my subsequent rewriting, or for the few points where my interpretation may differ from that of one or the other of them. I cannot thank them enough.

PHOTO CREDITS

Young Leopold: Corbis-Bettmann. *Stanley:* Royal Geographical Society. *Sanford:* San-ford Museum, City of Sanford. *Telegram:* Sanford Museum, City of Sanford. *King Leopold:* Corbis-Bettmann. *Tiwa Mwe:* Royal Geographical Society. *Goodwill:* Royal Geographical Society. *Williams:* Archive Photos. *Ivory:* Sanford Museum, City of Sanford. *Conrad:* New York Times Co./Archive Photos. *Rom:* Collection of the Musée Royal de l'Armée, Brussels. *Rom with rifle: Les Vétérans Coloniaux 1876–1908: Revue Coloniale Illustrée. Van Kerckhoven:* Collection of the Musée Royal de l'Armée, Brussels. *Morel:* Anti-Slavery International. *Antwerp:* Hulton-Getty. *Casement:* Ar-chive Photos. *Shanu: Au Congo: Comment les Noirs Travaillent* by Charles Lemaire. *Sheppard:* Presbyterian Church (USA) Department of History, Montreat, N.C. *Nsala:* Anti-Slavery International. *Severed hands:* Anti-Slavery International. *Two youths:* Anti-Slavery International. *Chicotte: Regions Beyond. Women Hostages: Regions Beyond. Baringa village: Regions Beyond. Baringa razed: Regions Beyond. Meeting poster: Regions Beyond. Leopold and skulls:* Stock Montage, Inc. *The Appeal: Regions Beyond. Expert Opinion:* Stock Montage, Inc. *Rubber coils:* Stock Montage, Inc. *Guilt of delay:* Stock Montage, Inc.

INDEX

ABOUT THE AUTHOR

ADAM HOCHSCHILD was born in New York City in 1942. His first book, *Half the Way Home: A Memoir of Father and Son,* was published in 1986. It was followed by *The Mirror at Midnight: A South African Journey* and *The Unquiet Ghost: Russians Remember Stalin.* Hochschild's work has won prizes from the Overseas Press Club of America, the World Affairs Council, and the Society of American Travel Writers. His most recent book, *Finding the Trapdoor: Essays, Portraits, Travels,* won the 1998 PEN/Spielvogel-Diamonstein Award for the Art of the Essay. His books have been translated into five languages.

Besides his books, Hochschild has also written for *The New Yorker, Harper's Magazine, The New York Review of Books, The New York Times Magazine, Mother Jones, The Nation,* and many other newspapers and magazines. He is a former commentator on National Public Radio's *All Things Considered.*

Hochschild teaches writing at the Graduate School of Journalism at the University of California at Berkeley and has been a guest teacher at other campuses in the United States and abroad. In 1997–98 he spent five months as a Fulbright Lecturer in India. He lives in San Francisco with his wife, Arlie, the sociologist and author. They have two sons.